COSMIC DANCER

THE LIFE AND MUSIC OF
MARC BOLAN

PAUL ROLAND

TOMAHAWK
Press

First published in 2012 by

Tomahawk Press
PO Box 1236
Sheffield S11 7XU
England
www.tomahawkpress.com

ISBN 13: 978-0-9566834-0-3

Proofread by Kenneth Bishton - kenbishton@talktalk.net
Edited by Bruce Sachs
Designed by Tree Frog Communication 01245 445377
Printed in the EU by Gutenberg Press Limited

Dedication
*This book was a labour of love and therefore it is fitting that I dedicate
it to my beloved wife, Claudia.*

Author's note

When I wrote *Electric Warrior* in 1979 (the first complete Bolan biography to be published), I relied upon the extensive archive of interviews I had accumulated over many years in which Marc told his story in his own inimitable way. I was proud to have been able to unearth a wealth of obscure but historically important material dating back to his solo recordings in the mid-sixties and to have tracked down and interviewed several key people involved in his early career who had not been interviewed before. And this at a time when there was no Internet and interest in Bolan appeared to be at an all-time low. However, being 19 at the time, I did not possess the insight that I would like to think I have acquired after writing more than 30 books as well as hundreds of articles and reviews over the past 30 years, including substantial Bolan features for Sounds, Record Mirror and Uncut. It is only now that I feel that I can do justice to a subject that deserves a thorough and exhaustive reappraisal.

I feel particularly privileged to have been close to a number of those in whom he confided, specifically June Bolan who acted as my manager for a brief period in the early Eighties, and Andy Ellison who afforded me the ultimate compliment by asking me to write songs for a John's Children reunion album because he considered my style to be the closest to that of his old friend.

I was also extremely fortunate to have had the chance to talk with Marc's parents in the months after his death who furnished me with details about his childhood and upbringing which, to the best of my knowledge, have not been touched upon to date.

I believe that my dedication as a 'fan', coupled with my critical facility as a music journalist has ensured that I have maintained a fair balance between fact and speculation, and that my additional experience as a recording artist has given me a deeper insight into Marc's creative process.

The following interviews were conducted by the author:

Keith Altham, Simon Napier-Bell, Rolan Bolan, Joe Boyd, Ray Connolly, Danielz, Andy Ellison, Simeon and Phyllis Feld, Harry Feld, Paul Fenton, Mickey Finn, Herbie Flowers, Stephen Gold, Mickey 'Marmalade' Gray, Tony Hall, Lani Herdmann, Bill Legend, John Peel, Rosalind Russell, Rat Scabies, Captain Sensible, Helen Shapiro, Steve Peregrin Took, Chris Townson, Brian Dunham, Freddy Hansson, Jorgen Angel and George Tremlett.

Acknowledgements

I have also made extensive use of my own archive interviews first published in *Electric Warrior – The Marc Bolan Story* (South Press 1979/Omnibus Press 1982) under the pen name Paul Sinclair and the following publications to whom I am indebted:

Zig Zag, Rolling Stone, Creem, Cirkus, The Observer, The Sun, Music Business Weekly, David Wigg (Daily Express and Daily Mail), Dick Tatham (Diana), Danny Holloway (NME), Chris Welch (Melody Maker), Ray Connolly (Evening Standard),

Maureen Cleave (Evening Standard), Legolas (Gandalf's Garden), James Johnson (NME), Valerie Mabbs (Record Mirror), Roy Hollingworth (Melody Maker), Rosalind Russell (Record Mirror and Disc), Geoff Barton (Sounds), Michael Watts (Melody Maker), David Hughes (Disc and Music Echo), Michael Benton (Disc), Robin Smith (Record Mirror),Tony Tyler (NME), Nick Logan (NME), Tony Norman (NME), Keith Altham (NME, Look Now and London Evening Standard), Anne Nightingale (Petticoat), Simon Napier-Bell (The Guardian), Bruce Harris (Words and Music), Penny Valentine (Sounds), Roy Carr (NME), Stevie Dixon (BFBS and Essex Music), Bob Hart (The Sun), Danae Brook (Evening News), David Neill (Record Weekly), Jan Iles (Record Mirror), John Blake (Evening News), Caroline Hedley (Daily Mirror), and Mick Brown (Daily Telegraph).

Plus those reviewers and publications credited by name in the text.

In addition I am grateful to the publishers of Record Mirror and Sounds for allowing me access to their files in 1978, to the publishers of Melody Maker for granting unlimited access to their archives in 1999 and to the staff of the British Newspaper Library, Colindale, London. Also to Allan Jones for allowing me to include interviews that I conducted for a lengthy feature in Uncut in 1997.

I also acknowledge the invaluable source material provided by the following:

Books

Dicks, Ted, *Marc Bolan – A Tribute* (Essex House, 1978)

Franzero, Carlo Maria, *The Life And Times of Beau Brummel* (Alvin Redman Ltd, 1958)

McLenehan, Cliff, *Marc Bolan – A Chronology* (Helter Skelter Publishing 2002)

Paytress, Mark, *Marc Bolan – The Rise and Fall of a 20th Century Superstar* (Omnibus Press, 2002)

Tremlett, George, *The Marc Bolan Story* (Futura Publications, 1975)

Wale, Michael, *Voxpop* (George Harrap and Co, 1972)

Welch, Chris, *Born To Boogie* (Eel Pie, 1982)

Documentaries

Marc Bolan - The Final Word (Universal 2007), 'Dandy In The Underworld' from *T.Rex On TV* (Demon Vision 2006), 'Cosmic Rock' from *Born To Boogie* (Sanctuary Visual Entertainment 2005), *Music In The Round: Rock of Ages* (ITV December 1971), *London Rock* (ITV, 1970), *Eleven Plus With Russell Harty* (ITV May 1972) *The One Show* (BBC November 2009)

Internet Resources

www.bolanicproductions.com (site for 20th Century Boy – The Musical' and other Bolan projects)

www.borntoboogie.net (site devoted to the DVD release of BTB)

www.marc-bolan.com (Official fan club)

www.trextasy.com (T.Rex tribute band)

www.easyaction.co.uk/releases/artist/T%20Rex (indie label with Bolan rarities)

www.thegroover.net (Bolan radio podcast)

www.angel.dk (Photographer Jorgen Angel's site)
www.marcbolanmusic.com (fan site)
www.marcbolanmusic.com/school.aspx
(page devoted to the School of Music in Sierra Leone)
www.rocksbackpages.com/artist.html?ArtistID=bolan_marc
(archive interviews on the web)
www.facebook.com/MarcBolanT.Rex
www.facebook.com/tyrannosaurusbolan
www.facebook.com/marcbolan
www.facebook.com/pages/Rexpert/144857602205077
www.wrinkledweasel.blogspot.com/p/wavelengths-2.html
(source of the Mike Hurst 'Wizard' quote)
www.paulroland.net (author site)
www.tilldawn.net/tomb
www.Marcbolanswiganbop.piczo.com

The author has made every effort to trace and acknowledge the original sources of reviews and interview extracts. However, in the event that a quote has not been correctly or fully credited, please contact the publisher who will seek to amend this in future editions.

All lyrics copyright of the following publishers:

'The Wizard' and 'Beyond The Risin' Sun' © Campbell Connelly and Co

'Sara Crazy Child' © Universal/Dick James Music Ltd

'Dragon's Ear', 'Strange Orchestras', 'Mustang Ford', 'Child Star', 'Weilder Of Words', 'Wind Quartets', 'O Harley', 'Cosmic Dancer', 'Rip Off', 'Get It On', 'Jeepster', 'Monolith' and 'Mambo Sun' © Westminster Music Ltd

'Childe', 'Chariots Of Silk' and 'The Time Of Love Is Now' © Lupus Music.

'The Lilac Hand Of Menthol Dan', 'Tenement Lady', 'Rapids', 'Left Hand Luke', 'The Street And Babe Shadow', 'The Groover', 'The Leopards', 'Sensation Boulevard', 'My Little Baby', 'Life's An Elevator', 'Spaceball Ricochet', 'Telegram Sam' and 'Dandy In The Underworld'. © Wizard Publishing (Bahamas)Ltd/Spirit Music Inc:

'Sycamore Of Sorrow' and 'untitled poem' from 'The Warlock of Love' ©Lupus Publishing.

Picture Credits:

The author extends his gratitude to Peter Barron, Mark Sheehan, Marc Arscott, Danielz and Caron Willans, and Gary Smith for granting access to their extensive private collections and for their time and patience in making these images ready for publication.

Finally, I would like to thank the team at Tomahawk Press for all of their help and support throughout this project:

Steve Kirkham for the thought put into the design of the book; Kenneth Bishton for so carefully proofreading the manuscript; and my editor and publisher Bruce Sachs for his constant support and involvement.

The author and publisher thank artist George Underwood for permission to feature his beautiful painting 'Marc Bolan 1972' on the cover and also for permission to include his sketches of Marc on page 277 and Mickey Finn on page 293.

Foreword

"**H**ey man, come in, I'm just cooking some mushrooms on toast", these were the first words the young 19 year old Marc Bolan ever spoke to me. I'd just been dropped off outside a small prefab house, next to the dog track in the London suburb of Wimbledon, by my manager Simon Napier Bell.

I was instantly taken with this friendly and smiling cool looking young guy.

It wasn't long before we were sitting in his cramped living room, Marc crossed legged, playing some of his tunes on an acoustic guitar.

"This one is called Hippy Gumbo". I was transfixed as Marc sang some very strange songs, with words that seem to make no sense. We began to work together on a new song he had just started 'Midsummer Night's Scene'.

I was here to get to know MARC and to see if he would fit in with the wild JOHN'S CHILDREN. I wasn't sure.

Five O clock and Simon dropped by in his White Bentley to pick me up.

Fast forward....Same Bentley on an Autobahn heading for Nuremberg, Germany on the first leg of our tour with the Who. Marc is now a fully-fledged, wild young child.

To alleviate the boredom of the journey we play acting games, one of them involves MARC being a huge pop star managed by his Jewish agent played by Chris. We are all in hysterics as the game becomes more and more silly.

At one point SIMON butts in from the driving seat.

"Don't forget your best move would be to die.... tragically!"

"Yeah man...... that's good!" Marc replied.

Simon: "Maybe some kind of car accident... Yeah! I know. In a white Roll Royce...?

Marc thought about it for a moment, staring out at the endless Autobahn. "No man... It has got to be a Mini!"

Some years later I was running down the Kings Road, late for a rehearsal with the punk band I was in at the time, Radio Stars, when a purple mini swung round in the road and swerved along side of me.

The blacked out window wound down.

"Hey man what are you running from?"

I'd heard rumours that Marc had lost the plot and ballooned into a shadow of his former self, whilst in his exile in Monte Carlo.

But here was the same cool, fresh young Marc that I knew.

"You're in a new wave band aren't you Andy? Fancy coming on my new TV programme?"

Some months later, we did get to appear on Marc's show. It was great to see Marc again, the smiling, laughing young guy that had cheerily opened the door to me that spring day in Wimbledon. We made arrangements to meet up for a meal, shortly after the shows run, a few weeks later.

Sadly that never happened.

Paul Roland has written the definitive book about Marc Bolan; an overdue reassessment of his sadly short but significant part in rock and roll history, with an in depth, insight into his glorious and eccentric lyrics.

For me one of his most poetic (but I am biased), is one Marc wrote whilst in JC, from the track 'Sara Crazy Child':

> *'Broken dusty mother her face melted just like wax,*
> *Her once gazelle like features bloodied by the age axe.'*

There are so many bands right now and in the past years, where you can hear the echoes of Marc, shining through – a truly missed friend and innovator.

ANDY ELLISON
2011

Preface

"I'm swallowed in the swell of your yellow leafy breast… my crippled bended chest is shamed… stake me with steel."
Sycamore of Sorrow, poem by Marc Bolan, 1969

He had been staring at the painting for some considerable time, transfixed by its simplicity and stillness; a solitary sycamore tree framed by a cloudless night sky. In the distance a featureless hill and beneath, a few silhouetted bushes. It was certainly a curious subject for a picture. No suggestion of a breeze. No birds, nocturnal creatures, nor figures inhabited this gloomy landscape. But there was something intriguing and vaguely unsettling in the midst of the dense leaves – a sliver of the waning moon hung like a half closed eye, a portal perhaps opening into a greater reality?

He remained as still as the subject that enthralled him while the other visitors to the Louvre passed through the gallery in unseemly haste as if window shopping for culture. Both the tourists and the art students seemed to find the diminutive figure with the black shoulder-length corkscrew curls, satin jacket and dainty girls' shoes more intriguing than the treasures on display. Some whispered, "Could it be? No, surely not. Must be a lookalike." Others sniggered. An American couple cast a distinctly disapproving look when they noticed the mascara. "Such people! Not the type of person one sees in Gary, Indiana."

Which, one wondered, was the real work of art?

A plaque listed the artist as René Magritte (1898-1967), the Belgian surrealist who had set out to challenge society's preconceived perception of reality and in so doing was credited with being a seminal influence on pop art. Magritte's obsession was to deprive everyday objects of their meaning, reducing the familiar to a mere image. That notion would have appealed to the young man with the porcelain complexion and suggestively feminine features, but his interest in art had been perfunctory. Until now. A moment later his thoughts were cut short.

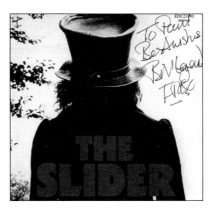

"Sound check in 20 minutes, man. We have to go."

The flustered roadie, entrusted with getting the errant rock star to the venue on time, was anxiously looking for the nearest exit when he was struck by the haunted look on the other's face. A mixture of otherworldliness and what else? Apprehension? Not exactly.

"You OK, man? You look weird."

The roadie caught the name of the painting as his charge shook his black locks and muttered something about being tired.

It was titled *Sixteenth of September*.

"Funny title for a picture of a tree."

Marc Bolan didn't answer. As the two headed for the exit, the roadie glanced back. Was it a trick of the light or did the framed silhouette remind him of the shot of the back of Bolan's head on the back cover of *The Slider* album?

Weird indeed.

Chapter 1
The Sixteenth of September, Nineteen Seventy-Seven

Bolan is alive today but he may get knocked down by a car tomorrow…
I guess my name will live longer than a record. I'm a lifestyle.
Disc, 1974

They should have taken the Rolls. But Bolan had lent it to an old mate, Dave Brock of Hawkwind, for the weekend, so they opted for the Mini. A squat, square bonnet Black Tulip (i.e. purple) GT1275 with the licence number FOX 661L. The Mini would be easier to park near the Speakeasy that night where Marc intended to check out an unsigned band he was considering producing, and then they could nip through the late evening London traffic to Morton's club in Berkeley Square to while away the early hours in the company of business associates and old friends. Besides, in the summer of '77, the Roller was considered too ostentatious for a rock star to be seen in, for it was a time when the one chord wonders fronting rock's cultural revolution were demanding the wholesale slaughter of the irrelevant, offensively self-indulgent dinosaurs who had been Bolan's contemporaries. But Marc couldn't part with the car permanently. He cherished it as a trophy of his hard earned success, physical proof that this working class chancer from Stoke Newington had joined rock's aristocracy. Besides, it was only second hand. He could never have justified shelling out serious money for a new motor of that class while his parents refused to leave their Putney council flat where his father still worked as a caretaker. For Bolan, a Rolls was a justifiable self-indulgence, a status symbol from which he could wave imperiously to the adoring throng and taunt those critics who had sneered at his claims to be as significant a figure as Clapton, Townshend or Hendrix. At the height of his fame he assured his fans that he only drove a Rolls-Royce because it was good for his voice, a self-mocking sentiment that they found endearing but which critics saw as self-aggrandisement in the extreme. But to Bolan's non-mechanical mind a 1957 white Rolls-Royce was also an incomprehensible work of modern art.

Part of the mystique of stylish automobiles derived from his love of early rock and roll – specifically Chuck Berry's 'Maybellene', Jackie Brenston's 'Rocket 88' and 'Speedo' by The Cadillacs – records which extoled the sleekly seductive allure of classic American cars that British teenagers had only seen in the movies. This obsession was compounded by the fact that Marc had never learned to drive for fear that one day he might end his days in a crash like his childhood hero Eddie Cochran. It was a mystique intensified by the impractical nature of his mind and his inability to grasp the principle of anything mechanical or mundane. In Marc's world rock stars didn't drive. They had chauffeurs. His had been the redoubtable Alphi who had doubled as a bodyguard to keep the screaming teenage girls (and boys) from getting too close to their idol with their sharpened scissors. Everyone in those days had wanted a lock of Marc's hair.

But times had changed. The screaming teens had grown up. Alphi had gone (critically injured in a car accident in January 1974) and the garage at the new house in Upper Richmond

Road West was empty. Marc missed the adulation, but in his mind he was still a star, the biggest pop star Britain had seen since The Beatles. And his drastically diminished coterie of devoted fans remained faithful despite their idol's declining fortunes and the steady dilution of the music that had once enchanted them.

A number of the New Wave bands such as The Damned and Siouxsie and the Banshees were not ashamed to admit they admired him, their endorsement suggesting that the dethroned King of Glam Rock might now enjoy a more enduring second career as Godfather of Punk, a role he clearly relished.

The appellation wasn't as ludicrous as it first appeared. After all, he had rarely used more than three chords himself and what could be more minimalist than 'Metal Guru'? He had returned the compliment by inviting The Damned as support on his *Dandy In The Underworld* tour (a prophetic album title if ever there was one), praising Siouxsie as a name to look out for in his weekly column for *Record Mirror* that summer and offering a number of token new wave acts, such as The Jam, Bob Geldof's Boomtown Rats and Billy Idol's Generation X a spot on his Granada tea-time children's pop show, *Marc*, which he had just completed filming. And now there was talk of a second series.

In America it was a different story. They had never taken him seriously. But in Britain he could still command a few column inches in the national press if the quote was sufficiently outrageous. But of more importance, after years of substance abuse and emotional instability he had regained his self-respect by ditching the drugs and submitting to a rigorous regime of diet and exercise. Friends feared that he had overdone it by slimming down to a near anorexic nine stone in an effort to restore his earlier elfin-like appearance. As Diaghilev had once said to Nijinsky, "No one likes a fat faun", an observation the acutely self-conscious Bolan had taken to heart. (He hadn't read the biog, but he'd seen the movie starring Alan Bates.)

Alcohol, however, was a different matter. White wine, champagne and cognac were a recreational diversion from the tedium of touring and a soothing treatment for pre-performance nerves, but like a lot of other things for which he had a taste, Marc was inclined to indulge to excess. Today, Thursday 15th September, he had started early. It began in the late morning with a bottle of wine shared with his dentist then continued over a light lunch with partner Gloria Jones and her brother Richard who had flown in to stay with the couple and their two-year-old son Rolan for a few days.

Bolan was in the mood to celebrate and it was not just the promise of a second TV series or talk of a late autumn UK tour that had mellowed him.

The protracted acrimonious wrangling over the terms of his divorce from his first wife June were now behind him, although the official decree had not yet come through. He was now living a real life with Gloria and Rolan. It looked as if he had finally found the stability he had been seeking all his life. He had played the Mod, the folky, the hippie and the Glam Rock star until the latter delivered the fame he had hungered for since the age of nine, but stardom was a fleeting, heady affair and when the party was over and the hangers-on had deserted him, it left a hollow in the pit of the stomach and a bitter sense of betrayal. If the worshipping crowds had really loved him, where were they now? Had it not been for Gloria, the former Tamla Motown singer and writer who provided Bolan with a soulmate in the truest sense of the word, he might have descended into an ever increasing dependency on the chemical stimulants to sustain the buzz after the crowds had gone home.

June had been a friend, lover, muse and shrewd business partner with more 'world' savvy than the shameless opportunist himself could have mustered. Her role in his initial success was matched only by his precocious untutored talent. But Gloria completed him both as a musician and as a man. Before he met her in 1973, when she became a backing singer for T.Rex, he had cocooned himself in a childlike fantasy world, "a goldfish bowl" as he called it, isolated from reality and sustained in that illusion by his inner circle of flunkies and followers. When he had driven away many of these sycophants with his boorish behaviour only Gloria and a few loyal friends remained to give him the security he craved and the sense that he was appreciated as a musician, which had earlier undermined his self-confidence, despite his protestations to the contrary. With the birth of Rolan he also had a reason to sober up and face his responsibilities for the first time in his life.

But this evening he could relax. Rolan was staying with Marc's parents so he could let himself go and Gloria would drive him home. He had given his regular driver the night off. By the time they arrived at the Speakeasy, the music business watering hole and venue in the West End off Regent Street, Marc was loud and legless. His old friend, DJ Jeff Dexter, had tolerated a lot of Marc's drunken rants in the past, but this evening he felt he'd been let down. The young band Marc had come to hear had been rehearsing for days to impress their hero and he was in no state to give them a fair hearing. Dexter was ashamed and embarrassed. When Marc and Gloria got up to leave, Dexter excused himself from the party. He didn't want to witness more of the same at Morton's.[1]

When they arrived at Morton's, just after midnight, Marc climbed unsteadily up the steps of the white-fronted four-storey Georgian townhouse to be greeted by the reception staff who were trained to treat members with due deference, whatever their disposition. Inside, the three joined Marc's manager Tony Howard and EMI press officer Eric Hall who were waiting in the upstairs restaurant where they had planned a welcome home party for Gloria. But Hall excused himself after less than an hour. He, too, couldn't abide seeing Marc in this state. But the intimate atmosphere, fine food and musical accompaniment mollified Marc and soon he was sweet and subdued, engaging in lover's small talk with Gloria and making plans for the future. After the meal Richard persuaded the pretty blonde resident pianist, Victoria, to accompany them down to the bar where they sat and listened as Gloria, at their insistence, played the piano and sang until closing time.

It was 4 a.m. when they finally emerged. The stars were out and so too the waning moon. It would have been wiser to take a cab, but Richard's hire car and the Mini were waiting. If they took a taxi someone would have to return later that day to collect their cars. And there were now four of them as Richard had invited Victoria home. It would be an uncomfortable squeeze in a black cab. So Marc climbed in the front passenger seat of the mini, shivering slightly in his thin fluorescent green-and-white top and orange lycra strides as Gloria settled herself behind the wheel. The streets were quiet. Half an hour at the most and they would be home. She turned the heater on and debated whether to tune in the radio or let Marc doze. When he was on tour he liked to pass a long journey listening

---

1 *Morton's is now part of the Marlon Abela Restaurant Corporation, or MARC.*

Evening News

LONDON: FRIDAY SEPTEMBER 16 1977, 8p

Pop star's car smashes into tree

Gloria Jones . . . in hospital.

MARC BOLAN KILLED

Marc Bolan . . . as fans remember him

By HUGH WHITTOW

POP star Marc Bolan, 29, was killed instantly in a car crash in Barnes early today.

He was a passenger in a purple Mini which hit a tree in Queens Ride, near the junction with Gipsy Lane, just after 5 a.m.

The driver was Bolan's common-law wife Gloria Jones, 30. The black American singer broke her jaw and was taken to Queen Mary's hospital, Roehampton.

She has not yet been told of Bolan's death.

Their 20-month-old son Rolan was being looked after by Bolan's parents.

The couple were returning to their home in Richmond Road West, Sheen, after dining at Morton's Restaurant in Berkeley Square.

Stretched out

Miss Jones's car had just crossed a hump-backed bridge over a railway line when it ploughed through a thin wire fence and crashed into a horse chestnut tree.

The 1275 Mini GT, registration number FOX 661 L, was a write-off. The front windows and windscreen were shattered and parts of the engine pushed into the passenger seat.

Mr. Richard Jones, Gloria's brother, was travelling in a car behind them.

He told police that the Mini was do-

Continued on Page Two

Bolan's life story and pictures — Pages 24 and 25

DEATH CAR . . . the mini in which Marc Bolan died this morning. Police who towed it away said the car was a write-off.

TWO PAGES OF TV: 26, 27 ========== **ENTERTAINMENT: 28**

to archive recordings of DJs Alan Freed or Wolfman Jack, otherwise it would be London's own commercial station, Capital Radio. But he seemed so content and quiet, it would be a shame to break the mood.

They pulled out and turned left towards Kensington. Richard and Victoria followed close behind. Unfamiliar with the route, Richard kept the red rear lights of the Mini in sight along the King's Road, over Putney Bridge and along Queens Ride, parallel to the railway line bordering the south side of Barnes Common. The densely tree-lined road was a notorious accident black spot. It was ill-lit and surprised speeding motorists with a sharp bend hidden from view by a hump-backed bridge. There were no crash barriers at the bend, just a wall of trees to shield the houses behind from the glare of headlights. Then a mile or so from their destination, the red rear lights disappeared.

Richard slowed as he approached the bridge. Ahead he could see steam. A moment later he cleared the bridge and braked sharply.

The Mini had left the road and hit a tree. The impact had forced the engine into the passenger side killing Marc instantly.[2] He lay lifeless in the seat which had been twisted round to face the rear. The right side of the engine had trapped Gloria by the foot. She was unconscious but still breathing.

There was little Richard could do but assure his sister that an ambulance was on its way and hope that she could hear him. A light had come on in one of the houses and then another. Someone would be phoning for help.

WEEKEND STANDARD   *Evening Standard*   **LATE PRICES** STOP PRESS

47,471   London: Friday September 16 1977   6   8p

Mini driven by girlfriend hits tree

CRASH KILLS MARC BOLAN

MARC BOLAN—he took the full force of the crash sitting in the passenger seat.

THE WRECK of the purple Mini in which Marc Bolan died.

Standard Reporter

ROCK star Marc Bolan was killed today when a purple Mini driven by his girl friend left the road and hurtled into a tree on Barnes Common.

Twenty-nine-year-old Bolan, of T Rex fame, was sitting in the front passenger seat.

The car was reported to have been travelling between 40 and 50 mph, and the impact flattened the engine compartment snapping off the gear lever and forcing the steering wheel up to the roof. Bolan took the full force.

His girl friend, American singer Gloria Jones, 30, and mother of his two-year-old son Rolan, was taken to Queen Mary's Hospital, Roehampton, with a broken jaw and face injuries.

Not wearing seat belt

A Barnes police spokesman said : " As far as we know neither of the occupants of the car was wearing a seat belt."

Miss Jones was said by a hospital spokesman to be fairly comfortable. "She has her jaw wired up and she is on the mend."

Her manager Tony Howard said : "She does not know yet about Marc's death. She is in deep, deep shock. The doctor's advise against telling her.

" Gloria had just got back from Los Angeles, where she had been for six weeks. She brought her in a car behind the Mini. He came round the bend and saw the crash. He pulled them out of the car. He was first on the scene."

TV shows go on

The party had been dining at Morton's in Berkeley Square. Tony Howard—also Bolans manager—joined them with his wife for coffee. He left at 3.15 am and Bolan left shortly after.

Marc and Gloria were driving back to their home in East Sheen.

Distraught, Mr Howard said: "The party had not been drinking. Marc had given up drink as part of a slimming exercise. He had recently lost two stone.

Mr Howard went on: "Marc was doing very well with his

Cont. Back Page Col. 1

● News on Camera—Page 3

---

2 *Marc's mother told the author that the full extent of her son's injuries had been kept from her, but that she had later learned that his chest had been crushed by the engine and that this was the primary cause of death, making the quotation from 'Sycamore of Sorrow' even more prophetic.*

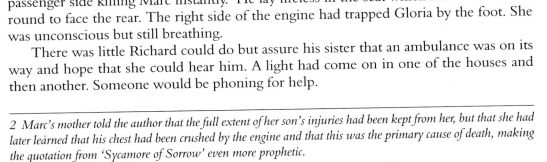

There was blood, oil and glass all over the inside of the car and in the road.

Victoria sat at the side of the road in shock. Richard was shaking.

It was then that he noticed the sliver of the waning moon in the heart of the sycamore tree. It looked like a closing eye.

Five years earlier Marc had remarked that life was as easy as 'picking foxes from a tree' ('Solid Gold, Easy Action'), a curious allusion which now took on an ominously prophetic meaning.

It was later alleged that Gloria had been driving with more than the legal alcohol limit in her blood, that she was tired and that in such a condition she was not able to negotiate the sharp bend at speed. It was also alleged that one of the tyres was 12 pounds under the required pressure and that two of the wheel nuts were loose which could have affected braking and steering. But these factors alone would not have proven fatal had there been crash barriers, adequate lighting and forewarning of a sharp bend. With no barrier to lessen the impact even seat belts could not have saved them.

On that night Fate, it seemed, had ensured that Marc would leave the stage as swiftly and painlessly as possible. Two weeks before his 30th birthday.

Marc had fulfilled the promise he had made to himself at an early age, to "live fast, die young and leave a beautiful corpse", a quote incorrectly attributed to James Dean which was in fact spoken by a teenage hoodlum played by actor John Derek in the 1949 film *Knock On Any Door*, a film Marc had seen several times.

Cosmic Dancer
I danced myself out of the womb. Is it strange to dance so soon?
Marc Bolan, 'Cosmic Dancer'

Marc Bolan considered himself to be unique and in one sense, he was right. Although he was not, perhaps, the most prodigiously gifted or technically accomplished artist of his generation, he was certainly one of a kind – which is arguably the more desirable – and as such, he was irreplaceable. But he was unique in another sense.

We are all fashioned to a greater or lesser degree by the circumstances of our birth and conditioned by our environment. Our parents instill certain values and attitudes and influence us by example, while the culture, religion and society that we are born into also leave their indelible impression on our personality so that each individual could be said to be a product of their time. Marc Bolan was no exception, even though he liked to imagine himself to be a magical being, the immortal Cosmic Dancer who danced himself out of the womb in his song of the same name and is dancing still among the stars. Marc had no interest in religion but he was a firm believer in reincarnation, the transmigration of the soul from body to body, until after a succession of lives the essence of the individual attains perfection and union with the Divine source. Such notions, shared by almost all of the earth's cultures, may not be as fanciful as they might appear.

According to the Jewish mystical tradition known as Kabbalah, which Marc was unfamiliar with but would have heard of while pursuing a passing interest in magic and mysticism, an individual who was created for a particular purpose is born at a predetermined time and place so that the configuration of the planets will influence their psychological make-up. The subtle influence of the celestial bodies on their inner being would stimulate the development of certain attributes at the expense of others to produce a balance of qualities and characteristics that will be peculiar to that person. He or she will then be predisposed to develop certain innate abilities and seize preordained opportunities when they arise as if answering the call of destiny. The more aggressively this person asserts their individuality, the more they will appear to be determining their own destiny until they have served their purpose. Such a luminous personality will fascinate the mass of 'common humanity' who will be intuitively drawn to it, some of whom will mourn its passing long after it has left this world.

The core concept in Kabbalah is the balancing of complementary attributes which we all possess but which we choose or are inclined to develop at the expense of others. A person who attains this equilibrium over the course of many lifetimes becomes a fully realised human being (Adam Kadmon, the cosmic man, the cosmic dancer) and has broken free of the cycle of birth, death and rebirth.

Prior to incarnation every individual will also have chosen their family and the more significant members of their soul group with whom they will interact, some of whom will assist them and others to work against them, testing their resolve and offering obstacles to be overcome. Although they will all be unconscious of the roles they will play, they may from time to time experience a sense that they have known each other at some other time and place, but will not be able to recall where or when.

If all this sounds too 'heavy' to explain the life choices of a mere pop star, then consider the following.

Bolan's Birth Chart

Our lives are merely trees of possibilities ('Dragon's Ear')

In 1978 Marc's publishers, Essex Music, commissioned a respected professional astrologer to draw up his natal chart in great detail. They withheld the identity of the subject from her and the fact that he was dead. She was told only that he was male and given his time, place and date of birth.

Her analysis of his personality proved uncannily accurate.

Marc was born at 12:30 on the morning of September 30, 1947 at Hackney Hospital in London, making him a Libran (September 23-October 23). The typical Libran, she observed, possesses natural grace and a fragile physical beauty which can manifest in the excessively vain male as narcissism. Such people crave attention and when deprived will wilt like a neglected flower. The typical Libran requires constant stimulation, appreciation and the devotion of admirers to sustain their self-image.

The chart suggested that this particular subject's sense of style would lead them, most likely, to a career in the arts where their determination to succeed should help them overcome any obstacles. Failing that, their impish charm and open, winning smile would ensure they got their way.

When given gifts they might not show sufficient gratitude because they may take their popularity for granted. But in general, individuals born under this sign can be extremely generous, although sometimes their generosity will mask an ulterior motive. They might hope for something in return, to curry favour or simply to feel needed. In this particular subject his angelic side hid a sharp sarcastic streak.

She went on to explain that her anonymous subject was a particularly strong Libran because he had four planets in that house and that would mean that he would be living in his head much of the time as Libra is an Air sign, governing the intellect and imagination. As such he would be an impractical person and constantly conflicted between his need for recognition and his desire to create work of beauty. His artistic impulse and his burning ambition would be a dominant theme in his life. If he was not allowed peace and privacy, his art would suffer, he would produce frivolous work and risk developing psychological problems.

The presence of Sagittarius rişing in the chart indicated that he would be constantly pursuing grand schemes which would invariably come to nothing as he was too restless to see them through. His artistic potential was "tremendous", but would be thwarted by his impatience and continual craving for something new.

In fact, his tendency to escape reality was one of the central themes in his chart and could lead to a dependency on drink or drugs. On an emotional level, there was a constant need to be loved and be in love and the dominance of the passive feminine aspect of Libra suggested that the subject might be bisexual.

Contrary to popular belief, astrology is not a means of divination, but from the subject's predisposition it is possible to foretell the direction a life is likely to take. When told that her subject was deceased the astrologer felt confident in saying that his death was "a sudden release" rather than the result of a prolonged illness. Of course, one could say that given his age that would be a pretty safe assumption, but the description she had given of Marc's personality had proved to be uncannily accurate.

CREEM

BOOGIE ALONG WITH BEEFHEART

CAN YOU TAKE 33" OF MARC BOLAN FOR NOTHING? GIANT COLOUR POSTER FREE INSIDE

DISCO 45

SONGBOOK SONGBOOK SONGBOOK SO

no. 6 5P

HIT SONGS FROM:

FREE 250 records
details inside

SONGBOOK SONGBOOK SONGBOOK SONGBOOK

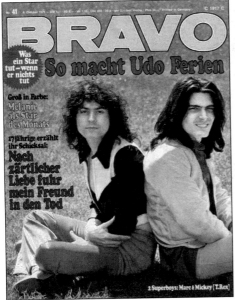

BRAVO

Nr. 41

So macht Udo Ferien

Was ein Star tut – wenn er nichts tut

Groß in Farbe: Melanie als Star des Monats

17jährige erzählt ihr Schicksal: Nach zärtlicher Liebe fuhr mein Freund in den Tod

2 Superboys: Marc & Mickey [T.Rex]

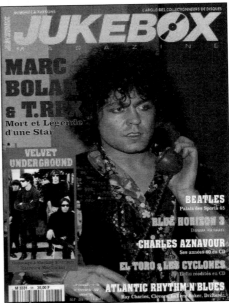

JUKEBOX

L'ARGUS DES COLLECTIONNEURS DE DISQUES

MARC BOLAN & T.REX
Mort et Legende d'une Star

VELVET UNDERGROUND

BEATLES
Palais des Sports 65

BLUE HORIZON 3
Dossier thématique

CHARLES AZNAVOUR
Ses années 60 en CD

EL TORO & LES CYCLONES
Enfin réédités en CD

ATLANTIC RHYTHM'N'BLUES
Ray Charles, Clovers, La Vern Baker, Drifters...

Chapter 2
Funky London Childhood

> *In the head of a man is a woman, in the head of a woman is a man,*
> *but what wonders roam in the head of a child?*
> Album cover verse from Prophets, Seers and Sages

When the baby was brought into the harsh artificial light and commotion of the delivery room in Hackney hospital just after midnight on the last day of September, 1947 there was relief that the child had been delivered safely and appeared to be healthy, if it's constant bleating was any reliable indication.

His parents were thrilled, of course, but in no mood to celebrate. For Simeon and Phyllis Feld, life was a daily struggle to pay the rent on their sparsely furnished four room flat in Stoke Newington, a working class neighborhood of East London. It was all they could afford on Simeon's wages of four pounds a week as a long distance lorry driver. Home on the upper floors of the dilapidated Victorian terraced house at 25 Stoke Newington Common had been cramped and uncomfortable at the best of times, but with only one coal fire for heating and no hot running water, it would be a test of endurance to get through the coming winter, one of the bitterest in living memory. That night the proud father bought a round for his friends at The Three Crowns to 'wet the baby's head' in the best East End tradition. No shorts. Just a couple of beers. He would have to be back on the road early the next morning.

Simeon, or Sid as he preferred to be called, was then 27 and the eldest of four sons born to Smithfield market porter Henry Feld and his red-haired Irish sweetheart Betsie (Bessie) whose maiden name had been Ruffell. Henry and Bessie settled first in Stepney before moving to Bethnal Green where their first son was born on August 22, 1920. 19 years later Sid left home to serve in the Dutch merchant navy as a steward during the war having been discharged from the British Army after basic training due to his poor eyesight. When he married Phyllis on January 31, 1945 at Fulham Registry Office she was just 19, the fourth daughter of Henry and Elsie Atkins, a Fulham greengrocer and a domestic.

A snapshot taken on their wedding day captures a smiling, unassuming couple who appeared to be content with their modest lot in life and looked as if they had the resilience to weather whatever the future had in store.

Phyllis and Sid shared the same birth sign (Phyllis was born on August 23, 1927), the same number of siblings and fathers with the same forename. But there was one significant element which the couple did not have in common. Although his mother was a Catholic, Simeon had been raised as a Jew whereas Phyllis was a gentile. This caused some tension in the Feld family, as Henry had hoped his son would marry in a synagogue as he had done, but Phyllis had no strong feelings about religion. She persuaded Sid that a civil ceremony would forestall any further argument as well as avoiding any awkward questions concerning the fact that she was already four months pregnant with their first child. However, she agreed that they would consider themselves to be a Jewish family if that's what her husband wanted.

According to the laws of Orthodox Judaism the children of a mixed marriage would not be recognised as such as the faith is passed down through the mother, but liberal or reform communities would have welcomed them. Phyllis was disinclined to take on the extra chores required to keep a *kosher* home, having more pressing matters on her mind, so she deferred to her husband as head of the family. Sid did not observe the rituals of his religion or acknowledge the high holidays, nor did he instill the teachings and beliefs in his boys, but his own background was rooted in the tradition and there were strong links to relatives who were then living in the neighbouring district of Stamford Hill. There was another factor however which made it impossible for Sid to sever all ties to his heritage, a nagging feeling that if he did so he would be betraying the memory of his own younger brother who had been brutally murdered in an anti-Semitic attack the year before Mark was born. It was in memory of his late Uncle Mark that the boy had been named.

Mark wouldn't have his mother's undivided attention for long however. Elder brother Harry was then just over two years old and curious to see his new playmate as soon as his parents brought it home from the hospital. At first Harry seemed doubtful that the mewling infant could be any relation of his. Harry was fair-haired with a high forehead like his father, whereas Mark took after his mother with a rounder face framed by a mess of dark wavy hair. Harry would grow tall and stocky while Mark remained small and sleight. The dissimilarity in both physique and temperament would become more pronounced as they grew, with Harry inheriting his father's quiet, self-effacing nature and Mark his mother's sensitivity and irrepressible enthusiasm. But the boys shared a strong affection for each other which Harry demonstrated on many occasions whenever older boys bullied his little brother.

As soon as he learnt to walk Mark was running, restless to explore and experience his surroundings. Unfortunately, it was not the ideal environment for an active and curious child. The only decent sized room in their portion of the house had to double as the boys' bedroom, the smaller being their parents' room at the rear with the kitchen and bathroom on the floor below. But at least the brothers could look out on the scrub of ground locals called the Common while their parents woke each morning to see only row upon row of grey tiled roofs and smoking chimneys. There were other tenants in the house, occupying the rooms below on the middle and ground floor who remembered the Felds as a very ordinary working class family who rarely quarreled and seemed happy enough. With Sid being away so often it was left to Phyllis to raise the boys. She was not demonstrably affectionate, but was devoted to them and ensured that they were as smartly turned out as she could manage.

But she had little time to entertain them.

They were expected to amuse themselves with the little they had. Their neighbour's children were allowed to explore the local bomb sites and play football on the common, but Mark was very young and his mother too over-protective to let him out of her sight. So he and Harry passed their preschool years sculpting dinosaurs out of plasticine, playing marbles, re-reading the few comics they possessed or playing with their toy cars on the floor of their room when the weather was bad, doing much the same outside when it was fine in the large flower bed that served as a garden. But neither was allowed to roam the streets, or cross the main road which was teeming with traffic.

The Felds had it hard, but they were better off than many in the East End who had been bombed out of their homes and had lost family members in the war. Many fathers, sons and brothers would not be coming back to make a home and raise a family. Those who returned might do so only to learn that a wife, sister, aunt, mother or child had been a casualty on the Home Front. It was not a time for celebration. Cynics would say the Americans had won the war and that Britain had merely survived. The country was exhausted after five and a half years of stubborn resistance, fighting a war it could not afford. The prevailing mood was to push on and hope things would get better. They certainly couldn't get much worse.

Thousands of those who survived the *Luftwaffe's* relentless air raids on London returned from the shelters to grim terraced houses with no indoor plumbing or electricity. Gas and water meters had to be fed regularly with small change or you would wake on a winter's morning in the dark with no hot water to wash in. The maxim of the post war period was 'make do and mend' which meant that clothes, shoes and even saucepans were repaired until they fell to pieces. The only recycling anyone practised in the late forties and early fifties was handing down their clothes and shoes to younger siblings. For the average housewife who spent six days of every week cleaning, cooking, scrubbing, shopping, polishing, waxing, washing, wringing and ironing, the war to make ends meet had not ended on VE Day. Rationing was still in force. Meals were basic, consisting mainly of meat or fish with vegetables or potatoes, boiled, fried or mashed. There were no children's meals or pre-frozen ready meals which we take for granted today, no fish fingers, pasta or pizza. Each item on the menu had to be bought from the butcher, grocer, fishmonger and baker whose shop became the social centre of the community. That meant a morning spent trudging from shop to shop and then preparing the food fresh for the evening meal. Supermarkets were an American phenomenon and would not be seen in Britain until the mid-sixties. In post war Britain a convenience store meant a shop within walking distance. It was a world in which spaghetti was considered exotic and you risked being labeled a gourmet if you put salad cream on your greens.

Even fizzy drinks were unknown then. Instead, children bought a packet of lemonade powder for a few pennies and poured it into an empty bottle to be diluted with water.

Fridges were a luxury, hoovers unheard of and the only television sets most working class families saw were on display in the windows of electrical appliance shops and department stores. Until the Coronation of Queen Elizabeth ll in June 1953 made owning a television set desirable and Hire Purchase plans made it affordable, the average British family gathered around the wireless for news and entertainment. Only the wealthy Westenders had a phone. In the East End you relied on letters and doorstep gossip for family news and only used a telephone box in an emergency.

The trams had largely been replaced by trolleybuses but there were still horses and carts to be seen in the streets, owned by rag-and-bone men who collected scrap metal from the bombsites during the week and sold shrimps and winkles on Sundays.

Working mothers trusted their neighbours to keep an eye on their children who would be allowed to play outdoors until dusk. Girls could earn a couple of coppers by offering to take their neighbours' babies out in the pram with a bottle of milk or milky tea to keep the infant quiet. This was the world Mark Feld had been born into, a world of self-reliance, a world in which you had to stand up for yourself if you wanted to get your share.

At night, when her work was done, Phyllis would read to the boys as they lay in bed, Mark's eyes tightly closed as he tried to visualise the exotic creatures which inhabited the fairy tales and bible stories that she retold in her own words so that he could understand. By the age of five he had discovered the pleasure of reading for himself, albeit through the improbable exploits of western heroes such as Casey Ruggles, Tex Ritter, Hopalong Cassidy and Rocky Lane whose adventures were being reprinted in black and white by English publishers. Every Sunday morning before Sid left to help his father set out the market stalls for other traders at Petticoat Lane, Mark would remind him to be on the lookout for more of these titles and Sid would do his best not to disappoint him.

With no savings or spare change to buy 'extras', it was down to Sid to make toys with whatever came to hand. One afternoon he came home with a set of pushchair wheels and some wood he'd found under a railway arch. By supper time he'd put together a cart complete with bottle tops nailed loosely to the front so they jingled as it drove over the cobbles. For Mark it was the start of his lifelong obsession with cars, but other local kids used their soap box cars to collect offcuts from the timber yard which they bundled together with string and sold door to door for firewood. Mark, however, was not interested in anything so crude as hawking firewood. He was happy to sit in 'Thunderwing' and wave imperiously to passersby.

Sid often drove through the evening to save having to spend a few shillings on a grubby B&B but it meant that he would arrive home too late to see the children. He'd look in on them as they slept before turning in himself, but on Saturday afternoons he made an effort to take them to the Common or to nearby Clissold Park. The 54-acre park was a favourite outing for the boys because after being cooped up in and around the house all week, they could finally run freely in the fresh air. There was also an enclosure where younger children could feed the deer and a family of rabbits or they could throw bread crumbs to the swans and ducks in the lake. Marc would often lull himself to sleep thinking about the swans. On their way home Sid would listen patiently as his youngest described his week's adventures and of his dreams of owning a grand house to match The Mansion, the name locals had given Clissold House, the imposing villa built for a local merchant near the bandstand. In a sense, Sid was in awe of his own son. Both parents had had the most rudimentary education and would not have considered themselves imaginative or artistic in any way. The ideas that bounced around the boy's restless mind like pinballs gave his father hope that his youngest would amount to something, but what that might be, he could only guess.

At first they wondered if Mark might become an artist. His crude but kinetic attempts at painting and modeling were as confounding to his father's untrained eye as any modern work of art, but it was too early to tell. Most kids of that age knocked off explosions of colour that the average man in the street couldn't distinguish from a priceless Picasso. But they suspected he was gifted in some way. "He used to make things from plasticine," Sid said, "and did what he called painting…He'd hang his work over his bed and say: 'That's lovely' and I'd say, 'Yes it is… oooh, gawd!' And he wrote loads of poetry."

His maternal grandmother, Elsie, was convinced it was only a matter of time before Mark found his medium. Shortly before he began his schooling she looked into his large wide eyes and predicted that fame and fortune awaited him. He took her pronouncement in his stride, but the more he brooded on it, the more he felt that he had to live up to expectations.

"The first thing I really remember," he told a reporter at the height of his fame, "is going to a big green common. I remember sitting on the front porch at home. I seem to remember ten years of my life sitting on the front porch…and we had a big flower bed… There was always flooding in our road. We used to go swimming in the water or go upstairs!"

Holidays were out of the question, though the family managed the odd day trip to various seaside resorts. At Margate, Mark enthusiastically helped Harry to build sandcastles and the boys chased each other in and out of the water. But the amusement arcades were out of bounds. If their parents had saved enough during the year they might spend the afternoon in Dreamland, the fun park whose Ferris wheel drew the day trippers from the crowded beach, then it was back to the railway station to catch the last train back to London with a fish and chip supper wrapped in newspaper for the journey and a bucketful of shells for a souvenir.

The rest of the year, Stoke Newington was the centre of young Mark's world. The neighbourhood had a character all its own and residents were proud to think of themselves as separate from both Hackney and 'The Hill'. The parade of small family businesses in and around Rectory Road had a distinctly Edwardian look to them, as if lifted out of an H.G. Wells novel, many of them owned by Jewish immigrants – Wolinski's the bakers, Mrs Abrahams the grocer, the Bronsteins' fruit and vegetable shop, Faith Brothers the tailors and Negal's the tobacconist where Mrs Feld would buy sweets for her boys. But even sweets were a special treat because until 1953 they were still subject to rationing, the wartime restriction on imported goods and homegrown produce and materials that was not abolished until the following year. But Phyllis soon learnt that if she took young Mark with her, the butcher would slip in an extra slice or two of bacon for the boy and Mrs Abrahams might find a banana or orange which were considered exotic in Britain at the time.

Toys, too, were a luxury though unsophisticated by modern standards. Hula-Hoops, Frisbees and the Slinky, a step-walking spring, being the most popular with Nomura's battery powered tin man Robbie the Robot aimed at the more affluent families. Walt Disney's movie *Davy Crockett, King of the Wild Frontier* had spawned the mass marketing of fake racoon skin caps and other frontier-themed toys, the first success of the modern merchandising boom. For weeks Mark begged his mum to buy him the outfit. He would never ask for anything again. It would not be the last time that she would go without so that her youngest could have what he wanted.

The Felds didn't own a television until Mark was 15. Before then the major source of news and entertainment was the wireless and it left much to the imagination.

"Radio is the big forgotten influence – we were the last generation to be brought up before television became universal…When I was a kid I used to listen to all the *Billy Cotton Band Show* programmes…*The Goons, Hancock's Half Hour…Dick Barton Special Agent…*"

Then in September 1952 Phyllis took her youngest son by the hand and led him to the gates of Northwold Primary School just a few minutes' walk from the house. With its high surrounding wall and concrete playground this forbidding three-storey turn of the century structure resembled a Victorian workhouse. It had survived a hit during the Blitz when the pupils had been evacuated to the countryside and was now a second home to approximately 400 children, dozens of whom were the children of refugees from Nazi Germany. The infants had their classrooms on the ground floor, the juniors on the floor above and the eldest at the top. On bright days the sun streamed in through the narrow high windows which added to the Dickensian atmosphere. It was a spartan but functional environment. At least the teachers were tolerant on the whole and children didn't have to wear a uniform, which was just as well as their parents would not have been able to afford one.

The first day of school can be traumatic for any child, but Mark apparently summed up the courage to walk into the playground and make friends by summoning one of several alter egos he would call upon in moments of crisis. Whether it was Mighty Joe Young or war hero-turned-actor Audie Murphy on this occasion, no one knows, but five-year-old Mark braved the separation without complaint and was soon settled. He proved to be popular with teachers and pupils alike, although he subsequently invented a more dramatic entrance for himself.

"On my first day at school I got beaten up. On the next two days I got beaten up too. But on the third day I beat up the bloke who kept hitting me. It was all right after that! It was a nice school really. I remember liking playing with rubber bricks and making things with them."

His precocious sexuality was also in evidence at this early age, if his rather colourful version of events is to be believed.

"I remember the first lady teacher I had. She used to hang her petticoat up in the classroom. It was quite astonishing now I think of it. She never took it off in front of the kids. She must have taken it off during the break 'cos when we came back from playtime it was there hanging up!"

Every child was given a half pint bottle of milk each morning (until the practice was abolished by Margaret Thatcher in 1971) and a small hot meal at lunch time. In return they were expected to be quiet and obedient at all times, sitting in regimented rows behind their desks which had a china ink pot in the top and a channel across the top to hold a metal-nibbed pen. Lessons were learned by rote and limited to the three R's – reading, writing and arithmetic.

Mark was always fiercely proud of his roots, but in the company of journalists and anyone else he considered to be one of the educated classes, he would affect a cut glass English accent that had probably never existed outside the members enclosure at Ascot. Mark thought that by mimicking the heavily enunciated manner of speech known as RP (Received Pronunciation) practised by BBC announcers, it would be assumed that he was well read and that his every pronouncement was beyond reproach. It was a form of inverted snobbery and it was understandable that someone from the 'wrong side of the river' might put on 'airs and graces' as Cockneys were often portrayed in post war films and on the radio as comical caricatures or as somewhat shifty types that were not to be trusted. This affectation of Mark's was already evident in those first years at Northwold

Primary and was the cause of much amusement among his less pretentious classmates. So too was his penchant for spinning elaborate fantasies to ensure he became the centre of attention, a habit he never grew out of. He would grudgingly admit to having had the same interests as other children of his age, but then the urge to embellish the truth would prove too tempting.

"We had a gang. We were quite rough. I got knifed when I was a kid. Our gang was called The Sharks, like the guys in West Side Story. I was only eight, mind. We used to rush round the streets wearing our dad's army helmets – the ones they had in the war. I remember liking the gang, being part of it…I loved my childhood – looking back, I wouldn't want to swap it for anyone's. In a way I'd like to be young again – you can tell from my music."

The daily routine of school life was periodically relieved by the magic of the movies, at that time still the British public's primary source of entertainment and escapism from the working week. Phyllis would walk the boys to the ABC, a 1,900-seater cinema on Lower Clapton Road designed in the art deco style by architect William R.Glen, or take the bus to the Regent in Stamford Hill, another art deco picture palace which jutted out like a landlocked luxury liner between the adjoining buildings.

It was an impressive setting, even if the wooden seats in both the circle and the stalls meant that it could be an uncomfortable experience on those rare occasions when the main feature was longer than the customary 90 minutes. But the audiences for Saturday morning cinema club and children's matinees were too excited to stay in their seats.

At the ABC Minors and the Odeon Club a compere would lead the children in a sing-along, giving out cards to those celebrating their birthdays and encouraging everyone to hiss the villain and cheer the hero of the weekly serial, be it Flash Gordon, Zorro, the Masked Avenger or the Lone Ranger. These black-and-white low budget cliff-hangers dated back to the 1930s, but the kids didn't care. For this pre-TV generation who relied on the wireless at home for their entertainment, anything on a big screen had them riveted for the duration.

In fact, the whole movie going experience was staged to be an event. Outside, a uniformed commissioner kept the queues in order while buskers entertained them in the hope of collecting spare change. Once inside, smartly dressed ushers showed ticket holders to their seats while an organist played popular tunes until the house lights dimmed and the Wurlitzer sank beneath the orchestra pit.

A typical trip to the cinema in the 1950s offered a main feature, or two 'B' movies, a 'full supporting programme' including cartoons, Movietone newsreel, and, of course, the trailers for 'forthcoming attractions'. Even the Pearl and Dean adverts would be watched in reverential silence accompanied only by the slurping of Kiora orange juice through plastic straws and the noisy appreciation of ice cream.

And when the show was over, there might be time to sit in the café situated in the auditorium, or queue for a hair cut from the barber who did a steady trade in the foyer. But while other kids were subjected to a short back and sides, Mark and Harry were allowed to grow their hair, as long as it didn't touch their collars.

By the age of eight Mark had grown out of U-rated comedies, westerns and swashbuckling adventures and was pestering Harry to take him to see something more stimulating. He found it in the Universal horror films of the thirties and forties which were being reissued in double bills after having been banned during the war. The 'H' for Horror classification had just been superseded by the 'X' rating which restricted such films to those over 16. But the Universal horrors starring Boris Karloff and Bela Lugosi were being issued with an 'A' certificate, meaning that boys of Mark's age could often sneak in if accompanied by an older brother, or even alone if the commissioner was prepared to look the other way.

"I think I've seen every horror film that has ever been made." The first X film he admitted to seeing was *Serious Charge* starring his childhood idol Cliff Richard, then all the Elvis films and every obscure rock and roll movie he could track down. But he kept a soft spot for Cliff and also Al Jolson, whose biopic *The Jolson Story* remained a favourite of his into adulthood. Other films that he revisited whenever the opportunity arose included *Untamed Youth* with Eddie Cochran, Cliff's second film *Espresso Bongo*, *The Wizard of Oz*, *East of Eden*, *A Star Is Born*, *On the Waterfront* and *Sunset Boulevard*.

Of all the films Mark saw in those preteen years, there were a handful which made a lasting impression. Universal's 1943 remake of *The Phantom of the Opera* was a particular favorite. He would lie awake at night reliving the scene in which the disfigured composer played by Claude Rains seduces the beautiful ingénue (Susanna Foster) with the promise of stardom. Raines' rich, mellifluous voice and the force of his (unseen) presence exerted a fearful fascination on the helpless young girl. The frisson of seeing the phantom unmasked was only half the attraction. Mark empathised with the maligned genius, denied the recognition that he deserved and hounded to his death by an angry mob. To exercise that degree of control over another person intrigued him. The music was almost incidental. The key to immortality, he decided, was the power of one's personality.

This notion was enforced by two other movies which stayed with him long after he had left the cinema. The first was the science fiction classic *The Day The Earth Stood Still* (1951) in which a messianic alien played by Michael Rennie travels to Earth to compel humanity to abandon plans to accelerate its aggressive space race which is threatening the peace of the universe. Again, it wasn't the central theme of alien intervention in human folly or even the presence of a large robot armed with a lethal ray which appealed to Mark, but the idea that the world could fall silent and be enraptured by a single, all powerful presence.

The third in the trio of his seminal cinematic influences was *Rebel without a Cause* (1955) which stared the 24-year-old James Dean as the troubled teen at war with himself and the world. Unable to find meaning or purpose in his empty existence and frustrated by his inability to express his rage, he inadvertently brings about the death of his best friend and loses the girl he loves. Though Mark did not identify with the character's inner conflicts and was somewhat bemused by the intensity of his self-inflicted anguish, he was impressed by the brooding presence on screen. Dean's death in a car wreck that same year fixed his iconic image in the minds of a generation and made his young fans acutely aware of the fleeting nature of fame.

These carefree days of childhood ended when Mark moved into the junior school and was expected to demonstrate some degree of academic ability.

A school photo taken in 1956 shows a pensive, unsmiling nine-year-old looking into the camera, an open book on the desk before him. It is a revealing artifact because it would have been around this time that Mark first exhibited signs of mild dyslexia, a learning disorder which impairs the ability to read or write fluently. As with many cognitive disorders, there is a wide degree of difficulty, and Mark would have been diagnosed as borderline, if the school system had been actively monitoring pupils for learning difficulties, as they do today. But, in the 1950s, state schools, and inner city schools in particular, had no concept of special educational needs, or the funding to support children who were struggling. In Mark's case this led to his habit of asking others to read to him and of more import, attaching more value to the sound of words than their meaning when writing his own poetry and song lyrics. This imbued his more fanciful songs of the Tyrannosaurus Rex and early T.Rex period with a playfulness that was endearing, but it would later become a mere excuse for accepting the first phrase that came into his head. He dearly wanted to be a poet, but once he had experienced adulation and racked up a few hits he wasn't prepared to work at his craft any longer than was necessary.

Fortunately, dyslexia has no correlation with intelligence and so a pupil with mild difficulties in recognising letters and words would have appeared attentive and intelligent at other times. The real problems would occur in secondary school as the work load increased and pupils would be expected to write extended essays without assistance. These pupils would find homework stressful and would become increasingly anxious at the prospect of taking exams. This coupled with the emotional upheaval involved in becoming a teenager would manifest in a dismissive attitude towards formal education to divert attention from his or her perceived inadequacy.

Mark referred to his own problem only in passing but it was a revealing slip. "(School) wasn't a bad place to be when I was five and we spent our time building bricks. But when the teachers tried to get me to do figure work and writing I just freaked out." And no one thought to ask why.

Mark's stable home life ensured that his frustration and adolescent energy was channeled away from delinquency, but his willfulness and abundant self-confidence could not be constrained. Shortly after that troubling photo was taken he found an outlet that would help him to express his individuality in a unique form.

Chapter 3
All the Young Dudes

A very rare photo of Mark during the period he was reading Rimbaud and modelling himself on Beau Brummell (photographer unknown. From the private collection of Danielz and Caron Willans)

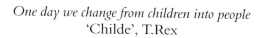

One day we change from children into people
'Childe', T.Rex

I t was a Sunday evening in September 1956 and Phyllis had just seen the boys to bed after their bath. Sid was sitting by the fireplace in the kitchen reading the paper when she joined him. She pulled up a chair and looked around for her sewing box and the socks she needed to darn. With the boys sleeping in what had been their living room, this was the only place the couple could unwind at the end of the day.

"Sid?"

"Hmm?"

"I've been thinking about what Elsie said about Mark being talented. Maybe even being famous one day."

He folded the paper and continued to read without comment.

"And I was thinking, maybe we ought to encourage him, support him in some way."

Sid cleared his throat, but didn't look up. "Buy him some more paints and coloured pencils, you mean?"

Phyllis began threading a needle and tried to sound as casual as she could whenever the prickly subject of money had to be discussed.

"No, not pencils."

"What then?"

"Well, it's his birthday at the end of the month and he's getting too old for toys. And now with me working weekends at the stall in Berwick Street and us having a few extra bob every week, we might get him something he could really use. To learn something. He's awful keen on music right now."

The paper came down with a rush as if her husband was swatting a fly. "You're not buying a bloody piano I hope! You won't get it up these stairs, woman."

"Will you calm down?! Who mentioned a piano? Did I say anything about a piano?"

"Alright, alright."

"As a matter of fact it's a guitar. And if you stop gawping at the sports pages for a minute you'll see the very one I have in mind on the back page."

There was rustling and then a severe intake of breath on the other side of *The Sunday Pictorial*.

"Blimey. That's nine quid, that is. Bet Formby doesn't have one that expensive."

"That's the ad Mark saw today and he got very excited about it. Anyway, it's nothing to do with George Formby. This is a guitar, not a ukulele. Ever since you brought him home that Bill Haley record instead of Bill Hayes, Marc wants to play like Haley and Elvis. All the kids want to be Elvis these days."

"Don't blame me for introducing him to that racket. Didn't I make him a guitar a few months ago out of orange boxes and elastic bands? He seemed happy enough with that at the time."

"That was just for fun. To jump around with and pretend. You can't make music with that thing. He wants to actually play an instrument and that contraption you made won't do. It's a fair bit of money, it's true, but there's the never-never. Half a crown a week and that's his birthday sorted."

Sid gave a long sigh, straightened the paper and settled back in his chair. It was one of the best decisions he ever made.

Had Mr and Mrs Hayes of Harvey, Illinois, not christened their youngest son William in June 1925, Mark Feld might not have become Marc Bolan, for it was the similarity in names between country singer Bill Hayes and portly rock and roll pioneer Bill Haley which led to Mark's first encounter with rock and roll.

One Sunday, in spring 1956, Sid had brought home a 45-rpm single by Country & Western singer Bill Hayes to play on the family's new radiogram, a massive piece of furniture which took up one length of the boy's bedroom. Sid had bought the record second hand from one of the stall holders in Petticoat Lane because he knew Mark was "mad keen" on Davy Crockett and would want to have the hit song from the film. Some weeks later he brought home a second record, a 45rpm extended play by the same singer, or so he thought.

"Dad, this isn't Bill Hayes," groaned Mark, taking one look at the cover, "It's Bill Haley." The name meant nothing to Mark, but he gave the record a play out of curiosity.

"One, two, three o'clock, four o'clock rock..!" The band hadn't reached the chorus before Mark realised he'd plugged into something totally new. Few knew at the time that Haley was little more than a tubby middle-aged hillbilly singer with a novelty dance hit who just happened to be in the right place at the right time. Until Elvis, Jerry Lee, Chuck Berry, Gene Vincent and Little Richard hit the airwaves with the real thing, Bill Haley and the Comets were in the front seat of the roller coaster that was heading their way at breakneck speed. Davy Crockett was for kids. Rock and roll was for teens and that Sunday Mark couldn't wait to grow up.

It's almost impossible for the 21st century consumer with the luxury of downloadable music on-demand, 24-hour music channels and more musical genres than Disney had Dalmatians, to fully appreciate the seismic impact the arrival of rock and roll had on youth culture in the mid-fifties. In fact, there was no such thing as youth culture at the time. You were either a kid, or an adult. Teenagers didn't exist as a recognisable group, unless you counted the Bobby Soxers who swooned and screamed at the crooners such as Sinatra and Johnny Ray. Until American DJ Alan Freed coined the name Rock and Roll to describe the suggestive juke joint jive that dancers did to this new brand of R&B, teenagers were an anonymous group of in-betweenies. Rock gave them an identity and a music they could call their own.

For those, like Mark, too young to see the movie of the moment, *Blackboard Jungle* featuring Haley's hit song, there was nothing to do but read about the riots that ensued as fans ripped up cinema seats and jived in the aisles. What made the new music all the more exciting was the venomous condemnation heaped upon it by the older generation whose righteous indignation made the Teddy Boys sound like a popular revolutionary movement set on overthrowing the establishment.

But by the time nine-year-old Mark Feld opened the largest of his presents on September 30, 1956, Haley had already been superseded in his affections by Elvis.

Presley personified the defiant, untamed spirit of rock and roll. The 21-year-old truck driver from Memphis, Tennessee, had been baptised in the bitter-sweet longing of gospel and as a child had listened at the open windows of the Holy Roller churches on the outskirts of town as the black congregations prayed and swayed for salvation. After school he hung around the house listening to the keening, yearning call of the white country singers on the *Louisiana Hayride* country radio showcase and at night he tuned in to the black stations playing 'race records', the blues and R&B.

It was an intoxicating, volatile combination and when Elvis shook it up on his early sides for Sun and RCA he unleashed a sound of raw, primeval power that put the fear of God into the older generation and electrified the young.

But it was not only the music that had made Elvis a teenage idol, nor was it his petulant Grecian good looks, the slicked down quiff and insolent curl of the lip. It was his smouldering, suggestive sexuality, the way he wiggled his hips as he sang and slung his acoustic guitar to the side so he could bump 'n' grind uninhibited by an instrument. The young Mark Feld recognised it the first time he saw 'Elvis the Pelvis', as the popular press called him, performing 'Heartbreak Hotel' on a tiny flickering black-and-white TV screen at a friend's house. Elvis had attitude. He was everything James Dean had been, but with the music to back it up. If Mark had a guitar he could imitate that snake hip shake. He could be Elvis. Maybe he could even pick up a few chords.

That autumn and winter Mark spent every spare moment standing in front of the bedroom mirror perfecting his Elvis impersonation. His voice had not yet broken and his chubby round face couldn't replicate the mean, lean and hungry look needed to be a teenage idol, but he got the shoulder shrugging and sneer down pat and he learned every word to the latest hits by his hero as well as those by Buddy Holly, The Everly Brothers, Chuck Berry and Eddie Cochran. Little Richard and Jerry Lee Lewis, however, didn't get a look in as they didn't play guitar. But then again, neither did Mark. When school broke up for the holidays the following summer, Stoke Newington's diminutive star had a rudimentary grasp of three or four basic chords, but oodles of enthusiasm. He also had absorbed the sound of those early primitive records at close range and at high volume by leaning in to the single speaker of his parent's radiogram as if willing himself inside the studio on the day they were made. For his school age friends, rock was for dancing. It was fun, the soundtrack to their life, but nothing more. To the young Mark Feld, records were not just for listening to. He wanted to live them.

Music was still a mystery to Mark. He had a vague notion that it was created from a combination of individual notes and chords galvanised into life by a rhythm like a runaway train, but there was something in the mix and in the whooping and wailing voice at the centre of the whirlwind that had little to do with crotchets and quavers. How did they create something as haunting and intense as 'Heartbreak Hotel' or 'Blue Suede Shoes' and make it sound as if they were making it up right there on the spot? But it wasn't just the song. He knew that Elvis didn't write his own songs and that the original version of 'Blue Suede Shoes' by its writer, Carl Perkins, was a pale blueprint of the King's reworking. So what did Elvis and his group, guitarist Scotty Moore, bass player Bill Black and drummer DJ Fontana, add to make it so different and distinctive?

But it wasn't just the music. Mark was enthralled by *the sound*. Something told him the way it had been recorded and where had a lot to do with what made the record special. That short, sharp echo that bounced back at the group off the walls of the studio, the percussive slap of the stand-up bass, the sting of Scotty's guitar licks, the cavernous wash of ghostly reverb that gave the singer an ethereal aura. And that indefinable ingredient that injected life into a track – 'feel'. It didn't sound as if they'd simply stood around a tape recorder. There was some kind of hoodoo going on. Every time he played it, he turned it up a little louder, leant in a little closer. The devil, they say, is in the detail and Mark was determined to root him out.

For Mark this was a solo trip, but for a time he shared his obsession with an older friend, Keith Reid who would later become lyricist with Procol Harum. Keith invited Mark round to his house after school and taught him a few chords. It was from Keith that Mark got the idea that by adding or subtracting one note to a basic chord shape or sliding the shape up or down the fretboard one could make another, more interesting chord. He was right in theory, but it wasn't true of every shape and only certain extra notes could be added or subtracted to create the more exotic sounding diminished, augmented and seventh chords. Either Keith neglected to tell his impatient friend this important fact, or Mark wasn't listening. Either way, this idiosyncratic method influenced Mark's guitar playing technique for the rest of his career.

Mark's father remembered: "They'd just sit together and write music from morning till night in our house. That's all they'd talk about – music. That and how they'd get on and what they'd do when they were well-known… He had this tape recorder and he'd sit there and do a song and you could hear him talking, often to himself through the wall. We'd just say, 'Hello, Mark's at it again.'"[1]

The boys soon tired of playing in their bedrooms and were anxious to make an impression on the outside world. Although Keith was a year or so older it was Mark who was the first to pluck up the courage to play in public. He befriended another local boy, Stephen Gold, who had also been given a guitar for his birthday. Stephen dragged Mark along to the first informal rehearsal of a group he was hoping to form with another friend, Melvyn Fields and two local girls who Stephen had met at Northwold Primary. Helen Shapiro and her cousin Susan Slater were a year older than the boys, but they both could sing in tune and they knew all the words to the Everly Brothers hits as well as some Elvis and Buddy Holly numbers, so they were in.

Shapiro was ten at the time but just four years later she would be signed to a major label contract and have a string of hits beginning with 'Walking Back To Happiness', in 1961. Helen remembers that Mark and Stephen were dwarfed behind their huge guitars, but the mere fact that they owned a guitar earned them respect at school. Being able to play it would have been a bonus. She played a plastic toy guitar with a ukulele tuning, Melvyn played snare and Susan's brother Glenn tackled the obligatory tea chest bass. Not surprisingly perhaps, bookings were a little thin on the ground. They played for their school friends during meal times in the summer holidays when some of the kids had to eat lunch at school because their parents were at work. They also played a few

---

1 *The songs Syd referred to were cover versions of rock and roll standards, or variations of hit songs. Marc's pre-Decca demos suggest that he did not write his own songs until 1965.*

numbers in a local café, were rewarded with a cup of tea and then asked politely to try somewhere else. But Helen disputes Mark's claim that they were called Suzy and the Hula-Hoops or that they even had a name.

"When I first saw him he was a chubby little kid with a huge quiff that he was so proud of because he could comb it down to cover his whole face. He swaggered when he walked down the street and he had a mouth on him. I remember him being real cheeky, very funny, a real comedian and a great little mimic. He could do a really good impersonation of Cliff Richard and Elvis. He was the first to discover Cliff, the first to get hold of a copy of 'Move It' which he loved. He was well into that first rush of British pop while the rest of us were just having fun. You can't be serious about making a career in music at that age, and I'm talking about when I was ten and Mark was a year younger. But he was dead keen, all fired up to have a go even if that meant playing at the local café for cups of tea or a coke. It was clear even then that he wanted to be famous. He was such a little show off!

"I never met his parents or went to his house as we weren't friends. He was far too cool to be seen in the company of girls! So I only saw him through the group, but later when we were teenagers, about the time I had my second record out, we both belonged to the Stamford Hill Jewish Youth Club. He would have been about fourteen then. There was always a fierce rivalry between the young guys from the different youth clubs and Mark came in one evening with a gang looking to throw their weight about and make a big impression. He was a tough little nut but he was always lovely to me. It was just a show of male bravado, toughing it out with the other guys, but that night there was a fight. Of course, Mark stayed out of it. He didn't want to get his suit creased!

"I met him again in '65 at a press party for *Fab 208* magazine and by then he had a new image – a donkey jacket, jeans and a Donovan cap and we just picked up from where we left off. He may have been calling himself Toby Tyler by then but he didn't pretend with me. He was always very natural and sweet."

With nowhere to play but their parents' front rooms the various members of the unnamed street corner skiffle group soon lost interest and Mark was left to practise his moves in front of the mirror once again. The group lost touch with their youngest member after they moved on to Secondary School that September.

Stephen Gold (erroneously referred to as Gould in earlier biographies) was Marc's closest childhood friend, but he has never spoken of their time together until now.

"I met Mark when I was about ten and he was nine. He was in the year below mine at Northwold Primary. One day he brought his guitar to school. I was also trying to learn guitar so we got talking and discovered we liked the same music – Elvis, Eddie Cochran and Gene Vincent. Then sometime later I saw him sitting on the wall in front of his house playing the guitar and he invited me in to hear his records. He had loads of 78s by Little Richard and Jerry Lee Lewis and we would listen for hours then his mum would make us a meal. One time she made us bacon and eggs and when I got home my mum went mad when she heard I'd eaten non-kosher meat, but Mark's parents weren't religious in any way. He considered himself Jewish because his father was and because all his mates were Jewish. The community around Stamford Hill and Stoke Newington was predominantly Jewish and Mark wanted to belong. He didn't go to Hebrew classes like I did, but when I got bullied at Hebrew Class it was Mark who told me how to deal with it. He was a real toughie. No one could push him around. All that stuff about him being shy was just an act. Believe me, he was ballsy. He told me to confront the other boy, to call his bluff, so I plucked up all my courage and I said exactly what Marc told me to say. I invited the guy outside to fight it out and the kid backed down. I didn't have any more trouble after that. Mark and I were together every single day after that, playing guitar in our rooms or browsing through the local record shop, 'R&B Records', near where we lived. Every Friday we would go there after school because that was when they got the new releases. Mark would come round to my house, which he could see from his bedroom, and he would teach me a few chords he had picked up.

"By the following year we formed a small group with some friends, Helen Shapiro and her cousin, another boy on tea chest bass and Melvin Fields who played cardboard boxes because he couldn't afford drums. It wasn't called Suzie and the Hula Hoops as Mark later claimed. We didn't give ourselves a name. It was just a bit of fun. But what I've never told anyone before was that Mark and I actually had an act together. We called ourselves Rick and Ellis. I chose the name Rick after my hero Ricky Nelson and Mark used the stage name Ellis after a local bohemian character he thought was glamorous because he lived on a riverboat and always had girls hanging around him. That appealed to Mark who was always after girls. All that stuff about him being bisexual or gay is complete rot. I knew him through his teens and we went everywhere together and I can tell you. He was not gay. He was a real man. All that camp thing was just to make himself more interesting for the press. We all affected that camp thing once we got into the entertainment business because it was part of show biz. But it was just an act."

Rick and Ellis were not going to let their age slow their ascent to stardom and so set their eyes on an audition at the legendary 2i's coffee bar in Old Compton Street.

On the cusp of the new decade, Soho had become the centre of the coffee shop culture and it seemed that there was one for every faction.

> I annoint my head with the blood of leaves to prevent my skull from growing rusty.
>
> as a knave in the tomb, with a mouth like a womb all wiseness is stiffled & bled dry, so I lay for one day in the way of the pray, the dreamy stream, where my knowledge becomes like a spring tree and takes root with the adornment of shadows upon the days waning back my self grows the tortured knowledge
>
> a misty century. This ② magicment has been my own since the sons of Romana breathed deep of the winds on the hill, and caped as I am in dripping saffonic yellows I'm a dancing soul, black bearded like the nomadic lords of our time

The Partisan catered for students and left wing intellectuals, Sam Widges attracted painters, Le Grand was THE meeting place for actors, writers and film makers and the 2i's drew tomorrow's pop stars. Outside, a white board beneath the thin red neon sign and the coca cola logos boasted that this unprepossessing café was 'The Home of the Stars' and if you doubted it there were framed photos of Cliff, Adam Faith, Marty Wilde, Billy Fury and Johnny Kidd at the back of the counter to prove it. It was said that Cliff had been discovered here, playing with his pre-Shadows combo, The Drifters, amid the miasma of cigarette smoke and steam, and that talent scouts from the five major record labels would vie with agents and managers to check out the talent playing on the table-sized stage in the cellar. By the time Mark Feld had plucked up the courage to enter the holy of holies, the lustre had faded from the espresso machine, the framed portraits were curling at the edges and the clientele was as tame as school kids in a soda pop store. Girls in twin sets and pearls crowded into the corner booths looking like miniature versions of their mothers. Boys in thick rimmed Buddy Holly glasses, starched shirts, slacks and pullovers tapped their brown suede shoes on the red tiled floor to a band that were so square their parents would have approved. Jutting through a hole in the wall behind the stage the fan remained motionless as there was no danger that the dancers would work up a sweat.

Stephen recalls the day of their inauspicious debut. "We persuaded Mark's mum to pester the manager of the 2i's coffee bar in Soho to let us play there one afternoon as Rick and Ellis. We were very nervous but also excited because there were a couple of guys from the Shadows in the audience. We only did two numbers, I think I sang 'Baby I Don't Care' and Mark did 'Summertime Blues' or another Eddie Cochran song. It went down alright because Mark knew how to carry himself and he had the attitude even then. He was very grown up and was very sure of himself. Of course we didn't get invited to play there again, but we hung around there a lot because at the time it was the place where a lot of Brit rockers had been discovered. But we weren't allowed downstairs again because we were too young."

Mark may have given his friend the impression that he wasn't bothered about the lukewarm reception they got, but when he got home it was a different story. Phyllis remembered that he found rejection hard to take.

"He was too young," Phyllis remembered, "I think they only did it to keep him happy. But he never let things like that get him down. He just came back, shut himself in his room for a while then came out and said, 'Well, I've tried that. I'll try something else now!'"

Stephen: "We made another appearance – I wouldn't call it a gig by any stretch of the imagination – as Rick and Ellis at the Casbah Café in Stamford Hill for a free coke and piece of cake. We also played outside the Stamford Hill Youth Club. It was dark so must have been early evening. But we weren't busking. We didn't do it for money.

"When we were ten or eleven we would take the bus every Saturday morning to the Hackney Empire where they were filming *Oh Boy!*, the TV pop show. We would get there for 10 o'clock when the doors opened so we could grab the best seats. We never missed a show. When Mark became famous he used to boast that he had carried Eddie Cochran's guitar at the Hackney Empire and journalists would nod politely but wouldn't believe him. I can tell you that story is absolutely true because I was there. We were standing at the stage door when a car pulled up and Eddie Cochran and Gene Vincent climbed out. Mark didn't miss a beat. He asked Eddie if he could carry his guitar case and Eddie said, 'Sure, kid'. The four of us went through to the back stage area and they thanked us, but that was all. I don't think he asked for their autograph. He just wanted to be in the presence of greatness. Mark made up a lot of stuff, he was a great storyteller, but that particular story is true. Another time at the Finsbury Empire we carried the Shadows guitars in for them, but Mark never mentioned that for some reason.

"Our other passion was the cinema. We would take the bus to the Super in Stoke Newington where we saw *Love Me Tender* and *The Girl Can't Help It*. My mum had to take us to that one because it was an 'A' certificate and we wouldn't have been allowed in on our own. We also went to the Regent in Stamford Hill, the Ritz in Clapton and the Savoy in Dalston. When we were still ten or eleven we were going all over the West End by ourselves. You could do that in those days. The number 73 bus stopped right outside Mark's house by the common and went straight into town where he would go to see his mum at her market stall and then we'd go round the shops looking for clothes and records.

"Mark's parents were the loveliest people. They were quiet but very friendly. His mum would have killed for him if she had to. They didn't have much money but they were very hard working and she bought him whatever he asked for – a pink shirt, records... whatever he wanted she would get it for him."

The following autumn Mark found himself in a new and harsher environment and separated from his friends. Having failed his 11-plus exams he was offered a place at the nearby William Wordsworth Secondary Modern in Wordsworth Road, Shacklewell, where he was immediately demoted to the lowest grade. Being discarded and labeled unteachable at that impressionable age had a devastating effect on his self-esteem. Although his parents hid their disappointment and reassured him that they had no doubt that he would distinguish himself in some way, Mark was clearly disheartened. He saw no point in making an effort and became lazy, surly and defiant. He fell in with a group of boys who encouraged him to play truant and he was soon singled out by the staff as a delinquent in the making and beyond redemption.

"I always had trouble at school... I always hung around with the rough kids. Perhaps it was because I was in the lowest class. They were sweet kids really. But they were always on their guard. That type's insecure really... They just wouldn't answer my questions at school. I mean questions about real life things – about the whole business of growing up... I knew if you got the drift, you could end up an accountant."

Despite his dismissive attitude to formal education, Mark frequently took refuge in the local public library on Church Street where he cultivated a love of poetry. He claimed to have read *Beowulf* at the age of nine (although that may have been on the school curriculum), but after that he embarked on a voyage of discovery, working his way through the classical and romantic poets – Keats, Shelley, Byron and Wordsworth before coming across Rimbaud, "the first poet who really rocked me. When I first read him I felt like my feet were on fire." Next came Kerouac, Dylan Thomas and Kahlil Gibran. They inspired Mark to begin writing his own poetry, but one day he chanced upon a book that was to have a profound impression on his outlook and interests.

The 13-year-old had recently caught a rerun of the colourful costume drama, *Beau Brummel* (1954) starring Stewart Granger as the 18th century dandy who rises to prominence and influence in Regency society by befriending the Prince Regent, then falls out of favour through his pride and arrogance. So when he saw a copy of *The Life and Times of Beau Brummel* by Carlo Maria Franzero (published in 1958) in the biographical section, he spent an idle half hour leafing through it before deciding to borrow it and read the whole story at his leisure.

It is scarcely credible that such a seminal influence on Mark's youthful attitude and ambitions should have been overlooked for so long. A glance through the first edition immediately reveals passages that clearly must have found a profound resonance with Mark's craving for recognition and his own emotional state at the time.

"Brummel felt beauty and elegance as a woman or an artist feels it," wrote Franzero.

Brummel had been a symbol of his age, more colourful than any number of dull politicians and boorish generals. His only failing was to have grown old and graceless. "It was a tragedy to have lived so long," mused his biographer, "he was now a king in exile who had outlived his reign." Mark would not have made the same mistake. He was taken by the image of the Dandy, that personification of elegance and ambition, the preening peacock who seeks admiration and whose first love will always be himself. Mark admired his new role model for fashioning a living work of art from such unpromising raw material. Brummel was "an upstart", the son of a valet, but also "a genius who gave his style and manners to a society that was by birth his superior." But greatness was a gift of the gods, not something to be grubbed about for in the dirt, or earned by sweat and drudgery. It should be intuitive, effortless and admired by the mass of humanity who could never aspire to it because, through no fault of their own, they lacked sufficient imagination. Even that most romantic of poets, Lord Byron, had acknowledged Brummel's influence when he sighed, "I would rather be Brummel than Napoleon."

Mark was cheered by the fact that the young Brummel had shown no academic ability, that at the age of 16 he had "shaken the dust of academic studies of his boots" in the belief that a "veneer of being knowledgeable" was infinitely preferable to "the weight of erudition." A "hero of elegant idleness" with no interest in the mundane world, Brummel had been admired for his "little affectations of speech" and forgiven his air of arrogance because it was seen as not disdain but "the imprint of the gods". Impudence was not to be confused with rudeness, but the "detachment of the genius" who believes himself to be superior to other men. Brummel was "a mass of contradictions", condescending and courteous, philosophical and capricious.

He had been mocked for his fastidiousness which he had taken to the point of neurosis, but in the belief that simplicity made a more immediate and lasting impression on society than ostentatious ornamentation. "The simplicity of Brummel's dress, like simplicity in writing, was only achieved with great artifice…that effect of spontaneity which can be achieved only by taking infinite pains."

His motto had been "Fortune favours the audacious" and that led him to nurture an unshakable self-belief. Mark too would be unswerving in his self-assurance and blinkered in his ambition. For is not ambition "the strongest impulse to greatness"? Like Brummel he would "go for the great world and be a star in that world". And he would chose his friends "with care and discard them with ruthlessness" when it served his purpose. Brummel refused to share credit with his tailor just as Mark was to do with the musicians he would work with, believing them to be mere craftsmen to be hired and fired at the whim of their employer.

Brummel's success, he noted, was achieved by his impeccable poise which, though it might have been a pose, nevertheless ensured he was noticed. "He created his own legend and imposed it upon the world," wrote Franzero.

Mark must have felt himself struck as if by lightning when he read the next line. "Never has England been in greater need of a new Brummel!"

The very next day he was contemplating how he might answer his country's call when Fate stepped in with a heavy hint.

As Mark recalled, he was sitting on the wall outside his parent's house watching the world go by, hoping the local Teddy Boys would compliment him on his togs – Everly Brothers shirt, black drainpipe jeans and two-tone shoes – when one walked right by and didn't even break his stride to say, 'Cool, kid'. A minute later and disappointment gave way to open mouthed astonishment as local Mod Martin Kaufman came into view. "He had on very, very baggy ginger tweed trousers, a pair of green hand-made shoes with side buckles and long points, and a dark green blazer with drop shoulders, one button cutaway, very short. I checked out later where all the stuff came from…The impact of having just seen what one thought was a real trendy looking Teddy Boy and then seeing this cat…I knew something was going on."

Already the ephemeral nature of pop culture had claimed its first victim. The Teddy Boys were as dead as the last decade and their music was now as anachronistic as their fashion sense. 1960 was the year Fate had finally managed to accomplish what the embattled establishment and moral crusaders had failed to do: demoralise a generation that thought it had found its voice. Within the space of a few months Elvis had been drafted into the army, Jerry lee Lewis was blacklisted for marrying his 13-year-old cousin, Chuck Berry was jailed on morals charges, Carl Perkins had been hospitalised after a car crash and Little Richard had denounced rock for religion. Buddy Holly had been killed in a plane crash the previous year and Eddie Cochran had died in a car wreck while on tour in Britain, on September 30, 1957, Mark Feld's 10th birthday, just weeks after Mark had carried his guitar from that very same car.

1960 began with rock music in decline and with only a half-hearted rear guard action to fend off the critics who were eager to write it off altogether. Pale imitators such as Pat Boone and Britain's own second rate sound-alikes from the Larry Parnes ('Parnes, Shillings and Pence') stable were re-recording watered down versions of R&B hits which the majority of Britain's teenagers hadn't heard and so accepted as the real thing. It was a very sad state of affairs and it killed off Mark's musical ambition for a time. Instead, he invested all his energy and every penny he could borrow from his doting mum in pursuing his new found aspiration to be the Ace Face of the East End.

He persuaded his landlady, Frances Perrone, who lived downstairs and owned a shoe repair shop opposite the library, to make a pair of snakeskin shoes in return for a sworn promise to turn down his radiogram whenever she was home. Then he charmed his mum into extending her HP commitments to include a new tailor-made suit from the local branch of Burtons. But both Perrone and the tailor quickly became exasperated at Mark's exacting demands and suggested that he look further afield if he wanted something really special.

"The only places I used to get clothes from were Vince's and Domino Male and these sort of places in Carnaby Street... they were basically very camp shops. I didn't understand that most of the people were gay."

In an interview conducted in 1971, Bolan confessed to stealing scooters to fund his clothes habit and raiding a store in Leman Street, Whitechapel to rip off their stock of Army surplus Levis, an incident no doubt embellished to enhance his roguish reputation.

"We just pulled up there on forty scooters... They were there, one wanted them and one took them. My scooter had zipped off without me and I just stuck the Levis up my jumper and I ran down the road and got a bus. My heart was pounding away. It was great knowing I was one of only a few people in England who had them. It was very funky."

In his new duds Mark ingratiated himself with the 'in crowd' who made the rounds of the Jewish Youth Clubs in Stamford Hill, but he soon outgrew the local scene and was pestering the older boys to tell him where they had their clothes made. Now in the last year of school, he cut classes to scour the back streets and alleys of Bow and Bishopsgate in search of Italian tailors, shoemakers and wholesalers who stocked imported American jeans. On Saturdays he did the rounds of Whitechapel or the West End with brother Harry, Stephen Gold or another school friend, Richard Young, and on Sundays he would take the bus with Phyllis to Leicester Square where he would cadge a few bob to meet his mates at a West End coffee bar where they would argue about which clothes shops to visit. Everywhere he went the pint-sized Dandy carried a rolled up umbrella under his arm like a sword stick, ready to fend off anyone who smirked at his lacquered hair or Italian suit. But although he acted tough, he would run when confronted by a rival gang. He had no stomach for rough stuff but would save 'face' by telling his friends that he'd made a strategic retreat to save his suit from being besmirched with blood stains. He was cool to the point of freezing out his friends, but they realized and accepted that even within their own clique there was intense rivalry for the leadership.

"I was at the forefront of that movement... I was always a star, even if it was only being the star of three streets in Hackney... You've got to be different... I remember wearing quite amazing things when I was younger. I used to have a black velvet jacket with a white satin collar and a gold walking stick with a white elephant handle... The only thought I ever had was, 'Oh. I just bought one suit this week – and I should've bought three.' I was, simply, quite knocked out by my own image."

This obsession with sartorial splendor had nothing to do with attracting girls. Mark showed little interest in the opposite sex at that time. All he thought about was cutting a figure that would get him noticed by the other Alpha males. Even music came second to looking sharp, although he found the lip-curling Cliff Richard an adequate substitute for the absent Elvis for a while.

Wearing the right gear was only part of a Mod's obligations. Being seen in the right place was the other. At night there was only one place to be – the dance floor.

Mark and his mates, who included future EMI press officer Eric Hall, and DJ Jeff Dexter, were mods before the term was in common usage. "There were no Mods as such, just people." The zoot suits with their side vents and tapered trousers which became associated with The Who and their generation came later. Besides, a dandy did not follow the fashion, he set the trend. The Hackney contingent of the early sixties looked to no one for inspiration or style sense. That is why in spring 1962 trend-setting lifestyle magazine *Town* sent reporter Peter Barnsley and photographer Donald McCullin to Stamford Hill to check out the local 'faces'. There they found 14-year-old Mark Feld and his mentors, Michael Simmonds and Peter Sugar, both six years his senior.

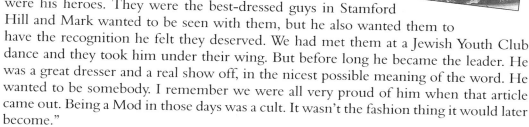

According to Stephen Gold, the *Town* magazine feature had been Mark's idea.

"Mark went to their offices and told them what was going on in Stoke Newington. They didn't have a clue until he told them. He instigated that article because Peter Sugar and Michael Simmonds were his heroes. They were the best-dressed guys in Stamford Hill and Mark wanted to be seen with them, but he also wanted them to have the recognition he felt they deserved. We had met them at a Jewish Youth Club dance and they took him under their wing. But before long he became the leader. He was a great dresser and a real show off, in the nicest possible meaning of the word. He wanted to be somebody. I remember we were all very proud of him when that article came out. Being a Mod in those days was a cult. It wasn't the fashion thing it would later become."

The idea that two young men would hang around with a precocious teen, a self-confessed "exhibitionist", intrigued Barnsley who didn't question Mark's more fanciful claims, such as travelling to Paris to buy a suit or putting down jealous class mates by telling them that he had been wearing their fashionable duds two years earlier. But on reflection the reporter felt saddened by the futility of all this misspent energy and activity. He concluded the six-page article which was published that September by asking, "Where is the goal to which he is obviously running as fast as his impeccably shod feet can carry him? It is nowhere. He is running to stay in the same place and he knows by the time he has reached his mid-twenties the exhausting race will be over and he will have lost."

Mark wasn't too happy about being portrayed as a shallow, self-obsessed poseur – at least that was the implication he read between the lines. He wasn't keen on the photographs either.

"He made us sort of look like convicts. He got very hard-looking pictures."

But it forced Mark to see himself as others might see him. The more he thought about it, the more he came to realise that he had taken the young Dandy trip as far as he could afford to at this point. There was no future in being a star in Stoke Newington if it didn't lead to something bigger. Ennui was setting in.

"By the time the Mod thing really happened, I was out of it… I was never a Mod… there was no such thing then."

He was also acutely aware that he was practically the only Mod that didn't own or ride a scooter. His phobia for all things mechanical had forced him to keep a safe distance from the gleaming machines beloved by his peers, a fear that was compounded when he was hospitalised after a minor accident while riding pillion on a friend's souped-up 'hairdryer'.

But the deciding factor was one Mark hadn't considered or foreseen. The turnaround time for a monthly magazine in those days could be anything up to six months. When the *Town* article finally hit the newsstands, the three 'faces' were looking decidedly outdated. It was time for a change of scene.

The move was precipitated by Frances Perrone's decision to put her house on the market in September 1960 obliging Hackney Council to find new accommodation for her tenants. The Feld's new home was a modest prefab bungalow in Summerstown, Wimbledon, within a stone's throw of the greyhound stadium. Mark's parents were pleased as punch with their clean, heated modern home – they even bought a TV to celebrate – but Mark was gutted. He had spent his youth establishing a name for himself and now he was a nobody. The humiliation he experienced when he returned to Stamford Hill to check on his old friends, was crushing. But as usual, he later re-imagined it as a seminal episode in a modern suburban myth.

"I'd been very funky to be around as a face, you know. I was still the heaviest face – the fact that I'd not been around and other cats could move in brought total resentment at having me back there. No one would talk to me and it made me very sad for about five minutes. But I could dig it. It was like I was too heavy. I was in that magazine. All that stuff had come out and I was supposed to be somewhere else… I'd ascended to Olympus. And suddenly I was there. The funkiest thing I could have done from a theatrical point of view was split. So I did. It was instant immortality."

Mark put a brave face on his disappointment and after locking himself in the box bedroom he still shared with his brother, he emerged with a new plan.

He would quit his new school, Hill Croft Secondary Modern, which he had enrolled in just months before the mandatory leaving-age, and resurrect his musical ambitions. Hill Croft had been as hostile an environment for Mark as his former secondary school, so he would be glad to see the back of it. "Because I had done modeling they called me a right cissy… I spent all my time then not going to school. I mean, I purposely didn't go."

In fact, he forced the authorities to expel him because of his poor attendance.

"We honestly didn't mind him being expelled," his father admitted. "He just didn't have any interest in school and so we encouraged him to go ahead with his music. Whatever he did, that music thing was the end of it. Marc idolised my Phyllis and she went out…and really worked hard so he could stay at home."

Without his mother's approval and indulgence her youngest would not have enjoyed the luxury of spending his days nurturing his new interest through Radio Luxembourg's weekly chart show, *Pick of the Pops* on the BBC Light Programme and BBC TV's only concession to the 'new music', *Juke Box Jury*. "We weren't upset when he was expelled because frankly he never went to school much anyway. And when he did he went wearing Elvis Presley clothes and winkle-picker shoes, which always annoyed him… I was in the same position as mothers whose sons go to college. They have to support them until they are 18 or whatever so I didn't mind supporting Marc while he worked on his songs."

His steel strung guitar was taken out of its cardboard case and tuned up. And instead of merely imitating the moves of his former heroes, Elvis and Eddie Cochran, he applied himself to the demanding business of learning the instrument. Every waking hour through the spring of '63 he devoted to working his way through Bert Weedon's *Play in a Day* guitar course, whose title Mark soon found out, to his chagrin, was a typical music biz come-on. There was clearly more to mastering the guitar than memorising basic chord shapes. One afternoon trying to copy The Shadows (who had just hit the top of the charts with 'Apache'), Duane Eddy and Link Wray was enough to convince the impetuous wannabe pop star that he would have to work at his trade like any other. Bluff, bluster and *chutzpah* would only get you so far. Without the tunes and a rudimentary grasp of technique, he wouldn't get his foot in the door of any of the publishers in Denmark Street, London's Tin Pan Alley. But there were short cuts. Instead of practising major and minor scales he learned the blues scale, a five note pattern that could be played anywhere along the fretboard provided you knew the root note of the dominant chord in the song. And there were barre chords which saved you from having to learn all the shapes 'Uncle' Bert recommended. Barre chords offered the means of moving one simple shape up or down the neck to produce more chords of that type (be it major, minor, major 7th, etc.) And there was God's gift to the lazy guitarist, the capo which allowed musicians with short stubby fingers to transpose chords to a higher key without having to press their index finger across the torture rack of steel strings. Uncle Bert may have been pushing his luck by promising young hopefuls that they could play guitar before bedtime, but given a little patience and persistence the average youth could arm himself with enough chords to play the typical pop song within a few weeks. 15-year-old Mark Feld was more tenacious than most and what he couldn't master, he approximated. It was an approximation which, if not strictly correct, sounded more exotic to his ears.

While Mark served his unpaid apprenticeship, his mother was learning that even her inexhaustible patience had its limits. One afternoon she returned from her new part-time job as a cashier at the Parsons Green branch of the National Savings Bank to find Mark lying in bed. When he asked what was for dinner, the normally docile Mrs Feld gave him some free career advice. The essence of her argument was that he wouldn't be living rent free for long if he didn't make an effort to contribute to the family food budget. His pride was hurt at the mere suggestion that he should dirty his manicured fingers with physical labour, but one look at his mother's steely gaze was sufficient to tell that she was deadly serious. He could have reminded her that he had recently earned a respectable fee modeling for Littlewoods Mail Order catalogue and posing for a cut-out for the John Temple clothes stores but then he remembered that she had shelled out the astronomical sum of 100 pounds to send him on a West End modeling course to qualify for those assignments. He pouted. It was settled. Mark Feld would be actively seeking employment the next morning.

The fifties had been a depressing time to grow up in Britain. Fortunately for Mark's generation they were too young to appreciate the cheerless climate they had been born into. By the time they were old enough to fend for themselves, the country was recovering from the privations of the immediate post-war period and benefitting from the radical social program implemented by Clement Attlee's Labour government. Attlee kick started the economy by nationalising British Industry and funding the Welfare State which made health care free for all. The poor were no longer reluctant to call the doctor out when their children were sick because they feared they wouldn't be able to pay his bill. Nor did they think twice now about having their babies in a state run hospital rather than risk the unsanitary conditions of their own home for the same reason.

By the time Mark and his mates were entering their late teens, they were spoilt for choice of employment, as their parents would remind them, including the option not to take a job at all, if they didn't mind the stigma of signing on for unemployment benefit at the local labour exchange. It was said that jobs were so plentiful in the early sixties that one could quit working after the morning shift and be in a new job after lunch. Leisure was no longer a luxury for the rich idle classes, but every working person's right after a hard day's graft.

In '57 the new Conservative Prime Minister Harold MacMillan had assured the nation that they had "never had it so good" and, though the previous administration argued that he did not have the right to take the credit for it, there was truth in the boast.

When Mark left Hill Croft Secondary school "by mutual consent" he felt in no hurry to earn his keep. When asked by the clerk at his first and only interview to sign on for work at Wimbledon Labour Exchange what type of work he was seeking he answered, "Poet", but added that anything else would be given serious consideration if it paid well.

He found not one, but two jobs within a week. The first was as trainee salesman for Edgars, the male outfitters in Tooting Broadway and the second was less glamorous, washing up in a Wimpy Bar. He kept the first for a fortnight before handing in his notice. The second gave a 240-volt shock to Mark's delicate system and he quit before the week was out.

"I had two hours sleep at night," he swooned when recalling the only 'real' jobs he'd ever done, "I did that for a week and had a mental breakdown – one of those Scott Walker numbers at 16. I was really wasted…I didn't know what I wanted to do, I had no direction at all, just that I knew something was going to be happening." Exhausted from his token gesture, he quietly returned to acquiring the skills that promised to pay more handsomely than any regular job.

Mark had convinced himself that music and not modeling was the means by which he would be a star, but there wasn't much to inspire him in pre-Beatles Britain. He hadn't yet discovered Howling Wolf and the Chicago bluesmen who recorded for Chess, nor had he felt the urge to root out the likes of Billy Lee Riley, Warren Smith and Sonny Burgess who were Elvis's contemporaries at Sam Phillip's Sun studios. Early Mods like Mark simply hung around dancehalls such as the Lyceum, the Scene and the Whisky A Go Go, posing to whatever the DJ was playing, which was almost exclusively American: R&B from James Brown, the soul-lite sounds of Motown and the sweatier sides from Stax interspersed with a gaggle of American girl groups from the Phil Spector stable. It was a dance scene, not a music scene and there was no homegrown talent to hold a candle to the Americans.

So it isn't so surprising that Mark made his fateful decision to put every fibre of his being into music after a screening of Cliff Richard's latest offering, *Summer Holiday*. Cliff may have been the personification of anaemic pop, but it was the idea of being adored for something as effortless as singing that initially appealed to Mark.

Although it has not been singled out as such by previous biographers, a far stronger influence on the young Mark Feld was Cliff's earlier outing, *Espresso Bongo* (1959), a cynical send-up of the music business in which Lawrence Harvey played a sleazy, unscrupulous (and overtly Jewish) manager who believes that a shrewd operator can make a star of any talentless teen. Although it was a crude satire, it conveyed an attitude that was prevalent at the time, that pop was just another branch of show business and that any schmuck could be a star if the public could be hoodwinked into buying into the hype. Pop was not yet recognised as an art form. Records were marketed as a novelty product and performers were 'properties' to be exploited. Singers were just another act to be booked on a variety bill. This attitude was to change after the arrival of Bob Dylan and The Beatles, but at first even the Fab Four considered a spot on the London Palladium to be a high point of their career.

Mark (far left) on a 'ban the bomb' march with Joan Baez and Donovan c.1965

Initially music was simply the means by which Mark would achieve his ambition, to be a bigger star than Cliff, but once he began hanging out at his local record store in Tooting Broadway listening to albums, instead of just gawping at the covers, he was burning with the fervour of the newly converted. Day by day as he played his way through Weedon's course book his finger-tips hardened and his ear became more attuned to the licks and fills that cropped up repeatedly on those early records. Within months he had an elementary style of his own and had learned a handful of songs recorded by his new heroes Dion and Bob Dylan. When his friend Dexter reminded Mark that he couldn't sing, he was told "any cat can sing". All Mark had to do was open his mouth and the gods would weep. The problem though, was not convincing the gods, but their representatives on Earth in the music publishing business.

When Dexter asked Mark how he was going to make it without an electric guitar and a group to back him, Mark brushed it aside by saying that rock was passé. Folk was the new thing. Oh, and by the way, he wasn't to be called Mark Feld anymore. He was now Toby Tyler.

Chapter 4
The Face of an Angel, The Mind of a Man

“ *I went to see Joe Meek and did the 'I wanna be a star Joe' bit… I'd never sung in fact, but I assumed I ought to be a rock and roll star or something.* ”
Marc Bolan, 1971

The first port of call for any budding British pop star in the early sixties was 304 Holloway Road, N7 – a seedy flat above a row of shops in the London borough of Islington. From the outside, Shenton's leather goods shop, sandwiched between Long Electricals and a branch of Lloyds Bank, would have been of no interest to the casual passerby unless they were in the market for a ladies handbag and matching accessories. But if you watched from the café across the street on any given day you would see half a dozen young men or more enter the shop and remain long after closing time. Locals suspected it might be a brothel or an illegal gambling club, until they noticed that all of the visitors were carrying musical instruments.

Once inside, the house band and assorted hopefuls passed through the beaded curtains behind the counter and negotiated the narrow staircase to the first floor to be greeted by a torrent of expletives from the highly strung Svengali of British pop as Joe Meek wrestled with the chaos that was his improvised studio. Joe was England's answer to Phil Spector – he had even adopted Spector's dark suit and sunglasses, although, to be truthful, so too had half of London's gangland. But unlike his American rival, Joe's empire was run on a shoestring. Backing singers were squeezed into the lavatory and the band in the front room, while the kitchen doubled as the control room. The one oasis of tranquillity was the makeshift office in what had once been the living room. Behind the plate glass window engraved with the initials RGM, Meek's business partner, the redoubtable Major Banks, could be seen blowing smoke rings from his cigar surrounded by the filing cabinets on permanent loan from his plastics moulding factory – the legitimate arm of RGM productions. "We're spending too much on blank tapes, Joe," the Major would remind his reckless partner every time a requisition for two dozen reels of BASF ¼-inch magnetic tape were thrust onto his desk, with an invoice demanding his signature.

"Can't run a recording studio without them, old love," would be the standard reply. "You can bet fucking Spector doesn't have to jump through fucking hoops every fucking week like I do," Joe would roar to whichever poor musician happened to be in range.

As for equipment, it was a Heath Robinson affair, a spaghetti tangle of cables and primitive effects boxes, many of them of Joe's own construction. It looked like the inner workings of the TARDIS, but remarkably it worked. In fact, it worked remarkably well. Thanks to its eccentric genius a handful of hits had been created from chaos, namely 'Just Like Eddie' by Joe's personal protégé and lover Heinz, The Honeycombs' 'Have I The Right?', John Leyton's 'Johnnie Remember Me' and, of course, 'Telstar', the multi-million selling instrumental which the musically illiterate and partially tone deaf producer had been forced to dictate to his long suffering session musicians by humming it over and over until they pinned down the key and worked out the parts.

In mid-January 1964, Mark climbed the stairs to the first floor, a new acoustic guitar in hand and a harmonica hanging in a holder round his neck. He had been to see a package show featuring The Ronettes and Marty Wilde supported by The Rolling Stones at the Tooting Granada a week before and had decided he had to make a move or face the prospect of having to take another 'real' job. Luckily, there was no receptionist to freeze out the cold callers. He advanced a few steps to an open door and looked in.

This was his first sight of the inside of a real recording studio and it wasn't what he had expected at all. If it hadn't been for the white baffle boards lining the walls, the abandoned instruments and microphone stands, he would have mistaken it for a storeroom. There were ornaments, lamps and other household objects from the flat that nobody had bothered to throw out. No gold records, no plush carpet and no engineers in white coats milling around machinery. Just a smartly attired man in a black suit leaning over a young boy who was picking out notes on an upright piano.

At first he didn't recognise Joe without his shades. "Yes?" It was evidently not a good time to call without an appointment.

"I've come for an audition. Marty Wilde said I should see you about making a record."

"Oh, he did, did he? Well, let me tell you, if any of Larry Parnes' puppets sent you, it must have been to take the mick." The name of his hated rival was spat with as much venom as Joe could muster this time in the morning. "And, by the way, I don't do auditions. This is a recording studio, not some showbiz agent's office."

"I've done some modelling and I wanna make a record. I'm gonna be bigger than Cliff."

"God! Do we need another Cliff? Don't answer that." Joe's first instinct was to kick the kid down the stairs, but he had to admit, anyone with enough front to walk in off the street and offer to play there and then might have something. And he was good looking, for sure.

"I can't listen to you now, son. I'm in the middle of a session and, as I said, I don't do auditions. But if you make a tape, I'll try to give it a listen. But ditch the guitar. I really can't use a folky. All that Dylan/Donovan shtick is strictly for students and they don't buy records." He advanced on the visitor who was beginning to feel as welcome as if he had been sent to serve a writ. "Have you heard one of my records? You must have, right? Do I use acoustic guitars? Not on your life. Skiffle's dead, son. Take a tip. Buy a real guitar and write some songs. I need songs. I could always use more songs. In case dear old Geoff deserts me. But you wouldn't leave Joe would you, Geoff, old love?"

A shy young man looked up from the piano and returned a sheepish grin. He looked as if his mother must have knitted both him and his sweater from the same ball of yarn.

"I've no use for covers. I can record covers till the cows come home, but then I'd have to pay some bugger royalties. What would I want to do that for when I have my own resident genius right here?" Geoff cracked another self-conscious smile. "Come back when you have a tape and some of your own songs, then maybe I'll give it a listen, alright? Gotta get on. See yourself out, there's a dear."

Mark hadn't a clue how to write his own songs at this point. He was still grappling with the handful of chords he needed to play Dylan's 'Blowing In The Wind' and Dion's

'Gloria (The Road I'm On)'. Neither was particularly taxing for a genuine fingerpicking folk musician, but Mark was looking for another short cut to success, not a musical education. He didn't buy into the protest movement's 'ban the bomb' ideology either, although he joined the odd march in the hope of meeting Donovan and hitching a lift on the current bandwagon. Opportunism and persistence were bound to pay off eventually, he thought. And his looks, of course.

He wasn't quite ready to go it alone so on his return to Summerstown he decided to look up an old friend.

Stephen Gold: "I answered the front door one day and there was Mark, a big broad grin on his face. The first thing I noticed was that all traces of his East End accent had gone. He was speaking like a public schoolboy. My uncle had tried to teach him to talk properly when we were younger and he'd obviously taken it to heart and had perfected this soft wispy tone. My uncle had told him that he wouldn't get anywhere unless he could give the impression that he was middle class and well educated. He would have to blend in with the successful crowd if he wanted to make it. So he taught him tongue twisters. Before that Mark was a 'Cor blimey!' Cockney.

"Mark told me he had arranged an audition with Joe Meek and asked if I had a group he could use to back him. As it happens, I did. So sometime in the next day or so we all went in a taxi paid by Mark's mum to Holloway Road and played for Joe. I played guitar, there was my bass player Barry Phillips and Melvyn on drums. By this time Melvyn could afford a proper kit. How we got it all in the taxi I can't remember, but we did. Mark sang. He didn't play guitar. He wasn't writing his own songs yet so we must have played some rock and roll standard. In fact, it must have been something we all knew backwards because we didn't have a rehearsal. Can you imagine? An audition for Joe Meek and we didn't bother to rehearse! I think Mark just wanted Joe to hear his voice. I didn't hear what they said afterwards because we were busy packing the equipment away. All I know is that Joe wasn't too impressed."

But Mark wouldn't take no for an answer.

He pestered Meek over the next six months which, if Mark's penchant for exaggeration is anything to go by, was more likely to have been six weeks, or even six days, but all he got was the proverbial brush off. He even called at the producer's house and talked his way inside.

Marc: "He had his bedroom with the budgerigar where he made all The Tornados stuff and for six months he said, 'Sure kid, record you next week'. And he never did."[1]

Frustrated but undefeated, Mark hung around the Rediffusion television studios in the hope of hustling a job as an extra on their weekly pop show *Five O'Clock Club*. There in the early autumn of '64 he met and befriended teenage actor Allan Warren who invited Mark to share his spacious flat near Earl's Court with another aspiring thespian Gregory Phillips[2].

Warren: "One day I met 'Toby Tyler' who was getting in on the pop scene. I liked

---

1 *This remark should finally scotch rumours that an acetate of a song titled 'Mrs Jones', which was produced by Meek, features the voice of the teenage Bolan.*
2 *Coincidentally, the flat at 81 Lexham Gardens was just a stone's throw from Tony Visconti's future flat at 108 where Tyrannosaurus Rex would rehearse.*

him and thought he had a lot of talent. He used to come round to my apartment most nights and play his guitar. Some of my friends used to laugh and say, 'Not another one trying to make it!'

"I rather saw him as a baby-faced copy of Cliff Richard –and frankly that's how Toby styled himself.[3] The idea was that if Toby made it, I would manage him."

Warren's abiding memory of Mark Feld (aka Toby Tyler) was that his new lodger never seemed to sleep. Day and night he was to be seen either reading or playing guitar with the curtains drawn to protect his sensitive pale skin from sunlight. Despite the dedication he was putting into playing the guitar, he didn't seem to have developed a style of his own, yet. But then Warren wasn't the best judge of pop talent. His personal taste was for West End and Broadway musicals, but he fancied himself as an impresario and he found Mark extremely likeable, despite his self-centred obsession. Unhappily, the producers of *Five O'Clock Club* were not convinced the world needed another cherubic-faced folk singer. But Toby's self-confidence was contagious and so after months of listening to his unremitting spiel and tiring of hearing his limited repertoire from breakfast to bedtime, Warren thought it time to call his bluff. He leafed through the phone book and picked out an inexpensive studio that would make a demo in two hours for less than 20 quid. Warren has spoken of booking a session at Regent Sound Studios in Soho's Denmark Street in December '64 to record 'Blowing In The Wind' and 'Gloria', but no tape of this session has surfaced and so it is assumed Warren has confused it with the Maximum Sound Session which saw Mark record the same two songs in January '65.

Maximum Sound Studios at 47 Dean Street in the heart of the West End did not live up to its prestigious location. Wardour Street, the centre of a thriving British film industry, was just a few hundred yards away and the offices of EMI and other major labels were within a short walk, yet to Mark's eyes Maximum Sound was only one rung up the ladder from Joe Meek's self-assembled operation. Two stereo reel-to-reel tape decks and a PA mixer were all that had been left behind when Pirate Radio Atlanta abandoned the studio to broadcast offshore. It was now little more than a jingle studio, but would be adequate for recording an acoustic demo.

In just over an hour Mark stumbled through half a dozen takes of Dylan's song before he attempted Dion's 'Gloria (The Road I'm On)' four times. His performance left engineer Vic Keary unimpressed, but in his own mind he had passed the test he had set himself, or to be more truthful the acid test that Warren had forced him to take. It was the rawest of recordings for sure, but it had something. It wasn't the touch of reverb Keary had added

---

3 *This comment would appear to authenticate the recent discovery of a previously unreleased recording Marc had made on August 28, 1964. The song, 'All At Once', was written by George Bellamy, guitarist with the Tornados and father of Matthew Bellamy of future supergroup Muse. It was recorded as a demo by Marc accompanied by an in-house band at IBC Studios in Portland Place near BBC Broadcasting House under the watchful eye of engineer Martin Haines. Both song and performance are a pallid imitation of Cliff Richard. No one who heard the tape showed any interest in releasing it and no acetates were made. The session is believed to have been paid for by Marc's latest 'manager', Jeffrey de-la-Roy Hall, a former World War Two fighter pilot. When Hall was finally tracked down by Danielz of tribute band T.Rexstasy he still possessed three previously unpublished snap shots of his youthful lodger and a copy of their contract. Unfortunately, the photos were lost when Hall's belongings were disposed of after his death.*

to make his small, thin voice bigger and more tuneful. It was a plaintive, haunting quality in his voice made all the more poignant by the lyrics which appeared to foretell his own death, the mention of Gloria and the chorus ending with "the road I'm on won't run me home". He didn't sound like Dion or Dylan and he certainly didn't sound like Cliff now. It wasn't a powerful voice, but it was distinctive. As he stepped out into the roar of the traffic on Tottenham Court Road he reminded himself what Elvis had said when asked who he sounded like. "I don't sound like nobody." Now Mark could say the same thing and he had the tape to prove it. Warren and his friends could say all they liked about the awkward amateurishness of his guitar playing and that god-awful rasping harmonica, but that wasn't a deal breaker. Session musicians could be hired to back him when the big day came. And better songs could be found. Maybe he would even write his own. But for now he was a real singer. And that was only one step from being a star, in his mind.

Convincing others that Toby Tyler was a bankable commodity was now down to Warren and he found it dispiriting to say the least. While Mark sat around the flat dreaming of imminent recognition his 'manager' hawked the acetates cut from the tape to several independent labels which had folk artists on their roster. They turned him down flat. Even a set of professional promo shots taken by Warren's friend, photographer Mike McGrath, didn't convince the image conscious A&R men.

"I took Toby's pictures on the balcony of my Earl's Court flat and outside in the Square", McGrath recalled. "He didn't say a word – Allen Warren did all the talking. When he was there he was like a shy silent schoolboy."

Mark, who had taken the name Toby Tyler from the 1960 Disney film of the same name about a young boy who runs away to join a circus, had posed in an outfit chosen to project the image of himself as a committed card-carrying protest singer – a suede jacket, white jeans, suede boots, rollneck pullover and a peaked cap – the spitting image of Donovan's kid brother.

Warren finally secured an audition for Mark with Columbia A&R manager John Burgess at Abbey Road on February 16, 1965. A pianist was at the artist's disposal, but whether or not he accompanied Toby Tyler on this occasion is not known. Mark might have accompanied himself on acoustic guitar or Warren may have played Burgess the demo tape recorded at Maximum Sound a few weeks earlier. In any event, no offer of a contract was forthcoming.

But Mark was not discouraged. There were now other distractions to entertain him.

A few months earlier Mark had met and befriended a young Irish-American actor, Riggs O'Hara, who had called at the flat in Kensington to visit Phillips. Riggs was a classically trained actor who had come over to England with the cast of *Guys and Dolls* in the late fifties and had taken small, often uncredited, roles in TV series such as *Richard The Lionheart* and films *The Victors* ('63) and *Promise Her Anything* ('65). He would go on to play Sinclair in *The Virgin Soldiers* ('69) before becoming a successful theatre director. With his fair eyebrows, flaxen hair, square jaw and muscular physique he could have been a stand-in for James Cagney and he had the gift of the gab to go with it. His blue collar Bronx background gave him an instant affinity with the Hackney hustler who he found charming and as full of the blarney as himself. He chose to overlook Mark's outrageous claim to be the new Olivier and decided it might be fun to play mentor to the wide-eyed wonder who was still trying to decide whether to be a thespian or a troubadour.

Riggs took Mark to parties, opening nights and on one occasion to the National Theatre on the Southbank where they saw Peter Brook's production of *The Royal Hunt of the Sun*. Afterwards, they went back stage to meet Robert Stephens who was playing 'Athuallapa' whose character was to inspire the song of the same name on the first Tyrannosaurus Rex album. "He was all blacked up and I thought he was a spade," was all Marc remembered of his first exposure to classical theatre. "Then he put his foot up and it was white underneath and it slayed him." But once Mark became less in awe of his new surroundings and the circles he was moving in, he devoured the edifying feast as greedily as a culture-starved urchin.

Marc later claimed that it was around this time that he tried his hand at acting. While waiting for Warren to secure the contract that would make him a star, Mark condescended to make fleeting and uncredited appearances on the children's TV show *Orlando* starring Sam Kydd. The non-speaking part was known in the trade as a 'walk-on' but it paid well enough, "ten quid a touch stuff". He had Warren's other flat mate Gregory Phillips, a regular cast member on the series, to thank for those.

"I did a lot of character parts like that. But they're so jive, all those things, anyway, and I never took acting seriously. I knew I wanted to do something and I knew that wasn't it... I couldn't see that as something that would turn me on. It was so slow... I did all that because I didn't really know what I wanted to do."

There was nothing sexual in the relationship between Mark and Riggs, nor had there been the suggestion of such with Warren, or any of the other chic young men Mark was seen with at that time, although Mark may have developed an adolescent 'crush' on these mentors that he secretly admired. "There was no way he was gay or even bisexual," Riggs assured an interviewer. It was the actor's assertion that his young friend put all his sexual energy into his career. Mark enjoyed male company because he craved their approval and they in turn enjoyed his company, adhering to Lord Henry Wotton's credo in Oscar Wilde's novella *The Picture of Dorian Gray*, "I choose my friends for their good looks, my acquaintances for their good characters and my enemies for their good intellects."

Besides, the female of the species required courting and that was too much like hard work. Sex appeal was merely animal attraction. It signified nothing. The attention of male admirers, however, was a mark of respect. It meant that one was worthy of attention and perhaps even envied.

Riggs was not presumptuous enough to presume that he was playing Professor Higgins to Mark's Eliza Doolittle, but it did not pass unnoticed that his Cockney charge was enunciating as daintily as the theatre crowd he was now mixing with on these occasions. Perhaps it might be fun to take him abroad.

And so one fine spring day in 1965, Riggs and his wide-eyed companion took the boat train to Paris.

"I was in Paris for about six months. A friend of mine had a big house which had about 40 rooms. He was a magician actually, very powerful man. Very learned man. I learned a lot of very important things off him, just sort of mythology, good things. I read a lot of books. He had amazing books there, books by Aleister Crowley and handwritten books and things like that."

According to brother Harry Feld, the truth was rather less glamorous. "He went for a weekend Citybreak to Paris with his actor friend," Harry confided to this biographer. "But when he found a slug in the bath at the hotel he freaked and caught the next boat home."

Facts, however, were not to be allowed to stand in the way of a good yarn. Over the years the legendary sojourn with the magician was elaborated upon with Mark recast as the sorcerer's apprentice.

"He wasn't a black magician," he would reassure the interviewer. "He had many old books about control of the environment by thought projection and he could transmit feelings so you could understand what he meant implicitly…which is magic to me. It was a Yoga magic rather than one involving sheep sacrifice at midnight on Glastonbury Tor… I learned by watching him for the five months I lived there. And I went on studying magic from books for two years… He could read people's minds and conjure up spirits, yet these things to him were normal things. I learned a lot in Paris. Rubbed out what school had done. It was there that I decided what I wanted to be.

"I saw someone levitate. He was standing on the floor and he raised himself about eight feet in the air. I've also done magical rites and conjured up demons… I once conjured up a spirit that wasn't very friendly. It came in the form of a Greek boy. I believe you can do whatever you want to…

"I definitely believe in reincarnation. I believe for a start that all my lyrical ability was learned in a past life as a bard."

At one point he planned an autobiography detailing his past life recollections. "When I read back what I've written it's just like an old man talking – it's just not me – it can't possibly be me… there is no way with my background, that one could account for it.

"I wrote out a rite calling on Pan to change me into a Satyr. Literally, with hairy legs, hooves and horns. But I realised I couldn't do it. What's going to happen? I'm not going to be able to walk onto an Arcadian hillside and go up to my cave and just hang out…the rite would have worked. I do know how to do it."

Riggs contradicts Harry's version of events and he should know as he was there. According to Riggs, he and Mark enjoyed an idyllic weekend, doing the night clubs, eating at swish restaurants, taking a leisurely cruise on the Seine and going to the theatre, which must have been a strange experience as Mark didn't speak a word of French. And there was the obligatory visit to the Louvre.

By the time they returned, Allen Warren and Mark had become estranged and the latter was not unhappy to be told that his squatter had decided to move out. Warren was philosophical. He admitted defeat, having had the demo turned down by both Columbia and a number of small independent labels. He had done his best and wished his young friend well.

It was shortly after the return from Paris that Mark claims he talked his way inside the hallowed halls of Decca and a fateful meeting with A&R manager Dick Rowe. Rowe had famously turned down the Beatles and was now inclined to give every young hopeful a chance, just in case.

Decca's headquarters was then a six-storey building on the south bank of the Thames at Lambeth. With its olive green interior and functional furnishings visitors might have mistaken their surroundings for their local labour exchange, which was not entirely inappropriate given the way the label treated their acts. When Mark walked through the door for his first audition, an officious commissioner demanded his signature in the visitor's book then watched him as he walked down the corridor to the A&R department, just in case he was tempted to pocket any pens or paper clips. But then, anyone under the age of 30 was considered suspect. Artists and their agents particularly so. The company had made its money developing radar during the Second World War and had entrusted its crusty managing director, Sir Edward Lewis, with investing its considerable revenue in recording classical music. Pop was regarded as a profitable, but insignificant sideline. Acts (the term artists was reserved exclusively for classical musicians) were rarely signed on merit. Groups could be trouble, breaking up before they had repaid their initial investment, although Decca weren't doing too badly from The Rolling Stones, The Moody Blues and The Zombies. But solo singers were given a chance because it cost comparatively little to give them a try out. The label had its own recording studios and orchestra on salary. It was a hit factory, but they needed to keep producing the hits. Singers were seen as a low risk, speculative investment with the potential to pay enormous dividends for a comparatively tiny outlay.

"I did a recording test… This was '64, late '64…and the song that I sang to him was 'You're No Good', which in fact was a Betty Everett record which had been out in America for six months before… I got it the week it was released in America because I had a friend over there who sent me the stuff over.[4] And I really dug the song… So I did the test and they said, 'Kid, with your face we'll make you a star.'"

What Mark omitted to say was that it wasn't his face, nor his performance of the Everett number which convinced Rowe to give him a chance, but his promise to come back with an original song, or face recording whatever material they thought suitable. There was no avoiding the fact. He had to write his own songs or call it a day. The thought of modelling again for Littlewoods, working as a cloakroom attendant at Le Discothèque in Wardour Street (which he had done briefly for tips) or – God forbid – plunging his pinkies in leftovers and soapsuds in the backroom of the Wimpy Bar – were just too hideous to contemplate. But he couldn't face the prospect of writing his own songs and finding out that they weren't up to standard. So he prevaricated. And there was still the business of finding a name that would swing it. Even at this late stage, Mark was convinced that the right name was as important as a hit song. It was all about image. Any chump could write a song. Couldn't they?

Shortly after leaving Lexham Gardens with his guitar and a couple of shopping bags stuffed with his clothes and notebooks, Mark moved in with Riggs who shared a spacious flat with actor James Bolam in Lonsdale Road, Barnes. For a few months in early '65 the three flatmates got on famously until Mark casually informed Jimmy, who was already well known for his work on *The Likely Lads* television series, that he would soon be recording his first single under the name Marc Bolan[5]. Jimmy was not flattered. In fact, he was incensed that his name had been appropriated by a ruthlessly ambitious

---

4 *It was Riggs who had given Mark the single, but it sounded more exciting to claim it had been sent from the States and the Decca test was more likely to have taken place in early '65 as it led to a contract being signed on August 9th that year. Marc was often purposely vague regarding the facts of his early life and would give contradictory dates, which has made reconstructing events a nightmare for successive biographers.*

5 *A report in London Life magazine dated September '65 claimed that a simple typing error by one of the secretaries in the Decca contracts department was to blame for the name change from Bolam to Bolan.*

and unprincipled upstart who proudly boasted he would be the most famous of the three. Mark admitted that the two surnames sounded very similar but argued that by altering the last letter nobody would confuse the two. Furthermore, there would be an umlaut over the 'o' to make it more French. Backpedalling rather awkwardly, he claimed he hadn't taken the name directly from Bolam, but had been thinking about a change months before when he saw an article on the famous French fashion designer Marc Bohan in a magazine. They would see who became more famous and that would settle it. Marc's lack of tact enraged Jimmy and embarrassed Riggs who found himself caught in the middle of a very unpleasant situation. It was decided Mark Feld had outstayed his welcome. He left Lexham Gardens soon after.

Riggs bore him no ill will and to prove it he bought his friend a small statuette of Pan as a leaving present in Camden market which was later photographed for the back cover of the first Tyrannosaurus Rex album.

Marc caught the bus back to Summerstown. There he read, wrote reams of poetry and planned his next move.

He did a great deal of thinking over the following weeks and concluded that his progress had been impeded by well-meaning amateurs who were not well connected with the wheelers and dealers in the music business. What he needed now was a professional manager. After all, Elvis had a million dollars' worth of talent until carny huckster Colonel Tom Parker made the deal that turned it into cold hard cash. And the Beatles, whose music hadn't made much of an impression on Marc, but whose success he coveted, had risen from provincial obscurity to international fame in a matter of months thanks to the efforts of their manager, Brian Epstein. The Stones too, were indebted to wheeler-dealer, Andrew Loog Oldham for their big break. It was the managers who made the deals. Marc would find himself someone who didn't mind getting their hands dirty and whose job it would be to convince a label that his client was the next big thing.

He found the man who would perform this particular miracle in the New Oxford Street offices of publicist Phil Solomon.

18-year-old Mike Pruskin was the bespectacled cousin of Lionel Bart, the composer of the hit musical *Oliver!* and several hits for Cliff including 'Living Doll'. That was the clincher for Marc. Pruskin had left school before taking his A levels to handle publicity for The Nashville Teens and Them (both Decca acts), but he chose to devote all his energy to his new client who appeared to have the winning combination of talent and aggressive self-confidence.

But until the royalties flooded in the pair would have to survive on their wits. It was decided that to minimise outlay they would share Pruskin's basement flat near Baker Street. With luck they wouldn't have to pay the £8 a week rent as the landlord had taken a shine to his new tenant and offered to forgo payment in return for free tickets to any West End shows that he might be able to blag from his famous uncle. But they couldn't live on hope and handouts for long. Marc would have to come up with original songs if he was going to stand a chance of a contract. Everyone was writing their own material. With original material they could approach a publisher and it would be for the publisher to secure a recording contract. Give the publisher a share, said Pruskin, and let him do the donkey work.

How difficult could this songwriting lark be, Mark wondered as he cradled the acoustic guitar in the half light of the basement apartment at 22 Manchester Street?

Pruskin had made himself scarce for a couple of hours to give Mark a chance to channel his muse.

He strummed the verse of the Dion song, half-heartedly at first, as if afraid it might rear up and bite him for fooling with it. It sounded moodier when taken slower, less folky. He began humming idly. The G, E minor, C, D sequence had been used a hundred times, a thousand times, but somehow the best variations overcame its limitations. How did they do that? Perhaps the trick was not following the chords too closely with the voice but using it as a foundation only. And what do songwriters write about? Longing for girls? Losing girls? Driving cars? Riding freight trains? He had no experience of any of these and he would have sounded insincere if he pretended that he did. He could hear well-meaning Warren and his friends laughing now. What do you know of the world, kiddo?, they would say. No, he had to find something they couldn't scoff at. Something that would make them sit up and take notice. Something exotic. Or somewhere exotic. Paris. That would do it. But no one would pay for a single with the title 'Slug in the bathtub'. He didn't want to be Bobby 'Splish Splash' Darin. Real stars don't make novelty records. He played a mental word game to delay the inevitable, scanning the alphabet for suitable subjects. When he reached the letter 'C' he dismissed Cars, Chicks, Clothes and Clubs because they had all been well covered. But Characters gave him pause. Riggs had been the most colourful character he knew. Riggs recast as a Magician, maybe?

"Walking in the woods one day, I met a man who said that he was magic."

Chapter 5
Misfit

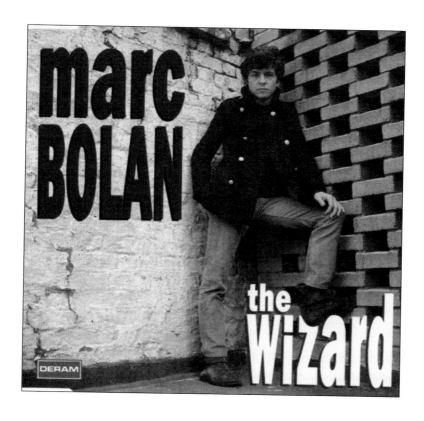

I t was an obscenely early hour to make a record. At 10 o'clock in the morning most musicians would still be in bed, sleeping off a hangover. But 17-year-old Marc Bolan could not claim that privilege. He was not yet a name, nor had he faced a live audience. And so, when the Decca executives decreed that morning sessions should begin at 10, their contracted artists, producers, arrangers and session musicians clocked in as ordered. Fortunately, the orchestral players, guitarist, bass player and drummer hired for Marc's first professional session on September 14, 1965, were old pros and could have read the score in their sleep. The magical element known as 'feel' wouldn't be needed today. It was strictly playing by numbers, and the numbers – or in this case the notes – had been scored by the dependable Mike Leander, an experienced arranger who would later make million-selling hits with Gary Glitter.

Greek-American producer Jim Economides, looking dapper in his customary surfing shirt and slacks, was also taking the session in his stride that morning, reading the newspaper, drinking coffee, chain-smoking and making small talk with the engineer and his assistant Mike Hurst while the mikes were being set up.

All in contrast to the singer who wiped his palms on his mohair slacks and paced nervously around the sterile West Hampstead studio, shadowed by his teenage manager who had come along to supervise the session they had worked so hard to secure.

Pruskin had been right. A third party had been necessary to clinch the critical deal. The shrewd former publicist had offered London agent Leslie Conn a 50 per cent share if Conn could secure a publishing contract. Conn had asked if there were any contacts he could follow up before canvassing names from his own address book and was told that Dick Rowe had once expressed an interest in their boy. One brief phone call later and Marc had the promise of a one single release with the option for a second. And there was one other favour Conn performed. He introduced Marc to another young hopeful he was representing at the time, David Jones (later David Bowie).

Right now Bolan would gladly have swapped places with his new friend. The clock was ticking and there were three tracks to get down in two hours, the standard work rate for Decca's resident popular music division at that time. What if his voice cracked? What if he shook so much he couldn't pitch, or sang off key? Pruskin may not have figured very significantly in the Marc Bolan story after this point, but that day he earned his share of the 15 shillings they would earn in publishing royalties from this debut single. He reminded his inexperienced client that the orchestra only needed a guide vocal to fix the tempo and once the backing was in the can he could have as many run-throughs as he liked. They planned to put three tracks down but only two were needed for the single and he had written them both. This was what they had worked for and it was going to sound great.

Leander, too, had every confidence in Bolan who he imagined as cast from the same mould as Cat Stevens, or a male Marianne Faithfull, both quintessentially English folk singers with pop appeal. Leander had worked out the changes with Marc over several sessions at his flat the previous week and had sketched in a simple but densely textured arrangement for a small orchestra with a tight rhythm section at the centre to propel it along. Xylophone flourishes, handclaps and a wordless ethereal harmony part for female backing singers completed the picture. Unfortunately, the composer hadn't provided a chorus, and couldn't be persuaded to write one even after Leander had pointed out that it was hooks not looks that sold singles. So the Musical Director had written a fill which he gave to the flutes and woodwind to break up the otherwise seamless string of verses. He also thought it desirable to insert a pause at a critical point for dramatic effect – the point where the chorus ought to have been – and an instrumental verse to act as a coda, but the track still clocked in under two minutes, which was uncommonly short for a single. When Marc heard the orchestra run through the arrangement for the first time, he was speechless. If only he had taken Leander's advice and written a chorus, it might have a better chance of being a hit.

But if hearing his song played by pros shook his studied cool, he was less impressed by the business-like attitude of the female backing singers.

"A couple of the Ladybirds, or the Vernon Girls, or someone did the backing. They talked about corsets and stuff, you know, between takes, knitting and things. My first big session that was, chicks knitting!"

Economides was an efficient if unimaginative freelance producer who had been brought in because he could be relied upon to keep the session on track and on time. But he was better known in the business for his eccentricities, namely having insisted a tailor measure him for a suit during a Beach Boys session, a band he claimed to have produced.[1]

When Economides was with Capitol in the States he had worked with surfer Dick Dale, rocker Johnny Burnette, pop idol Bobby Darin and harmony group The Lettermen, but he was afraid of being stuck with second division acts and so had emigrated to England to set up his own production company and pursue his interest in drag racing. A burly six-footer with black curly hair and a neat charcoal moustache, he towered over the seated musicians, his forthright manner and commanding voice ensuring that everyone put in their best efforts.

When the first backing track was down he waved Marc back into the vocal booth and

---

1 *Economides may have been present at a Beach Boys session, but he was not their producer and if he was prepared to claim credit for a Beach Boys session, it lends credibility to Mike Hurst's claim to have produced the first two Bolan sessions under his boss's supervision, although Bolan always credited Economides. Hurst: "Jim had done a deal with Decca for seven or eight thousand pounds to produce a number of singles for them, which he never did, because he got me to produce Marc Bolan and never came up with anybody else for them. Jim really liked him and asked me to do something with him. I did the first two records with Marc (The Third Degree and The Wizard). Marc was very raw when he came in. What he did was good but I didn't appreciate at the time that it could get better... What I recognised in him was the burning desire to be successful. If that's star quality, then he had star quality".*

told him to run through the first verse for level without the backing. Once the engineer was satisfied, they went for a take. One minute and forty-five seconds later the red light was flicked off and the producer's voice boomed over the monitor, "That's fine. Come in to the control room and listen to the playback."

Marc may have had his doubts about the production line methods, but he had to admit it was a tight track and he sounded assured in the midst of it, aided by a touch of natural echo. His trademark vibrato was not then in evidence, but it was a strong, confident performance. However, there was no time for congratulations. Time was money and the musicians had been booked for two hours. Not a minute more or their union would be hearing about it.

Everyone flicked over to the next sheet on their music stand and the red light came on again. One minute forty seconds later the flip side of the single was given the producer's tacit approval before Marc put down a second and final vocal.

'Beyond The Risin' Sun' was in the same vein as its companion, but with the added rasp from a sax way down in the mix, a more prominent xylophone to emphasise the exotic subject matter and the Ladybirds oohing for all they were worth having been freed from their knitting. Again, Leander had to disguise the fact that there was no chorus by creating a memorable hook from the instruments at hand. And again there was change from two minutes, twenty seconds to be precise. At one minute forty it was one of the shortest pop sides ever recorded (beaten only by Elvis's 'Let's Have A Party' at 1.36). If the lyrics were a shade on the twee side at least they were offset by a strong backbeat and Marc's delivery which boasted a conviction beyond his years. The glimpse of a fairy land "where people walk hand in hand" and where "unicorns and young gods play from the break of dawn to the end of day" was also saved from cloying corniness by a direct reference to Ray Bradbury's short story collection *The Golden Apples of the Sun*. Marc was reading SF as avidly as the back cover blurb on the latest Dylan album. It was from Dylan that Bolan had learned the art of linear narrative and the power of surreal imagery. But Dylan knew that even his most erudite listeners liked to be thrown the odd chorus now and again.

The session wound up on schedule with the recording of a third track, a cover of Fred Neil's folk standard, 'The Bag I'm In', which has remained unreleased to this day. But one look at the lyrics with their reference to being late for work and the atom bomb and it's clear that the song, which was later recorded by US freakbeat combo H.P.Lovecraft, was out of tune with the two original Bolan compositions.

What the inclusion of this cover does reveal, though, is that Bolan evidently did not have enough original songs at that time to offer an alternative if 'Beyond the Risin' Sun' had not worked out on the day.

Much relieved and eagerly anticipating the imminent arrival of fame and fortune, Bolan and Pruskin retired to Manchester Street to hold court to the world's press.

Meanwhile, the Decca publicity machine concocted as pretty a piece of fiction as their copywriters could conjure up. Their press release was a masterpiece of sixties hyperbole.

"Marc Bolan was born in September 1947. After 15 years had passed he travelled to Paris and met a black magician called the Wizard. He lived for 18 months in the wizard's chateau with Achimedes (sic), an owl, and the biggest whitest Siamese cat you ever saw.

"He then felt the need to spend some time alone so made his way to the woods near Rome. For two weeks he strove to find himself and then he returned to London where he began to write. His writings mirror his experience with mentionings of the magician's pact with the great god Pan. In London, walking down King's Road, Chelsea, in the dead of night he chanced to meet a girl named Loog who gave him a magic cat. This cat, named after the girl, is now his constant companion and is a source of inspiration to him. Now the wizard's tale is set down for all to hear on Marc's first recording for Decca."

The notion that Marc had acquired a familiar, like the witches of old, was only slightly less ludicrous than the claim that he had made his own way from Paris to Rome where he lived alone in a forest communing with nature. The cat was in fact named after Andrew Loog Oldham, manager of the Rolling Stones, and it lived out its life in the Putney council flat where Sid Feld worked as caretaker until his retirement. Roadie Mick O'Halloran told the author that Marc had admitted elaborating on his meeting with the Wizard, but that he had met an occultist in Paris, that his name was Bobu and that it was he who had predicted that Marc would not live to see his 30th birthday.

A small poem accompanied two photographs of Marc looking every inch the pop poet in navy blue reefer jacket, black jeans and suede boots.

Standing alone in the wood, with the golden palace bleeding scarlet tears into the sunset
I thought of all the treasures in the magic palace.
And all the emptiness in my stomach.
And I smiled secretly remembering the Wizard's words.

However, despite all of Decca's efforts, the world was in no rush to beat a path to yet another Bohemian beat poet's basement lair, although in October the London Evening Standard sent their showbiz reporter Maureen Cleave with a brief to check out what made the new generation of pop hopefuls tick. She found her chosen specimens precocious but not unappealing.

"They wear black jerseys and pale corduroy trousers, and they are much more agreeable than you might think from the way they talk. There is a cat asleep on an old fur hat on the windowsill; a green telephone and a self-portrait by Mr. Pruskin.

"He and Mr. Bolan have been working industriously, methodically and intelligently for the last eight weeks on turning Mr. Bolan into a pop singer. They are as certain of success as the good knitter who follows the Fair Isle pattern, knowing the result will be a gorgeous splash of colour."

Pruskin gushed, "People want to be like Marc: He's leading them somewhere."

"And I don't know where I want to go myself," added Marc. "I had this thing about Greek Gods: the whole idea about centaurs and horses with wings just knocks me out."

He was asked to elaborate on the story of his wizard friend and duly obliged.

"I met this man who was a black magician and who had a big chateau on the Left Bank; I only left it about eight times all the year I was there. I learned about the black art but being evil didn't particularly appeal to me. I think this man was getting old and wanted to work his magic through me. He liked my mind. I used to watch them when they cast spells. They crucified live cats. Sometimes, they used to eat human flesh just like chicken bones. From a cauldron…Personally, the prospect of being immortal doesn't

Marc with Mike Leander in the Decca studios recording 'The Wizard' (photographer unknown. From the private collection of Danielz and Caron Willans)

excite me; but the prospect of being a materialistic idol for four years does appeal. With this image we are putting out, I know I can communicate. If I have a couple of glasses of wine and I'm relaxed, I know I can come through. I know it sounds ego, but it's really scary: if I go into a room and there are ten girls, nine of them will fancy me. I've never failed yet with girls…I look forward to growing old, to being mature and knowing good wine. I want to savour life; I want to have grey hair like Cary Grant."

When the single was finally released in November '65, reviews were encouraging rather than ecstatic. George Melly, writing for *The Observer*, compared Marc's facility with words to the 19th century poet Walter De La Mare which did wonders for Marc's ego, while *Disc* summed up the response of the music press. "On the strength of this strange young man's looks and weird background I suspect that we'll hear more of this odd record about meeting a wizard in the woods who knew all. I prefer the other side, 'Beyond the Risin' Sun' which has more tune. Jim Economides, ace producer, does lovely things on this. I'm a bit put off by the way this boy sings with Dylan phrasing, but that's all."

It is revealing how little the reviewer knew of the recording process. It was Leander who was responsible for the way the record sounded. Economides (or Mike Hurst, if you prefer) had done little more than supervise the session and approve the arrangement.

The consensus was that the now 18-year-old Bolan was a name to watch, but that he hadn't found his voice or his own style yet. As disappointed as Marc may have been by the lukewarm reception for his first release, he suspected they were right.

His performance on the showcase TV pop show of the period, *Ready Steady Go* on November 12, seemed to confirm that he was simply not ready for the big time.

"I did *Ready Steady Go* – it was live then – but the band played in the wrong key and missed the intro out, it was a terrible disaster, the whole thing. And the record wasn't a hit, no way, it didn't deserve to be."

It was a sobering experience to say the least and a painful reminder that he hadn't paid his dues, to coin a phrase, and would not earn the respect of his contemporaries or the all-important music press until he had faced a live audience.

A week later he took a bath, to borrow another show business idiom, at the Glad Rag Student's Ball held at the Empire Pool, Wembley. The same venue would see the realisation of his dreams seven years later, but this evening it was an unmitigated disaster as Bolan was shaking so hard with stage fright that he couldn't strum and sing at the same time. He was heckled and booed by an estimated 8,000 rowdy students who were angry that the headliners, The Kinks, and their special guest John Lee Hooker, had pulled out at short notice leaving them to listen to a nervous unknown. Marc's torment was intensified by the knowledge that his ordeal was being recorded for future broadcast, but fortunately his parents remembered that the screen went blank on the day sparing their son any further embarrassment.

A second performance at the more intimate Pontiac Club in Putney was disrupted when a fight broke out and Bolan had to cut his brief set short. Television appearances on *The Five O'Clock Fun Fair* and *Thank Your Lucky Stars*, however, passed without incident, although that was due to the fact that performers were required to mime to pre-recorded backing tracks.

It was at this point that Marc met journalist Keith Altham who eight years later would became his publicist.

September 14th 1965 Marc's first professional recording session (photographer unknown. From the private collection of Danielz and Caron Willans)

"I knew him when I was a journalist on the *NME* and we used to frequent a bar called The Brewmaster in Leicester Square. It was around 1965 and he was about 18, 'the Mod about Town', when he used to do modelling, about the time he had his contract with Decca. He came in with a single, 'The Wizard' and he used to try and brag to us and say 'Gotta listen to this, fellas. I'm going to be the greatest thing since Elvis Presley'. And we thought, 'Nice little bloke, Marc! Sit down and have a coca cola.' He was the kind of hustling figure one never really expected to do the amazing things he later did. I liked him.

"He never had a strong voice, so I suppose he made a virtue of an idiosyncrasy that there was in his voice, like most singers do.

"If I think about him as a person – I think there was something special about him. You see somebody like that who is a pushy little guy as he was, but you're not certain, as the years go by, whether you actually knew it at the time or whether you were thinking of it in retrospect. There were some strange things about Marc. He was a sort of precocious talent – a sort of boy/man thing, because he lacked a formal education. I've met other people who are artistic but not formally artistic... It's an innocence, a kind of naivety that children have and that we lose as we grow up. There was this very young childlike quality about him, the way that children see colours better than we do, their sense of smell is better and their reactions to certain things are faster. The inability to put things down in grammatical sequence you could see in his writing – he was dyslexic almost – was a part of that. He was reacting in a very honest, unaffected way that children do to emotional situations. "I don't think he traded on it, or that he was even aware that he possessed it. It probably gained him other qualities as well that he wasn't aware of. He tended to think they were almost supernormal talents. He put quasi-mystical interpretations on them. I think it was much simpler than that. He was intuitively right about whether somebody was good, bad or whatever, although he wouldn't be able to tell you why, or explain the logic behind it."

If Marc was feeling sorry for himself, he didn't have time to brood on it. On the last working day of 1965, he was invited back to the Decca studios to demo a batch of new songs from which Mike Leander hoped to select a follow up single. As soon as Marc put his guitar down it was clear that Decca's Musical Director was disappointed. He made encouraging noises, but regretted that none of the four fragments recorded that day ('The Soldier's Song', 'Reality', 'Rings of Fortune' and 'Highways') had the same potential or appeal as 'The Wizard'.

Both 'The Soldier's Song' (aka 'Song For A Soldier') and 'Reality' have never been released but the author has heard both and can understand why Leander failed to see their potential. Both are heavily influenced by Dylan almost to the point of pastiche. Whatever had initially appealed to Decca's A&R executives and persuaded them to give Bolan a chance was conspicuously lacking in these two songs which were derivative and lacking the all-important hook that was needed for a potential hit single. Interestingly, the melody of 'The Soldier's Song' is strikingly similar to the outro to 'My People Were Fair' which suggests that it had stuck in Marc's mind and that he was reluctant to waste a good tune.

Leander ended by suggesting that Marc scrap all of these and write something more up tempo, preferably with a chorus. Gutted, Marc slunk back to Manchester Street to be commiserated by Pruskin, Loog and a new confidant he knew he could rely upon for moral support, Theresa Whipman.

'Terry', as she preferred to be called, had her own flat in Maida Vale, but shortly after meeting Marc became a regular visitor to Manchester Street. She was what Marc's parents would have called a tomboy, but when Marc and his bob-haired girlfriend were side by side, the effect was something less readily defined. He had the more feminine features, the soft wispy voice, while she seemed and sounded the tougher of the two. They even dressed alike. The implication from his journal entries suggested that the attraction was not entirely sexual as he saw her more as a soul mate and unpaid secretary, available day and night to note down his latest lyric, poem, play, short story or film script. "She's not beautiful, she's not ugly," he confided to one notebook. "Yet her heart-shaped face smiling resembles the dawn." She was a treasured companion and extremely useful to him as his dyslexia impaired his ability to write at speed. Or at least that was the excuse he used when he felt too lazy to scribble his ideas down. She was present when he wrote many of the early songs and sat in on every recording session. It is Terry he can be heard yelling at on the intro to 'Jasper C. Debussy.' ("Fuck off or keep cool, you know.")

He could also be cringingly coy and as hopelessly romantic as a schoolgirl. In a letter to the girl with the "ballerina body" dated sometime in 1968 he gushes, "Here's to the gates of my very own castle happy where I'll live with foxes and ponys and my true love. Here's to my true love who live with me when I'm me." (The grammatical errors are indicative of his marginal dyslexia.)

After all his florid protestations of love she would be unceremoniously dumped the day Marc met the media savvy June and was never mentioned again. But during this first phase of his career, when his own sexuality was still unsettled, he wasn't looking for a lover. He needed an adoring admirer to listen to his dreams and with whom he could share the ideas streaming from his increasingly fertile imagination.

The biggest influence on Marc during this period was Bob Dylan, the educated middle class son of a doctor from Duluth, Minnesota, who had begun by labouring under the ghost of Woody Guthrie, the world-weary voice of the oppressed, until he tired of being a spokesman for the silent majority. In '65 Dylan cast off the expectations and obligations foisted on him by the protest movement to pull pop music up by its boot straps, forcing it to grow up fast and evolve from an inarticulate howl of teenage angst in to an art form. He enjoyed pricking the pretentions of those who took it all far too seriously, but he could also lapse into pretentious self-indulgence and be wilfully obscure when the mood took him. His imitators did likewise, but few had the same facility with words or the persistence to practise their craft even when it seemed that no one was listening. Dylan was clearly the master and Bolan one of his many acolytes, but Marc's quintessentially English verse, woven from the classical mythology and the children's tales of Kenneth Grahame and C.S. Lewis, gave his lyrics a pastoral quality that was distinctly different to Dylan's verse which was rooted in biblical parables, Steinbeck's novels and the iconography of the mid-West.

In the first weeks of '66 Marc was fooling around with a simple A major, C, E7 chord progression and mimicking singer Roy Orbison's quavering falsetto to help him pitch and sustain the longer notes. It certainly made him sound different and would confound the critics that said his phrasing was too similar to Dylan. Dylan had trademarked the lazy drawl. This exaggerated vibrato was something unique. The riff too was sounding promising, a simple A major chord given emphasis on the offbeat by alternately lifting and holding down the middle note to create A/A7. The words also came effortlessly – inspired by a tag line from the *Perry Mason* TV series that was popular in Britain at the time. Whenever Mason (Raymond Burr) asked his Private Investigator Paul Drake if he was ready for the next case the latter would wearily reply, "Why am I getting the third degree here?" Buddy Holly had done likewise with a catchphrase from John Ford's *The Searchers* ('That'll Be the Day') so Marc felt he was in good company. By the time he had finished there was even a line that could charitably be called a chorus. Mike Leander would be happy. And Jim, too.

A session was arranged and the new song, 'The Third Degree' recorded in a couple of takes together with a flip, 'San Francisco Poet'. Marc doubled on acoustic guitar backed a group of session musicians that included John Paul Jones, four years away from forming Led Zeppelin with fellow session muso Jimmy Page. Marc subsequently claimed that the latter track (for which Jones swapped his bass for an organ) had been a demo, but there is nothing in the sound or performance to suggest that. It's more likely to have been an initial run through or a rough first take which they were forced to pass as a master when time ran out. But at 2 minutes 29 seconds the A-side broke the important two-minute barrier beloved of pop radio and it had an identifiable hook: "Philosophising mad psychiatrist closing up my mind in darkness, beware of the Third Degree".

The stripped down sound and back to basics instrumentation was in stark contrast to the ornate orchestrations of his debut single. This was a band (albeit comprised of hired hands) and Marc was dictating the pace and 'feel', not a baton-wielding Musical Director. His infectious enthusiasm can be clearly heard on the vocal adlibs that bleed through from the backing track (listen carefully and you can hear him shout "Yeah, go man!" after the guitar solo). Admittedly, his playing wasn't on the same level as the pros. His scrappier guitar had to be overdubbed by a tighter rhythm guitar, but there is no denying the energy level had been ramped up a notch propelled by Jones's bass line. With Marc singing on the live backing track it was possible for him to double track his vocal which thickened his voice and gave it more presence. Galvanised by the thrill of making a 'real record' he opened up on the final verse and let the new tremulous vocal soar as he hit the line, "Fantasy baby's all I got, I'm as sane as you, believe it or not."

Marc had found his voice.[2]

Decca must have known they had a potential hit on their hands and an artist who was distinctly different from Dylan, Donovan, Cat Stevens or anyone else the critics cared to name. Yet, incredibly the label didn't get behind it. Perhaps they believed a second single didn't merit as much effort as a debut, that they had done the ground work and the second single would sell on the back of the first, or maybe Dick Rowe was displeased that Economides had taken his business elsewhere, refusing to record in Decca's own studio. Whatever the reason, the single was pressed, shipped and forgotten.

Marc became disillusioned. He had taken setbacks in his stride before now, but this latest rebuff was a bitter blow to his ego. He'd had two singles released by a major label, appeared on TV, been interviewed by the national press and even survived a hostile audience – twice. Now he seemed to be back at square one. Matters were not helped by having to do a moonlight flit from the Baker Street basement when his manager couldn't find the few quid owing for the rent. It was the end of a promising partnership. Back in Sommerstown with mum and dad was a humiliating retreat, however you looked at it.

"I spent a year trying to get away from Decca. They wouldn't record me to be quite honest! They wanted to do a number. It was one of those 'You've got to be commercial, kid', numbers, which I couldn't really foresee. I didn't understand what they were talking about. At this point Dylan had just happened and The Byrds were big and those sort of things and that was obviously the avenue I should be taking… eventually I got away from them."

---

2 *Marc enjoyed teasing gullible journalists by claiming he had found his distinctive vocal style by playing Billy Eckstine singles at 78 rpm, but Eckstine's 'velvet voice' was not to Marc's taste – at any speed. The only jazz singer he listened to was Al Jolson who's biopic The Jolson Story had been a childhood favourite of his. Mundane though it might be, the fact of the matter is that Marc simply exaggerated a quality inherent in his own voice.*

Back home in Wimbledon he withdrew into himself, sustained by a diverse diet of poetry, prose and his favourite meal, mushrooms on toast.

What he needed, he concluded, was a manager with a proven track record and a roster of artists who were making records and making money, hand over fist.

Chapter 6
Ready, Steady, Go!

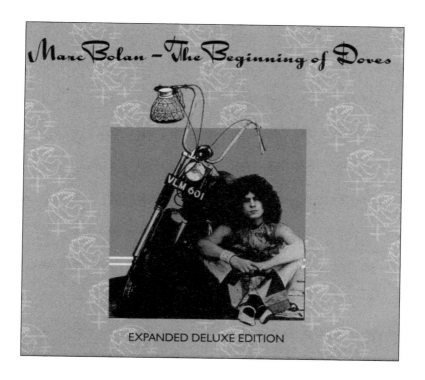

I'm sick of modeling and living off wizards.
Marc, October 1965

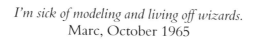

Marc's timing was fortuitous. When he called at the London home of Simon Napier-Bell in late September 1966, the 27-year-old former assistant film editor (who, incidentally, had attended the same Harrow grammar school as Conservative MP Michael Portillo) was considering parting company with his only clients, the Yardbirds. The group's singer, Keith Relf, had been telephoning long distance night and day to complain about conditions on their Australian tour and at one point refused to go on stage without a clean pair of socks. Exasperated and exhausted by Relf's unreasonable demands and the band's constant bickering, their manager, an avowed atheist, had been reduced to praying that something would turn up to relieve him of the responsibility of playing nanny to the group. That afternoon his appeals were answered.

Bolan had phoned only minutes earlier to ask if he could pop round with a tape, but when Napier-Bell opened the door his visitor, dressed like "a Dickensian street urchin", sheepishly admitted that he didn't have one, but he had brought his battered acoustic guitar and could perform the songs right there and then if his host had ten minutes to spare. "You wouldn't want to miss the chance of signing the next Elvis, would you?"

It was an offer Simon couldn't refuse.

"He curled up cross-legged in a large armchair which made him seem even smaller and played them on an acoustic guitar. He had about four albums worth. He was on a very high ego trip at the time. He really didn't think he needed to make a record. He thought if we just put some posters up then people would see his photograph and he would just happen. And I said, 'No'. I thought a record would be a good idea. So he said, 'OK, but it's just me and the guitar'. He had done that one record with Decca. He was pre-running what he later did when he left John's Children and went acoustic. But I thought it wasn't a very good idea, but if that's what he wanted to do, we'd give it a try. And I loved all the songs."

Marc excused his rudimentary guitar playing, but was clearly proud of the songs. His host had the impression that song writing wasn't a craft he had worked at. Marc had merely opened up his mind and plucked out the finest blooms he had cultivated in the fertile soil of his imagination. He appeared to be as astonished at their quality as his one-man audience.

Contrary to the impression given in earlier biographies, Marc had not picked his new manager at random. *Ready Steady Go* editor Vicki Wickham, who had arranged for Marc's appearance on the show the previous year, had recommended her former song writing partner when Bolan had phoned her to complain that Decca had dropped him and that he was at a loss as to what to do next. Wickham[1] and Napier-Bell had co-written the English lyrics for Dusty Springfield's number one hit 'You Don't Have To Say You Love Me' (adapted from an Italian tune Dusty had heard at the San Remo festival) and it was Wickham, one of the unsung movers and shakers of the sixties scene, who had suggested Simon move into management. By putting the two in touch she thought she might be doing both a favour.

Napier-Bell was no novice to the music business, though. On the strength of the publicity he generated for his first clients, an inter-racial singing act, Scott and Ferraz, he was asked to manage The Yardbirds who had recently parted with their original manager, Giorgio Gomelsky. He renegotiated their shamelessly stingy contract with EMI for a record fee of £25,000 and a 12% royalty and in doing so claimed that he learnt the first hard lesson of music biz management – never trust a record company. Through various accounting clauses and conditions he discovered the label could avoid paying royalties on overstocks and that there was no limit to these 'excess pressings'. Furthermore, the advance he had secured was recoupable against royalties. It was nothing more than a glorified loan. When Simon asked The Yardbirds' lawyer why he hadn't refused to sign such a deal he was told, "If I told my clients to refuse to sign unfair contracts, none of them would have a deal." Napier-Bell told Bolan many other music business horror stories that evening and apparently found an eager and attentive listener.

In the fifties an artist who dared to ask for royalties would be laughed out of the office or told, 'You want royalties? Go to Buckingham Palace'. Payment would be limited to a nice lunch now and then if they were lucky, and a few luxuries to keep up appearances, to sustain the illusion of success – publicity parties, photo shoots, a posh nosh and maybe a hand out, 'an advance' on royalties which would never come. Then when the record sales dried up or the artist got wise, they would find themselves with a huge bill for 'corporate hospitality'. For those for whom success seemed too good to be true, there would be a nasty shock. It was. That is when they first heard of the Devil's own accounting scheme known as cross-collateralisation in which the profit from the last record would be offset against the advance that was still to be recouped from the current release. This 'balancing of the books' (known in criminal circles as 'cooking the books') would invariably leave a debit amount on the annual royalty statement, if the artist were ever privileged to see such a thing. Did the working class oik with a guitar really think that the record company were going to pick up the tab after all they had done for him? What did they think the company was – a charity? The music business is like any other, Simon told his new discovery, and it exists solely to make money. And the bigger the business, the more likely it was to attract the interest of criminals who were looking for a means of laundering their cash. The mafia had their dirty hands in almost every corporate pie. Try to wriggle out of a contract and you'll likely find yourself dangling by your heels from a window on the top floor. All the gloss and glamour is nothing but a flytrap to catch the grubs that the label will bleed dry to make the stockholders rich. Records offered the highest mark up in the entire retail industry. Ten cents worth

---

1 *Wickham went on to manage Morrissey and Marc Almond.*

of vinyl selling for 10 dollars. That's a 10,000 % profit.[2] If you think about it, the cost of the product was being deducted from the artist's earnings. And in what other business would the employer be legally entitled to tie the employee to them for five or ten years and sell them on to another company without their agreement? It was positively medieval. And don't forget, kiddo, for every ten acts they sign, only one will succeed. Still want to be a star?

Bolan didn't flinch. Does a prophet fear martyrdom after he sees the vision of the heavenly kingdom? "Talk all you want Simon, I'm gonna be so big, they won't dare to rip me off or I'll bring the whole rotten mess crashing down round their ears. Better still, I'll set up my own label and keep all my earnings for myself."

Bolan might be looking for a surrogate parent-cum-fairy godmother to pamper, protect and wave a magic wand to make his dreams come true, but he was not fazed by Simon's stock of horror stories. Simon realised that his new protégé may look like a pixie and talk like a poet, but he was street-wise. He would stay the course. After his wearisome experiences with The Yardbirds, Napier-Bell needed someone who would accept advice and trust to his instincts.

Simon drove Marc straight down to De Lane Lea Studios at 129 Kingsway, Holborn, that very night for an 8 o'clock session during which his new discovery demoed 14 songs in just under two hours, Marc insisting on performing live with no overdubs. The tracks were 'Hippy Gumbo', 'Jasmine 49', 'Black and White Incident', 'Cat Black', 'Charlie', 'Hot Rod Mama', 'Mustang Ford', 'Pictures Of Purple People', 'The Perfumed Garden Of Gulliver Smith', 'You Got The Power', 'I'm Weird', 'Observations', 'Eastern Spell' and 'Horrible Breath'.

Of these, four songs would be re-recorded for the first Tyrannosaurus Rex albums, but ten would remain in the vaults. Two of the 14 concerned cars, four were quirky character sketches and three were descriptive fantasies revealing an original mind in full flow.

The studios had recently been fitted out with a customised state-of-the-art Sound Techniques mixing console, and could claim the Rolling Stones as regular clients, so this was no bargain-basement session. (Just one month later Jimi Hendrix would record his first single 'Hey Joe' within these same walls.) If there had been a chance the tracks would be overdubbed with other instruments at a later date, the guitar would have been miked for stereo so it could be spread across the soundstage. But the minimal mono, one mike set-up was clearly intended as a demo session. Even someone as new to the business as Bolan was at that time would not have been as naïve to imagine that an album could have been made from these raw recordings.

"So we recorded all the songs with just him and the guitar. Then when it was finished he again said, 'Well, that's it, now I've done an album it's really going to happen.' He was really ridiculously egotistical to the point where you were furious with him, but he was so totally charming that you had to accept it as probably true."

---

2 *The seemingly-inflated figure of 10,000% profit may be Napier-Bell's own typo or that of the journalist who edited it. The exact quote – "The Artists were never the product; the product was discs – 10 cents' worth of vinyl selling for $10 – 10,000 per cent profit – the highest mark-up in all of retail marketing." – is from The Observer, January 20, 2008.*

Marc's claim that he had just recorded his debut album was not entirely preposterous – his guitar playing was surprisingly assured (false modesty aside) and his vocal performance was strong. It is also worth noting that he had recorded a sufficient number of songs that evening to fill two sides of an LP, although these versions were so short that all 14 totalled just 26 minutes, barely sufficient to spill over to the second side. He would also remind Simon that Dylan had recorded his first couple of albums straight off the bat in a single session, but from a technical standpoint there were several reasons why these recordings could not be released. For one, his guitar tuning was highly suspect, his timing erratic and as is self-evident from the number of vocal explosions that the performance hadn't been recorded with a pop shield – a prerequisite for all professional recordings.

Simon was irritated by Marc's impatience and his impulsiveness which might have seen the songs released before they had been given the treatment they deserved. He could see it was going to be a constant struggle to keep his new client grounded so they would have the time to consider the best approach, but he also admitted to being seduced by the broad, open-hearted smile and childlike innocence of such a preciously talented young man.

Afterwards Simon took Marc to dinner and gave him the second half of a long lecture about how to survive the minefield that was the music business. But Marc was no wide-eyed innocent, either. In fact, Simon was astounded by his perceptive assessment of other stars and impressed with the reasons he gave for crossing Brian Epstein and Andrew Loog Oldham off his hit list of potential managers. Then Marc subjected Simon to a provocative series of questions devised to measure the BS quotient of any potential candidate. When the interrogation became too personal for comfort, Simon called for the bill and promised to phone when he had a chance to listen to the songs and decide what to do with them.

"I eventually persuaded him that we had to do something more to the songs, so we decided on 'Hippy Gumbo' which we took and did with some strings."

The song was about a 'schoolboy crush' that Marc had had for another man (presumably Allen Warren or Riggs O'Hara) which forced him to face his latent bisexuality. But when the opportunity arose to confess his feelings and consummate their relationship Marc chickened out. So he made a voodoo doll and burned it in effigy to exorcise the feelings that confounded him. It was this encounter to which he was no doubt referring when he later confessed, "When I was 15 I wasn't very sure of myself. I wanted to find out, so I went with a bloke. It was so that I would never have to look back and wonder what I'd missed out on. I felt I should try anything once…Anyway, I checked it out and I prefer chicks."

Until 1967, the Criminal Law Amendment Act of 1885, under which Oscar Wilde had been prosecuted, was still in force which made it an offence for consenting adults to practise homosexual acts, even in private. The Act, commonly known as 'the blackmailer's charter', would have been a significant deterrent to anyone contemplating a same sex relationship and for someone with Marc's 'hang ups' the shame of prosecution would have forced him to suppress any attraction he might have felt towards those attractive young actors who had taken him under their wing in the mid-sixties.

"A lot of people thought he was gay," Allan Warren has said, "but he wasn't. He was bisexual… He flirted with the gay scene but he was more there for decoration." The gay scene appealed to class-conscious Marc because no one enquired into his background and if they thought him pretty and cute, they would introduce him to their friends in the theatre and music business. Simon Napier-Bell didn't deny that he found it more fun to manage a group of pretty young men like John's Children who were singularly lacking in talent than the sweaty blokes in the Yardbirds who had some to spare.

Although Simon had initially been bowled over by the simplicity of the rockier songs, it was 'Hippy Gumbo' with its brooding, haunting refrain and sinister nursery rhyme-like lyric which had lingered in his mind. It was re-recorded, probably with a click track or metronome, so the additional instruments could be added at a second session at De Lane Lea in October. Rock musicians could be relied upon to ride any fluctuations as the track progressed, but classically trained string players would refuse to play on a track that did not stick strictly to the tempo given on the first page of the score.

"I took it to every record company – and you must remember there were only four major record companies in England then (EMI, Decca, Pye and Philips) and if anyone was in a position to do anything with it I was. Nobody liked it. So finally I went back and told him and he was completely shattered. He wasn't even expecting to be turned down now. He was absolutely certain of himself. But I didn't lose faith in him. He lost more faith in himself than I did in him."

In the end EMI agreed to release the record by the back door on their subsidiary, Parlophone, in the hope that Simon would return the favour by getting tough with The Yardbirds who were on another label owned by EMI, Columbia, and were wasting increasing amounts of studio time arguing among themselves.

The Parlophone press office secured a spot for Marc on *Ready Steady Go* and it just happened to be the edition that saw the British television debut of Jimi Hendrix. Marc claimed to have been sitting in the control room with the producer when Hendrix performed 'Hey Joe' live in the studio. "This old lady really freaked out and said 'Turn the backing track down!' because it was really loud. All the machines were shaking and they said 'But there is no backing track'…And that really interested me." It was that incendiary performance which convinced Marc that his future lay with the electric guitar.

The appearance on *Ready Steady Go* failed to persuade the record buying public to part with their 6 shillings and 8 pence (about 33p), although Marc was heartened to hear Hendrix say that he dug the voice and predicted a big future for him. "I thought 'bullshit', you know," but a couple of years later when Marc got seriously into Hendrix he recalled the comment and considered it a highlight of his early career.

But despite the blessing of the gods, the record sank without trace. If truth be told, the label thought it too weird to categorise and if they couldn't classify it, they made no effort to promote it. It simply fell between the cracks.

The press release contained the best review the single was to get.

"Bayou fog seems to creep out of the phonograph as you play it. The combination of simplicity and sophistication is rather reminiscent of *Porgy and Bess*. It features guitar, strings, kettledrums and Marc singing in a voice that is as Creole as Gumbo itself. Just how and why Marc wrote a Creole song is a mystery, but it may have something to do with his French background. For although Marc was born in London, both his parents are French and he lived in France as a child."

Quite what Phyllis and Sid made of this nonsense one can only imagine. However, the blurb offers one nugget of information which appears to confirm Marc's avowed dislike of jazz and discounts the persistent myth that he had discovered his voice by listening to Billy Eckstine records at 78rpm.

"Taste in music: rock and roll and Chet Baker. 'I've never heard Chet Baker, but he looks great. I have all his album covers.'"

Mention is rarely made of its flipside, 'Misfit', although it was the first time Marc's bleating 'Larry The Lamb' voice is heard throughout an entire track in high register as opposed to 'The Third Degree' where it was used a subtle effect to lift the song towards the end. It is likely that this higher pitched vocal was achieved by speeding the track up 3%, a common trick used by producers in the sixties and early seventies when they wanted the artist to sound younger, or the track to sound tighter and more exciting.

One more solo single was recorded in the first months of '67, but was shelved when Napier-Bell couldn't secure a release. 'Jasper C. Debussy' again featured John Paul Jones and sidemen including sometime Stones' pianist Nicky Hopkins, whose pumping piano style added an authentic barrelhouse boogie to the track which broke into a manic waltz rhythm in the breaks. Jasper was a caricature of a Music Hall villain, a "grim-faced sword fencer looking for a fight" with a silhouette like Cyrano de Bergerac who got his kicks tying defenceless women to the railroad tracks. The stuttering 3/4 time breaks between the verses and the addition of a Farfisa organ added a hint of the fairground or silent movies where such hissable villains would tie the heroine to the tracks in order to lure the lantern-jawed hero to the scene. There was nothing like this in the charts, or on an album for that matter until The Beatles issued 'Being For The Benefit Of Mr Kite' the following year. Even Dylan rarely mined this potentially rich seam of subject matter. Marc had moved away from conventional rock and roll and was now in a Grimm fairytale world of his own making into which only Syd Barrett might stray if he was on the right drugs. But Bolan didn't need mind expanding chemicals to fire his imagination. He was tripping on adrenalin and the exhilaration to be found in word play. It was one of the great misfortunes of his career that he did not develop this narrative ability, but instead offered only teasing glimpses into a fantasy world during the Tyrannosaurus Rex period before abandoning poetic imagery altogether for superficial surrealism in the mid-seventies. 'Jasper C. Debussy' was just one of many intriguing tracks which were denied a legitimate release until it was too late to do him any good.

After the failure of 'Hippy Gumbo' and the abortive release of its follow up, Simon thought it might be a good idea for Marc to join another group that he was managing, John's Children, who were without a guitarist at that point. But he knew Marc wouldn't be keen on joining a band if he couldn't be the leader and while he still saw himself as a solo star ripe for discovery at any moment. There was also a more pressing, practical problem – Marc had never played electric guitar and didn't even know the most basic power chords. Playing open and barred acoustic guitar chords on an electric guitar produces a thick, muddy indefinable sound so any self-respecting electric guitar player would have to be able to play the sparser two and three note variations known as fifths or power chords.

But Simon knew that Marc was both too stubborn to admit he didn't know how to play electric guitar and too lazy to learn a new set of chords. He would avoid the subject by claiming that it was only a matter of months before the music business came to its senses and acclaimed him a star. Like a parent that needs to get a child to take its medicine, Simon devised a strategy that would get the result he needed and save face as far as Marc was concerned. He took him along to a Yardbirds' session in the hope that he might learn by example. By pure chance they happened to sit in on a session in which the normally flashy Jeff Beck played a single note solo that was both economical and extremely effective. It did the trick. Marc put his solo career on hold and allowed himself to be persuaded that joining a group might be good experience. "I said I thought it was a good idea if he worked towards where he wanted to go by joining a group. He would be in a band, he would make some contacts and some of their fans would become his fans. He could play lead guitar. I wanted to get him back into the idea of rock. His songs were so obviously rock. It worked very well. It restored his ego enough that he wanted to leave them but that was good."

Chapter 7
A Midsummer Night's Scene

Andy on stage during the ill-fated German tour. Marc is seen with a borrowed cherry red Gibson SG. (photographer unknown. Courtesy Andy Ellison Collection)

"Around the 'Desdemona' period I was really getting into guitar playing as an idea. I abandoned it because they sold my guitar. But, had they not, I would have been an electric guitarist. I would never have been an acoustic guitarist.
Marc to Danny Holloway, NME 1972

Their own manager called them 'the worst band in the world' and he wasn't being flippant.[1]

John's Children compared themselves to The Who, but that would be The Who without Townshend, surely? The band freely admitted that drummer Chris Townson was the only competent musician in the group – he even deputised for Keith Moon, the only drummer to do so during Moonie's lifetime. And frontman Andy Ellison could certainly whirl a mike as lethally as Roger Daltrey while risking self-inflicted GBH to entertain a crowd. Ellison practically invented stage diving a full decade before it became fashionable and would launch himself into space when there were only a dozen or so bodies willing to catch him. Sometimes there was no one to break his fall. But as for the other two in Leatherhead's only protopunk power pop quartet... the best that could be said for guitarist Geoff McClelland was that he was willing – willing to spend an entire recording session in search of the right solo – while bass player John Hewlett could always be relied upon to put on a good show. Which was just as well, as he was seriously lacking in the musical proficiency department.

Napier-Bell had chanced upon the boys while on holiday in St Tropez and offered to pay their fine to save them from a vagrancy charge. He had also suggested the name change (from 'The Silence' to 'John's Children') because it was the only way he could think of keeping Hewlett in the band. Johnny boy was just too good looking to lose. The fact that he couldn't play to save his life, was incidental. Image was everything. And if the band couldn't play, their manager would dream up diversions so that no one would notice. Fights were staged so that they could cut their set short before they ran out of songs. And if that failed, Geoff would fake a fainting spell.

To compensate for their musical shortcomings Napier-Bell had fallen back on that old showbiz stratagem – shock tactics. He suggested singles with provocative titles that would guarantee press coverage to make up for the lack of airplay. He even faked a

---

1 *Andy Ellison disputes this version. He told the author in 2011, "As usual, Simon's throw away comment that none of us could play, and the singer couldn't sing, has now been taken as gospel, re-hashed and perpetuated to death. Simon would always embellish the truth to make a good story and this is one that has stuck.*
Before Marc arrived you will find we were a tight outfit of very capable musicians, John played the perfect incredible low volume bass parts that added to the overall unique JC sound and Geoff was far more competent than Marc at the time. We actually played worse when Marc arrived.
You will find that most mod clubs, even today, when the DJ plays the earlier Johns Children stuff, eg 'Come and Play', 'But She's Mine', 'Smashed Blocked', 'Just What You Want' etc. at full volume, the place goes wild."

live album, tastefully titled *Orgasm*, with screams looped in from the Beatles' *A Hard Day's Night* (it would remain unreleased until 1970.) It was Napier-Bell who would goad them into upstaging The Who on their one and only European tour which resulted in the group having their equipment confiscated. But even after the loss of their instruments and the departure of their star guitarist, Simon wouldn't admit defeat, persuading the remaining members to pose nude behind discreetly placed flowers for the cover of their next single. Malcolm McLaren was a model of restraint by comparison. John's Children were forerunners of the musical nihilists who would perpetrate the great rock and roll swindle almost a decade later, but it is doubtful that they would have earned more than a footnote in rock history had they not crossed paths with 19-year-old Marc Bolan.

By February 1967, the fourth member, guitarist Geoff McClelland, was beginning to take the musical element too seriously. When he deliberated over a 20 second solo for the best part of an hour the group gave him a dishonourable discharge and brought Jeff Beck in to knock it off in a single take. Now they urgently needed a permanent replacement. Preferably one who could play and would look good in the white polo necks and jeans Simon had chosen to emphasise their corrupted choirboy persona.

The group had two releases already under their belt when their manager introduced them to McClelland's replacement. 'Smashed Blocked' (retitled 'The Love I Thought I'd Found' in the US) had been a minor hit on the West Coast and 'Just What You Want, Just What You'll Get' had kept the group's name in the music press. A third single, 'Not The Sort Of Girl You Take To Bed', was cancelled when Bolan was brought in.

Hewlett: "Marc had done a couple of singles like 'Hippy Gumbo', but he hadn't really worked. He was floundering. He wanted to be in a band, but he also wanted to be a poet. I had the strongest personality in the band, but Marc had all the good songs."

Ellison's initial impression of their new guitarist was that he was incredibly young, inexperienced and introverted. In an interview with this writer in 1997 Ellison recalled, "He really wasn't a good guitarist, but he managed to get some weird noises out it. His technique was incredibly basic, but his songs were simple and instantly memorable. And his voice was totally unique."

Kit Lambert, The Who's manager, had agreed to sign John's Children to his own label, Track Records, on condition that they find a Pete Townshend figure to write hits and play the guitar god. Whatever qualities Bolan possessed at that time, it is fair to say he was not yet an axeman of note. On more than one occasion Chris Townson would tune his guitar because even amidst the chaos and cacophony the drummer could hear it was almost a semitone out. (An excruciatingly off-key BBC *Saturday Club* session taped in June that year supports his story.) But Bolan was not about to let his limitations hinder his ambition.

At their first meeting their newest recruit proudly boasted that he had gone one step further than Jeff Beck by writing an entire song using only one chord. Better believe it, because it was going to be a massive hit.

Marc described 'Desdemona' to the band as having a riff like 'Jailhouse Rock', but to be more accurate, he had borrowed its semitone slide from Jody Reynolds' 'Endless Sleep' (a song he himself would cover ten years later). The lyrics were almost conventional compared to his previous flights of fancy – perhaps in a deliberate effort to be 'more commercial', but there was a hint of puckish mischief in lines such as "the touch of your hand can turn me on just like a stick" and, of course, the notorious chorus "Lift up your skirt and fly" which ensured it got banned by the BBC. Marc's allusion was to his heroine's habit of leaving the scene on her broomstick, but as far as the pipe smoking grey beards at the Beeb were concerned this was not suitable material for the innocent ears of 'Uncle' Pete Murray's pop pickers.

The few positive reviews it had from the weekly pop press were not enough to compensate for the lack of airplay.

"The member of the group who answers the lead singer (Marc Bolan) has a great voice. I'd like to hear more of him." Alan Freeman, *Melody Maker*.

The minimalist approach extended to the arrangement, which pared down the sound to a spat between Bolan's two-note riff and Townson's fluid drum pattern without which the track would have been, literally, monotonous. Buried low in the mix Hewlett hung on the root note, anchoring the verse until the one chord chorus kicked in, while Ellison delivered the lyrics as if they actually meant something. But the main attraction was Marc's stuttered reply "D-D-D-Desdemona" behind the lead vocal. It was one of the rare times he shared a lead vocal with a male singer and it served to emphasise the contrast between a standard rock vocal and his eccentric warble.

Bolan and the band may not have been aware of the fact, but they were among the first performers to practise what Lou Reed was preaching on the other side of the pond in New York, "One chord is fine, two is pushing it, three and you're into jazz."

Townson remembers that the first time Marc plugged in his borrowed cherry red Gibson SG he cranked it up to 10 and was almost floored by the slab of sound that burst from the speaker cabinets which were taller than he was. (Marc was not as short as has been claimed. The passport issued to him in 1967 gave his height as 5' 7".)

"We were a tight group of competent musicians before Marc arrived. Simon perpetuated the myth that we were shambolic."
Andy Ellison. (photographer unknown. Courtesy Andy Ellison Collection)

Andy, Chris and Marc survey the damage after staging a pillow fight to distract the audience from the fact they had run out of songs! (photographer unknown. Courtesy Andy Ellison Collection)

During Bolan's brief stint with the group they recorded an album's worth of his material, including several re-workings of his earlier songs. 'The Perfumed Garden Of Gulliver Smith', 'Hot Rod Mama', 'The Third Degree', 'Sara Crazy Child', 'Lunacy's Back', 'Jasper C. Debussy', 'Mustang Ford', 'Hippy Gumbo', 'Sally Was An Angel' and 'Midsummer Night's Scene' with Marc sharing or alternating vocal honours with Ellison, but not always using his original lyrics.

But only two originals were given an official release while he was with the group. 'Desdemona' was released as an A side in May '67 backed by a Hewlett/Townson song 'Remember Thomas A Beckett' on which Bolan did not appear. The second, 'Sara Crazy Child', was side-lined for the B-side of 'Come And Play With Me In The Garden' in August 67 (a remix/re-edit of 'Remember Thomas A Beckett' with new words!), while a third Bolan song, 'Midsummer Night's Scene', had been scheduled for release in June with 'Sara Crazy Child' as its flip, but withdrawn after the band gave away a boxful at their club in Leatherhead, making it one of the rarest and most sought after singles in pop history. According to Napier-Bell, an album, provisionally titled *Playing with Themselves*, was prepared for release only to be "thrown on a fire by workmen who were clearing out the offices of Track after the label folded". It would have included the following songs: 'Midsummer Night's Scene', 'Mustang Ford', 'Hippy Gumbo', 'The Perfumed Garden of Gulliver Smith', 'Leave Me Alone', 'Sara Crazy Child', 'Sally Was An Angel', 'Daddy Rolling Stone', 'Jasper C. Debussy', 'The Third Degree' and 'Hot Rod Mama'.

'Midsummer Night's Scene' began like a mantra, gradually gathering momentum until it turned in on itself and disappeared like Alice down the rabbit hole into a parallel dimension.

It wasn't as well executed, nor as slyly subversive, as other examples of early psychedelia, such as Tomorrow's 'My White Bicycle', Pink Floyd's 'Arnold Layne' or The Small Faces' 'Itchycoo Park', because as a group John's Children were too ham-fisted to carry off the subtle self-mocking aspect with style, but it was an interesting artefact of the era.

Marc gained little from working with the band other than the experience of performing before a live audience on less than a dozen occasions, including an anarchic performance at the legendary Technicolor Dream at Alexandra Palace during which he balanced his guitar on his head for most of the 20 minute set before whipping it with chains. There were also two appearances at the band's own club in Surrey and four dates in Germany before the fateful gig in Ludwigshafen. The latter ended with water hoses being turned on the crowd after the group taunted them with chants of '*Sieg Heil*' during the aptly titled 'You're A Nothing' and showering the front rows with feathers from pillow cases stolen from their hotel.

A reporter from the *Mannheimer Morgen* was almost at a loss to describe the scene.

"John's Children proved to be very unruly infants. They were dressed in white, the same shade as the face of the owner of the hall as they leapt around the stage... Amps toppled over making nerve shredding sounds and the stage lighting also came down. While all this was happening the drummer courageously continued. So these are John's Children. 'Poor John!'"

Ellison: "When Marc was in John's Children he was very quiet. We had to teach him to join in the orgy on stage. He was so nervous about performing that he would drink himself stupid on red wine just to get the courage to get up there. Then he'd burst into tears when we told him off about it and promise never to do it again. We would drop acid a lot, but Marc refused to touch drugs while he was with us. He said he didn't need them, but we could tell that he was scared. Scared of losing control, or perhaps he was scared of finding out about himself. Whenever the car we were touring in broke down we would run around like kids but he would stay inside and scribble in his notebook. Then when we dropped acid he would politely refuse a tab saying, 'I'm quite high already'. For about half an hour after a gig he would be buzzing, but then he would soon go back into his shell and you couldn't talk to him then."

Drummer Chris Townson grew increasingly frustrated with Marc's refusal to participate in the mayhem.

"He was not the sort of guy you would hang out with," Townson told me. "He wouldn't get pissed and go clubbing with us. In fact, he made me slightly uncomfortable because he made me feel a bit guilty about putting the musicianship second to all the nonsense that went with being in a band in those days. It threw me. We were always outrageous on stage, but he was completely wrapped up in himself, in his own little world.

"He was self-conscious to start with, so he created his own corner of the stage with screens of silver baking foil which he claimed would create amazing feedback, but which we all reckoned was a ploy to separate himself from the antics of the rest of the band. He would tune his guitar down and beat it with a big chain, but it was definitely a separate issue from what we were doing.

"One thing that struck me about Marc, though, was that he was single-minded. He was so focused. He was determined to make it and everything else was of no interest to him. He would often say that he wanted to be the biggest star ever and we all believed him. Nobody laughed, even though he looked so slight and unimpressive. It sounds a cliché, but there really was something different about him.

"I remember one incident especially. Simon's Bentley had broken down while we were on tour in Germany and we were waiting to be towed to the nearest garage. Simon, Marc and I started to play this game in which I was Marc's manager and Simon was the big record company boss that I was trying to get a deal with. We were wheeling and dealing in these stereotypical Jewish voices which was rather insensitive, I know, but at the time it was just the way people in the music business imagined that managers and agents talked. Marc never said anything that suggested he was uncomfortable with it. In fact, he was well into it. And the more he went on describing his plans to be a big star, the more it sounded like he really knew what he was talking about and that it wasn't a game anymore. He was going to have hits in Britain, then conquer America. It was a very logical progression that he'd worked out. This was how he saw himself in the future. He just knew he was going to make it – and it wasn't going to be with John's Children. But then right at the end of this fantasy pop star game I asked him what he was going to do after having all these hits. How would he become a legend and I think it was Simon who said, half-jokingly, he'd have to die in car crash like Eddie Cochran in his Rolls. And then Marc said, calmly, 'No, not in a Rolls; in a Mini.' It seemed an odd thing to say at the time. There was silence for a minute while we wondered why he'd said that, then we got talking about something else and the game was forgotten."

If Marc appeared reluctant to join in the chaos, he didn't give that impression when giving one of the few interviews the group secured at the end of their aborted German tour. "We don't just do a musical performance it's a 45-minute happening sometimes we're barely conscious of what we're doing. It's like a big turn-on séance between us and the audience. I've seen Andy go quite mad like a witch doctor in the tribal dance. He leaps off the stage and runs round the audience or sometimes he attacks one of us. In Dusseldorf he got in a fight with John and they both fell 15 feet off the stage onto Andy's head."

In the same interview Townson described Marc's contribution by saying, "He usually sits in a trance in the middle of the stage, except when he's jumping about like a flea."

And Hewlett acknowledged the part his songs played in whipping them all into a frenzy. "Marc's songs are part of it, their superdimensive (sic)… not just double meanings, but millions of meanings. Take 'Desdemona'. A lot of people say that 'Lift up your skirt and speak' is dirty, but it's not. Marc wrote those words coz they gave him a buzz… they weren't meant to mean anything."

Marc might have chosen certain words and phrases for their sound rather than sense, but it would be wrong to dismiss the resulting songs as frivolous, ephemeral pop. He often created a long convoluted backstory for each song like a method actor who develops a biog for his character, because without it he can't find the motivation to bring him to life. In Marc's case, he needed to know "where the cat was coming from" if he was to sing the words with conviction. The listener, of course, was only given half the story and that made these songs all the more tantalising. Who, for example, was 'Sara Crazy Child' and why had she "forgotten how to dream"? Marc told Simon Napier-Bell that she was a slum girl who had been taken from the Brazilian jungle and sold to a brothel keeper in the big city. Her father had died in a brawl before he could find her and bring her back. Meanwhile her mother was left to scavenge for scraps to feed herself and her five children. Of course, Marc might have been winding up Simon up by spinning him this yarn only to deliver a couple of verses, smirking secretly at his manager's incredulity, but it seems more likely that he did indeed have more ideas than could be squeezed into a three-minute song. He wrote or dictated reams of poetry and prose into numerous notebooks during this period, but he lacked the self-discipline and stamina to agonise over or tease out the 12 or 15 stanzas that such a story would require, as Dylan had done. Instead he allowed the germ of an idea to blossom in his mind, but left much unsaid in the song.

And like all the best verse, with or without music, it was the ambiguity and evocative imagery which added to its appeal.

Her brother, the jukebox king with his venom mouthy sting and his knowledge twisted hair and his 1920 stare, he lived beneath the roadway in a minotaurus lair, in private he's a young boy, but in public he's a bear. (from original hand written lyric for 'Sister Crazy Child' later retitled 'Sara Crazy Child')

Other lines were remarkably rich and suggestive of the story line he had described, although they were not appreciated as being so at the time.

Broken dusty mother, her face melted just like wax, her once gazelle-like features bloodied by the age axe, the sepia picture postcard of the twosome of her own, granite-like they submitted to the guillotine of their home.

The use of the single word 'dusty' and the allusion to the girl's olive skin in an earlier verse were all that its author felt was needed to imply their Brazilian origins, while the words 'broken' and the phrase 'her face melted just like wax' were enough to suggest that the mother was grieving and that tears were streaming down her face. Her youth and beauty has been cruelly ravaged by time and all she has to remind her of her children (the "twosome of her own") is an old photograph (a sepia picture postcard). But then the scene abruptly changes to an image of the mother eating a dry tasteless fragment of food (her teeth being the guillotine) – life must go on even if it is a life of impoverishment and scavenging for scraps.

A compelling case can be made to support Bolan's claim to be a poet, the evidence is there from the earliest songs and 'Sara Crazy Child' can be entered as 'Exhibit A'.

Talent however, is rarely enough to get ahead in the music business. Bolan allowed the opportunity to make John's Children his own slip through his fingers because he lacked the leadership that would have motivated them and distilled their excess energy into creativity instead of chaos. Instead, he shyly offered them his songs with no specific instructions as to how they should be played, nor did he see the need to oversee the mixing which would have been his chance to stop Simon from gleefully performing postproduction surgery with a razor blade and reels of editing tape, after which the group had to relearn their own songs. Simon's argument was that as their manager he owned the tapes, and having paid for the recording he felt free to erase tracks or restructure the song as he saw fit without consulting the composer or the musicians. The rest of the band were too busy chasing birds and getting drunk to give a damn and Bolan, who was doing neither, was too timid at that time to assert himself.

After he left the group in June 67 they continued using his backing tracks to which they added new lyrics and instruments. Townson felt guilty about it for years afterward, admitting, "We butchered his numbers".

According to Andy, it wasn't the German fiasco that had prompted Marc's departure, nor even the tampering with his songs that must have irked him, but the simple fact that the group broke up a few months after their return to England. Despite Marc's dissatisfaction with the cavalier manner with which his material was being treated, he remained with Napier-Bell for some months after the German tour and recorded at least one more session with the group in June '67.

'The Lilac Hand of Menthol Dan' (aka 'Dan The Sniff') was intended as the A-side of a single that would re-launch his solo career, but was shelved when Bolan decided to take a detour and ditch his plans to be a rock star – at least for the foreseeable future. The song remained in the vaults during his lifetime, but deserved a posthumous release if only for the insistent riff purloined from Eddie Cochran and the manic chorus delivered in a quavering falsetto, "Dan, Dan, Dan, you don't understand, you got the face of an angel but the mind of a man." It is noteworthy too for being one of the rare instances in his early career where he opted for an easy rhyme instead of taking the time to find a better line. The contrived and cringe worthy "He stood on the burning bridge all because he stole a fridge," betrays the fact that he couldn't be bothered looking beyond the first thing that came to his mind even though it sounded as phoney as a sour note given the setting and subject matter. He wouldn't make that mistake again until he gave up trying and cruised through the last years of his life in neutral.

And what made him decide to go unplugged?

"The Ludwigshafen gig was heavy-duty mad hysteria," Ellison laughs, "And it blew Marc's mind. After that he figured it might be less traumatic if he played acoustic guitar instead. I think what actually convinced him to form Tyrannosaurus Rex was seeing Ravi Shankar sitting cross-legged on the stage with his bongo player on our way back to England after being thrown off the Who tour. I remember we were all impressed by Shankar, but Marc was completely spellbound. So he got a similar thing together, found that it worked pretty well and started to get paying gigs. But he had always liked the idea of being a big hero. I think he felt the acoustic act was becoming a bit of a formula after a few years and he couldn't wait to get back to playing the electric guitar again."

Marc left John's Children after just six months without having added a single lick or power chord to his limited musical vocabulary, but he'd woken up to the fact that there was no more joyful noise on Earth than a cranked up electric guitar saturated in feedback.

It is customary to see Marc's early solo recordings and his work with John's Children as raw, primitive experiments undertaken on the long rocky road towards evolving his own style, but if he had been given the opportunity and the means to compile an album from this first batch of songs in 1967 (re-recording the demos as Napier-Bell suggested and excluding the weaker songs and those he would later rework for the first Tyrannosaurus Rex album) he would have a debut to rival, if not better, Syd Barrett's *The Madcap Laughs*.

Chapter 8
Middle Earth

"The ensemble makes a tiny rumble."
'Strange Orchestras'

Sometime around 10.30 p.m. on February 24th 1968, Brooklyn-born record producer Tony Visconti descended the steps to an underground club in London's Covent Garden, aptly named Middle Earth, in search of something special, something different from the psychedelic groups he had heard back in the States. The previous year San Francisco had given birth to numerous Bay Area bands such as The Grateful Dead, Big Brother and the Holding Company, Quicksilver Messenger Service, Jefferson Airplane and Love before the spirit of the so called Summer of Love spread to the East coast and even as far south as Texas, tinting everything from folk-rock to avant-garde in pastel hues and heavy eastern vibes. But for Visconti, an ardent Anglophile, the British brand of Psychedelia was more appealing. Although straight rock bands such as The Who, Cream and even The Stones were now flirting with kaleidoscopic sound collages and paisley-patterned themes, the likes of Pink Floyd, The Zombies, Family, Traffic and Tomorrow were on a different trip entirely. They had a childlike innocence and occasionally a hint of whimsical eccentricity that the American found endearing. He was confident that he could find an unsigned English act that was unlike any of those who were defining the new music and determining the direction rock would take in the future.

Middle Earth had been named after the mythical setting for J.R.R. Tolkien's epic literary fantasy *The Lord of the Rings* which was required reading for all hippies, but there was nothing picturesque about the dark cavernous cellar that had once been used by Covent Garden traders to store their produce. The rancid stench of rotting fruit from that morning's market could still be smelt outside as the brightly coloured crowd queued at the front door which bore an imitation stained glass sign with the name of the club and the price of admission – one pound for guests, ten shillings for members. No posters, no illuminated neon sign, no indication of who was playing that night. If you were 'in', it was assumed you would know. There were ads in *Oz* and *International Times* if you needed to check it out and handbills flyposted around town. But word of mouth was the preferred means of communication. And it was free. Only weekend hippies had money for the music weeklies because they were the only ones to hold down paying jobs. The rest of the tribe existed on their benefit cheques, saving rent by sharing a squat, or on handouts from their families who hoped the Age of Aquarius was a passing phase of adolescent insanity. And anyway, hippies didn't go to see a specific band the way their older brothers and sisters had done. They went to where it was 'happening', smoked their joints and dug the sounds. Few would remember who had been playing – even the bands were often too stoned to recollect anything more than the vaguest impression of their own performance. If the drugs were good, the gig would be 'way out'. If the drugs were poor, it would be a 'bummer'. Either way they were unlikely to get paid.

But Visconti kept a clear head. He didn't want to risk clouding his judgement with weed or anything stronger. Inside, there was a crush at the ticket office, a matt black booth framed with ultraviolet strip lights so the 'management' could read the invisible 'passout' stamp in the dark. From there the staircase was packed with heaving bodies queuing to descend into the dark like the Eloi, the ingenuous inhabitants of a future Garden of Eden described in H.G. Wells novella *The Time Machine*. But instead of being imprisoned by the cannibalistic Morlocks, these Flower Children were here to pay homage to their pagan gods – The Crazy World of Arthur Brown, Eric Burdon, Soft Machine and their visiting American counterparts Jefferson Airplane, The Byrds and Captain Beefheart. The Byrds famously halted their set half way through one night, demanded the house lights be turned on and then announced they would be playing

Bluegrass from then on. But everybody else played the game.

There were three stages so that when one band finished their set, another was ready to begin. While they played, coloured globules of liquid light were projected onto the white walls behind them. Large screens projected old movies during the breaks and a stall sold apples for those who wanted to add their own dressing. Mingled with the pervading damp was the pungent, intoxicating fragrance of incense and hash. Those few who were disinclined to partake were probably high anyway if there is any truth in the dangers of passive smoking. Bands were not the only acts on offer that year. Entertainment was also provided by The Exploding Galaxy dance group and The Tribe of the Sacred Mushroom who performed a dramatisation of the *Tibetan Book of the Dead*. Nice. And of course there were the DJs – Jeff Dexter and John Peel, the latter fresh from his stretch aboard Radio London. Dexter and Peel shared the same taste in music with one exception, Peel detested ska, but, as Dexter repeatedly reminded his friend, no one could dance to the rootless rambling rhythms of acid rock. So the soundtrack from 10.30 p.m., when the doors opened, to 11 p.m. when the first band went on stage, was a mixture of psych and bluebeat. The Heads who didn't want to writhe would wander around as if in a trance and stare at the colours seeping out of the speakers. That night Peel was attracting attention for the wrong reason. He had been given a hamster called Biscuit by his new friend Marc Bolan and several of the more sensitive customers were pointing out that hamsters do not enjoy going round and round on a turntable. Dexter was too busy to intercede on Biscuit's behalf. He was introducing the next act, Tyrannosaurus Rex. If Visconti was expecting a heavy blues band to take the stage – and what else could possibly labour under a name as formidable as that – he was in for a shock.

Seated cross-legged on a Persian rug, like the Sultan's storytellers, were two slight figures, one clutching a pair of bongos, long straight hair lying languidly over his gaunt features, his eyes hidden by shades; the other dressed in a silk shirt and waistcoat, an impish grin breaking across his cherubic face as he brushed aside the black cascade of curls to speak into the microphone. Visconti strained to hear but couldn't make out a word. It was a soft voice like the rustle of autumn leaves. A murmur of recognition or approval filtered through the 200 or so celebrants who sat as disciples before the master. If it hadn't been for the battered guitar and bongos Visconti might have thought he had stumbled on a meeting of the Hare Krishna cult. Then the music began, a sound from deep underground, a hypnotic drone as if the earth was giving up its most precious secret, two wordless voices chanting a mantra, their bodies rocking gently, throwing mad shadows on the wall behind. "Mamamamamamama, mamamamamamama, mamamama Mustang Ford, it's all put together with alligator leather…."

This was no spiritual ceremony, it was rock as religious rite and this diminutive shaman was evidently its High Priest. The words were unintelligible, at least to American ears, although the audience were hanging on every syllable as if the mysteries of the universe were being imparted wrapped in a melody that was both new and ancient at the same time. It was music full of eastern promise, mystic gypsy traces and something akin to the melancholy cry of Jewish cantors which Visconti had heard through the open windows of the synagogues on the streets of New York.

"Die die die die, die die die die, die die die die dah."

A homogenised stew of sound invoking all these traditions and none because it was not a studied synthesis of cultural influences such as that created by the Incredible String Band – the closest comparison the producer could think of at that moment – it was bubbling up from nowhere without rhyme or reason. It was beautiful nonsense such as children might make when imitating something they had heard but not fully understood. Sure, the words were an incoherent mass of garbled grammar, but it was the effect that counted. Was it good? That hardly mattered. It was magical.

Critics would later accuse Tyrannosaurus Rex of being excessively twee and lacking emotion but they failed to understand that the emotional core of Bolan's acoustic music came from his evocation of a lost idyll and the longing to return to it. Joe Boyd, producer of The Incredible String Band and other sixties British folk acts, hadn't been able to relate to it because he couldn't identify the tradition that it had emerged from and so found it false, but that was the essence of its appeal. It was the music of Middle Earth as Marc imagined it to be and therefore as valid as the culture, language and history of Tolkien's imaginary world.

When it was over Visconti approached the bongo player but was rebuffed. "Talk to him, man, he's the leader." So he made as casual an approach as he could manage only to be told that he was the eighth producer to offer a deal that week. But the little shaman took his business card anyway, tucking it in the pocket of his waistcoat and promising to call if John Lennon didn't make a firm offer on behalf of Apple by the end of the week.

Tyrannosaurus Rex had not risen fully formed that summer, but had emerged from a ramshackle five piece cobbled together in great haste and with only the briefest rehearsal within weeks of Bolan's advert appearing in the June 11 issue of *Melody Maker*. It was an impossibly naive act of faith by someone who had only just scrambled from the wreckage of John's Children and was either trusting in Fate to find the right people at the right time, or who believed in the shamanistic potency of jamming. Marc sensed that all artists were psychic to an extent, mediums that only had to open themselves to cosmic forces to channel the music of the spheres. But Marc's fellow "astral flyers" (drummer Steve Peregrin Took, guitarist Ben Cartland, and an unidentified bass player) were flying blind on this journey of self-discovery and couldn't get it together without a song to steer by. Their one and only performance at the Electric Garden (soon to be renamed Middle Earth) on July 22 billed as 'Marc Bollam and Tyrannosaurus Rex', was an unmitigated disaster.

"It was dire," Took told me in a rare interview in 1978. "I answered an ad in *International Times*[1] and met him outside a tube station. I thought he ran light shows or something. There were four of us. Marc had an electric guitar but there was another guitarist called Ben (Cartland) who had a beard and kept turning green from stomach ulcers. He thought he was Pete Townshend and went crazy, knocking over my double drum kit. The bass player was a lot older than the rest of us. I was 18. Ben was 28 so this guy must have been in his thirties. And he smoked a pipe! I just knew these guys were wrong from the start. We played some of Marc's old songs, stuff he'd done with John's Children, and standard 12-bar blues variations but it didn't happen – it was the wrong people. I don't know how Marc got involved with them – it was a mistake from the start. We couldn't afford anyone else 'cause we weren't making much money. We fooled around with a violinist once. That didn't work out either. So I was forced to sell my drum kit to pay the rent. As fate would have it a pair of bongos sufficed."

The (unequal) partnership with Took was crucial to the creation of the elaborately embroidered tapestry of sound that complemented Marc's often obscure imagery. Without Took's contribution, the three Tyrannosaurus Rex albums that they made together would not have been so richly textured. Took not only brought an increasing

---

1 *Took, who was not the most reliable source for small details, was probably referring to the* MM *ad.*

variety of unusual percussion to the studio, he also embellished the songs with mellifluous chromatic harmonies and eccentric 'character' voices he had picked up from listening to *The Goon Show* on the radio as a child.

Steve had not had an easy childhood. Born in Eltham, South-East London on July 28, 1949, Stephen Ross Porter was a chronic asthmatic who also suffered from eczema which caused his skin to flare up in red itchy blotches. Inevitably, he was taunted at school and retreated into a world of his own which involved making up elaborate stories to entertain his brother. When their father deserted them, Stephen withdrew ever deeper into his fantasy world until, as a youth he found hope in the hippie ideal and some of the answers he was seeking in the eastern philosophy it espoused. A gentle, easy-going 18-year-old he made no objection when Bolan renamed him Peregrin Took after a character (Frodo's loyal friend) in *LOTR*.

Shortly after the Electric Garden debacle, Bolan, too, withdrew into a fictional world where seemingly insignificant creatures faced their fears and overcame evil forces. Although he did not have the stamina to plough through the thousand-plus pages of Professor Tolkien's epic saga, the idea of small, stout-hearted hobbits undertaking a heroic quest appealed greatly to him, for he too was embarking on a quest to battle the cynics and critics who refused to take him and his music seriously. (Marc coined a generic name for these imaginary opponents – Scenescof – and was to face them in several songs). *LOTR* was to inspire reams of his unpublished prose and also the 'Children of Rarn' song cycle which he demoed, but left incomplete once the string of hits demanded he produce more of the same. (It was left to Tony Visconti to orchestrate one of Marc's most enchanting and ambitious pieces – another case of his best work being shelved until after his death.)

In *LOTR* Marc found a seemingly inexhaustible source of inspiration for his songs which until that point had been confined to a brief peek into the rose-tinted realm of illustrated childhood classics such as the 'Narnia' chronicles of C.S. Lewis, Kenneth Grahame's *The Wind in the Willows* and Aesop's Fables. Tolkien's densely detailed history of a fictional land and its myriad inhabitants supplied Marc with a ready-made world and a library of arcane lore to draw upon at will. Tolkien had mapped the topography, now Marc would chronicle both its wonders and its darkest depths. The history and lore of Middle Earth imbued the early Tyrannosaurus Rex albums with a rustic arcane charm, but the first evidence of its influence on his lyrics preceded the duo's debut disc. 'The Beginning of Doves' was one of a batch of songs the pair were to record with Simon-Napier Bell before Simon admitted there was no part for him to play and no profit to be had, if Marc was going to play the good hippie.

In the summer of '67 Marc was still under contract to his old manager who was keen to hear what his protégé had been up to. Of more importance to Marc was the standing offer of free studio time in return for ownership of the master tapes. What had he to lose? So having rehearsed a set, Marc and Steve rolled up at Spot Studios in South Molton Street, W1, one humid August evening and recorded eleven short songs in an hour.

This first session is noteworthy for several reasons, besides capturing the earliest recorded performance of Tyrannosaurus Rex, who Marc named in memory of his childhood fascination with dinosaurs and a short story by SF author Ray Bradbury. It preserved spirited run-throughs of two songs that would become a permanent fixture in their set ('One Inch Rock' and 'Hot Rod Mama'), as well as alternative approaches to older songs ('Sarah Crazy Child', 'Beyond The Risin' Sun' and 'Jasper C. Debussy') and the only known recordings of half a dozen numbers that were not to be found elsewhere ('The Beginning Of Doves', 'Sleepy Maurice', 'Rings of Fortune', 'Lunacy's Back', 'Misty Mist' and 'Sally Was An Angel').

At this first session Marc encouraged Steve to fill every space with assorted percussion or vocal harmonies because he was afraid that, if he left room, a record company might add instrumentation at a later date against his wishes and spoil the sparse soundscape he was aiming to create. (Ironically, Simon would add instruments to the earlier solo recordings for a posthumous release, 'You Scare Me to Death', in 1982 but was remarkably faithful to Marc's style. The album offered a taste of what might have been had Marc trusted him to complete these early recordings at the time.)

Of the eleven songs recorded at that first session, 'Lunacy's Back' and 'Misty Mist' are arguably the weakest, melodically speaking, and both are poorly executed, necessitating a second session some days later to nail these to Marc's satisfaction. But the first is noteworthy if only because it is an early example of Marc's fondness for romanticising mundane and even squalid events – in this instance an alcoholic haunted by visions of his past which appear in the beer spill on the bar and a puddle of gasoline in the street. Such images are reminiscent of Dylan Thomas and James Joyce whose work Marc would certainly have dipped into, even if he didn't have the interest to pursue it further, but is more likely to have been inspired by a scene from the comedy film *Hobson's Choice* in which an inebriated Charles Laughton is taunted by reflections in a puddle. (Whether an artist takes their inspiration from a popular piece or from high literature does not affect the value of their own efforts – the source is irrelevant, serving merely as a stimulant to their own creativity. The result is all that matters.) This juxtaposition of the romantic and the mundane would be most fully realised in 'Graceful Fat Sheba' on the first Tyrannosaurus Rex album where a perspiring butcher's assistant is described in terms that draws a comparison with Rubens' corpulent courtesans. Marc's poetic pretensions may have elicited derision from the critics, but one can only despair at the dilution of his verbal powers as he pandered to an increasingly younger audience in later years.

But perhaps the most significant track is the title song. 'Beginning of Doves' was the only lyric to refer directly to Tolkien's epic, but it also established the template for many of Marc's acoustic songs – a fragile melody hovers in mid-air like a hummingbird before swooping down to settle for a strong, simple chorus. No solos. No instrumental breaks. Their combined voices was all the orchestration that was required and always in perpetual motion, the torrent of Marc's half-intelligible words allowed to settle and permeate the brain while a pattering of assorted percussion, a pixiephone and Chinese Gong gilded the spaces in between.

The trademark Tyrannosaurus Rex sound was finally coming together.

On the remaining tracks the pair are clearly finding their way and checking each other out, with Bolan giving Took room to see where he can insinuate himself into the tightly packed but largely improvised arrangement. For Marc the studio offered a blank canvas with the luxury of retakes, overdubs and the profound satisfaction that comes with creating something better than he could ever have imagined it would be. One day the audience would be gone, but the music would remain.

Napier-Bell: "*Beginning of Doves* was done after the disastrous gig. He brought a rug and joss stick and said he was going to be what he was. I said, 'OK, we'll record you' which we did. I said, 'We really ought to do an album of this stuff because it would be cheap and could be beautifully recorded,' and he said, 'I don't want it beautifully recorded. I just want to sit on the floor with one microphone'. I persuaded him to use two so it would at least be stereo. There were a lot of good bits on the *Beginning of Doves* album which Track eventually released in '74, but it was a very early stage. It had solo acoustic numbers which were the original demos recorded at that very first solo session in '66. Then there were the Tyrannosaurus Rex tracks from this much later stage. All the tracks except the solo demos were done after he left John's Children.

"All the Tyrannosaurus Rex tracks from that first session in August '67 are overdubbed by Marc and Steve. There wasn't anyone else on that album. The girl's voice that you can hear very faintly at the beginning of one track was his girlfriend at the time. When this record was originally going to come out in '71 under the title *Hard on Love* we started the whole thing off with Marc saying 'Look, fuck off or get out' and we put that on the front and went into 'Jasper C. Debussy' and it had a great impact. It was said to his girlfriend and that's why it was to be called *Hard on Love* originally. He really said it with viciousness, but when he was nice he was nice. He put an injunction on it in '71 and the funny thing was he said that the bit of talking at the beginning of the record was recorded when he was no longer under contract to me. He said it was recorded at a concert at Wembley. He'd mistaken it for that because I had put a lot of echo on it to make it sound really big. He said it had been at a gig when 20,000 teenage girls had come to see him. The judge was horrified and Marc lost his sympathy. We said, 'He's mistaken, your lordship. It was said to his girlfriend.' By then the judge was so anti-Marc that the injunction was taken off and we released it without the very beginning bit and re-titled it *The Beginning of Doves*.

"I let him out of the contract in early 1968 after Tyrannosaurus Rex had started as I couldn't help him. He just wanted to sit around on a carpet and do what he was doing. He was even rejecting the idea of recording. If he was projecting himself as the unworldly hippie living off air and joss sticks, it wasn't going to do him any good having a manager. He needed to be unmanaged if he was going to have any validity."

Bolan was now free to reinvent himself as the cosmic pixie or bopping elf and busk with Steve in Hyde Park. It was there that they were spotted by DJ Jeff Dexter who offered to give them a gig at Middle Earth – once he'd recovered from the shock of seeing his old friend decked out like a Tibetan lama. But it wasn't just the physical transformation from sullen-faced Mod to miniature Maharishi that gave Dexter pause. All traces of his East End roots, not to mention reality, had been airbrushed out of Marc's new image and replaced with precious cultured tones and fashionable references to counter-culture gurus such as the Lebanese poet Kahlil Gibran and the English visionary William Blake. While they wandered through the park, Marc went into a long monologue, dropping names for effect more frequently than some of his acquaintances dropped acid, and as he went on Dexter had the impression Marc may not have read as much as he claimed, but had dipped in and out as the fancy took him. He was a magpie, taking elements that appealed to him from various sources to enrich his own inner world, but not feeling it necessary to go deeply into any one in particular. Tony Visconti made a telling observation once when he admitted that in all the years he and Marc worked together, he had never once seen him with a book. Yet, Marc surrounded himself with books and liked to be photographed with leather bound volumes of Blake, Gibran and Shakespeare, but he was too wired to sit for long and digest what he had devoured so greedily. For the same reason he was unable or unwilling to attempt meditation when all his acquaintances were experimenting with spirituality and natural ways of getting high. Had he done so he would probably have found the patience and peace of mind to see his countless unfinished projects through to completion and to have been less inclined to panic and pander to the lowest common denominator when he fell out of favour.

Though the critics might snigger at the fey philosophy of the Flower Children who urged the world to 'Make Love, Not War' while the Vietnamese were being barbecued with napalm, anti-war protests were spilling into the streets of every major European city and students were being shot dead on American University campuses, they were at least, sincere in their aspirations. Marc was not committed to the cause, but neither was he the cynical opportunist he has been painted. It was the scene at the time and Bolan, naturally, wanted to be in on it. In '67 everything seemed possible – at least for one brief, glorious year-long summer.

The hippies saw themselves as the harbingers of a new golden age, the Age of Aquarius, in which they would re-establish the Garden of Eden on Earth, free from the corrupting influence of mass, crass commercialism and the fossilized dogma foisted on humanity by institutionalised religion. In this impossibly idyllic new world everything would be free: free love, free food, free acid and. of course, free music. Drawn by the promise of paradise on Earth, several million young Americans converged on San Francisco in the summer of 1967 for huge tribal gatherings in Golden Gate Park that were dubbed the human be-ins, while their brothers and sisters in Europe did likewise, organising free festivals that celebrated the advent of this new era of 'harmony and understanding'. Across the free world young people rallied to the cause, dropped out of college and turned their backs on conformity to follow the pied piper and self-styled prophet of peace, Dr Timothy Leary, who had urged them to 'turn on, tune in and drop out.'

Turning on and tuning in was understood to mean loosening up and losing one's inhibitions with the aid of LSD, the then legal mind-expanding drug that promised to free them from the chains of routine and responsibility. It would light up their brains so they could see the world in its true colours, or open the 'Doors of Perception', as author Aldous Huxley described it in his highly influential endorsement of acid experimentation.

The music made under the influence of LSD, was dubbed psychedelic, a clinical term that had been applied to describe the altered states of consciousness induced by the drug. Psychedelia aimed to recreate in sound the same sensory effects as a mind-expanding acid trip and, for that, the groups needed to free themselves from the restricting three-minute pop format and boy-lusts-after-girl lyrics. As a result, songs became longer, interminably longer. In fact, they were no longer songs, but streams of consciousness pouring forth from the infinite depths of inner space, or self-indulgent, pretentious, pseudo-mystical dirges depending on the quality of the acid on offer.

Marc refused to take acid and had no patience with endless improvisation (although he felt less inhibited after discovering Hendrix), which was just as well as he didn't have the technical ability to indulge at the time. And having only recently found a way to stretch a song over two minutes, he was reluctant to stray beyond the three-minute mark. For these reasons, as much as for the quality of their material, Tyrannosaurus Rex were embraced by a section of the underground who saw the duo as a healthy alternative to the heavier bands who were dominating the scene. Their only serious rivals were Donovan, whose music was becoming increasingly twee, and The Incredible String Band, an acoustic duo who were so intensely authentic that they probably thought Chuck Berry was a quaint Gaelic custom.

Just before Tony Visconti's fateful first meeting with Marc, he and Steve had tried their luck with the ISB's producer, Joe Boyd who was much respected among the folk contingent for his work with Shirley Collins, Martin Carthy and Dave Swarbrick. But it wasn't Boyd's folk credentials that sold Marc on the idea. He hoped that Boyd's involvement might lead to a meeting, or even a collaboration of some sort with Syd Barrett who had replaced Dylan as his new musical guru. Boyd had produced the Floyd's debut single, 'Arnold Layne', and so was one step away from the new messiah. Marc had modelled both his music and his new look after the Floyd's resident genius who had unwittingly opened a Pandora's Box of new toys for his playmates to experiment with. It was Barrett, more than any other figure, who took the idea behind The Beatles' 'Strawberry Fields Forever' and made it the starting point for an excursion into the hinterland of English pastoral Psychedelia where childhood nursery rhymes took on a disquieting quality, neighbours kept sinister secrets and scarecrows threatened to intrude on your dreams. Marc couldn't compete with that. He hadn't taken enough drugs to see the world in that way, so he did the next best thing he could think of to show solidarity with Syd. He grew his hair in Grecian ringlets and hoped some of the magic might rub off in return.

The audition with Boyd on November 6 had been arranged through Marc's new publisher, David Platz of Essex Music, who had taken Marc on when he was still in John's Children in the hope that his new signing might mature into a pocket-sized Pete Townshend. Platz was understandably confused by the transformation from guitar god to acoustic sage in just a few short months, but was willing to see what might come of a session with the American.

It has been stated in earlier biographies that Boyd supervised two sessions at the Sound Techniques studio in Chelsea, the first on November 6 at which three songs were recorded ('Dwarfish Trumpet Blues', 'Child Star' and 'Highways'), followed by a second session on December 12 when only one song was completed ('Chateau In Virginia Waters'), the latter with session bass player Danny Thompson who Marc has referred to as a cellist! But Joe Boyd disputes this. While admitting that his recollection is understandably vague, he is certain that there was only one session.

"To be honest, I only remember one session," he told me. "The one with Danny Thompson's bass which I put through a Leslie Speaker. I think it was a kind of a try-out to see if we clicked, with the possibility of a single release if it went well. It was for Track Records. The idea came from Kit Lambert who thought that Marc and I might work well together, but I don't think I had much response from them afterwards. The next thing I knew, the pair were signed to EMI and I assumed the whole thing was forgotten. I have no memory of the first three songs, although 'Child Star' rings a distant bell. It may have been the second track we recorded in December because I think there were two songs recorded at that session, 'Chateau In Virginia Waters' and another. Maybe the November session was a kind of simple demo leading up to the more full-on professional agenda in December. I was pretty happy with the December session, but I confess I wasn't entirely convinced by Marc. He seemed to be acting out the hippie persona rather than being it. I wasn't sure I wanted to work with him on a long-term basis."

Boyd was not discouraged by Bolan's insistence on recording live in the studio with minimal overdubs and by his refusal to consider augmenting the sound with other instruments. "I was OK with minimalism, if that's what they wanted. I don't remember any dispute about this. I supposed that they wanted me to produce because of what I was doing with The Incredible String Band – and, at that time, I hadn't made *The Hangman's Beautiful Daughter* yet, so most of what I did was pretty straightforward, without too many layers.

"It was a kind of dialogue between Marc and me, as I recall. He had strong ideas about the songs, but responded well to my bringing in Danny Thompson. Danny was a bit frustrated with them, I think, as they tended to vary the structure from take to take."

Steve Took didn't leave an impression on the producer. If he had ideas regarding the arrangements, he must have made them before they came to the studio.

"I don't have a clear memory of him making significant contributions. Bolan was clearly in charge. I just remember Marc being a kind of over-eager puppy with the whole UFO/hippie scene and I was never convinced that it was more than a fashion thing with him."

Thompson had been brought in by Boyd to bolster what he considered a scrappy and insubstantial sound. To Boyd's ears the duo sounded as shapeless as they looked, like two rag dolls that had been found at the bottom of a playbox. On Boyd's suggestion Took was given a more prominent role, sharing lead vocals on 'Chateau', but the small differences in phrasing only made the pair sound under rehearsed. The acoustic double bass was a welcome addition, bolstering the bottom end, but it didn't gel. Boyd was right – this wasn't folk, it was rock hammered out by two raggedy-assed hand puppets. Platz settled the bill and waited patiently for Tyrannosaurus Rex to get their act together.

★★★★★

"I was always interested in the freaky things, the unique music rather than the obvious. That attracted me to T.Rex. I'd never heard anything like them." (Tony Visconti)

There is no greater disciple to a cause than the newly-converted and Visconti burned with a missionary zeal. So when Marc called him first thing the next morning after their meeting at Middle Earth, Tony didn't give the standard response. If they didn't have a tape, they could come round in person to the Oxford Street offices of Straight Ahead/ New Breed Productions and Tony would insist that his boss, Denny Cordell, give them the undivided attention they deserved.

Visconti found Cordell in his customary pose with his feet up on his desk admiring his new brogues. Shoes were a passion for the producer who was considering blowing a sizeable sum of his royalties from 'A Whiter Shade of Pale' on an entire wardrobe of new footwear to rival the collection amassed by Imelda Marcos.

(Cordell went on to collect an estimated £5 million from his share in Procol Harum's most successful single, or "five cool and funky big ones", as he liked to call it).

Comparisons with the Phillipino dictator's wife were not entirely gratuitous. 24-year-old Cordell, Argentinian by birth, saw himself as a benign despot with the attendant privileges, though with his long mane of silvery hair and full Druid beard he gave the appearance of being a modern day King Arthur. He was a 'lovable rascal' to those he bestowed his favours upon, and an 'unprincipled scoundrel' to those who would accuse him of hoodwinking them out of the lion's share of their earnings. He had reputedly made a five-figure sum from producing The Moody Blues 'Go Now', a Bessie Banks song he had discovered and suggested that they record. When the band challenged the legality of the agreement Cordell had drawn up himself, they discovered it was watertight. What he lacked in musical ability and technical expertise he more than made up for in charm, cheek and business acumen. Visconti had been headhunted by Cordell who originally had Phil Spector in his sights, but settled for the talented unknown because he was available and considerably cheaper. Visconti learnt a lot about the business form Cordell, but not so much about production as his boss was absent from the studio due to business and marital problems for much of the day, leaving his eager young apprentice to oversee the sessions. It was for this reason that Cordell was happy to trust Tony with the nurturing of a new act whose minimal production budget would be subsidised by the income from his "bread and butter band", The Move. With the cash from The Moodys and The Move, Cordell had set up his own independent production company New Breed Productions and a subsidiary, Straight Ahead Productions in partnership with publisher David Platz. Essex Music would cover all recording costs in return for ownership of the masters and all publishing rights. All New Breed/Straight Ahead acts would be licensed to Regal Zonophone, a label owned by EMI. All they needed now was for Tony to discover and cultivate an act of his own.

"I think I've found the act I want to produce. In fact, I know I have."

Cordell seemed amused. "Already?"

Tony enthused about the previous night's performance, but faltered at the description. He simply couldn't find the words.

"Only two, you say?" Cordell was confused. He couldn't imagine an acoustic duo making hits, and hits was what oiled the machinery and made the MD happy. "You're never alone with a grand," was Cordell's maxim and he hummed it whenever he smelt more in the wind. But this act didn't sound like it would make him a lot of new friends. "Only two," he repeated. "Well, at least they'll be cheap to record. OK, let me know when they're playing again and we'll go and see 'em."

"Actually they're playing another set in a couple of hours."

"Lunchtime gig, eh? Pub is it?"

"No."

"They're not busking in the bloody tube station, are they?" Tony shook his head.

"Where then?"

"Here."

Tyrannosaurus Rex performed their entire set from the previous night in Cordell's office that morning. They even brought their Persian rug with them. Marc said little, pausing between numbers only to tune his acoustic guitar (which he had bought for £12 at a flea market) with a pair of pliers as the peg holding the G string was missing. When they had finished they rolled up the carpet and left.

"Well, what do you think?" Visconti beamed. Now he could be certain that he hadn't been unduly influenced by the atmosphere in the club or any mood-altering pharmaceuticals in the air. They were unique.

Cordell admitted that he simply didn't understand what he had just witnessed, but he agreed that they should sign them as their "token underground group". However, there wouldn't be much of a future for them if Platz didn't get behind them. The publisher would have to see them live and gauge the audience reaction for himself.

"They're certainly different, I'll give you that," Platz conceded after a visit to Middle Earth. "But I don't know. What the hell was that? It wasn't folk. It wasn't rock and it wasn't your everyday singer-songwriter shtick. But more important, will it sell?" Visconti was not expecting to have to haggle. He assumed everybody would see what he saw in them and hear what he had heard. In the end it was Visconti's enthusiasm that won Platz over. That and the awe-struck audience.

"Well, at least that's a few hundred record sales guaranteed," the publisher conceded.

Chapter 9
My People Were Fair

My people were fair and had sky in their hair...
But now they're content to wear stars on their brows

We make two sorts of music – loud and freaky and soft and pastoral.
Marc to Derek Boltwood, NME, November 1968

In the late sixties it was fashionable for bands to retreat to the countryside before recording a new album in the belief that they could draw inspiration from their rustic surroundings and channel the natural energy of the Earth. At least that was the line their record companies sold them because they knew it was cheaper for a group to get their act together in a remote rural location where there were fewer distractions. And groups were taking considerably longer to write and record what they hoped might be their own *Sgt Pepper*.

In March 1968 Marc Bolan was not in a position to make such demands, although the duo was moving up the bill at Middle Earth. They had also supported Donovan at the Albert Hall that month and were booked to headline at the Purcell Room on London's Southbank in April. So when the time came to record the first Tyrannosaurus Rex album Marc and partner Steve Took packed their odd assortment of instruments in a couple of plastic carrier bags and caught the tube train to Advision Studios in New Bond Street in London's bustling West End. There they unrolled their Persian rug, dimmed the lights, lit a joss stick and imagined themselves giving an impromptu performance in a clearing in a forest somewhere over the hills and far away.

Given a budget of just under £400 they had only four days to lay down the bulk of their live set with the assistance of 'novice' producer Tony Visconti and expert engineer Gerald Chevin. Four days was precious little time to record an entire album, albeit an acoustic one with minimal overdubs, and there would be little chance of retakes, but £400 was all that Cordell was willing to risk. With no room for error, Visconti had insisted that the pair rehearse at his Earl's Court flat in the days prior to the recording so that no time would be wasted in the studio.[1] Marc and Steve dutifully turned up, several evenings in succession, to the amusement of Visconti's dinner guests and played the entire album through several times while Tony made notes and offered suggestions, such as when Marc should try finger picking instead of strumming to leave space for percussion and to give light and shade to what would otherwise have been a repetitive backing. In this collaborative atmosphere Marc found the inspiration for a new song, 'Debora', which was immediately seized upon as the strongest candidate for the first single but would have to be squeezed into the same session.

Steve didn't contribute to the discussion, but both Marc and Tony were enthusiastic about the harmonies that he came up with and the vocal ticks that he introduced to add to the air of otherworldliness.

---

1 *A reel-to-reel recording of the final rehearsal is still in the producer's possession.*

Steve: "He just wrote a song and I did what I wanted round it. Gave it the treatment, you know. We just did it in our front rooms. I played organ a bit. I guess he wrote a lot that we never actually used, but then you do. It was very workable. We got a lot of communication going. You can when there are only two of you."

To all intents and purposes there were now three members of the group. Visconti was not satisfied to sit back and supervise a session then collect a cheque as several successful producers were prone to do. He enjoyed being an active contributor to the creative process and if that meant having to submit to the Marc Bolan 'Scenescof' test, then so be it.

"Before we got together and started recording, Marc was very inquisitive about me and wanted to know what sort of person I was. We played guitar together and found we liked more or less the same type of music: Phil Spector, The Beach Boys and The Beatles."

But if Marc's melodies were imbued with a sixties pop sensibility, his lyrics owed little to the music he was listening to. For inspiration he visited every gallery, museum and monument in London to furnish his songs with Greco-classical references, supplementing these with scenes from books on mythology and children's fairy stories which he skimmed for ideas and atmosphere, but rarely read all the way through. But Marc was not interested in narrative songs, nor in character studies. He was an impressionist, content to suggest a scene and leave the rest to the listener's imagination. And if he couldn't find the right word to convey what he wanted to say, he'd make it up or combine two similar sounding words if they sounded musical. There was a child-like joy in the way he played with assonance and alliteration and with words which he felt evoked a scene that needed no further explanation. For Marc, names such as Atahuallapa, Aznageel, Conesuala and Pan had a pictographic meaning, like runes. Their very utterance would draw back the veil between this world and the next. And he would cheerfully juxtapose argot with the antique, sixties slang with pseudo-Shakespearean phrases if it meant that his music would be distinctive and harder to define.

'Hot Rod Mama' had been chosen to open proceedings and it made the ideal introduction. With its emphatic chugging rhythm, familiar twelve-bar structure, simple lyrics and a melody lifted from 'Speedo' by the Cadillacs, it lured the listener into believing that this might be another standard folk-rock offering, though the eccentric vocal suggested it could be an acquired taste. It was only on the final verse that the transition was made from the commonplace (anachronistic references to hot rods, baseball boots and Levis) to the uncharted lands of legend with mention of pan pipes and an elixir-of-life pill.

The second track, 'Scenescof', also played it comparatively safe to allow the newly initiated to become familiar with one of the most extraordinary voices in rock (comparable only to that of Family's frontman Roger Chapman whose debut album had been released the previous year). Two verses were all that was needed to run a variation on the oldest theme in the book – the bad guy stole my baby. But the artless indifference of the singer suggested that there might be more to this scene than the words conveyed.

It is only with the third track, 'Child Star', that we realise we're not in Kansas anymore. The 13-year-old subject of the song is a prodigy whose talent is bestowed upon him by the dead composers who won't let him rest until he has transcribed their unfinished symphonies. He is worked to death like a latter-day Mozart by his ruthless agent , but his spirit lingers in the garden that he loved. Though cruelly exploited and unappreciated by the masses during his lifetime ('The awesome people stare, they're unaware of all the angel sounds they see and hear'), death brings belated recognition of his extraordinary gifts and also regret ('and when you died at just thirteen they wept and wrung their hair'). Mourners wring their hands, of course, not their hair, but it's a typical Bolan trait to use the wrong word and let it stand because it sounds better or defies expectation. This confusion of similar sounding words was the result of his mild dyslexia, but it becomes one of the many endearing and intriguing characteristics of his compulsive wordplay.

On one level this is a song of self-pity as Marc identifies with an unappreciated talent, while at the same time he marvels at his own comparable abilities, specifically his penchant for tongue-twisting lines that few could have spoken, let alone sung, and for which he can find no explanation other than his belief in angelic inspiration. The album rejoices in such verbal contortions, just one of several examples being "So sad they should be owning a man who's thicker than the forestry from which they began" ('Weilder of Words' – Marc's misspelling).

In a similar vein, 'Strange Orchestras' teases with a concept derived from *Gulliver's Travels*, but is transplanted to an English glade where tiny Lilliputians play miniature instruments while being stalked by a cat that looks like a dinosaur in comparison to them. But even little people have feelings and the harpist is seen lusting after a young boy. It's nonsense, as John Peel, has said, but it's clever nonsense and the chorus of pixie voices lends it a perverse character all its own.

'Dwarfish Trumpet Blues', 'Knight' and 'Weilder of Words' also benefit from the multi-tracked vocal ensemble which appears to consist of a choir of unruly infants, a couple of animated ventriloquist dummies and several refugees from an unspecified region of Eastern Europe – all voiced by Marc and Steve. One can imagine that such idiosyncratic sounds would not be to everyone's taste, but even the detractors were going to have to admit, this was different. Only the Hare Krishna chant at the end of 'Frowning Atahuallpa' sounded contrived and out of character with the rest of the album.

The last song to be taped was the single, a catchy pop song in the Donovan mould masquerading as an eastern style raga. It was Marc's answer to 'Jennifer Juniper' and was fashionably attired in the trappings of the period. 'Debora' joined a long list of classic songs with girls' names in the title – Dion's 'Runaround Sue', Paul Anka's 'Diana' and Buddy Holly's 'Peggy Sue' being three of Marc's personal favourites, a fourth, being his own 'Desdemona'. The words were sketchy, to say the least, and the theme, if there was one, was obscure. The fashionably intellectual critics who sought to increase their readership by dissecting Dylan and Beatles' lyrics in search of hidden meanings would have been hard pressed to find any in these insubstantial images. The more pretentious might have interpreted the subject's gaunt "sunken face" and her heavily lined features which are compared to the contours of a map as clues that she is one of the hollow-eyed heroin users to be seen hanging around the Tube stations hoping to score, while references to a zebra and a stallion could have been veiled allusions to heroin (known commonly as 'horse'). Another might have seized on the line that has the mounted writer looking down at his lover and mourning the loss of her looks as evidence of the singer's sexual obsession and concluded that the girl was frigid because she is turning her head away during intercourse. In truth, Marc probably had no specific idea in mind. 'Zebra' and 'conjuror' were simply the only two words he could think of that rhymed with 'Debora' and the rest just slipped out as he strummed. They sounded good and so that was OK with him. There were times when Marc had aspirations to be a poet and there were times when he simply wanted to boogie – acoustic guitar or not. Marc didn't do gloom. It didn't pay to get too philosophical if you wanted a hit single.

Penny Valentine reviewed the single favourably for *Disc and Music Echo* describing it as "a new weird sound" and "pretty in a strange way". Peter Jones in *Record Mirror* enthused, "This is ever so clever, ever so different", while Derek Johnson in the *NME* admitted it was probably "too offbeat to succeed…very clever and intricate" and "probably too complex to register".

If they had not had 'Deborah' set aside for a single it is hard to imagine which other tracks might have been released (presumably 'Hot Rod Mama' or its companion 'Mustang Ford') because the remainder are clearly album cuts. Each a prime example of pastoral English pop-psych but lacking the instrumentation that Bolan's back-to-basics policy imposed upon them and which the budget restrictions denied them. One can

only imagine how 'Chateau in Virginia Waters', 'Afghan Woman', 'Graceful Fat Sheba' and 'Frowning Atahuallpa (My Inca Love)' might have sounded had Visconti had the budget and Marc's approval to add a woodwind ensemble, a string quartet, a flute or perhaps even a mellotron to the mix. But this is the way Marc wanted his debut album to sound. Well, no, not quite because there was an unforeseen technical problem that undermined all their hard work. When Marc heard the test pressings he was distressed to hear how harsh it sounded.

"It was the first LP he'd ever produced and it was done at Advision on an 8-track, the first in the country, and they didn't know how to use it. The stereo was awful. When we were doing it, it sounded good, but when it was on record it sounded very thin and nasty… I like the feeling on the first LP but, as a production, I can't listen to it."

Perhaps the most appropriate artist to design the cover would have been Victorian illustrator Arthur Rackham, but as he was indisposed (i.e. deceased) the task fell to George Underwood, a friend of David Bowie. It was Bowie who recommended Underwood when Marc mentioned that he was looking for an artist to create the cover. "People ask me what I was on when I painted that," Underwood smiles, "So I tell them I was on all fours on my mum's living room carpet." The only guidance he got from Marc was, "I want something like William Blake," so Underwood took a long hard look at his bookshelf and chose a volume of Gustave Dore etchings for inspiration. He found what he thought Marc might like in two illustrations for Dante's *Inferno* from which he abstracted a damned soul beseeching a flight of evil spirits for mercy, a green-skinned serpent-tailed demon and a phalanx of naked men carrying their own tombstones under the baleful gaze of a winged devil. Into this hellish scene he added details gleaned from the album with portraits of Bolan and Took to show that they presided over this fantastic subterranean realm. The package was completed by an inscription in a Gothic font written by DJ and friend John Peel who had also read the brief children's story (written for Marc's niece) inserted before the final track:

Tyrannosaurus Rex rose out of the sad and scattered leaves of an older summer. During the hard, grey winter they were tended and strengthened by those who love them. They blossomed with the coming of spring, children rejoiced and the earth sang with them. It will be a long and ecstatic summer.

Underwood admits that, on first hearing, the album took him by surprise, but that he found Marc very charming, if a bit vague about what he wanted for the sleeve.

"We had arranged to discuss the artwork at Visconti's flat, which went fine. Then later in the evening I remember Marc and June sitting cross-legged on the floor just staring into each other's eyes for about ten minutes as if nobody else was in the room, or in the universe!, which I thought was a bit bizarre. David was there and Tony, of course, and neither commented on it. Maybe they were used to it, but it was a bit too cosmic for my liking. Otherwise it was a really nice relaxed evening, a meeting of like minds, and we got a lot done. There was a feeling that we were all going somewhere and that this was the start of it. David was then doing his mime thing, but that was just a phase. I had known David since we were nine years old and I knew how ambitious he was, but he was still working on how he could achieve stardom and that's one reason he was attracted to Marc. Marc knew where he was heading and was already getting attention. None of us were making money, but we were filled with great ideas.

"Marc and David were already good friends by then, but they didn't record much together as far as I know. David wasn't collaborating with anyone at that time. He was very self-contained and concerned with getting his image together. Marc too. He was on the cusp of having his first hit, 'Debora', and Bowie didn't want to be seen to be in his shadow. He was determined to cast a bigger shadow, to overtake Marc, so there was this friendly rivalry between them.

"Steve Took didn't come to that first meeting, but then Marc was the driving force behind Tyrannosaurus Rex. I met Steve shortly after, but he didn't say very much. He struck me as very introverted, a bit listless and laid back, working at half-speed, but then he was stoned most of the time. I got the impression Steve wasn't the most reliable person to work with. Possibly he was more casual about things whereas Marc was incredibly ambitious.

"I was into other types of music so it took me a few listens, but that first album grew on me. Like a lot of people at that time, we were all into Black American music – David, Marc, Tony and myself – and we would go and see blues legends like John Lee Hooker whenever they were in town. Marc seemed to be able to detach himself from that and create his own mixture of blues, folk and rock. In my opinion his music wasn't as profound as some of the stuff being made back then, but it was very different and so right for the time.

"Marc had a more than passing interest in art and his taste was eclectic. He liked anything that evoked the world of fantasy and dreams, which included William Blake, Arthur Rackham and Dali. He also had a hankering to try his hand at drawing in his own individual style. Years later he did a rough sketch of himself sitting on a dragon to give me an idea of what he wanted for the *Futuristic Dragon* album.

"He also did some little scribbles and drawings for me in his own style which showed that he had some artistic aspirations. They were pretty good. He could have been a fair painter if he had the training and had acquired the basic techniques. At the time I dismissed them as just ideas for the LP cover, elaborate doodles, as it were, but later I could see that they were more than interesting. Everything Marc did bore his own distinctive stamp – his poetry, his hieroglyphic handwriting and his music."

Contrary to public perception, pop and rock stars have not always been selected by a panel of 'experts' on a televised talent show, or manufactured and marketed like a new brand of soap powder. The majority broke through only after years of struggle, playing poorly paid gigs in small venues with little or no promotion and having to hump their own gear in and out of the club, grabbing a beer and a burger before scrambling into a clapped out van for the long haul to the next gig. Bolan and Took did it the hard way, but they did it with the invaluable assistance of John Peel who insisted that, whenever he was booked, Tyrannosaurus Rex was added to the bill. And he made sure they were paid. At first it was no more than petrol money, but after 'Debora' became a minor hit, grazing the Top 30 in May '68 and nudging the first album up the charts to number 15 in July, their fortunes increased dramatically. Peel estimated that he did about 25 gigs with the duo before they found an agent to book gigs in their own name.

Peel was initially hooked by the voice ("I've always been drawn to extreme voices") which he had first heard on an acetate of 'Hippy Gumbo' that Bolan had sent to Radio London, the pirate station broadcasting in the Thames Estuary until the British Government closed it down in the summer of 1967. Peel was then presenting *The Perfumed Garden* which gave him *carte blanche* to play whatever took his fancy, including unreleased recordings and unsigned acts. But the days of the pirates were numbered and, in August, Peel was poached by the BBC to lend credibility to its new 'pop' station, Radio 1, in a bid to sink the pirates once and for all. Back on shore he called Bolan who was then living with his parents in Wimbledon and had included his phone number at the bottom of a thank you note illustrated with a fairy tale castle.

Peel: "Marc came round to my flat and sat on the floor and sang some of his songs. I must say they registered immediately... I knew deep down inside that he was something special. He was sort of happy, unique and rather simple in his writing style.

"I remember trying desperately to get him onto a TV programme called *How It Is*. I said, 'Bolan's soon going to be producing number one hits', but they just fell about scoffing, saying, 'With that funny, squeaky little voice? It'd be like having Larry the Lamb!'"

Marc: "I met John when he came off Radio London, and he was like us – he couldn't get any gigs... John got a gig at Middle Earth when it opened, and we went along and played – just acoustic and bongos – unamplified. Then gigs started to happen... £10 sometimes, really heavy bread!"

There was a time when Peel was seriously contemplating signing Tyrannosaurus Rex to his fledgling Dandelion label, but both and he Marc knew that this one-man operation couldn't give the group the financial support and promotional push they needed to get off the ground. However, Peel did pay for their first photo session in Holland Park, a favourite haunt of Syd Barrett, and he lobbied the BBC selection panel to approve the first of many radio sessions on his influential *Top Gear* show, sessions which were crucial in selling the group to a sizeable section of the record buying public. But his endorsement brought criticism from many irate listeners who found the duo irritating in the extreme and accused the DJ of having a financial interest in the group.

When Peel was approached to contribute to an extensive feature I was writing for a national music magazine in 1997 he was already weary of his 'legendary role' in his late friend's success.

"I stopped talking about Marc some time ago. I've always had lots of requests from T.Rex societies and fanzines and it's become almost an embarrassment, really. It's just one of those things I'm reluctant to talk about. I'm not really one for reminiscing and I don't much care for being a professional friend of the dead. Marc was a very good friend to me and then he stopped being a very good friend. After he became famous, he just dropped us (I include my wife in this because we were all good pals)... There wasn't really an explanation – I guess people just move on to other things... I always knew there was a harder side to him, but it didn't reveal itself until he started having hits. He was very good and now he's gone.

"I was drawn by the sound of it all, not just his voice, but the sound he created with the words that he chose and the way that he sang them. They didn't seem to make much sense when they were read out loud, but with the music they fused to make something more than the sum of the parts. It was highly original. I couldn't make out much of what he was singing about, but it sounded mystical, though if you studied it there wasn't much substance. Marc was more into the whole hippie thing than I was and he seemed sincere about it all. He seemed to be always looking ahead towards something beyond the horizon, but that didn't mean that he didn't believe in whatever he was doing at that particular moment. He wasn't cynical about it. He really seemed to believe in it but he certainly wasn't naive."

Marc and Steve recording at Trident Studios 1968. Took's chromatic harmonies gave the early albums a unique pixified tone.
(photo: Ray Stevenson, Rex features)

While the national music press found the duo a delight, if hard to categorise, the Underground press were beginning to complain that they were in danger of becoming popular, an unpardonable sin in their eyes, punishable by excommunication.

In June, *International Times* damned the duo with faint praise for the lack of variation in their hour-long set at the Royal Festival Hall at which they were supported by Roy Harper and David Bowie. "They have a beautiful sound, but too much of it all at once… gets boring."

Just prior to the album's release Marc gave his first full-length interview to a short-lived underground magazine appropriately titled *Gandalf's Garden*.

"I relive my childhood through my songs," he confessed. "There are so few books like *The Lord of the Rings* and the 'Narnia' books, that once you've read them, you want more, and there just aren't any around. So I just write my own things. I'm very unmusical… When I write, the words and music come together, normally very roughly, but I start getting high on it and just can't stop… I never feel that it is just me doing it, it's more like my astral self. I do believe in the Guardian Angel scene. I don't think there's anything I do that isn't directed."

Asked if he had a guru like The Beatles' Maharishi, he told the interviewer that the kind of guru he would listen to wouldn't be the traditional figure from the East but an old man of the woods.

"But that person is within me anyway… I see (God) as a monster sun that opens in the middle and you could get sucked into it and out the other side. Where you come

out, I don't know, that's only my
imagery, but it's a preparation for
birth... You are born and born
again until you reach the ultimate,
until you reach another scene, get
into another dimension. I have no
doubt about reincarnation."

To another journalist he
admitted that he didn't put much
thought into creating a unique
sound.

"I didn't realise it was unique.
I've always sung like that really.
I suppose we are trying to imitate
the instruments. It's just a
development of my mind. I never
used to like singing, but now it's a
great fulfilment, like flying. I think
it mirrors what I feel inside. My
guardian angel does all the writing; I'm sure it's not me."

Nevertheless, Marc got all the credit when it came to the reviews which were very
encouraging.

Record Mirror categorised their style as "jug-band Psychedelia" and the sound as
"same-y" but "original" and concluded by stating that it "deserves to be a big seller".

Disc and Music Echo began by reminding readers that this was the first album from
"John Peel's favourite group" and called Bolan "gifted" and "prolific" concluding, "the
strength of the album lies in his excellent, totally individual songs of love, beauty, fantasy
and nature".

The relative success of the single and the healthy album sales together with the
unstinting support from John Peel and better-paid gigs were all the encouragement Marc
needed to write a slew of new songs. So many, that a second album was scheduled for
release only four months after the first. It was unheard of, to release two new studio albums
within such a short period, but Marc complained that he couldn't sit on the material for a
year and that a second set would capitalise on the interest generated by their first. It would
also help to establish them as a fixture on the circuit and in the minds of the music press
who had seen many groups break through only to break up shortly afterward. Having
recouped their £400 and seen a minor hit single from it, Denny Cordell and David Platz
had no objection to a second album being released so shortly after the first.

Prophets, Seers and Sages – the Angels of the Ages was recorded at Trident Studios in St
Anne's Court, Soho, over several months in the summer of '68 and released in October.

This time the cover was a simple black and white photo depicting Marc and Steve as
two strolling players who had just decamped from their gaily-coloured caravan to give
a recital to the faerie folk. Marc stood bare-chested in striped blazer with what appears
to be a scimitar tucked in the waistband of his black jeans, Steve is attired in full length
magician's cloak, a jester-headed children's rattle at their feet.

Contemporary critics were tempted to dismiss it as a continuation of the first album, but those who did so had given it only a cursory listen. True, there was little that could be added to the sound while Marc insisted on limiting the instrumentation to acoustic guitar and percussion, but the increasing complexity of the songs and the more densely layered production marked a significant progression from the rustic simplicity of their sparse sounding debut.

The improvement is evident from the opening cut, a vigorous re-reworking of 'Debora' goaded into fifth gear by more sharply defined percussion and strengthened by double-tracked vocals. But Bolan was still resisting all attempts to persuade him to embellish the songs with other acoustic instruments. At one point Visconti made a home demo of 'Debora' with recorders and bass to illustrate how beautiful the tracks could be, but Bolan stubbornly refused to compromise his own ideals.

Elsewhere on the album, there is an effort to vary the dynamics by the use of contrasting time signatures and subtle shifts in rhythm within a single song, which is akin to ethnic music even though it's patently obvious this faux-naif folk-rock is not remotely authentic.

'The Travelling Tragition' is perhaps the most perfectly realised example of their mock-hybrid music, an amalgam of quintessentially English folk with anachronistic Yiddish vocalisms giving way to gleeful child-like abandonment ("boom de boom, de tra la la, de rat a tat tat").

Then just when it appears they are in danger of becoming too precious to exist in the same world as mere mortals, Marc breaks into one of his infectious pop-goes-to-Hobbiton tunes and we're grounded again. 'Stacey Grove', 'Conesuala' and 'Salamanda Palaganda' being three prime examples of his astute pop sensibility melded to the fragrant imagery of the era.

Occasionally the playful jumbling of words produces an unexpected delight as in this image of a woman whose bowed head is momentarily hidden from view behind a veil as she drinks a liqueur made from herbs and flowers.

"She hooded deep in chartreuse, a falcon glimpse of white teeth separated by lace cinnamon folds." ('Wind Quartets')

This album too has its share of tongue-twisting lines of alliteration which retain their potency almost half a century later, even if their meaning remains stubbornly obscure.

"Medieval doublet, elk horn ornamented woodland trumpet." ('O Harley')

Allen Evans of *NME* complimented Bolan on his "beautiful lyrics" but confessed that after 14 tracks of acoustic guitar and "monotonous percussion" the songs had become "virtually indistinguishable" from each other. It was a view that was not shared by the anonymous reviewer in *Melody Maker* who observed, "Innocence is what Rex is all about, innocence mixed with a search for ancient wisdom…It could be so pretentious except when it's in the hands of a genuine bopping imp."

The cluster of deceptively simple songs revealed a wealth of delicate melodies and stunning imagery for those prepared to suspend their disbelief, but it has to be said that there were also moments of excruciating tweeness ('The Friends' being one cringeworthy example), but it was all delivered with such sincerity that it seemed indecent to snigger and the exquisite moments far out-numbered the ostentatious, so the latter could be overlooked. Only the closer 'Scenescof Dynasty' sounded a sour note. This *a capella* rap was a track few would have played more than once. Had it been replaced by the instantly appealing single, 'One Inch Rock' with its Betty Boop scat vocal and a less eccentric performance of the outtake 'Nickelodeon', it would have been a substantially better album. But labels were still uncomfortable including singles on LPs in the belief that fickle record buyers might be put off having to buy the same track twice. 'Deboraarobed' was an exception because it was a re-recording and tricked up like a new track by being reversed at the end.

That said, given the choice between owning a copy of Pink Floyd's *Dark Side of the Moon*, the critic's choice for best album ever recorded, and the garden of delights that we are invited to explore in *Prophets*, more than a few people would be happy to opt for the latter.

Chapter 10
King of the Rumbling Spires

*Bolan used to hang around in our office and sit on the floor, strumming his guitar,
flirting with our secretary, June, who, of course, he later married. He was a
great Syd (Barrett) fan. I was quite fond of him. He was a big pain in the arse,
of course, very full of himself. I always liked that thing where he called himself
the Bolan child, this magical, mythical name. It was really from his doorbell in
Ladbroke Grove. It had his name and our secretary's surname, Child, so it read
Bolan Child and fans used to think, wow, he is the Bolan Child!"*
David Gilmour, guitarist with Pink Floyd, October 2008

Every artist has their muse. Marc had Poon, the statuette of Pan he had been given by Riggs on the day they parted. But Poon was a mere talisman, a lucky charm that served as a physical reminder to Marc that he had been blessed by the gods. If he had a muse, it was June Child, the former lover of Syd Barrett who became Marc's lover, best friend, big sister, business partner, unofficial manager and advisor, although Marc was never one to take advice. Whatever suggestions she made he would routinely dismiss, and then later claim as his own. And when he did so she would smile and say nothing. That was perhaps her greatest contribution. Although he wrote several songs about her and the contentment he had found with her, her most significant contribution to his creativity was her willingness to listen to his first sketches for songs and assure him that they were entirely original. If she hesitated for a moment to praise them, or dared to suggest that there might be a similarity to a record he had recently been listening to, he would scorn the implication with the insolence of a child who had been caught red-handed with his hand in the cookie jar and dismiss her with a wave of his hand. She would return to her book or magazine and he would disappear into Toadstool studios, his makeshift curtained-off cubby hole to revise, returning 10 or 20 minutes later with a triumphant grin and a gleam in his eye that said, 'Now you'll never guess where I got the idea for this one!' But if anyone accused him of ripping off Chuck Berry, Ricky Nelson or Howling Wolf, June would be his first and most ardent defender. "There's nothing new under the sun," she would say. "Every artist takes inspiration from somewhere." Marc was an assimilator, a "wonderful sponge" as she called him. He absorbed influences and ideas by osmosis and because his versions were not conscious or deliberate copies, he felt that he needn't credit anyone else. Riffs were a building block for a song and not subject to copyright. The melodies and the words were the essence of music and were floating in the ether to be plucked out by a visionary such as himself. Riffs and licks were in common usage, and in 'borrowing' these the artist was acknowledging his roots, nothing more. The melodies and the words had been channelled through the mind of Marc Bolan and that made them his unique creation. Marc was in accord with Jerry Lee Lewis who once rebuffed inquisitive critics by saying, "I played on those records. What more do you need to know?"

June was gentle, considerate, soft-spoken, fiercely loyal and protective of those she loved. She kept the world away from their door so that he could have the privacy and peace to work on his music, which she knew was special. And for that she was willing to sacrifice anything. She even looked the other way when he strayed, knowing that together they shared something no one else could intrude upon or compete with. She didn't suffer fools gladly and had no patience with anyone she suspected of trying to pull the wool over her eyes. It has also been said that she could turn on the tears when confronted by an angry producer who was being forced to accept a royalty cut or a manager who was being sacked, but she would say that she had to be ruthless because Marc didn't have the courage for confrontation.

Their alliance appeared predestined from their first meeting. June (born 23 August 1943) also came from a working class Jewish background. Her father was an engineer and her mother worked as a cleaner. They lived on the top floor in a council flat in Parsons Green with her younger sister, but in 1955 June managed to secure a place at Holland Park Secondary Modern which was a flagship Comprehensive school and there she received a first class education and acquired a cut-glass accent and celebrity friends. But it came at the cost of estrangement from her family with whom she then felt she had little in common.

In spring 1968, she was working as a secretary to Peter Jenner and Andrew King of the Blackhill Enterprises agency who were representing Pink Floyd.

Marc and his muse. (Photo David Dagley, Rex Features)

She had already parted from Barrett because of his acid-fuelled erratic behaviour and was living with another man. Syd's ever-increasing demands on her time and nerves had sapped her energy and so Marc's almost pathological fear of drugs was one of the aspects that attracted her to him. When Marc walked in to Blackhill's Alexander Street office wearing his mother's trousers, a pair of flying boots and a red-and-black striped blazer, she was typing in an adjacent room, but she felt a presence. Something throbbing at the back of her head, prompting her to stop whatever she was doing and find an excuse to interrupt the meeting.

It was his eyes that transfixed her and rendered her speechless. She mumbled something about making them coffee then left. Marc was telling Jenner and King about the cult following they had, the deal with Regal Zonophone, the invaluable exposure they were getting from the Peel sessions and the comparisons with their current clients. "What the Floyd do with electric instruments, we do acoustically," he told them, to which they nodded politely, but seemed unconvinced. When Marc left, June was asked if she had heard anything by Tyrannosaurus Rex as Marc had neglected to bring them any recordings, trusting in his salesmanship alone to broker the deal and assuming that everybody must have heard his music by now. She found herself giving the second half of his sales pitch. She had only heard a couple of songs on Peel's *Perfumed Garden*, but it was certainly different. It was only a matter of time before they broke through big-time and if Blackhill didn't pick them up, someone else would for sure. It was agreed that she and Andrew would catch their next appearance which was to be at Ealing College the following day.

They caught the second half of the lunchtime set which was performed without a PA. Marc's vocal mike had to be put through a 30-watt guitar amplifier and kept in place with a coat hanger and Gaffa tape. But Jenner saw the potential – and the potential profit to be had from an acoustic duo which could be billed like a band but sent on the road for a fraction of the cost. June drove them all back in Blackhill's Bentley, dropping Marc off at his parent's place in Wimbledon. Then an hour later she had a phone call from him asking her to come straight over. Thinking it was business, she drove back only to be greeted by a lovelorn poet who told her, "I'm in love with you and I don't know what to do about it."

They sat out in the garden, shared a bowl of muesli and gazed longingly into each other's eyes. There was the strongest feeling that Fate had brought them together and that it would be futile to fight it. Two days later June drove back to Summerstown in her Hillman van and collected her new man. She couldn't bear to be away from him for one more day. She'd left her former partner with only a cursory explanation before packing her toothbrush and a change of clothes. For the next four nights they lived, ate and slept in the back of the van parked on Wimbledon Common.

Marc would probably have been happy to have continued a nomadic existence, living on nature and the odd trip to the local corner shop, but June knew they needed a base and a phone if she was to make those all-important connections.

She found an attic flat at 57 Blenheim Crescent in Ladbroke Grove for £28 9s and 6d a month, a trifling sum at the time but it would still be a stretch on her income. Still, there was a pawnshop round the corner that could come in useful. And Marc and Steve would soon be getting £20 a gig.

The three-storey town house with the white facade would have been a fashionably elegant residence at the turn of the century, but like so many houses in the area it had

Bolan built up a considerable cult following between '68-'70 by performing at every club, college and festival that would add Tyrannosaurus Rex to the bill. (Photo: Jorgen Angel, Denmark 1970). Inset: Marc in his 'Warlock of Love' cloak at Glastonbury Tor 1969 (photographer unknown. From the private collection of Danielz and Caron Willans)

been partitioned off into flats and had now found itself in the midst of the hippie counterculture that had spilled over from Notting Hill Gate. But it was only half an hour from Central London and a short drive from the Blackhill offices. Marc and June occupied what would have been the servants' quarters on the top floor. It was to be their home for the next three and a half years. They had to share a toilet on the landing and there was no bath or hot water, except for whatever they could boil in the kettle for washing each morning, so they arranged to visit Tony Visconti once a week and avail themselves of his facilities.

When the royalties began to trickle in they rented the floor below for a total of £11 a week and knocked through a wall to enlarge the living room. Threadbare rugs were spread on the bare floorboards and posters of Marc's idols, Hendrix and Clapton, were tacked on to the wall.

June: "The only thing we possessed that was worth anything was his guitar and that was a cheap Japanese Gibson copy. He had a small reel-to-reel tape recorder, but he wouldn't let me near that because all his ideas were on those tapes, so when we needed to pay the rent I would take the guitar to the pawn shop then redeem it a few days later if we got a royalty cheque or a fee from a BBC session. If nothing had turned up he could always have found a new guitar or borrowed one, but the tape recorder was not to be touched."

The first sign of June's positive influence on Marc's music came in August that year when a second single was released to capitalise on the interest created by the album. 'One Inch Rock' was pint-sized pixie pop propelled by a walking bass line that looked back to 30s jump 'n' jive. The initial inspiration was Cab Calloway's 'Minnie The Moocher' with the 'hi-di-hi-di-hi-di-hi' refrain replaced by Marc's best Betty Boop impersonation, 'Doo-de-doo-de-die-die', although the underlying influence is Bob Dylan, a suspicion made transparently clear in the line, 'I asked her name, she said Germaine' which is pure Dylan. But Dylan didn't dance and Marc, as he readily admitted, was "always a bit of a wriggler". After just one album the Bopping Elf was already itching to jump down from his toadstool, but he would have to be patient. There was a glut of guitar groups on the circuit wringing sounds from their instrument that Marc could only dream about. He had a reputation now and couldn't wing it like he'd done in John's Children. If he were going to compete with them on any level, he'd have to learn a few more licks.

'One Inch Rock' was one of the few times he spun a straight story and one that revealed a wicked sense of humour as a youth is seduced by a witch who reduces her victim in size and imprisons him in a can where he meets and falls in love with another miniature captive, a girl. The idea came from a scene in the macabrely comic 1930s horror movie *Bride of Frankenstein* in which mad scientist Dr Pretorius takes a morbid delight in exhibiting his homunculi grown 'from seed' in glass jars. At one point the miniature King escapes so that he can be with his Queen and Pretorius recaptures him with tweezers and drops him back in the jar.

The lyrics are uncharacteristically commonplace for a Bolan song, but even here there is a subtle touch that would go unnoticed by the casual listener. The witch has "luggage eyes" which is Bolan's way of saying she has bags under her eyes, meaning she is old and tired. Unfortunately, such nuances appear to have gone unnoticed by the music press who found Bolan's vocal incomprehensible in the extreme.

Reviewers were unanimous in their praise, but it is a curious fact that while the music weeklies agreed it might be another minor hit, none of them made an attempt to describe the record. All talked in generalities using words such as "happy", "light-hearted", "interesting", "catchy" and "commercial" which could have applied to any contender for the singles chart that week.

Penny Valentine admitted that it had taken her longer than many to appreciate the group and now that she was "hip" she found it "endearing" and "individual" but she still couldn't understand a word Bolan was singing!

The single peaked at number 28 and stayed in the top 30 for 7 weeks. A respectable performance for a quirky acoustic song, but hardly the hit Marc was hoping for.

Meanwhile the duo's concert appearances were still being seen as something of a novelty act with their January 13th appearance at the prestigious Queen Elizabeth Hall being described by Chris Welch of *Melody Maker* as "Noddy meets Pete Townshend."

The arrival of an unexpected royalty cheque at the end of that first year together elicited great squeals of delight and gave Marc and June the means to move into the more spacious flat below, but one night there was another reason for screaming. As they lay in bed June thought she heard breathing and turned to see the colour draining out of Marc's face. He whispered, "It's moving!" and pointed at the Tyrannosaurus Rex poster on the opposite wall.

Marc: "I was afraid. I knew I was doing it. I knew my imagination had brought it to life. I also knew afterwards that had I not stopped looking at it, it would have destroyed me. The Tyrannosaurus Rex would have eaten me and there would have been blood on the bed. Since then, I've been so strong I believe nothing could hurt me."

This was one of the reasons why Marc refused to take drugs. It wasn't only that he feared losing control. He was terrified what his hyperactive imagination might unleash if allowed free reign. It was another reason why he didn't practise meditation when Visconti suggested it, although had he tried it, it would have grounded him and given him peace of mind. His fear of what might await in the dark was one reason why he was attracted to a strong personality like June. He sought protection even more than companionship. Every night before going to sleep he would recite the same short passage from the Old Testament that his mother had taught him.

Thou shalt not be afraid of the terror by night, nor of the arrow that flieth by day, nor of the pestilence that walketh in darkness, nor of the destruction that wasteth at noonday' to which he would add 'God's love on the room, amen.'

He carried a copy of this verse with him at all times written in his own angular script.

June: "We used to stay up night after night because he was petrified of going to sleep: he was afraid that if he went to sleep he might never wake up…. the big fear in his life was dying in his sleep… because it wasn't a very splendid way to go." He had told June's mother that he wouldn't live to see his 30th birthday and she sensed that he wasn't saying that to impress her. Sometimes they would stay awake for up to three nights in a row playing scrabble or backgammon. She would read to him from *Lord of the Rings* or *The Song of Solomon* or recite the poems he had written onto tape after she had typed them up. If he chanced to doze off, she would wake him as she promised to do, after half an hour so that he could see everything was all right, then he would doze off again. Later, when they could afford a phone he would call his friends in the early hours of the morning to pass the time till morning. And if he had a new song he'd call Tony whatever the time and ask if it was OK to pop round and play it to him. Visconti rarely refused.

When Steve Took spiked Marc's drink with STP at the launch party for the UK edition of *Rolling Stone*, Marc felt betrayed and his sense of security was irreparably damaged. Although June bawled Steve out for it, the incident had eroded the trust between them. It was thought that Marc decided to split with Steve and seek a new partner because of Took's increasing drug dependency, his erratic behaviour on their first American tour and his demands to have his songs recorded, but these might have been tolerated had it not been for the spiking incident. It made Bolan feel vulnerable and fed his latent paranoia of losing all he had worked for.

While Marc worked on new songs for the third album, June went back to work at Blackhill, arranging the practical aspects of upcoming appearances at the first Isle of Wight festival and a free concert in Hyde Park supporting Pink Floyd and Jethro Tull, which Marc would claim as his idea. And it probably was. He had played there so many times for free, one more appearance wouldn't worry him.

> a mansion forged on foundations
> of fire, a wallet
> of indigo & a pitchfork
> of carnelian gold
> where the dying gifts to
> me from the
> bird man of arzadia
> once skylord in the
> halls of Pan,
> Diamond domed
> courts,
> marbled & green have
> long since been ruinous
> the home of the mountain
> goat & winters boys

> m.2
> simple & starless, wanderers
> of the moors forever.
> seeking wisdom in the
> guise of Dewella, goddess
> of the needy pathways
> and wooded dells,
> daughter of the great
> ganatik river, fluid
> & silver, upon the
> swans of green she
> has been seen at
> midnight.

But he was becoming tired of being hired out for a nominal fee, or playing for free to demonstrate his hippie credentials and, in the spring of 1969, one year after joining Blackhill, he stormed into Peter Jenner's office and informed him that the group would not be going out for less than a hundred quid. When Jenner gave him half a dozen reasons why that would be impossible, Marc told him he was terminating their agreement with immediate effect and taking June with him. (Jenner remembers a less dramatic exit with a scribbled note torn from the back of an envelope being shoved under his office door after closing time informing Blackhill that Bolan was leaving them.)

Irritated by the casual, un-businesslike way they had been treated for the past two years on the counterculture circuit, June suggested they try a more traditional organisation, the Bryan Morrison Agency, on condition that they publish a book of poetry that Marc had been planning for some time.

Marc had been writing poetry since his teens and made no distinction between verse and lyrics, but a review of their recent Royal Festival Hall performance by the *Sunday Times'* arts critic Derek Jewell, had given him the idea that he was overdue for recognition as a poet. Jewell had been less than flattering in his assessment of their performance, but in comparing Marc to Ezra Pound, he had inadvertently given Marc all the encouragement he needed to petition Morrison to finance a slim volume of verse to be issued by the agency's publishing arm, Lupus. Poetry has never been a best seller in Britain, but Morrison had no ambitions to elbow 'legitimate' poets from the bookshelves. He imagined it being bought, as much out of curiosity as anything, by the 20,000 or so punters who had purchased a copy of the first two albums and hopefully another couple of thousand copies to those who would come to see the group live and would consider it a souvenir of the occasion. Marc couldn't give 'a monkeys' how it was marketed, or whether it was a risk underwritten by his growing reputation as an underground artist, it would be the fulfilment of a burning ambition.

THE WARLOCK OF LOVE
BY
MARC BOLAN

With a new love in his life, a modest place they could call their own and a number of prestigious appearances pencilled in for that summer, including their first concerts on the continent, Marc had become more than usually productive.

The creative process was not something he agonised over and the songs were not consciously crafted. It was simply a case of getting into the mood and being receptive. "If I get a particular feeling, then it has to come out. I can just sit down and get a song written down straight away. It takes me as long to do it as it takes to physically write it down. As soon as I start to think about it, then I might as well forget it. Once I've got it down, I usually play it to myself about 20 times on the trot, getting the music worked out and then tape it on my little recorder. Maybe we use it – maybe not."

When the poetry project was approved he immediately warmed to the task, rummaging through cartons of old exercise books and spiral bound notebooks brought from Summerstown to compile the book that would establish him as the equal of Dylan and Lennon. Shakespeare, Shelley, Lord Byron and the like didn't come into this. Dylan and Lennon had published verse and Bolan wanted to be recognised as a literary figure on a par with his peers.

When *The Warlock of Love* was published in March 1969 it became an instant bestseller and therefore beyond criticism in its author's eyes. Its contrived, archaic style screams pseudo-intellectual on every page and would have benefitted tremendously from the input of a courageous copy editor, but Marc would have had none of it. Freed from the rhythmic constraints imposed by a musical setting and the need to rhyme he rambled incoherently, spewing out disconnected phrases that sounded like a parody of his own lyrics. It must have struck the casual reader as pretentious nonsense, but the fans found it profound.

Birdling suckled on the tongue of the wiseone
who has tutored you in meadows, learned laughter
looks he bequested you.

If nothing else, it gave a generation of fifth formers hours of amusement poring over its impenetrable Tolkienesque imagery and may even have prompted some to write their own.

There is a seam of almost child-like wonderment in its random jumble of deconstructed sentences (*The hobbly nobbly skull of the knave…*), and an infantile delight in being wilfully obscure which makes long sections of the book extremely heaving going. Some of the crueller critics were tempted to quote Macbeth, "'tis a tale told by an idiot, full of sound and fury, signifying nothing". However, Marc was no fool. He may have been self-educated, but his verse revealed a passion for abstract painting in words, which would have made him worthy of the title, the Picasso of poetry, had anyone thought to bestow it upon him.

The author and journalist George Tremlett agrees that the book would have benefitted from having a more critical eye run over it before being passed for publication.

"On the whole I think it's very good if a bit obtuse and very obviously influenced by Dylan Thomas. I put this to him and drew the allusions and cited the compositions I thought he had been inspired by, to put it politely. He wasn't livid, but he wasn't amused. He disagreed strongly, but there's nothing wrong in having roots, nothing wrong in having influences."

Having fulfilled his ambition to be a published poet Marc now felt the time was right to be more direct in his songwriting. "I slowly began to cut the words down. Most poets do."

The first evidence of this more economical approach came in the form of the third album, *Unicorn*, and the single that preceded it, 'Pewter Suitor'.

With its manic acoustic refrain, falsetto yelps and furiously fluttering bongo rhythm, 'Pewter Suitor' was arguably the most whimsical of the group's singles. Reviewers, unfamiliar with their previous offerings would have been forgiven for thinking that the BBC children's TV characters Bill and Ben had made their own single to upstage their ITV rivals Sooty and Sweep, especially if they tried to decipher the words. As John Peel so eloquently put it, Tyrannosaurus Rex "were elfin to a degree beyond human understanding".

Puppet sounds aside, 'Pewter Suitor' was a beautiful song, but it was not single material. "It was an album track," Marc later explained. He had been persuaded to release it against his better judgement and bitterly regretted it as its failure to chart would make it more difficult to secure airplay for the album.

The album's opening track, 'Chariots of Silk', would have made a more appealing single, but it would have meant dropping it from the LP as the self-imposed ban on including singles on an album was still in force. And that would have deprived the record of one of its many highlights, the others being 'The Pilgrim's Tale', 'Evenings of Damask' and 'Iscariot', a triptych of subdued and wistful elegies to an era that had never existed.

Even an old 'familiar' (in both senses of the word), 'Cat Black', the least promising of the pre-John's Children material, was transmuted from the basest matter into gold with a new set of lyrics and a Spector-like 'pocket symphony' production featuring Visconti on piano, Took on drums and Marc trilling a harmonium in the outro.

The formula, and it was in danger of becoming one, was much as before (even down to the inclusion of a second short story narrated by John Peel), but with the addition of a full drum kit, piano, bass guitar and Fonofiddle there was an increasing sophistication to the sound and the production values were noticeably higher. As before, the strength of the songs came from the synthesis of words and music which melted into a magical invocation to summon forth the forces of nature.

A mad Mage with a maid on his eyebrows hunteth the realm for a God who could teach him the craft of decanting the glassy entrails of a frog. ('Chariots of Silk')

It was a pity that Marc used 'decanting' (to pour from one container into another) instead of 'divining' (to foretell the future from signs), but in '68 it was assumed any errors were not only intentional, but highly significant. Every innocuous pop song was believed to hold a hidden meaning and every new album was greeted as a work of art. No one was paying much attention to elementary grammatical errors and, if they noticed one, it would have been interpreted as a profound message for mankind.

During their regular trawl through the record shops in Camden Town and long evenings listening to Ricky Nelson and Gene Vincent records at Peel's flat, Marc would occasionally ask his host the meaning of a particular word he was unsure of, but after being told it was not the right one he would stick with the original because it sounded better. Neither Peel, June nor Tony Visconti would dare to suggest that Marc consult a dictionary or a thesaurus as that would dampen his romantic ardour; besides, their *enfant terrible* was having too much fun playing with words to care what the world thought of him.

Exhibit B: *"the black chested canary who as a moose could sing bass." ('Chariots of Silk')*

It didn't trouble Marc that his lyrics made little sense when read aloud. As in ritual magic, it is the intention behind the act that empowers the incantations and works a psychological transformation in the participants. The earnestness and vitality with which the lyrics were sung gave them a resonance that transported the listener to an elder age. Those who entered the magic circle found themselves ennobled. Those who remained without were unmoved. There is a saying in esoteric circles, 'For those who believe, no proof is necessary; for those who disbelieve, no proof is enough.' The same could be said of the music made by Tyrannosaurus Rex.

Had two outtakes, 'Demon Queen' (reputedly featuring David Bowie on autoharp) and the unfinished sketch 'Ill-Starred Man' been completed and substituted for the superfluous ''Pon A Hill' and the dreary 'Stones for Avalon', the LP would have earned a place on every list of Classic Albums. As it was, *Unicorn* was an album burnished in the glow of the late afternoon sun and redolent with wood smoke.

The rural idyll it evoked was the result of a brief holiday in Cornwall and Wales. Marc: "I was very close to the earth…It was a period of clarity and purity- and *Unicorn* was very much into my soul – it was all me. It was the first time I got into production as well…the drums gave me a real buzz because I wanted to get a Phil Spector sound."

Not everyone appreciated the group's distinctive sound. It was even known to be the cause of marital quarrels.

"In spite of the uneasy peace or the domestic rifts that ensue whenever I play their records, I must admit to deriving a certain enjoyment from the joyful music of the monstrous duo… I can't imagine why the Rex should attract such loathing… To me it's just a happy warming sound, absorbing, refreshing and stimulating." Nick Logan, *NME*.

It was difficult to imagine where they could go from here without radically altering their sound or approach. Until the day Marc arrived for an afternoon session clutching a Fender Stratocaster. Visconti took it in his stride. He'd noticed Marc eyeing his electric guitar with envy lately and had wondered how long it would be until he bought one of his own.

Visconti: "It was Marc who wanted the change. One day he turned up with an electric guitar and I knew how to handle it. I knew how to record electric guitar. If he needed bass I'd play bass for him. If he needed strings I'd write the string parts for him. I covered all the directions he wanted to go in."

For their first electric single, 'King of the Rumbling Spires', Marc took a leaf out of the Grimm Brothers' book of morbid fairy tales. After adding a tastefully overdriven guitar, organ, bass and Took's highly individual and unusually muscular approach to drumming, the track was possessed of a demonic fury. Instead of simply providing a back beat on the snare as conventional drummers would have done, Took gave the toms a drubbing that drove the VU needles into the red. "More than a song, this is tantamount to a poem set to music," raved Derek Johnson in the *NME*.

And it was intoned against a primeval slab of sound sent crashing through the undergrowth like a rampant beast that had broken free of its chains.

Tyrannosaurus Rex was reborn and bopping, to borrow the one memorable line from *The Warlock of Love*. Nobody would accuse them of being lightweight again.

★ ★ ★ ★ ★ ★ ★

"If I started to believe I was a splinter of God's head I'd be zapped and mown down by lightning. And what good would that be? I'd never get into the charts then!" (Marc Bolan, 1968)

In the summer of '69 Marc was worried that he might tarnish the image he had cultivated of himself as an elfin emissary of the underground and was anxious that he should not be accused of 'selling out' by going electric. In his mind it was as seismic a shift in direction as that taken by Dylan in '65 when he ditched the Dust Bowl poet persona, but few noticed when Bolan added an electric guitar and fewer still cared, so long as he continued to sing of fauns and fairies. Nevertheless, during an interview to plug the new single, he felt the need to reassure his audience that he hadn't compromised his ideals.

"It doesn't actually sound that different, just more funky. We always played pop music anyway and to me it's completely fair to use electricity. But we won't be loud. We'll be using two 15-watt amps."

With two minor hits, three steady selling albums and a 25-date US tour planned for August, the portents looked promising, but behind the scenes not everything in the garden was lovely. The good vibrations that had provided the soundtrack to the Summer of Love had given way to discord and the realisation that there would be no happy ending for the Beautiful People. Acid casualties were beginning to outnumber the survivors and the hippie disdain for commercialism had become a pathetic excuse for promoters not to pay bands, or to palm them off with dope. The world was not a paradise on earth, far from it. News of the Manson cult murders in California exposed the sordid underbelly of the hippie dream, while images of the escalating violence in Vietnam, student protests against the war and civil rights riots in American cities depicted a society at war with itself.

Closer to home, Steve's merry prankster routine was becoming tiresome and was putting a serious strain on the relationship between Marc and his new management, Enthoven and Gaydon. EG were in a different league to the one-man organisations Marc had been dealing with up to this point. They handled King Crimson and would be taking on stadium rockers ELP in the near future. They had no time or patience with dope heads who couldn't make their gig.

Had the US tour not been postponed, a crisis might have been averted, but the delay meant that Steve had time to kill and he did so in the company of his friend Twink, drummer with the Pretty Things. Twink invited his self-destructive friend for a recording session to complete his solo album, Think Pink, the afternoon before the rescheduled flight. When the session wrapped, the pair went to celebrate at the Speakeasy where King Crimson were holding court with the press. After availing himself of the free booze and other substances on offer, one half of the world's smallest group was in no fit state to make the morning flight. Ron the roadie had to break in to Took's flat to drag him out, but it was too late. He missed the flight. By the time he arrived in Los Angeles, Marc and June had decided they couldn't rely on him anymore and would have to find a replacement. Any loyalty Marc had felt towards his partner evaporated when Took explained that he'd missed the flight because he had been recording with someone Bolan despised, Twink being a true believer in the counterculture that Bolan couldn't buy into. And to add insult to injury, Twink had the temerity to help Took get two of his songs into shape after Marc had said they weren't good enough for inclusion on the next Tyrannosaurus Rex album. For someone with a critically low tolerance threshold, this was the ultimate 'Fuck you'. Bolan wasn't going to let anyone question his authority or judgement. Took had to go.

But this was only the beginning of Bolan's troubles.

Whoever had booked the dates stateside on behalf of Blue Thumb, the group's new US outlet, evidently hadn't given any thought as to whether or not the bands were compatible. Audiences who had come to wig-out to The Grateful Dead, Country Joe And The Fish and Janis Joplin had no patience to sit quietly through an acoustic set, or to strain their necks to see a singer who was sitting down and not putting on a show.

Polite applause was not the reaction Marc had flown across the Atlantic to hear. Press interest was also muted and interviews were scarce, although Billboard acknowledged them as being "unusual", "engrossing" and "spellbinding". But for Steve it was the Promised Land. Every form of high was offered in the spirit of transatlantic cooperation and not wishing to give offence, he accepted gleefully. Took has been unfairly described as Bolan's 'yes man', but on that first US tour he earned his nickname by saying 'yes' to every chemical trial he was asked to participate in. As a result he freaked out, stripping to the waist on stage, beating himself with a belt until he drew blood and smashing up the few items of equipment they had. It might have been funny had it not been so sad.

"We would get to the end of the set and we would do 'The Wizard' which was my licence to freak out. I'd scream such things as 'I want a woman', throw my bottle up in the air and then I used to smash up my maracas and the occasional drum if I didn't like it. I'd sling things across the stage and then I'd pick up my chair and, oh yeah, I used to throw my gong up in the air, kick it and bite it and dribble all over it, you know. Which I found great fun…"

Marc wasn't laughing though and when Steve broke several bones in his hands one night trying to demolish a metal chair on stage, it was the end of the partnership. Fortunately, Took found the prescribed painkillers also made him insensitive to the bad vibes radiating from Marc and June who abandoned him after the last gig in Seattle on September 20 where they had supported It's A Beautiful Day. Took had gone off into the night with a girl without telling them where he could be found if needed and they hadn't asked.

After three weeks hanging around LA and tripping, Took was arrested for wandering along a freeway and deported for not having a valid visa. When he returned to Ladbroke Grove he found a bill for £2,000 waiting in the letterbox from EG management for 'breach of contract' and a brief letter informing him that his services were no longer required. There was no suggestion that promoters had refused to pay because of Took's antics and no extra expenses had been incurred on his behalf. The demand was evidently a ploy to discourage him from pursuing a claim for unpaid royalties, or his share of the money that had been made on the tour. Sadly Steve was in no state to understand what had happened to him. He threw the letter in the bin and went in search of Twink who offered his friend more painkillers.

Chapter 11
A Beard of Stars

"**Y**ou stupid cunt! Who said you could shave your beard off? You've ruined everything!" When Bolan was angry he pursed his lips, narrowed his eyes and furrowed his brow. And he was very angry indeed.

"Jesus, Marc. I didn't think it would be such a big deal." Mickey Finn was not used to being yelled at, but he'd only just been given the gig as Steve Took's replacement and he didn't want to blow it by talking back to the boss. When accused he'd get defensive and quiet. He shrank from confrontation, or laughed it off. Humour was his best defence, his weapon of choice, but he was disarmed by the intensity of Bolan's anger. He hadn't seen him like this before.

"Big deal? Of course, it's a fucking big deal! The album's called *A Beard of fucking Stars* isn't it and now you don't have a fucking beard!"

Bolan drew himself up to his full height and glared at his new partner, his limpid green eyes darkening. Finn, an inch taller, stared back, unblinking. It was a scene straight out of a Bugs Bunny cartoon.

Bolan caved first, convulsing into fits of girlish giggles.

"I could get a false beard from a joke shop for the cover shoot," Mickey offered.

"No, no forget it man. We'll just rename it *A Naked Chin of Stars*." Bolan collapsed into more giggles.

Within a few weeks Mickey had grown sufficient stubble to justify the album's title and have the photo session rescheduled.

Marc and June had advertised for a replacement for Took in the October 4 issue of *Melody Maker*, but Finn had materialised before they could wade through the 300 applications.

'WANTED to work with T.Rex a gentle young guy who can play percussion, i.e. Bongos and Drum Kit, some Bass Guitar and Vocal Harmony. Photos please.'

The last item gave the game away. Image was essential. As it turned out, Mickey's shortcomings as a musician were overlooked when he was introduced to Marc by mutual friend and photographer Pete Sanders.[1] Not only did Finn answer to the name of an illegal knock-out potion (a cool name being a good omen as far as Marc was concerned), he was also the very embodiment of the noble King Aragorn in *Lord of the Rings* as Marc had always imagined him.

"Mickey couldn't sing a note," June admitted, "but he looked beautiful." He also happened to bear a passing resemblance to Steve Took which might prove useful. Perhaps no one would even notice that anything had changed.

---

1 *Other sources name the mutual friend as John Lloyd or Nigel Waymouth, while Mickey has said he met Marc by chance in The Seed restaurant where he was working as a mural painter at the time.*

TYRANNOSAURUS REX
A BEARD OF STARS stereo album. EMI
Regal Zonophone SLRZ 1013. Essex Music.

Mickey possessed a natural sartorial elegance, dressing his slender frame in soft pastel-coloured clothes and accentuating his prominent cheek bones, dark eyes and pallid complexion beneath wide brimmed hats.

But he was more than a pretty face, although the press wouldn't be given the chance to find out. Those who did manage to corner him backstage were impressed. Journalist George Tremlett felt that Finn was frequently and unfairly dismissed as Bolan's sidekick.

"Mickey Finn had one of the best gifts for language of anyone I'd ever met. He had a better facility for words than Marc Bolan himself. Bolan was very career conscious, determined to sell a lot of records, determined to be a star. He was very careful not to let people around him become too prominent – understandably – but in Mickey Finn's case, it did him a considerable injustice. Marc was a very dominant person.

"Mickey was kept in the background away from the press by publicists who blocked all requests for interviews with Finn by repeating that Marc spoke on behalf of the group. But on the three occasions that I managed to interview him Mickey proved a fascinating conversationalist and was in some ways a more interesting character than Marc. He shared Bolan's belief in extra-terrestrial life – both claimed to have actually seen UFOs – and he was passionate about surreal art and the films of Fellini which Marc told me he'd seen a dozen times. But Mickey had a much wider range of interests. He loved to travel and had been on a voyage down the Nile. He was widely read, played chess and was a connoisseur of fine wines and gourmet cuisine. He continued painting and drawing even after T.Rex became successful but it was his gift for language that was so impressive. It was almost impossible to capture the way he spoke on paper because he would reverse sentences in mid-speech and jumble phrases as they came tumbling out of his mouth."

Mickey had a magical effect on Marc who came to regard him as his personal talisman. Fate appeared to have brought him into the frame at the perfect moment to form a Kabbalistic triad with Marc and June, Marc being the Magus, balanced by the outer pillars of Force and Form. Without their stabilising influence, Marc's creativity could not be grounded and channelled into something constructive. That is why Finn's limited contribution was rewarded with a 50 per cent share of all appearance fees. His mere presence was believed to guarantee good fortune, until the time came when Marc ceased to believe in magic and it deserted him.

Michael Norman Finn was born in Thornton Heath, Surrey on June 3 in the same year as Bolan, 1947. His father was an engineer and had hopes that Mickey would become a graphic designer, but Mickey too failed to finish his education, although he got as far as the first year at Croydon College of Art before he quit to find 'a proper job'.

"I used to get some still life, say a pineapple, to draw on the Monday and that was supposed to last me all week…but by the end of the day I might be feeling a bit hungry, so I would take a bite out of the pineapple – and then I'd draw the pineapple with one slice missing – by the Friday, I would have just the core left – so then I would draw the core."

When he was called before the Principal and informed that his attitude was not likely to earn him sufficiently high grades, he shrugged and said that if that was the case, he'd better leave immediately.

Like Bolan, he also dabbled in male modelling but considered it uncool when a sharp suit and short back-and-sides gave way to shoulder-length hair, beards and kaftans. By '67 Mickey had earned a reputation as a painter of murals, graduating to work on the Apple boutique in Baker Street and Granny Takes a Trip in the King's Road. He also earned a steady income from painting the cars of friends who wanted their motors to look like John Lennon's Rolls-Royce which had been decorated in the red, yellow and green swirls of a circus caravan. But his two consuming passions were rock music and motorbikes. Mickey loved speed and the sensation of the cold air on his face when he hit 100mph, but it was the solitude of riding through deserted streets and country roads at dawn after a long recording session or a gig that gave him the greatest pleasure. He'd never lost his love of fifties rock and roll either, but had picked up The Beatles and The Stones after leaving college and by the time he met Marc in October '69 he had dabbled with playing drums for a loose collective of painters and musicians who called themselves Hapshash and the Coloured Coat.

It appears Mickey was visiting Sanders in the attic flat at 57 Blenheim Crescent when the photographer remembered that he had to show Marc some proofs. When Mickey mentioned that he liked fooling around on bongos, Marc didn't need the matchmaker to point out the possibilities.

When I met Mickey in 1997 he was haggard and had difficulty talking as the result of alcoholism and ill health. His long shoulder-length hair was cut short and he seemed to have withered a couple of inches. But he remembered that first meeting. "We went for a macrobiotic meal at The Seed, a restaurant round the corner from where he was living at the time, and just clicked straightaway. He had this long curly hair by then and was wearing girl's shoes, which was kind of strange, but he talked real soft so it sort of went together. It was part of the image he wanted to create. He had created this image of the hippie poet, but he was driven, you know, determined to make it and it convinced me that we would be going places. The strangest part was that I felt as if I'd always known him. He gave off this incredible kinetic energy and you were fired up by him, no matter how tired you might be. I liked what he was doing with the music. He didn't have to convince me. I had to convince myself that I'd be up to it because I knew I couldn't sing and play as well as the other guy he'd had. But Marc didn't seem to care. So if it was alright with him…"

Marc was equally enamoured of his new musical partner.

"I've got a little studio set up in the flat and Mickey comes over on his 650cc Triumph and we just blow for a couple of hours. It's all very relaxed… we play together very naturally… Mickey and I could pick up guitars and play for fifteen hours straight without getting bored. I could never do that with Steve."

Enthoven and Gaydon whisked the pair off to a fashionably rural retreat in North Wales to get it together and by the last day of October '69 Mickey had grasped the rudiments of bongo playing and could be coaxed into playing bass and adding backing vocals. Even so, it was often quicker for Bolan to replay and re-sing Mickey's parts than ask him to re-do it until he got it right. Finn's prominent credit and portrait on the back cover of the LP gave the impression that this was an equal partnership and that the group dynamic was as before. Nothing could be further from the truth. *A Beard of Stars* was, in essence, a Marc Bolan solo album with minimal contributions from Finn and Visconti. Fearing his former partner might apply for an injunction which could delay the release, Marc shelved several tracks he and Took had recorded prior to the US tour and erased Took's contribution from another. Fortunately, he had a surfeit of songs to choose from and so was able to replace the missing tracks at short notice. But it's a pity that songs as strong as 'Once Upon The Seas of Abyssinia' and 'Blessed Wild Apple Girl' were replaced with an obvious filler, 'Organ Blues', and the bleak 'Wind Cheetah'.

Deprived of Took's lustrous harmonies, pixiefied vocal effects and percussion embellishments, *A Beard of Stars* was noticeably sparser than its predecessors. But that was also its strength. The rudimentary bass lines, multi-tracked acoustic guitars and toy organ (sounding remarkably similar to a harmonium), provided an uncluttered backdrop for Bolan's heavily enunciated vocals, placing him centre stage. In contrast to the busy verbal jousting of earlier albums, backing vocals were kept to a minimum, which brought the lead vocal and lyrics into sharper focus. These too were pruned back to two or three verses and the language simplified.

It was an invitation to cast off one's inhibitions and join in the rites of 'the Old Religion' whose devotees needed no encouragement to dance skyclad by the light of the magical moon. Complementing the earthy paeans to Pan there were also princely songs of courtly love and a poet's reverence for the mysteries of life. ('A Day Laye')

There was even a place for two delicate scene-setting instrumentals, a 'Prelude' and an interlude (the title track) on which Marc demonstrated his new proficiency on lead guitar before stretching out on the climactic 'Elemental Child' for which he climbed down from his toadstool and indulged in Hendrix-style histrionics. The choice of title suggested he wanted to be seen as a serious disciple of Jimi Hendrix whose 'Voodoo Chile' had heralded the advent of the screaming Heavy Metal guitar solo, though Bolan knew he was not in the same league and it was to torment him when he became a rock star. But while his ambitions could be channelled into a five-minute freak-out within the context of a recognisable song, it seemed churlish to deny him the right to rock out with the best.

In retrospect, however, it is the economical lyrical fills on tracks such as 'Pavilions Of Sun', 'Great Horse' and the unfussy wah-wah accompaniment to 'Lofty Skies' which prove most effective and exemplify the inimitable Tyrannosaurus Rex sound.

Marc was still wandering the dark woods on the borderland between Narnia and Mordor, encountering all manner of dragons, dwarves and magical beasts. But there was a new urgency to the tracks, a ramping up of the energy level accentuated by the addition of raw amplified guitar. The change to electric had been inevitable; it was only a matter of time before he tired of the all-acoustic arrangements and attempted to emulate his new heroes, Hendrix and Clapton.

"Even when we did 'Debora', it was always 'next week I'll plug my Stratocaster in'. But I couldn't play well enough then to make the noises that I wanted to hear."

NME acknowledged "young Mr Bolan's emergence as guitar star extraordinaire," but their rivals didn't hear anything radically different from the previous Tyrannosaurus Rex albums.

Marc was still willing to acknowledge his technical limitations at this point, though he was impatient to emulate his heroes. What he needed was the approval of a genuine guitar god before he felt safe in striking out on his own. Who better to bestow the blessing than 'God' himself, Eric Clapton, whose fiancé, Alice Ormsby-Gore, happened to be June's best friend? A phone call was all that was needed to secure an invitation to visit the next time the couple who called themselves Bolan-Child found themselves in the area.

The very next day they were waved through the gates of Clapton's Surrey estate. But the guitar stayed in the car. For once Marc listened to June and didn't push his luck. It was a low key, informal affair – an invite to hang out while Alice and June chatted over tea and maybe shared a little dope. Eric was rehearsing with Blind Faith. Marc could sit in so long as he showed due deference and didn't open his mouth. It was the longest couple of hours in Marc Bolan's short life. There were no words of encouragement or predictions of future stardom for Bolan to brag about later, as had been the case with Hendrix. All he could say afterwards was, "I sat at the feet of the master". He had kept his mouth shut, but his eyes open, wider than they'd ever been and he had memorised two or three licks that would become his trademark. Yes, Bolan had his limitations but he would be an industrious pupil.

"I don't claim to be a guitarist," he later declared in a rare moment of modesty, "but I've got flaming hands and bleeding fingers. I steer the guitar like a ship and sing with my eyes closed. When I'm bopping it feels great."

When it was time to leave, Marc excused himself in his best upper class accent and followed June to the door, but as he stood by the car he hesitated and looking back at the house he pulled the guitar case from the back seat. He couldn't resist the chance to have his photo taken with his beloved Les Paul in God's garden.

As the 'Swinging Sixties' drew to a close it became apparent that the hippie dream of a new Utopia had given way to bitter disillusionment. As early as October 1967 a group in Haight-Ashbury had held a mock funeral to bury their ideals when they realised that Love and Peace were being marketed as fashionable accessories for just another youth movement. But for those still sleepwalking through the sixties, there was a rude awakening at the Altamont Racetrack in California on December 6, 1969, when a member of the audience was murdered within sight of The Rolling Stones by Hells Angels who the band had hired as 'security guards'.

With no one in the mood for Tolkienesque fantasy and the 'electric elf' himself now faced with the fact that hippies didn't buy records in sufficient quantities, it was time for 'the world's smallest group' to get themselves a makeover.

Bolan simply couldn't afford to be seen clinging to the coat tails of a lost cause. He needed to change and to be seen to do so. There had to be a radical overhaul of the music to widen its appeal and a long overdue abbreviation of the group's name to something more readily pronounceable. And all without losing their sense of identity (!) – but which way to jump?

Rock was splintering into two opposing camps, on the one side were hard rock outfits such as Deep Purple, Black Sabbath and The Who and on the other, prog rockers like ELP, Yes and King Crimson who had ambitions to blur the boundaries between classical and rock music with symphonic rock and endless extended solos. And in the middle, straddling both the left and right hand path, were Led Zeppelin, masters of both wistful folk and primal hard rock. Bolan could only look on with envy as these behemoths burst out of the club circuit and into 30,000-seat stadia, shifting vinyl by the container load. As Bolan couldn't compete with either, perhaps the only course open to him was to mine a new vein entirely. Even while he had been bleating out prayers to Pan, Marc had kept one eye open and focused on the singles charts and lately he'd noticed that the big groups had turned their back on 45s to concentrate on the more prestigious album market. Zeppelin even refused to release singles in the UK and Yes would have been hard pressed to squeeze one of their intros into a three minute single. There was a new generation of record buyers who were being ignored by the serious musos and this younger audience couldn't afford to buy albums. But they had the pocket money to purchase singles. And the competition for their cash was decidedly second rate. The singles charts of January

1970 were clogged up with lightweight playground pop by acts who had no discernible identity and would have struggled to score at the Eurovision Song Contest. A shrewd businessman could make a killing if he could create a new brand of pop with the instant appeal of these bubblegum groups and the impudence to make it convincing.

The year of Bolan's breakthrough began on a bum note. On January 8 1970, Visconti had invited him to a David Bowie session hoping that the friendly rivalry that had existed between them since '65 might spark something special. It did, in the form of an elegant guitar part on 'Prettiest Star' that was crucial to the song's success, so much so that, three years later, Bowie asked Mick Ronson to replicate it note for note when he re-recorded the song for the *Aladdin Sane* album. But the session began badly as Marc and June arrived in a foul mood, spoiling the party atmosphere. That Thursday also happened to be Bowie's 23rd birthday so Marc and June's uncharacteristically selfish behaviour was doubly distressing for David. And it ended with June telling Bowie that his song was "crap" and that the only good thing on it was Marc's solo. It has always been assumed that the source of this ill-feeling was Marc's envious resentment of his rival's success with 'Space Oddity' and it has been cited as an example of his spiteful nature ever since. But what was not known until now was that the reason for Marc's animosity was not his rivalry with David, but a row he had had with June on the way to the studio. June resented being dragged along to someone else's session and she was livid that Marc was giving his time and talent for free when he was entitled to a fee as a member of the Musicians' Union. June was annoyed with Marc for being 'soft', as she saw it, and as she couldn't take it out on him, she vented her frustration on Bowie. Marc could be driven to tears quite easily if his own plans were ruined, but he was curiously insensitive to the feelings of others and so never felt the need to explain his behaviour that day to David.

The success of 'Space Oddity' had rankled with Bolan whose latest single, 'By the Light of a Magical Moon', was released that month to a chorus of indifference. Marc had an unwavering belief in his own abilities whereas Bowie seemed to bend with the wind. David's flirting with mime and Anthony Newley-styled novelty songs such as 'The Laughing Gnome' led Marc to believe that his friend wasn't serious about the music, so when 'Space Oddity' took off on the wave of interest generated by the Apollo moon landing, Marc was seriously pissed off. In his mind Bowie had scored a bulls eye and hadn't even been trying. Marc gave interviewers the impression that he wasn't concerned by the lack of commercial success, but he was becoming increasingly frustrated that he couldn't crack the charts. "It had four plays in eight weeks," he moaned, "but I think our time for singles may come again. "

In the meantime Marc thought he might be able to turn his fortunes around by making his relationship with June official. He may also have been hoping to heal the hurt she was feeling after he had admitted to a brief affair with singer Marsha Hunt and at the same time assuage his own guilt at having strayed. For someone at the centre of the sixties counterculture, Bolan was uncommonly conventional in his attitudes, eschewing drugs and free love for the security and stability he needed to work on his music. "I never felt the need for any sort of psychedelic drugs or hash…the way I live my life I've got to have a very open head."

There was also some embarrassment on his part in owning up to being a married man.

Acoustic duo Tyrannosaurus Rex were a cheap act to book and they were soon able to afford their own PA system. (Photo: Ray Stevenson, Rex Features)

"It felt like something interesting to do one day, to be quite honest… Just felt like an event, you know, a reason to have a champagne lunch…"

It had certainly been an impulsive decision. On January 30, 1970, just two days after making a formal application for a marriage certificate, they tied the knot at Kensington Registry Office. There wasn't time to organise a reception, or the desire to make a fuss, so only a handful of friends attended – Jeff Dexter, Mickey Finn and his girlfriend, June's closest friend Alice Ormsby-Gore, and photographer Pete Sanders who forgot to bring his camera. Fortunately, someone managed to borrow one and it was left to a young Indian boy who happened to be passing at that moment to take the only snap of their wedding.

But even immediately afterward, Marc felt the need to deny that he had made a commitment.

"We're not married; I'm not a 'married man'. I'm still waiting to get hair on me chest, you know, let alone be married. But we're two human beings who like being together. We've had times, of course, when we haven't wanted to be together and we haven't been and we've probably been with other people, no doubt… but June's the funniest chick I ever met and while she fills that role I shall be a happy married man, family man with slippers and a dog and a pipe."

The hesitancy with which he stumbled through the awkward subject of being unfaithful to her betrays not only guilt, but also a desire to avoid the fact that he wasn't as dissolute, or as free as a rock star was expected to be. Marriage also ended all speculation as to his true sexual orientation, as far as he was concerned.

The asexual romantic aspect of the music he made during the Tyrannosaurus Rex period avoided the 'difficult' subject of sexual identity and it could be argued that the pastoral environment he created inhabited by fairies, fauns and satyrs should have offered a clue as to his true nature. It was the realm of a Victorian child, a Peter Pan world where no one had to grow up and face the harsh realities of life or the 'sordid' subject of sexuality.

June has described him as very childlike and even confessed to having had an abortion because she couldn't imagine him coping with family responsibilities at that time, but also because she felt that she couldn't have handled "two children", the other being Marc.

By March 1970 *A Beard of Stars* was ready for release and an impromptu performance at the offices of *Melody Maker* was given to announce the return of the sorcerer and his new apprentice. Unfortunately, the duo arrived at lunchtime when the journalists had decamped for the pub, so only Staff Writer Chris Welch and the office manager were there to witness the debut of the new line-up. Marc perched cross-legged on a desk dressed in yellow satin trousers, star patterned shirt and girl's shoes, threw back his head and launched into a sampling of new songs from the forthcoming album while Mickey thrummed on desk tops and chairs. Welch was mightily impressed with the new material, but before he could give his verdict there was a hammering on the wall and annoyed cries from the adjacent office of *Cycling* magazine. But Marc wouldn't have long to wait for a more appreciative audience.

All the omens indicated an auspicious new beginning. The Regal Zonophone acts would be relocating to Fly Records, a new venture formed by David Platz in partnership with Track's Kit Lambert and Chris Stamp and a larger budget had been earmarked for promotion and the printing of picture sleeves to make future singles more appealing to younger buyers. But when word reached Marc that Lambert and Stamp were less than enthusiastic to hear that the first release on the new label would be 'those old dinosaurs' Tyrannosaurus Rex, he determined to make them eat their words.

His streamlining of the group's sound was not a calculated strategy for stardom, or part of a grand plan to get rich, more a realisation that he had to kick start a new phase in his career or risk remaining a cult figure. "What struck me in the end after, like, two years of doing that, was that there were so many people who didn't know who we were… I felt very stuck… I'd done four albums and we're boogying along, we were very comfortable, you know? And I don't like to be too comfortable… I'd got to a metal wall and the albums were hitting the wall, charting and disappearing… I don't deny money, but the excitement is what I do it for, honestly, like fulfilment."

But once he noticed that there were more young faces in the audience and that the once reverential silence between songs was broken by girls calling his name, he grasped the opportunity to exploit a gap in the market with the ruthless astuteness of a commodity broker.

Marriage to his muse seemed to settle Marc who immediately began work on a fifth album, one that would appeal to 'the heads' and the younger fans, but what he really needed to come up with was that elusive all-important single.

Visconti did not believe in magic, but he was willing to try anything to help Marc achieve the breakthrough that he deserved. During the making of *A Beard of Stars* the producer had copied a snippet of screaming teenage girls from a Beatles soundtrack and mixed it into the single, 'By The Light of The Magical Moon', in the hope that the good fairy might be listening. It was all in fun. He didn't seriously believe he could attract good luck that way and, of course, he didn't. But he wasn't wrong to try. The secret of ritual magic is to act as if whatever you desire has already happened. A vague wish is not enough. The desired object or event has to be visualised in detail to imprint the image on the ether and then it must be empowered with an emotional charge over a sustained period if there is to be any chance of bringing it into being. Good intentions are never enough. It was obvious to all those who had invested their faith in Marc Bolan that the only person who could perform that particular miracle was the poet-sorcerer himself.

The last day of June was extremely close. It was particularly so in the city, far from the coast. Even with all the windows wide open there was barely a breeze. In their third floor flat Marc and June could only draw the curtains for shade, lie back on the high-backed plush brown sofa and fan themselves with magazines. If only the storm would break. Something was in the air and it wasn't revolution. Even thunder and lightning would be preferable to this oppressive heat. It was stifling outside and too sticky to stay in. Too hot to move, in fact. It drained them of energy and left them listless. The only thing to do was to stay still and sweat it out. It was even too hot to get up and turn the record over. Ricky Nelson had been singing 'It's Late' for the past 20 minutes as the auto-changer lifted the needle and returned it to the beginning after the fade over and over and over again. June stopped fanning her face for a moment and gave Marc a look he knew well.

"OK, OK, I'll turn it off."

Once he was up and had switched off the turntable June stretched herself full length, leaving him only the armchair which was occupied by a stack of albums he hadn't got around to sorting. But in this heat he couldn't muster enough enthusiasm to move them. So he did what he always did when he was bored or restless or inspired.

The makeshift studio under the stairs was airless but, as there were no windows, it was a couple of degrees cooler. He cradled the acoustic, ran the plectrum across the strings to check the tuning and began strumming through the three-chord sequence that had been needling him all afternoon to see if anything could be teased out of it. When you live in Ladbroke Grove there's no going down to the crossroads to cut a deal with the Devil. You just have to roll your sleeves up and get down to it. A, D, E – the old three-chord trick. It had been good enough for Ricky Nelson and James Burton, Elvis and Scotty Moore, Carl Perkins, Jerry Lee and every black mother who played the blues and lived it too. They'd wrung endless variations from it and done pretty well out of it by all accounts. There had to be another permutation if he looked hard and wanted it badly enough. And God, did he want it badly.

June hadn't noticed he'd come back into the room. She was leaning over the side of the sofa looking for another magazine when she saw him standing at her feet. He was grinning from ear to ear. "I've got it!"

The next day a session had been scheduled to continue work on the first official 'T.Rex' album, tentatively titled *The Children of Rarn*, which would feature some of the songs he had already written for the epic song cycle, but all thoughts of that project had now been swept aside. Marc was itching to try out a new song while it was still hot and Visconti knew better than to try to persuade him to put it to one side until they had finished what they'd begun the last session. Marc had a strong superstitious streak and was afraid that, if he didn't nail a track while it was still burning a hole in his pocket, the moment would be lost and the magic wouldn't materialise.

There was no question of demoing the new song as he had done that at home. He'd finalised the structure and roughed out the parts for bass, which would stick to the root notes of the chords, and the staccato guitar lick that would lend it a percussive momentum. The track would come together in the studio as it always did and the spontaneity of doing it for the first time and for real would be captured in the grooves.

He had an almost mystical belief in the first take being the only one that mattered. If asked to do another he'd say, "I put my soul into that take, literally. I couldn't do it again."

The amp was miked and another set up to capture his guide vocal, although it was more than likely that the scratch vocal might be kept and another double-tracked to smooth out any dodgy notes. If there was any spill, feedback or buzz from the guitar amp, then so much the better. A touch of tape echo on the guitar mimicked the sound James Burton and Scotty Moore had perfected back in the fifties and all was ready for take one. The experience gained from making four albums in two years had sharpened the Bolan/Visconti production team into a model of business-like efficiency.

The guide track would be knocked off in as long as it took Marc to play the song, he'd rarely need a second take. Then a second guitar part, doubling the first, would be overdubbed with a cleaner tone and more bite before Marc or Tony added the bass. Mickey would add tambourine, bongos or whatever he'd been allowed to contribute and that would be the backing track in the can, done and dusted in under an hour. Then Marc would record a lead vocal which would be mixed with the original guide vocal and bounced onto a new track, freeing up the two original vocal tracks for backing vocals. That could be done in 20 minutes. Marc would usually record his own backing vocals, a single harmony line tracked two or three times, singing a third above the root note of the chord, then these would be bounced to a spare track and the original backing vocals erased to free up the last couple of tracks for handclaps and additional guitar fills. If a spare track was required for strings then the guitar solo would have to be dropped in and punched out again on the lead guitar track as there were only eight tracks to play with. The whole process could be done in less than three hours.

"What are we calling this one?" asked Visconti over the monitors as Marc adjusted the strap of his Les Paul, sprayed orange to look like the vintage Gretsch Eddie Cochran had played.

Marc cleared his throat. "Ride A White Swan".

Chapter 12
Twopenny Prince

'Ride a White Swan' was the hit that almost didn't happen. After it had been recorded Visconti realised that it needed strings to add the sheen of sophistication to offset the rough-edged aesthetic. But they'd already spent their allocated budget for session musicians adding violins to 'Diamond Meadows' and 'Beltane Walk', two obvious highlights from the forthcoming album. So the producer was forced to ask David Platz for an additional one hundred pounds to bring the four string players back for a second session. He had a hell of a job convincing the publisher that it wasn't an extravagance but an essential element to ensure the single's success. Though once Platz heard the finished mix he agreed it was money well spent.

There was a lot riding on the success of the single, which was scheduled for release on October 9, 1970, the first official release under the abbreviated name. Little could be left to chance. A full colour picture sleeve was planned, but proved too costly so a black-and-white version was substituted at the last minute. The original B-side ('Jewel') was dropped in favour of two tracks ('Is It Love?' and a rather tame cover of 'Summertime Blues') to make Fly's first release a maxi-single. The Beatles were the only band to have put decent songs on the B-side and that was only because they had so many top drawer songs to spare. No one else offered added value on the flip side, but when your fans are mostly 13- or 14-year-old kids with only 10 shillings (50p) pocket money a week to spend, it only takes that extra track or a collectible picture sleeve to influence their decision. And it was the kids, not the late teens and twenty-somethings who made 'Ride A White Swan' a hit after hearing it playlisted on Radio 1.

Others contributed too, of course. DJ Jeff Dexter had played a pre-release white label promo of the single during his shift at the Isle of Wight pop festival over the August bank holiday weekend ensuring that 600,000 people went home with the song embedded in their heads. And Peel wrote a quaintly whimsical review in *Disc* in which he threatened to unleash his 'flock of highly trained hedgehogs' to deliver retribution on those who hadn't bought the single by Christmas. But it was play-listing of the single by daytime DJs on 'the nation's number one' pop station that did the trick. John Peel was not the only Radio 1 DJ to be bewitched by the Bolan magic. In the crucial early weeks of the single's release Marc and Mickey were invited to record the first of five prime time sessions for the BBC, securing priceless exposure for both the single and the upcoming album. As result 'Ride A White Swan' entered the Top 40 on October 31, but it would be 11 long weeks before it glided up to the number 2 spot.

As sales gathered momentum, Marc was confronted with unquestionable evidence of his changing fortunes and shifting audience demographic on the 'ten shilling tour' of the UK which June had arranged for October and November to capitalise on the single's success. The 'heads' were now unquestionably in the minority. Every song was greeted with cries of 'Marc! Marc!' and even tuning up brought squeals of delight.

"I couldn't believe it the first time I went out on stage and saw all those little white faces. No one is going to convince me that their enthusiasm for Rex is a bad thing. If there is going to be any revolution in pop, it must come from the young people and, if you ignore them, you are cutting yourself off from the life-supply of the rock music force."

Marc's new publicist, the indefatigable B.P. Fallon, witnessed the first incident of fan mania at Nottingham's Albert Hall on October 9, the first night of the tour.

"That's when the rock and roll tide turned and Boley started becoming a Rock and Roll icon. We talked about it after the gig. It was an inexplicable feeling."

Sales forecasts indicated 'Swan' would climb higher in the first week of November which convinced the producers of BBC TV's chart show, *Top of the Pops*, to invite T. Rex for what would be the first of three appearances on November 12. A two and a half minute spot on the only national pop show broadcast on British TV at that time, practically guaranteed a hit. All the acts had to do was stand on their marks and mime to the pre-recorded track. Now only a strike by BBC cameramen, the Musicians' Union

or a distracting 'trendy' routine by Pan's People stood between Marc Bolan and certain stardom.

Sometimes it takes a seemingly insignificant detail to make all the difference between a success and a sensation. That final touch came from Marc's new personal assistant and stylist, Chelita Secunda, playing fairy godmother by sprinkling a tear of glitter under Bolan's eyes just moments before he went before the cameras. It was a spur of the moment decision, an inspired final touch, and a foretaste of an entire musical fashion trend that would be known as Glam Rock. She had no idea what she'd started.

Actress and singer Toyah Wilcox was 12 years old when she turned on the TV that Thursday evening and caught her first sight of a new star.

"Here was a man with corkscrew hair, with eye makeup, a hint of lip gloss and a glitter tear drop. And in that moment my very strict, almost Victorian, upbringing changed forever."

The very next day she rushed out and bought the single, her first, feeling very grownup now that she could go into a record store and choose something she wanted and could pay for with her own money. "I was only allowed to play it in my bedroom where I had a little Dansette and would dance around the bedroom manically trying to get rid of my pre-teen energy and wondering how I was going to marry Marc Bolan!"

Her experience was typical of tens of thousands of pre-teens the length and breadth of Britain that winter. "He broke the mould and for me part of that rebellion was that he dared to be quite feminine. Woah! He wears makeup, he wears satin, he's gentle in the way he speaks. It was a very gentle rebellion, a very poetical rebellion. Growing up in Birmingham where men were very butch and had very long, unclean hair and then Bolan came along and you could tell here was a man who smelt of carnations and roses and wrote poetry. Was it any wonder we were completely bowled over by him?"

Bolan, as astute and self-aware as he was, had no idea the impact he had made on a generation. Toyah and her friends were not the only girls to wash their hands of their greasy denim-clad boyfriends and set their sights on a more sensitive guys ("If a boy looked like Marc, he was heavily in!"). Nor was she the only person of that generation to attribute their decision to pursue an artistic career to the inspiration they found in Bolan's image, attitude and music. "Bolan allowed me to make that journey. He gave me the right to my individuality. I owe it all to Bolan."

That sentiment would be echoed by artists as diverse as Marc Almond, Boy George, Morrissey and The Ramones to name but a few who were turned on by the image and the sound and couldn't care less what the words meant. "Nobody understood the lyrics," Morrissey admitted. "That was never important. He didn't know what he was singing about, I'm sure. It just sounded good."

Bolan, too, was seduced by his own image and once Chelita introduced him to designers Zandra Rhodes and John Lloyd he found the creation of his new look as exciting as making hits. Defending his use of make-up he reminded interviewers that women have always preferred sensitive romantic men. Who was the greatest star of the silent screen, he asked them? Rudolph Valentino and he wasn't exactly butch, was he?

"People are really works of art and if you have a nice face you may as well play about with it. It gets boring otherwise. Two hundred years ago men covered themselves with something scented or wore powdered wigs and faces. If someone is prudish enough not to realise that it's all been done before they're very stupid."

Within days of that first *TOTP* appearance, 'Ride a White Swan' was blasting out of every boutique and record store the length and breadth of Britain. Bolan's time had come.

"'Ride a White Swan' is another 'Summertime Blues',' wrote Chris Welch in *Melody Maker*. "(It) cunningly recaptures the drive and simplicity of late-fifties pop."

Marc had made what could be considered a dry run for 'Swan' during the *Beard of Stars* sessions when he recorded a deliberately frivolous pop parody, 'Oh Baby', partly for fun and partly to prove to himself that he could write a blatantly commercial song if he wanted to. The Tyrannosaurus Rex version was never released, but just for kicks Marc gave the song to Visconti who put his own vocals to a new backing track and released it on the Bell label under the name Dib Cochran and the Earwigs backed with a Bolan-Visconti instrumental 'Universal Love'. It was a throwaway novelty single and none of the participants were surprised when it disappeared without a trace, but the ease with which Marc had cooked it up and the fun he had had recording it planted a seed in the back of his mind which grew into a nagging doubt that he might be wasting precious time playing penniless poet to the heads. In idle moments he imagined himself on *Top of the Pops* grooving in front of a million viewers and knocking Middle of the Road and the New Seekers off the top spot with a song so simple it practically wrote itself. And then he began to wonder why he had been putting so much effort and so much of himself into records that made no impression on anyone outside the hippie community with which he was becoming increasingly at odds and had even less in common. He liked the idea of going back to Nature, but only if he could take his electric guitar and his record collection with him. He was happy to live on a diet of lentils, pulses and Romany Soup, but the thought of getting his hands grubby and growing his own food instead of nipping round to the shops was his idea of hell on Earth. And the thought of not being able to wash his hair with hot water and shampoo and have a fresh change of clothes every day was the kisser. The gypsy life was appealing only in principle. In reality he kept a distance from "the itchy people" and druggies made him distinctly uncomfortable. He had supported Steve Took when his friend was busted for possession and sent to Ashford Remand Centre because Marc saw the use of recreational drugs as a weakness of character that could be overcome with the right treatment, like shoplifting or alcoholism, but as soon as he realised that drugs were potentially lethal he came to despise addicts for their lack of self-control. As for environmental issues, he had no interest, other than a vague wish to see an end to world hunger and war, and he didn't share their sense of community, nor wish to be part of one which shared its worldly goods and its women too, no doubt. He had worked too hard to give it all away to hangers-on who told him they were all brothers and sisters under the skin. In short, he was too uptight and traditional in his values to be a good hippie. He'd had enough of their hopeless idealism and his patience was wearing thin.

He had come to an impasse and the frustration was unmistakable. 'Ride A White Swan' was to be 'make or break' for Bolan. "What I did really was a gamble, 'Either we've got to get a hit record, or I'm going to be a writer'… I was beginning to get bored with what I was doing, the way I was doing it… So I thought, 'Well, fuck it, I'm going to put it out and if it's not a hit there ain't no way that I'm ever going to get a hit record, just no way.' It was a two minute thirty second funky, snappy, toe-tapper… and also lyrically I was pleased with it… I was well prepared for it to bomb… and it was a hit in three weeks."

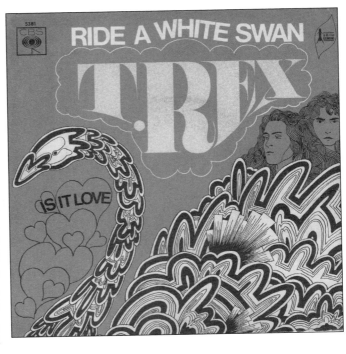

In truth, it took some months to really take off, and it almost didn't make it. In the week before Christmas it dropped out of the Top 10 despite the label's assurances that sales were increasing. Marc went ballistic and nagged June to phone *Music Week*, the industry trade paper and complain. "He didn't really need me to do the business side of things. He could have handled everything himself, but he didn't think it looked right for the star to be hassling people. A star should be distant and unapproachable. I was the front man to keep the press and record company people at bay until he was ready to charm them, but I was under no illusion that he could have handled his own affairs. He couldn't change a light bulb or manage his bank account, but he was perfectly capable of running his own empire. He just didn't like confrontation and arguments. He was the best manager he had in the early days. It was only later when it became so huge that he was forced to trust someone else to take care of the day-to-day business and even then he couldn't leave them to get on with it while he concentrated on the music as he should have done. He was always torn between being an artist, a star and a businessman and they were three distinct and incompatible aspects of his personality. He should've delegated more and concentrated on the music, but he couldn't leave the other side of the record business alone. By exposing himself to all that and trying to control all aspects of the business his optimism was eroded and cynicism and suspicion set in."

But Marc had been right to trust his instincts regarding the chart position for 'Ride a White Swan'. *Music Week* investigated and discovered there had been a miscalculation. The following week the single was back in the Top 10 and higher than before. By the end of January 1971 it stalled just short of the top spot, held off by Clive Dunn's novelty hit 'Grandad', written ironically by Marc's future bass player, Herbie Flowers. The gamble had paid off and there would be no stopping him now.

"I've suddenly tuned into that mental channel which makes a record a hit and I feel at present that I could go on writing number ones for ever. Let's face it, the majority of hits that make it are permutations of the 12-bar blues and I've found one that works."

As for accusations that he had sold out by going electric and was now dumbing down his music to seduce the pre-teens? "All we are doing is strengthening the songs… I do write quite strong melodies actually but treated acoustically, the melody isn't so recognisable… All I've done really is recreate John's Children, or what I wanted John's Children to be when I was with them at the beginning, and I'm writing exactly the same stuff as I was five years ago… I can play it now and I couldn't before… I could only play 'Desdemona'."

When the realisation hit him that after five years of false starts and false hopes he had finally realised his ambition, it was almost too much to take in.

Visconti: "When that record 'Ride a White Swan' made number two we nearly passed out. I mean, that was one moment that Marc couldn't cope with success. He lost his equilibrium for a little while there. Then all of a sudden, about two weeks later, he realised he was a star at last."

George Tremlett was one of the few journalists to see an artist with real potential beneath the pancake make-up and posing.

"I was asked to write an article for *Teenage* magazine around the time 'Ride a White Swan' came out and went to interview him in the King's Road offices of his agents Enthoven and Gaydon. The thing I remember particularly was that he was wearing a blanket that was supposed to be a cloak, but which was obviously a cut-up blanket. I liked him. I genuinely liked him because he had a gift for words. He created his own folk-lore in those early songs and that is very rare in rock. He was totally natural. He respected his audience. He put out records to sell, but he cared about what he was doing. You've got to have almost superhuman drive to succeed in the music business and I think he had that. He worked bloody hard for it.

"David Bowie certainly recognised what was there, he could see it. I don't think many of the press could. Critics can be very cruel and they really put the knife in when he suggested he was as significant a figure as Townshend, Dylan or Lennon. But given time he might have been.

"He was so many years younger than Lennon who had the education that Marc hadn't had. Lennon was an Art School graduate, so was John Paul Jones and most of Led Zeppelin, 10CC and Queen. And here was Bolan, struggled up from the backstreets and his dad a caretaker in a block of flats, no great educational advantages, fighting tooth and nail and as good as any of them.

"But he hadn't got the pieces together yet. He had an instinctive ability for structuring songs, but he didn't have any interest in politics or current affairs and he had no serious emotional issues to express, so his lyrics appeared very superficial compared with those of his contemporaries. Bolan had a comparatively easy and comfortable life growing up, so he hadn't suffered the pain of loss that so many of rock's greatest songwriters exorcise through their songs. And though he was astute when it came to manipulating the media, he didn't have an understanding of the real world and what it means to struggle to survive. But he had a very realistic attitude to the music business. He accepted that artists can have flops and still survive, emerging stronger and with a greater sense of identity. He told me that one day pop musicians such as Lennon and McCartney and Neil Young would be regarded as the classical composers of their time and that even left-field 'alternative' artists like Captain Beefheart would be acknowledged as seriously as Stockhausen. It was all down to melody, he told me. The strength of their melodies would ensure their songs survived whereas the symphonic rock bands would be forgotten because their music had little melodic content. Such statements annoyed the serious music journalists, but he was proven right."

Other journalists were not convinced by the fey Puckish mannerisms and the talk of mysterious magical rites and levitation. Ray Connolly, author of *That'll Be the Day* and *Stardust*, was then writing for *The London Evening Standard*. He had interviewed everyone that was anyone in the music business at that time from Elvis to Hendrix, Jim Morrison, Jagger and The Beatles and was not impressed by Marc's cultivated otherworldly charm.

"I found it all rather contrived to be honest. It was a bit silly because the things he told me were patently not true. He claimed to be able to levitate, which might have wowed the young female reporters at *Fab* and *Rave* magazine, but I'd interviewed the real heavyweights and Marc just didn't measure up. I liked his music. I could see why his singles were hits and he was clearly very talented, but I didn't understand why he felt the need to put on this act with me. I said to him, 'If you can really levitate and do all these things you claim you'd learnt from a magician, then do it now in front of me'. And of course he said he wouldn't because he didn't feel like it. It was so childish. I thought he was a silly little boy in that respect anyway.

"The giants of the music industry all had one thing in common which had ensured that they outlasted the talentless manufactured acts and it wasn't talent. It was that they were all grounded. Even someone as sheltered as Elvis or as high on music and seemingly 'spaced out' as Hendrix were no fools. Hendrix had been a paratrooper and Elvis had been a truck driver so they knew the realities of life, whereas Bolan didn't seem to me to have a grip on reality. He was one of those people who thought he was a star before he became one, what we now call a wannabe, and I didn't think that was an expression of self-confidence, more a pose. He may really have believed that he was as good as Lennon and the rest, but those artists wore it lightly. Bolan felt the need to tell you how great he was and that was certain to rub hardened cynical writers like me up the wrong way. There was no one else like him for bullshit. I was also amazed at his 'front', his cheek in telling me that he was already a millionaire when he was living in a dark and dingy flat in Notting Hill Gate at the time. That's where I went to interview him and it was the kind of place a student might squat in. I remember thinking at the time that I had a better flat and I wasn't a millionaire by any means. Part of the problem might have been that John Peel oversold him and presented Marc as this uneducated genius, a true intellectual which he certainly wasn't. He picked up bits and pieces and made an interesting collage out of it, but there wasn't much beneath the surface. At the time I thought he was a little boy copying the bigger lads, but later I thought, 'No, he can do it. Now I get it'. And I felt sorry for him, having such a short career."

December 1970 had seen the release of the self-titled *T.Rex* album which peaked at number 13 in the New Year and boasted a cover that doubled as a fold-out poster of Marc and Mickey in porcelain-white face make-up. Fans didn't know whether to play it or pin it to their bedroom wall.

T.Rex was a transitional album and one that had been written and recorded in some haste judging by the high proportion of 12-bar variations on offer and the presence of two old songs, re-recordings of 'One Inch Rock' and 'The Wizard'. The latter might have justified the remake had Marc not stretched two slender verses to almost nine minutes of shamelessly self-indulgent vocal improvisation, something that could be excused in a live setting but on record tested the patience of even the most loyal fan. This was one time Tony Visconti let him down. As the producer he could have reigned in Marc's excesses and suggested that he substitute stronger songs that had been rejected or left unfinished from earlier albums. God knows, there were enough of them and all far superior to the lacklustre 'Is It Love?', 'Seagull Woman' and 'Summer Deep' which wouldn't have made the cut on *A Beard of Stars* or *Unicorn*. Even Marc had to make excuses once he realised how lightweight the album sounded in comparison to the effervescent single.

That's not to say that there were no nuggets to be had, there were more than enough to justify its release; 'Jewel' and 'Beltane Walk' were strutting woodland rock with a nod and a wink to Jimmy McCracklin's 'The Walk' and numerous other R&B sides of the forties and fifties, 'Suneye', 'The Time of Love Is Now', 'The Visit' (a dry run for 'Cosmic Dancer') and the coquettish 'Diamond Meadows' seemed to have been drawn from the same wishing well as 'Dove' and 'Great Horse', but the lyrics were, on the whole, undeniably slight compared with the rich imagery of the earlier offerings.

But the real problem, and one which Marc readily acknowledged, was that it was a rock album, but one sorely lacking the presence of a rock band. Without the muscle that a real rhythm section would have provided several of the leaner tracks sounded anaemic and undeveloped, a deficiency which is compounded by Marc's overly prissy diction that veers toward self-parody.

It hasn't aged as well as the four 'legitimate' Tyrannosaurus Rex albums but at the time it received glowing reviews.

"People may argue that T. Rex's sound is no longer mystic and pure, but I for one am thankful it's not," cooed Penny Valentine in *Sounds*. "The former was getting a little jaded around the edges...not to say boring."

Disc and Music Echo called it "superb" but assured readers that "T.Rex haven't gone over to pure rock. There are still lovely peaceful numbers with Marc's beautiful lyrics."

"Beautiful" was the word with which *Melody Maker*'s Ray Hollingworth chose to use to sum up his reaction to the Prelude, 'The Children of Rarn', which he described as "a flying number, hovering over history and yet flying towards a scientific dream". When Hollingworth had returned to Earth he concluded it was a "valid rock album" which he predicted would make Bolan "exceedingly big in 1971".

Record Mirror noted, "the influence of early rock and roll and R&B is very much to the fore. But through all the changes, T.Rex remain a very individual band."

This was all very welcome, but without a permanent bass player and drummer Marc couldn't take the next logical step.

"I was overdubbing like mad on all the records and I wasn't getting the feeling I wanted."

Marc Bolan WAS T.Rex. It was the brand name he chose for the gender bending bump 'n' grind that he originated and dressed up in satin 'n' tat for the early seventies pop party they called Glam Rock. But without bass player Steve Currie, drummer Bill Legend and, to a much lesser extent, Mickey Finn, the eleven Top 10 singles (four of them number ones) and three hit albums he made at the peak of his powers would not have had the sensual swagger that made them so seductive. Currie's sinewy bass lines locked into Legend's deceptively simple back beat to create a laidback groove that gave Bolan the space to strut and swagger, pout and preen as he played the two penny prince of panache, the self-styled saviour of pop. And overseeing the creation of that inimitable sound was Tony Visconti, the unofficial fifth member of T.Rex who was able to recreate the hot-wired vibe of the early Sun sides that Marc was striving to replicate in the spring of 1971. Bolan was both the motivator and innovator, but he needed the band to earth his irrepressible energy and give his songs a discernible shape and momentum.

In November 1970 Currie had spotted an intriguing advert in the back pages of *Melody Maker*, "Bass player wanted to augment guitarist and percussionist". It didn't name the band or give a P.O. Box but invited all interested parties to a school hall near the Elephant and Castle in South London which gave Steve the impression that it must be another "Mickey Mouse outfit", the kind that he had been wasting his hopes on for the past five years. But as he had to drive down to the capital from his home in Hull to audition with Manfred Mann that same day, he thought he might as well check out the "Mickey Mouse" act while he was at it.

Marc's new publicist, B.P.Fallon, remembered that "all kinds of real dorks" had applied, but that Steve Currie made an immediate impression, being polite and so easy-going that no one was sure whether he wanted the job or not. He was a highly competent musician and was able to fit in with whatever Marc demanded of him. After jamming for 20 minutes he was told "we'll give you a call" and left, thinking no more about it. Back home in Hull he received a call from Tony Visconti asking if he'd consider joining, but Steve confessed he didn't care too much for the "jingle-jangle" acoustic music that he'd heard from Tyrannosaurus Rex and was still keeping his options open with Manfred Mann. But Tony knew a good bass player when he heard one, being a more than competent bassist himself, and wouldn't let it rest.

Steve: "He took me down to watch Marc and Mickey play a couple of gigs and I could tell something was missing; that they needed a tight rhythm section behind them for the kind of numbers they were doing.

"To be honest, I didn't really want to join them. There was such an aura around Marc; I thought he was some kind of a freak and I just couldn't imagine myself working with him at all."

But the next day, over a cup of jasmine tea at Blenheim Crescent, Marc played Steve a batch of new songs and reassured him that the old acoustic days were over, that T.Rex were going to be "a funky little rock and roll band". Those were the magic words Steve was waiting to hear. He took the gig and the next day married his girlfriend on the promise of a steady wage of 30 quid a week, £50 per gig and double that for recording sessions. He joined Marc and Mickey on stage for the first time at the Civic Hall, Guildford, on Tuesday November 24th.

Bill Legend was offered the same deal when he accepted the drummer's job at the end of February 1971, although he got an unexpected bonus in the form of a new name. His real surname had been Fifield, but Bolan rechristened him Legend after the band that he'd been in, a band produced by Visconti. It was Visconti who had brought the Barking-born drummer and former Sunday school teacher in for the January 21 recording session at Advision when Marc, Mickey and Steve had stalled attempting to record their new single as a three-piece. It was clear from the first run-through that 'Hot Love' wouldn't come to life without drums, but once Bill was installed behind the kit it was patently obvious that they could never record a single without drums again. It was so easy and felt so good that they immediately put down the backing track for another 12-bar variation, 'Woodland Rock', after a couple of run-throughs. And that, bar some editing and overdubs, was the flip side taken care of in the time it took Marc to scribble the lyrics on the back of a track sheet. A typical Tyrannosaurus Rex-styled outtake, 'King of the Mountain Cometh' was paired with it and the second T.Rex maxi-single was in the can.

Just prior to mixing, Marc took a call from ex-Turtles singers Howard Kaylan and Mark Volman (aka Flo and Eddie) who were in town with Frank Zappa for the *200 Motels* tour. They were promptly invited down to the studio to add backing vocals to 'Hot Love' but not until Frank's after-gig party wound up around dawn. The pair had first hooked up with Bolan in September '69 when the Turtles and Tyrannosaurus Rex shared a bill at the Grande Ballroom in Detroit. Back stage they discovered a mutual affection for the Marx Brothers and so when Howard and Mark came to England the following year they offered to sing backing vocals on the 'T.Rex' album.

Volman: "He kept telling us he was going to be super big."

Kaylan: "Oh yeah, now Marc isn't one of the most humble guys we ever met, but neither are we, so that gave us a really good rapport."

Volman: "Marc baby knows that he didn't have a hit record until we sang on his records!"

Kaylan: "He knows that WE made him everything that he is. So everything has worked out real well." (Much laughter). "A very shrewd little elf, very shrewd."

Flo and Eddie were to feature on the *Electric Warrior* and *Slider* albums, where their West Coast harmonies added a translucent sheen, but they found themselves unavailable after they realised that Bolan expected them to continue making a guest appearance on his albums for free, after which Marc and Visconti dubbed the falsetto parts.

Events were now moving so fast that nobody had thought to make an official offer to Bill to join the band. He was still gainfully employed as a graphic designer when T.Rex performed 'Hot Love' on *Top of the Pops* in mid-February leaving Mickey to mime behind the kit. A month later it was number one and would remain there, repulsing all challengers for an incredible six weeks.

'Hot Love' was a flawless gem in pop's crown and one that Elvis would have given his last pink Caddy to cover. In fact, the "Take it out on me mamma" middle 8 break was pure Elvis (and if it wasn't, it ought to have been). However, the real masterstroke was the tagged on singalong coda which was a blatant imitation of 'Hey Jude'. Bolan was sampling snippets and soundbites from the rock and roll songbook long before the terms were coined and retro became fashionable and he was doing it with a wink that defied the critics to condemn him. It was good time bubblegum boogie and anyone who reproached the new prince of pop was showing their age.

'Hot Love' was aimed squarely at a younger demographic, the so-called 'teenyboppers' who didn't remember The Beatles, couldn't understand the prog rockers and considered The Rolling Stones too old and ugly to interest them. As the irresistible chorus rolled on wrapped in languorous strings, a seamless blend of single-note harmonies and crisp handclaps, Bolan assured his listeners this was 'Cosmic Rock', but it bore no relation to the greasy thumbed space anthems that their longhaired elder brothers listened to. It was as smooth and sweet as a brandy and coke with the guitar blended into the strings and a break so brief that it couldn't be considered a solo. As for the lyrics, there was nothing that would tax the intellect of a twelve-year-old. They were delivered in a refined tone that was the musical equivalent of a fragrant note passed from the back of the class by a shy, sensitive boy who'd read poetry and whose intentions were strictly honourable – no awkward fumbling behind the bike sheds with the "twopenny prince" in his "Persian gloves". This was a crush that could never be consummated and that made Marc Bolan all the more desirable. There was the only merest hint of sweaty sex in the orgasmic gasps of the final verse which made it even more alluring to girls just awakening to their own sexuality and desperate to save themselves for the 'right kind of boy', one who wouldn't just use them and move on. Bolan projected the image of the 'right kind of boy', one in whom they could confide their secret desires, albeit in their dreams.

Nina Myskow, editor of the biggest selling teen weekly, *Jackie*, recognised Marc's cute and cheeky boyish appeal as her reader's ideal and agreed to pay an enormous sum to secure the rights to publish a three-part double-page poster in successive issues of the magazine. Everybody, it seemed, wanted a piece of Marc Bolan and some were prepared to pay a great deal for it.

"Chart cert," declared *Record Mirror* in their gushing review of 'Hot Love'. "Bound to do as well, if not better than 'Ride A White Swan'," agreed *Sounds*. "I'm sure you'll feel compelled to sing along," raved the *NME* and *Melody Maker* concurred. "Bolan rushes back into the chart battle with a sound to appeal to all pop purists."

But not everyone was seduced by the remodelled Rex. John Peel had been overjoyed at 'Ride A White Swan's' success, but was 'lukewarm' to the follow up, despite a magazine claim that he cried when it reached number one. He saw it as evidence that his old friend was prepared to dumb down and dilute the music that had once been so unique to secure commercial success. But for Bolan it was nothing more than a logical progression. He had no illusions about creating great art.

"I wanted to write a rock record – I know it's exactly like a million other songs, but I hope it's got a little touch of me in it too. It was done as a happy record and I wanted to make a 12-bar record a hit, which hasn't been done since 'High Heel Sneakers' really… I've never done anything in music that I didn't honestly believe in so I don't believe I've ever let any of my fans down… had I not done what I did when I did it, I would probably have ended up as another James Taylor, playing acoustic and singing gentle little songs."

Ironically, it was singer-songwriters that American audiences craved at the very moment Marc and the band flew over to play their first US tour as a group. The month long tour, which began in Detroit on April 9, proved to be an anti-climax for everyone except Bill and Steve who were thrilled to be playing in the States in medium-sized auditoria and staying in first class hotels. But for Marc it was hard going as the largely unresponsive audiences greeted Britain's new sensation with little enthusiasm and reviewers carped on about the lack of virtuosity that they expected from a band supporting the likes of Mountain and Johnny Winter.

"T.Rex's music is built on the contrast between Marc Bolan's expressive stylized unreal vocals, his inhumanly electronic (sic) guitar technique and the adamantly idiotic rhythms of the percussion section. The great mystery of the group is how they can create a head-splitting wall of sound, with no appreciable melody, and simultaneously maintain that there is a certain order...even an obscure kind of beauty." Nancy Erlich, *Billboard*.

The Americans were tiring of heavy bands after three years of psychedelia and heavy blues rock and were turning in increasing numbers to introspective artists such as Joni Mitchell, Don McLean and Neil Young as an antidote to late sixties excess. Matters were not helped by the fact that the band was still being billed at some venues as Tyrannosaurus Rex because notification of the change in name had come too late for the promoters. Fans who turned up to hear *A Beard of Stars* might have accepted a bass and some wig-out weirdness on 'Elemental Child', but a drummer was too much, too soon. They didn't cry 'Judas', they just left quietly. It was a fitting end to the Tyrannosaurus Rex era.

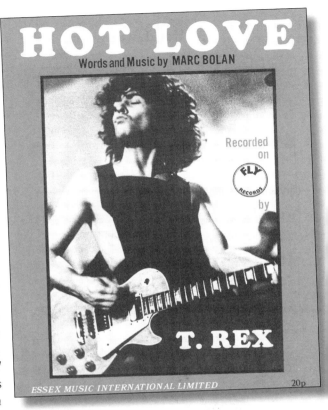

BOLAN

The rise to fame of a 1972 Super Star — in words and pictures

✱

A Melody Maker special

25p

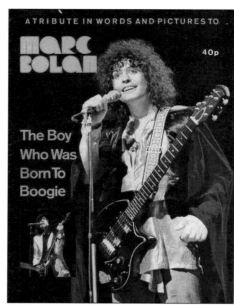

A TRIBUTE IN WORDS AND PICTURES TO

MARC BOLAN

40p

The Boy Who Was Born To Boogie

Nr. 34

C 1917 C

BRAVO

Michael Schanze bringt Schwung ins Fernsehen:

Selten so gelacht!

Foto-Love-Story:

Wenn beim ersten Mal die Liebe fehlt

Großes Farbfoto: **Christian Anders**

25 Fragen-25 Antworten:

Wie gut kennst Du Ryan O'Neal?

Marc Bolan

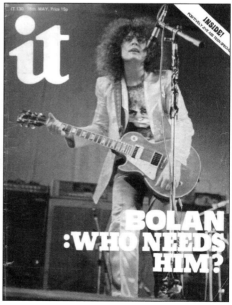

IT 130. 18th. MAY. Price 15p

it

INSIDE!

BOLAN :WHO NEEDS HIM?

Chapter 13
Electric Warrior

Tony Visconti was homesick. He had not been back to Brooklyn since he had emigrated to England in 1967, so when T.Rex flew out for the first dates of their US tour on April 6, 1971, he took the opportunity to ask Denny Cordell for a long overdue vacation. Tony missed his family and was more than happy at the thought of not having to spend the next fortnight sitting in a smoke-filled studio. But even his mother's Italian cooking was not enough to keep the producer away from meeting up with the band when they arrived in New York to play three nights at the Fillmore East, a showcase event arranged by their new American label, Warner Reprise. Backstage Visconti learned that Howard Kaylan and Mark Volman had booked the group into Media Sound Studios on 57th Street with no particular plan in mind other than to give their English friends the opportunity to try out a top flight America studio. He made it known that if there were a prospect of a serious recording session, he would like to be in the control room. In this casual manner work began on what would later be recognised as one of rock's classic albums, *Electric Warrior*.

The first couple of tracks had actually been laid down at Trident Studios in London on March 16, but there was no intention at that time of stockpiling songs for the next LP. Marc was keen to record while the songs were still fresh and excited him. He was afraid that if he waited until he had an album's worth his enthusiasm for them would fade.

He took a lined school exercise book with him wherever he went, crammed with lyrics and chord sequences that he would try out whenever the band found themselves in the studio. Visconti has said that Marc would open the book when a new series of sessions began and work methodically through it until they had enough tracks. Then he would shut the book until the time came to record the next LP. There was never a master plan or overall concept when it came to making T.Rex albums.

Song writing was effortless and as natural as breathing and the ideas came flowing out of him. But when asked to describe the creative process, or identify the sources of inspiration he could be as vague as a lovesick poet. "There are magic mists within certain chords. You play a C major chord and I hear 25 melodies and symphonies up here. I've just got to pull one out. It's all there. There's no strain."

That autumn he told *Beat Instrumental*: "I play about for a couple of hours before I move into new dimensions where I'm being creative. I record everything then." Which was his way of saying that he did what all great songwriters and composers do to get the juices flowing – they begin by playing random chords or melodies in a relaxed, distracted fashion until they settle into an almost meditative state. With the rational part of their mind asleep at the wheel, the intuitive aspect is then free to take over and channel ideas

Setting up in Rosenberg studios, Copenhagen March 1972. Note the Dallas Rangemaster effects box on top of the guitar amp with which Bolan created the distinctive guitar sound on 'Electric Warrior', 'The Slider' and 'Tanx'. (Photo Jorgen Angel)

which the more fancifully-minded might interpret as a gift from the gods. In short, the greatest artists are those who don't think too much about it.

Bill Legend was on hand when inspiration came unexpectedly in New York while they were killing time in their hotel before a sound check.

"Marc invited me to his room to hear a new idea and when he finished he asked me what I thought of it. I said it had possibilities. That was 'Get It On'. Then he asked if I had any drums in my room so we could work on it and I remembered I had a snare that I was repairing, so I went to get that and then we ran through it, working out the structure and breaks so we could record it the next chance we had. But it was very rare to have a chance to try things out with him like that. We almost always heard songs for the first time in the studio and had a few run-throughs while Tony was miking up the instruments and tweaking the controls before a take.

"Marc wanted that live feel like the old rock and roll records had in the fifties. He thought that it would kill the energy to build a track up one instrument at a time like a lot of the bands were beginning to do then because they had more tracks than they really needed and so much time to spend in the studio. Marc was of a mind to bang it down and tart it up later. And that suited us. We rarely needed more than half a dozen takes and more often than not two or three would get it.

"There's a fantastic atmosphere on *Electric Warrior* because the backing tracks were done live with the band facing each other and bouncing off each other. We had to keep our wits about us and watch for his visual cues. Marc was jumping about, banging his Cuban heels on the wooden floor and giving little cries of delight which you can hear in the background. He was just bumbling over with energy. You can't replicate that when you record the instruments individually. It's just not real."

When they returned to England with the tapes on May 3, 'Hot Love' was half way through its six-week reign at the top of the charts. It was selling 28,000 copies a day, every day. Both Warners and Fly were eager to get a new album in the stores while interest was running high. Bolan was beginning his dizzying ride on what Ray Davies called The Money-Go-Round, that relentless cycle of recording, touring and promotion that record companies and management schedule on the artist's behalf, often years in advance. The band had barely time to catch their breath before they began a 14-date UK tour. So Visconti was left to trawl through the tapes with engineers Roy Thomas Baker (future producer of Queen) and Martin Rushent (later producer for the Buzzcocks and Human League) until Marc could take time off to add his vocals and extra guitar parts.

Whatever a mojo was, Marc worked it hard on *Electric Warrior*, an album that oozed self-confidence. From the sultry Creole shuffle of 'Mambo Sun' to the swirling strings and spiralling sax that chased the fade on 'Rip Off', the mid-tempo tracks trucked along in a groove that seemed machine-tooled to fit his thin reedy vocals, while the raunchier numbers, 'Jeepster', 'The Motivator' and 'Get It On' were lean, mean and hungry, the way rock used to be. 'Get It On' rode on one of the most readily identifiable riffs in rock, at once sensuous and sophisticated. The guitars were chunky, tastefully distorted, but never leaden, the parts pared down to the bone and the lyrics likewise. Marc kept his solos short and sweet and they were all the more effective for it.

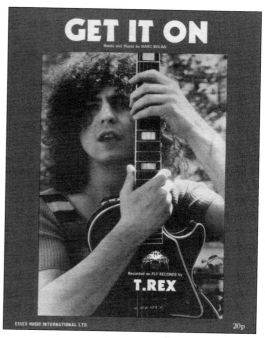

Even the slow-burning 'Lean Woman Blues' smoulders with an earthy intensity with amp buzz, cable crackles and all manner of sonic debris retained in the mix to add authenticity.

"We've got a really raunchy guitar sound and recorded them in a way that they can't now be altered. There is no way I can blow the energy on them, by looking at them later and being in a different mood."

Visconti had formulated the trademark T.Rex sound, but it was Marc's choice of valve-powered Vox Supreme and Vampower MK1A 100-watt amps that shaped his fat and funky signature guitar sound. The valves' amps gave him a much warmer distortion than the transistor amplifiers which were becoming increasingly popular in the early seventies, though he was to switch to HH amps a year later for *The Slider* because HH offered a far longer sustain. The combination of the low output of the open coil pickups on his 1958 Gibson Les Paul guitar ensured he squeezed out plenty of bite for the licks and solos and could also grind out a thick wad of sound for the staccato stabs and sustained power chords. Although he owned a couple of dozen guitars (including a Burns Flyte, Gibson Flying V and a Veleno aluminium guitar plus several acoustics - a Gibson Hummingbird, a Gibson J-160E and an Epiphone acoustic) he rarely used anything other than a late sixties Olympic Fender Strat or a Gibson Les Paul[1] in the Visconti era. The secret components in the chain were two Dallas Rangemaster effects boxes which sweetened the signal coming out of the amp giving greater separation so that power chords had both weight and clarity and didn't blur into a sticky morass. Bolan bought them because he had seen Clapton use one, but Tony Iommi of Black Sabbath and Ritchie Blackmore of Deep

---

1 *In 2011, the Gibson Guitar Corporation finally acknowledged one of their most celebrated customers by issuing a limited edition customised Marc Bolan edition as part of their Signature series.*

Purple also swore by these small silver boxes which had an input jack, an on/off button and volume control in the front and an output jack at the back. Marc also fed his guitars through a series of effects pedals including a Dallas-Arbiter fuzzbox, a Vox Wah-Wah pedal, an MXR Blue Box, an Electro-Harmonix Screaming Tree and a WEM echo unit. But his choice of guitars, amps and effects only coloured the sound. His playing technique determined the distinctive character he created by the way that he played chords and the vibrato he wrung from single notes. He may have had a limited repertoire of licks, but he used them to tremendous effect on *Electric Warrior*.

Steve Currie: "He was an amazing rhythm guitarist. If you listen to 'Hot Love' and 'Get It On', they're classics of really four to the bar straight foot-tappers."

And though Mickey Finn may have seemed little more than a visual foil at the time, his conga patterns were as essential to the trademark T.Rex sound as Visconti's arrangements. When upfront in the mix and intermingling with the drums, as on the semi acoustic 'Planet Queen' and 'The Motivator', the congas gave the rhythm tracks a supple spine for the guitars to groove to.

Top flight session musicians were brought in to add polish to the intentionally rough and ready backing tracks. Ian McDonald of King Crimson added rasping sax, Burt Collins a mellow flugelhorn and Rick Wakeman garnished 'Get It On' with cascading piano runs before the ubiquitous string section was brought in to paper over the cracks. But there was no danger of the songs being smothered in saccharine sweet violins. Visconti shared Marc's taste for the 'pocket symphonies' of Brian Wilson, Kim Fowley and Phil Spector, all of whom used orchestration sparingly. It was agreed he would keep the string parts simple and untreated so they would sound as natural as the acoustic guitars.

Visconti's scores were an integral element of the T.Rex sound and as vital to Bolan as George Martin's contribution had been to The Beatles.

"If I have a special idea on how I want to use a song I'm quite dictatorial, but if I don't, I give the song to Tony and see what comes out of it. 'Cosmic Dancer' was a track I did that way and I thought the arrangements were amazing."

On 'Cosmic Dancer', one of the album's four acoustic numbers, the strings are largely understated, leaving the track with room to breathe and build slowly, the droning cellos interjecting with staccato phrases that mimic guitar licks so that even this introspective acoustic song retains an edgy vitality. Ethereal backing vocals and flecks of backward guitar add to the soft focus setting while Marc delivers even his most off the cuff lines with conviction. ("What's it like to be a loon? I liken it to a balloon.") For the fans who hung on his every word, such statements sounded as profound as poetry, even if they didn't hold up to closer scrutiny. But the critics who claimed that he was neither significant nor sincere had missed the point. Bolan was pop's Mad Hatter (a character he would adopt for the next album cover and in a sequence for the concert film *Born to Boogie*), a sensualist and surrealist for whom the sound of words was to be savoured. Bolan was not as self-consciously clever as Dylan, nor as caustic as Lennon, but he enjoyed twisting words into funny shapes and reducing lyrics to the level of a nursery rhyme if it scanned.

The problem with the stream of consciousness method is that it throws up a good deal of undigested rubbish along with the occasional nugget and it takes a critical eye to sift the 24-carat gems from the clinker. Unfortunately, Marc frequently accepted the first rhyme to pop into his head and made no distinction between randomly generated nonsense ("Mountains of the moon remind me of my spoon" – 'Rip Off') and inspired abstract expressionism ("You're built like a car, got a hubcap diamond star halo" – 'Get It On'). The 'diamond star', incidentally, referred to the sun glinting off the chrome. It wasn't an image that he consciously crafted. It popped into his mind as he followed a train of thought and described the image that arose spontaneously.

Even during the glam rock years Marc repeatedly referred to himself as a poet and his early lyrics are certainly rich in evocative imagery, but *Electric Warrior* reveals that he had a greater claim to being one of the most original lyricists in rock. Rock lyrics do not always have to be meaningful just so long as they scan and sound good. And Marc certainly mastered that particular art.

"Just like a car you're pleasing to behold. I'll call you Jaguar if I may be so bold." ('Jeepster') Rimbaud and Dylan Thomas would certainly have had *Electric Warrior* in their record collection had they been around in '71.

It is highly significant that *Electric Warrior* is the only Marc Bolan album that does not feature his face on the cover. The iconic sleeve, conceived by June and designed by Hipgnosis from a photo taken at the Albert Hall, Nottingham, on May 14th, distils the artist to a formless essence, an aura of primal energy plugged into a massive guitar amp as if drawing on the life force. The visual allusion to the monolith featured in Stanley Kubrick's enigmatic sci-fi movie *2001: A Space Odyssey* was intentional. In the film the smooth black stone slab appears at critical moments to trigger the next evolutionary step in mankind's journey back to the source, its appearance signalled by the opening bars of Richard Strauss' *Also Sprach Zarathustra*. The movie inspired Marc to write a song that turned out far better than it ought to have done considering its humble origins. 'Monolith' was a slow, stately hymn to cosmic consciousness which he reconstructed from the unlikeliest of sources, Gene Chandler's 1961 million-seller 'Duke of Earl'. No one else would have been so ingenuously ambitious as to assume that they could condense such a profound concept in a three-minute song using a clichéd fifties chord sequence. But carry it off he did and with some aplomb. "The throne of time is kingly, a kingly thing, from whence you know we all do begin." It was Bolan's answer to 'Space Oddity' and he couldn't wait to hear how Bowie would respond.

'Duke of Earl' wasn't the only classic oldie to be revamped. Howling Wolf's 'You'll Be Mine' provided the basis of the verses for 'Jeepster' which was branded with the Bolan trademark, a descending bass line doubled on bassoon and cellos and imagery that no Chicago bluesman could have dreamt up. "You slide so good with bones so fair, you got the universe reclining in your hair."

"We did that in New York, in the studio where Paul Simon did 'The Boxer'. And all those bits on it like 'dun dun dun bop bop' is me banging on the floor. It had a real wooden floor like a cathedral. So it's got this bit of tap dancing on it."

This time there was no mistaking the orgasmic shrieks. Bolan was getting off on the buzz of being a bona fide rock star.

"I am my fantasy. I am the 'Cosmic Dancer' who dances his way out of the womb and into the tomb on *Electric Warrior*. I'm not frightened to get up there and groove in front of six million people on TV because it doesn't look cool. That's the way I would do it at home. I'm serious about the music but I'm not serious about the fantasy…I'm just a rock and roll poet man who's just bopping around on the side… I've always been a wriggler."

In '71 few journalists on the British teen-orientated music weeklies such as *Disc* and *Record Mirror* would have been familiar with the Howling Wolf track, but everyone would have known Chuck Berry's 'Little Queenie'. For that reason Mickey suggested Marc should name check the song in the fade to 'Get It On' with the kiss off, 'Meanwhile I'm still thinking'.

"I wanted to record 'Little Queenie', but it wouldn't have worked again, so I wrote my own song to it. I put that on the end so that someone like you would know and wouldn't say, 'What a cunt, Bolan ripping off "Little Queenie"', because in the end it's only the feel of the song… The actual backing track of guitar, drums and bass, Howard (Kaylan) and Mark (Volman) and I took about ten minutes, then we double tracked which took about another five… The only thing that took time was the lead guitar track… the trouble was that I was playing too much, overplaying all the time and it took some time to work that part out. Rick Wakeman did a piano part on it too… just came in, heard it and played… took about five minutes and that was that."

Already the myth-making had begun. Soon name dropping would be routine as Marc sought to secure his place among the rock aristocracy, sales figures would be inflated to counter criticism and song writing would be reduced from a craft to a casual conveyer belt process as image management took precedence over music. Already he was referencing his own records. "I've got stars in my beard and I feel real weird." ('Mambo Sun') and self-mythologising, "I was dancing when I was twelve,"('Cosmic Dancer'). But at this point it was still playful and endearing. Within a year it would be endemic as he became seduced by his own image and self-confidence mutated into self-glorification. Nobody would worship Marc Bolan, rock idol, as ardently as Bolan himself.

And it was all so unnecessary as *Electric Warrior* and the unbroken run of Top 10 singles he knocked out between '70-'73 demonstrated that he was a force to be reckoned with, an original in a business teeming with cheap clones and imitators. He had an inimitable vocal and guitar style and a captivating way with words that enriched his songs with imagery that fascinated his fans and confounded his critics. Yet he always felt the need to be his own cheerleader as if he wouldn't be taken seriously unless he made the case

himself. He was a delightful contradiction - an original, despite his wholesale borrowing from past masters, a self-possessed media savvy star with a headline grabbing quote for every interviewer, a man who was not ashamed to admit he cried yet claimed he was not sentimental. But he was also painfully insecure, despite his success. He was obsessed with the idea that it could all be taken away from him and that fear only increased the brag and bluster that threatened to isolate him from his friends and fuelled his increasing consumption of brandy and cocaine.

Few artists handle fan adulation well, especially when they are just out of their teens themselves, and the pressure to deliver more hits only intensifies their insecurity, but if they are also insulated from reality by sycophants and advisers who feed their egos, then the descent into a drug- and alcohol-fuelled fantasy world is inevitable.

Steve Currie: "There was one particular person, close to him, who was bad for him. He created the Marc we all loved to hate; he turned Marc into a machine. He put the germ into Marc's head that he was the greatest thing since sliced bread."

Tony Visconti: "He lived and created his own environment and had everyone around him add to it. You had to nurture his fantasies and help them along. You could never burst his bubble."

Elton John, who appeared with T.Rex on the *Top of the Pops Christmas Special* that year promoting 'Get It On', put it more kindly, "He lived in a wonderful fantasy world which he never let go of."

The reviews for *Electric Warrior*, which was released on September 24, were uniformly excellent and deservedly so.

"T.Rex have never been one of my favourites, and until 'Get It On' I had more or less ignored them, but I was entirely converted when I heard the tapes of their new album… It's tougher and funkier, more energetic than I'd imagined." Martin Hayman, *Sounds*

"Bolan has so cunningly utilised a panorama of influences…that anyone who has travelled a similar path will find his head spinning from one nostalgia to the next… a finished product very much '71 and very much his own." Anon, *Sounds*

"Marc Bolan and his friends seem to be causing a great deal of upset and confusion lately. 'Boo, rubbish' is the cry, which is a shame because Marc's music is getting better all the time… *Warrior* is a quaint and curious twisting of the skeins of pop, a gathering and weaving, which makes it not in the least significant, but decidedly enjoyable." Chris Welch, *Melody Maker*

"Whether or not you feel you have a legitimate grievance that Bolan has butchered the spirit of Tyrannosaurus Rex, you must admire his composure and concede his sincerity… What Marc has done here is…draw upon the range of rock and roll influences that is the diet of any child of rock… But I'm not sure that he hasn't been a little too clever… Much as I can admire Marc for refusing to be swayed by the critics, it would be damaging if he reacted by cutting himself off and trusting only his own head." Nick Logan, *NME*

It was at this point that Marc needed the stability of genuine friends, but several of the most significant figures in his life began to fall behind.

John Peel and producer John Walters no longer felt obliged to play Bolan's records if they didn't like them. They felt they couldn't justify playing a single that didn't move them just because they had aired every record he'd sent them in the past. Marc took it as a rejection and made a point of not answering Peel's next call. An assistant informed the DJ that Marc was too busy to come to the phone. Peel didn't phone again.

Peel later admitted to mourning the passing of the Marc Bolan he had befriended in the Tyrannosaurus Rex era, but in the summer of '71 Bolan himself had no time for reflection or sentiment. He was living in the moment and the moment was pregnant with possibilities.

Chapter 14
Children of the Revolution

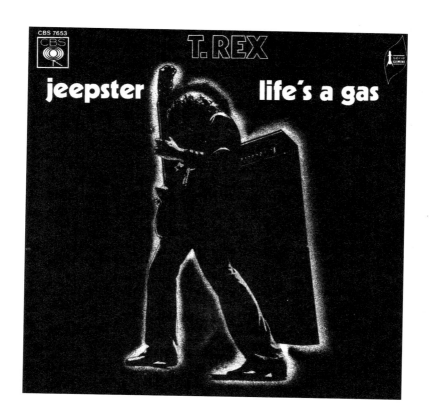

Marc Bolan might have died in Bournemouth in May 1971. It was touch and go for a while. It was the first night of the UK tour and the Winter Gardens' security guards were entirely unprepared for a full-scale riot by dozens of screaming, scratching and clawing teenage girls who trampled over each other in a frantic scramble to reach the stage. Some had come armed with scissors to cut off a lock of their idol's corkscrew curls and others were so overwrought, they didn't know what they wanted or what they were prepared to do to get it. Any one of the elderly security staff could have manhandled a fan to safety, but there were so many. It seemed as if the first ten rows had left their seats and rushed the stage and would stop at nothing to tear a piece from Marc's gold satin jacket, or rip his hair out by the roots. In desperation the security staff locked arms and braced themselves, but the hysterical horde was too much for them and the metal barriers soon gave way under the combined weight of heaving bodies and thrashing limbs spilling the girls into the orchestra pit and taking an official or two with them. Fortunately, the injuries were mostly superficial, cuts and bruises and the occasional sprained ankle or wrist. But that was just the first wave. As the uniformed staff helped the walking wounded to the First Aid station, a second wave stormed the stage and had to be held off by a dozen policemen who had been seconded just in case things got out of hand. They proved a more formidable obstruction and the girls had to content themselves with pressing against the human barricade and screeching at the top of their lungs.

And all through the din the band played on, barely audible above the ear-piercing screams.

When the last song was over the screaming didn't stop. If anything, it intensified as the fans feared they might never see their idol again and ecstatic cries gave way to wailing and sobbing. Several girls had to be treated for shock and others for injuries sustained in the scramble to capture one of the plastic tambourines Mickey had skimmed into the crowd during the encore. The band could still hear the din in the hall as they made their way backstage to the dressing room. Normally they would have wound down with a coke or beer and a cigarette, packed away their instruments and invited a small group of fans in for autographs, but there was no question of hanging around tonight. It was bedlam out there and they would have to make their exit as quickly as possible before the fans realised they weren't coming back for another encore. But already it was too late. A large group was besieging the stage door.

"It was truly frightening," Mickey told me. "And I don't scare easily! I'd heard about this violent reaction at Beatles and Stones gigs in the sixties, but of course I never imagined I might one day be in the thick of it. You think that having fans would be great, but it was too much. And some of them came with screwdrivers to steal bits off the cars. It was just madness and we were in the middle of it."

Leaving their gear behind for the roadies to take care of, Marc, Mickey, Steve and Bill huddled at the exit peering through the small glass window at the scene outside. Once the phalanx of police were in place the doors flew open and the band ran the gauntlet of girls to the waiting hire cars, leapt in and locked the doors behind them.

Mickey: "That was the worst part. Now we were trapped and the fans threw themselves on the bonnet and the roof. They were ripping the windscreen wipers off, pulling at the hubcaps and door handles and unscrewing the number plates. You couldn't just drive through them and hope they'd let go. They might get hurt. I think that's what we were frightened of the most, that someone would get hurt and it would have been our fault. We weren't frightened for ourselves; it was too unreal. But then we heard the tires bursting under the weight of the bodies and the roof started to buckle. That was when we thought we might not get out alive."

"I couldn't believe it the first time I went out on stage and saw all those little white faces" Marc Bolan (Photo Alan Mosser, Rex Features)

Fortunately, the police managed to pull off the fans and the car edged forward until they were clear and the driver could give it some gas. Back at the hotel someone came up with the brilliant idea of getting the group out while the last chord was left ringing and that became their strategy for the rest of the tour.

But even that didn't save the band from determined fans. In Newcastle, Mickey was pulled off stage and lumps of his hair ripped out, at another venue the group were besieged for an hour and a half before the police managed to clear a space through the crowd, at Bradford they had to be smuggled out in a police van and in Glasgow it took one hundred and fifty police to keep the mob at bay. By the end of the tour eleven cars had been severely damaged and four had to be written off completely, their chassis having cracked under the weight of bodies.

The scenes were repeated that summer at even larger venues during the July tour.

"Marc opened the set with an amazing solo electric guitar number using pedals and feedback," wrote *Sounds* reviewer Steve Peacock of the Lewisham Odeon show on 9th July. "I got strong memory flashes of Hendrix as he stood alone on that stage... I can't imagine anyone who could remain unmoved by it all...and while I wouldn't want rock music to be solely T.Rex, I wouldn't like to be without them."

Val Mabbs of *Record Mirror* recorded the moment Marc paused during his acoustic set to explain "how people are troubled by the direction they've taken, but how he understood."

Perhaps he did understand, but he couldn't have anticipated the snide and spiteful carping that began to appear in the press from those who envied his success.

"I'm sure a lot of Rex aficionados have found themselves wavering recently in the face of all the anti-Rex sniping," wrote supporter Nick Logan in a review of 'Get It On' for the *NME* that July. "But there is a simple cure... listen to the music... there's a lot more to this multi-textured single than space here permits me to go into."

Sounds scribe Penny Valentine agreed. "Boley does it again. I don't care a damn if people think he's sold out..." and *Record Mirror* called it "an absolute cert for the top...a giant hit".

Being essentially a singles act, T.Rex were insulated from the mainstream rock audience who liked their heroes to work up a sweat, but their paths crossed at the Weeley Festival at Clacton-on-Sea over the August bank holiday and it was not a pleasant experience for either party. It was Marc's Newport moment.

"As if following the Faces' incredible showstopping performance wasn't more than enough," wrote Roy Carr later that week in the *NME*, "T.Rex had to contend with... equipment failure and a barrage of abuse." Bolan, it has to be said, gave as good as he got. "Eventually his dissenters were silenced by Marc threatening to leave the stage... T.Rex are a strange band. When electrified they encompass the basic rudiments of rock music... They emit a naïve enthusiasm." Carr concluded, "You can't compare either Bolan or T.Rex to other bands, they are a power unto themselves and an essence that needs savouring on more than one hearing and at far better conditions than at Weeley."

Luck hadn't played much of a part in Bolan's success. It was mainly down to hard graft, talent and the support of influential insiders such as John Peel. But he did have one incredible piece of luck at the most critical point in his career. As 'Get It On' (backed by 'There Was A Time' and 'Raw Ramp' on the flip) soared up the charts to secure his second British number one in July 1971 and become his only million-seller in the states, Marc learnt that his contract with Fly was due for renewal. He couldn't have been in a better bargaining position if he'd planned it. But he needed someone to negotiate on his behalf, someone sharp enough to squeeze every percentage point he could get by playing all interested parties off against each other. Someone who could play the game of brinkmanship without blinking.

31-year-old Epsom-born public school graduate Tony Secunda had a reputation as one of the toughest managers in the business. He had guided the careers of The Moody Blues, The Move and Procol Harum and was a close associate of Denny Cordell. It was Secunda who had taken Roy Wood and his Brummie band to Carnaby Street the day they arrived in the capital and had them kitted out in sharp suits. It was Secunda who encouraged Roy Wood to write hit singles. And it was Secunda who staged the publicity stunts which garnered the group a lot of free press. He dreamed up a contract-signing photo session that was guaranteed to get the press queuing round the block as the band put their signatures on the back of a half-naked girl. And he thought up the headline grabbing 'pornographic postcard' which landed the band in the High Court defending a libel action brought by Prime Minister Harold Wilson. The band lost the case and Roy Wood forfeited his royalties for 'Flowers In The Rain' to charity in perpetuity. They sacked Secunda soon after. He was high risk, but he made almost all of his clients very rich and that prospect appealed to Bolan.

When Cordell and Platz invited Bolan and Enthoven to lunch at the Venezia restaurant in Soho in September '71 to discuss terms for the renewal of the contract they had no idea there was a silent partner hovering in the wings. After the deal had been agreed, Platz received a phone call from Secunda informing him that he was now acting as Marc's manager and that the deal they'd just hammered out was off. Secunda demanded an excessive royalty that Essex Music couldn't justify under their agreement with EMI and he was adamant that the only territory on offer was the UK. Separate deals would be made for other countries. Platz had no choice but to pull out. Secunda had forced his hand and was now free to go straight to EMI and negotiate a very favourable licensing deal which guaranteed that Marc would own the copyright in his master tapes and pocket all the publishing royalties. He would have his own label, The T.Rex Wax Co, a production company to be named Wizard Artists, and a publishing company, Warrior Music Projects. It appeared to be a deal to die for, one which other artists could only look on with envy as Bolan consolidated his supremacy in the charts, in the concert halls and now the boardroom.

Secunda: "We sat down and totted up all the thousands of dollars that would come from different sources – and he just couldn't believe it… Bolan's eyes just got wider and wider."

Instead of developing a long-term relationship with David Enthoven, John Gaydon and publisher David Platz, Marc had opted for short-term wealth and the chance to control every aspect of the monster he had created. Music industry insiders whispered that it might prove a case of 'too much too soon' and that there was always a danger that the beast might turn round and bite back.

But from here on Marc was riding high and wouldn't look back, unless it was for inspiration.

Following a short trip to Germany to appear on pop shows *Starparade* and *Beatclub*, the band played a couple of concerts in Holland before kicking off a 15-date UK tour on October 18th, their third British tour of the year.

"Magic is a hard thing to summon up for a Sunday after lunch afternoon audience," conceded Penny Valentine in *Sounds*. "So if anyone deserves the award of the month, it's Marc Bolan… Musically and visually T.Rex can't go wrong and Bolan is an ace at giving a crowd of kids who were in nappies during the original rock era all that knee-trembling, hot-panted feel that Presley, Holly, Chuck Berry and others brought to that age."

Martin Marriott of *Disc* was also won over by the band who had to battle on above the deafening noise of screaming teens.

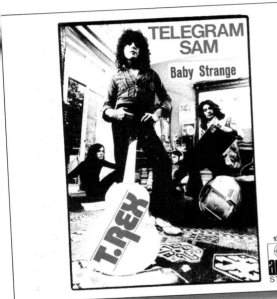

"In days past when a group found themselves with an audience of ravers and dancing fans, the music very often suffered. But not so in the case of T.Rex… T.Rex opened with 'Cadillac', a wild rocker, and from then, until the 'Summertime Blues' encore a happy madness reigned."

The day after the first part of the tour ended Bolan and the band were booked on a flight to Copenhagen where they spent three days recording tracks for the next album including the proposed follow up to 'Get It On', 'Cadilac' (Marc's misspelling). On the fourth day (November 4th) they were already back in Britain for the second leg of the tour.

Marc had been advised to record abroad for tax purposes but was wary of trying out a new studio until Visconti recommended Rosenberg Studios in Denmark where he had recently recorded another English band, The Strawbs. The studio had moved to new premises in the interim, but Tony had faith in the affable in-house engineer and producer Freddy Hansson who would later work with Roy Thomas Baker and Queen.

"As soon as the group arrived we went to work at full speed," Freddy told me. "Marc was very eager to get on and get his ideas down as fast as possible. He wasn't rushing it, but he was so full of energy and enthusiasm, it was hard work to keep up with him. But the whole band was hot and that ensured those first tracks were really powerful.

The studio was small. Just a low ceilinged room with dampening on the walls at one end where we could get a dead sound and bare bricks and plaster at the other so we could turn the amps round and use the reflection off the bare surfaces. I had to work with the limitations of the environment by placing mikes in unusual places to create space and natural echo, though sometimes we would use the garage next door to get a certain sound on the drums or guitars. And I had a mixer that I'd built myself. All that added to the distinctive sound that no one can recreate exactly today, even with expensive effects.

'The Slider' sounds special because of the musicians who played on it, the way they were recorded and the place where that recording was made. It's unique.

We decided to saturate the tape to get that warm overloaded 70s rock sound that you can't get with digital recording today. We had the meters in the red when we were recording the backing tracks so they would sound raw and live, but with 'sweeteners' over the top like sax, keyboards and strings. So 'Telegram Sam', 'Metal Guru' and all those classic tracks sounded on the surface like teen pop singles, but underneath they are aggressive rock and really kick.

Marc was serious when he was working but he was also very funny. And there was no 'I'm the boss and you'd better do as I say,' at all. He was always taking care to keep the other musicians happy. He would call a break and suggest they all have something to eat, or he would send his driver out to get chilled champagne for them. He was careful not to work them too hard because he knew he would get the best out of them if they were well fed and had time to relax. It was important to him to keep them in a good mood. I didn't see what they did when they went upstairs to the rest area as I had to stay behind with Visconti and work on the tracks, reducing (bouncing) two or more guitar parts or double tracked vocals onto one track to free up some more for future overdubs and tweaking the sound using compression and gating so that the extraneous noise from the amps didn't leak onto the track - that sort of thing. So I can't say if they were real good friends but they had to like each other otherwise they couldn't have worked that well together.

They had a routine but it was very flexible. They might start work at 10 in the morning one day and finish at 5, 6, 7 or even later, but the next day they might decide not to start again until the afternoon. It depended if Marc was eager to get something new down on tape, or whether he was still working on something. He had come with finished songs and fragments of others which would either come together in the studio while they were running through them, or he would go back to the hotel in the evening and complete them. There were probably a few tracks that he wrote from scratch during the sessions but you can't rely on writing a whole album in the studio, that would put any artist under intolerable pressure and it isn't practical. So he had quite a lot of the album written when he arrived.

Once they had set up, he would stand in the main room and play through each song on the electric guitar so the others could learn the chord changes and the structure and then they would run through them until Marc was satisfied that they had the right feel and tempo. Tony would sit on the sidelines and make the occasional suggestion and then they would record in one or two takes. It was very rare to make more than that as Marc wanted to keep it fresh and vital. He wanted it to sound as if he'd just made it up and not as if they had rehearsed and rehearsed until it was so polished that there was no life left in it. Then after the backing track was down Visconti would come up with ideas and play parts on the piano that he was thinking of writing for strings or saxophone or other instruments. But he wouldn't suggest that Marc add a middle 8 or anything to the songs. Marc knew his fans wanted a strong chorus or hook and not too many verses and no frills. And Tony respected that. But as far as arrangements and which instruments were added, it was pretty much an even split, an equal partnership between Marc and Tony. They made a very creative team. Bill and Steve would also contribute bits and pieces,

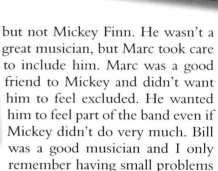

but not Mickey Finn. He wasn't a great musician, but Marc took care to include him. Marc was a good friend to Mickey and didn't want him to feel excluded. He wanted him to feel part of the band even if Mickey didn't do very much. Bill was a good musician and I only remember having small problems with the drums which were easily fixed, whereas Steve Currie never made a mistake that I can recall. He got his part right first take. Marc too, was a brilliant musician. All those guitar parts he would multi-track just blended together so well. I thought he was a fantastic guitar player. And when it came to vocals, he was deliberately loose. Visconti never said, 'try one more Marc, that one was a bit ragged', because it was that looseness which made it sound like a T.Rex record. It was deliberate.

I contributed some ideas too, such as adding handclaps and small things like that so we made a good team. I liked Marc and I learned a lot from working with him and Visconti.

The sessions went very smoothly and we managed to get rough mixes of the whole album, but they took the tapes with them and added some overdubs elsewhere. That was just the way they worked then.

When the group came back the next year to record 'Tanx' it was just as well organised and they were the same professional people. I didn't see Marc drunk or arguing or being aggressive. He was very together and in no hurry. He knew he had to develop the sound and was willing to try all of Tony's suggestions, as far as I can remember. There was a definite intention to make that album sound different to 'The Slider' and all these years later I think they both stand out as very special records."

On November 5th Fly released 'Jeepster' b/w 'Life's A Gas' without Marc's approval and it almost brought him a third number one, but was held off the top spot by comedian Benny Hill's novelty hit 'Ernie'.

The November tour ended with two shows at the Liverpool Stadium on November 11th. At the first, six o'clock show, the audience were noticeably younger and appeared to be uncertain as to whether or not they were 'allowed' to leave their seats to dance in the aisles or rush the front of the stage. At the second, the crowd were older, the girls gathering to chatter and giggle and the boys ganging together to look cool and distance themselves from the screamers. When the band hit the stage the place erupted and all traces of tiredness evaporated.

During the short acoustic set the screams, shouts and general mayhem died down as the audience caught their collective breath, straining to hear those precious few words the object of their desire was imparting personally to them. And still a couple of girls managed to break through the cordon and rush the stage, throwing their arms around his neck until they were forcibly dragged off to the side of the stage and thrown back into the sea of upturned faces, the envy of their friends for they were among the few who had touched Marc Bolan.

At the end of year the music industry trade papers were reporting that the group's singles (excluding the unofficial number 2 hit 'Jeepster') had outsold those released by both The Who and Hendrix combined. Altogether, T.Rex accounted for 3.5% of the total UK record sales that year. Advance orders for 'Telegram Sam', the first single on the new T.Rex Wax Co label had already hit 97,000 and EMI had stockpiled a quarter of a million copies in anticipation of demand weeks before the official release date of January 1972.

When asked to account for his monopoly of the singles market Marc offered a simple explanation:

"When we started in '67 everyone was doing Cream, Hendrix, and it was very much hard rock. The only way I could break through was to be something completely opposite. By the time it got to be 1970 everyone was playing acoustic. Had I not done what I'm doing now, I would have ended up like Cat Stevens, which is not what I want to be. I'd much rather be a cock rock star."

'Telegram Sam' may not qualify as cock rock but when coupled with 'Cadillac' and 'Baby Strange', it delivered the goods, becoming the group's third number one, priming the Bolan-Visconti hit factory for a string of similarly styled hits. All three tracks had been recorded in Denmark for tax reasons and continued the policy of offering value for money maxi-singles to the cash-strapped teenyboppers who now comprised the bulk of Bolan's record buyers. It was the archetypal T.Rex single, bubblegum boogie at its most appealing, powered by a raunchy rock revivalist riff and a catchy chorus swathed in saxes and strings. It was irrefutable evidence that Bolan could cast an enchanting spell with three or four chords and a neat turn of phrase. Lyrically it name-checked his inner circle: Sam was Marc's main man, Secunda; Jungle-faced Jake his black assistant Sid Walker; Golden nosed Slim, a coke dealer; Purple Pie Pete was photographer Pete Sanders; and Bobby, the 'natural born poet', was of course Dylan, although Marc sometimes sang 'Purple Browed Beep' in praise of publicist B.P. Fallon. There was even a verse to himself ("Me I funk but I don't care. I ain't no square with my corkscrew hair") as Marc savoured his own success and acknowledged the influence of Howling Wolf in the fade out.

Bolan had instigated Glam Rock but his music outlived the ludicrous fashions that exemplified the era, the skyscraper stack-heeled platform boots, satins, sequins and Max Factor face paint. Glam Rock more accurately described the ephemeral tongue-in-cheek, high-camp, good-time party pop exemplified by Gary Glitter, Mud, Sweet, Kenny, Hello, Alice Cooper and the Chinn-Chapman stable with their pneumatic big 'n' bouncy beats, playground chants and Neanderthal cries of 'Heeeeey!' Bolan's boogie was cut from a different cloth, but he was lumped in with the rest of the glitter gang and dismissed as a teeny-pop phenomenon until time, a certain nostalgia and his premature passing burnished his early seventies singles with a glow that would have confounded the critics and also his original audience.

ESSEX MUSIC INTERNATIONAL LIMITED   £1·25

Rejecting accusations that his music appealed mainly to young girls Marc countered, "I hope that anyone who is seriously into music takes what I do seriously." But being a teenage idol demanded sacrifices.

In the midst of all this Bolanmania, as the press had dubbed it, one of Marc's most cherished projects, one which if completed could have been his masterwork, was side-lined and eventually forgotten.

The Children of Rarn was a Tolkienesque/Narnia inspired acoustic song suite that had been gestating since '69, but was considered too 'old hat' by the time of Bolan's big breakthrough. Originally it was to have been a double album with an accompanying book, but every time he needed an extra track for an album, Bolan would borrow a song from the suite and, by autumn 71, only about 15 minutes of music was left unrecorded. Rather than abandon it altogether, he demoed what remained one October evening in Visconti's flat using the producer's nylon strung classical guitar. Marc had hinted that it would be a monumental rock opera, his answer to *Tommy* and *Sergeant Pepper*, and the culmination of his Tyrannosaurus Rex period. But it was clear that what he had recorded that day was only a sketch of the main songs and that a lot more work would be needed to develop the individual themes and link them with instrumental passages. There was no doubt in Visconti's mind that he and Marc would be up to the task, but there was the question of time and whether or not Marc would be prepared to transpose the songs so that interest could be generated using contrasting keys. Of more immediate concern to Marc was the worry that his audience wouldn't understand or accept it. It was hard enough to get them to quieten down during his acoustic spot. He couldn't imagine them listening in rapt silence to an 80-minute orchestrated acoustic album about a prehistoric race of hobbit-like creatures going into battle on primitive motorbikes! The potential audience for this particular project had turned their back on him after 'Ride A White Swan' and it was too late to win them back, even if he had wanted to. And so *The Children of Rarn* was forgotten. Every time work was scheduled to begin on a new album Visconti would ask if it was going to be *The Children of Rarn* and Marc would smile and say not this time, he had to give the kids 'a rocker'. It was only after his death that the producer dug out the demo and sketched in his ideas based on what he knew of Marc's intentions and his own thoughts as to what should be added. As Visconti observed on the posthumous compilation containing the piece, "It could have been very beautiful." And it was.

Real life in the Bolan camp was not as idyllic however. The American *Electric Warrior* tour which began in Seattle on February 10, 1972, was a very mixed affair. T.Rex headlined at each of the nine mid-sized venues and drew respectable sized crowds on the strength of the stateside success of 'Get It On' (retitled 'Bang A Gong' to avoid confusion with a similarly titled single by American act Chase). It went on to become a million-seller but it was Marc's only top 10 US hit. The audiences were enthusiastic and the reviews were generally very favourable. The problem was that the Americans expected a lot for their money, long sets, showmanship, pyrotechnics and dazzling displays of instrumental virtuosity and T.Rex came up short on all counts as far as the more critical members of the audience were concerned.

"More than 5,000 people, including Mick Jagger and one of the largest contingents of reviewers/writers to see a rock show here in months, jammed the Hollywood Palladium Tuesday night to see if T.Rex can generate…some of the extraordinary excitement in this country that's it's achieved in…England.

"The answer was quite possibly, but probably not overnight. T.Rex had to be satisfied with a split decision at the Palladium.

"As Jagger watched, hidden from the audience by amplifiers, T.Rex…showed several reasons for its success, part of them musical, part of them in the glamour surrounding the lead singer/writer/guitarist Marc Bolan…

"Despite these strengths, however, Tuesday's concert didn't generate anything like the hysteria that apparently occurs at the group's English concerts…. but the Palladium concert was the first stop on the US tour… the hysteria may just be a matter of time. The ingredients are there." Robert Hillburn, *Los Angeles Times*.

Jagger went backstage after the Palladium show and warned Bolan that 45-minute sets would not cut it with punters who demanded at least double that. There wasn't much Marc could do about it without padding the set out with more acoustic numbers and so he persevered, hoping to win them over. It was hard work. On record his solos were succinct, short enough for the kids to sing along to and short enough to retain their interest. But when he indulged in a sprawling ten-minute solo on stage, it was immediately apparent that he was no Hendrix, there just weren't enough ideas to justify an extended workout and Marc's habit of assaulting his guitar with a tambourine didn't always convince those who had seen the original in action. Back home he only had to tune up to elicit squeals of delight, but on the other side of the pond they were more discerning. T.Rex were caught between two extremes – the British teenyboppers who only wanted an image to fixate on and the American audiences who had to be won over.

John Allen of *The Washington Post* gave a measured response to their concert in the capital on Sunday 20th informing those readers not familiar with the name that T.Rex were still a cult group in the US but were in the process of expanding their following. He made a valid point by saying that one of the band's biggest hits, 'Hot Love' had not been released in America (two more were from the as yet unreleased *The Slider*) and yet despite the audience being unfamiliar with about a third of the short set they were "brought to their feet" during a night of "well played but loud, loud rock music." He also noted that "Bolan displayed a skill on the guitar that none of the group's six albums had shown," which was something of a back-handed compliment as three of those albums had been acoustic and only one of the six had been recorded with the band.

It all augured well for the future, but Marc was impatient to conquer the continent in one campaign and couldn't accept that making a career in America required building support one tour at a time.

The customary backstage tipple to calm the nerves before a show soon became half a bottle before the soundcheck with the other half polished off during the long tedious wait before show time. It was said that he finally abandoned his no drugs policy during that tour and very quickly picked up a serious cocaine habit, made worse by snorting low grade, cheap coke. According to Tony Secunda, it was Marc's erratic behavior caused by his increasing coke habit and his consumption of cognac and champagne, which killed off his chances of ever making it big in the States, and it all came to a head on the night of a prestigious showcase performance at New York's Carnegie Hall on that February tour. According to Secunda, his nervous client succumbed to a bad case of stage fright and locked himself in the dressing room toilet with two bottles of champagne which he emptied half an hour before he was due to appear. It was too late to sober him up and so Marc staggered on stage only to fall over during the first number. By the time he had been helped to his feet some of the celebs were already heading for the exit.

However, reviews of the Carnegie Hall concert refute Secunda's version of events.

Bob Kirsch of *Billboard* wrote, "Headlining for the first time in New York, Britain's T. Rex showed why they are causing more commotion in England than any band since The Beatles… Bolan's a true showman… an excellent musician and a capable singer… By the time a frenzied 'Summertime Blues' encore ended, (T.Rex) had treated New York to one of its most uninhibited and enjoyable evenings in a long time."

The New York Times was not impressed, but they made no mention of Marc being drunk, falling flat on his face or of celebrity guests leaving before the end.

"Sunday night had all the elements of hyped superstardom," sniped Don Heckman. "One is constantly aware of the mannerism rather than the music… And the ego behind it all."

Marc's tour manager and Personal Assistant, Mickey 'Marmalade' Gray, broke a 20-year pledge not to talk about his friend, to assure this author that such stories were untrue.

"Secunda made that story up because he was bitter that Marc had fired him. So much tosh has been written about Marc by people who blithely accepted such stories at face value because it fitted in with their image of a flamboyant, outrageous rock star on the edge. Marc was certainly a bundle of nerves that night, but he had only one drink to calm himself down and he definitely didn't collapse on stage. His drinking didn't really become a problem until much later when his marriage to June ended and his music suffered as a result of the problems in his personal life.

"But even then, he never made an arse of himself. Marc's problem was that he had a very low tolerance for alcohol. Steve and Mickey could drink till all hours, but Marc would be legless after a few glasses. The truth behind all those drinking stories is much less dramatic and destructive than it has been made out to be. Marc was really a victim of his own image."

June offered a simple explanation for her husband's increasingly violent mood swings. "He started taking cocaine in New York during the *Electric Warrior* sessions in the belief that it would just give him a buzz and a rush of energy to enable him to keep going. Cocaine makes you thirsty, but the drug offsets the effect of the alcohol so you don't get drunk, just aggressive and impossible to reason with. He phoned me to confess, because he felt guilty, so I knew from then on what was affecting his behaviour. "

Marc would be on a natural high one day if the gig went well and the reviews were good and down the next if the opposite was the case.

The Detroit and Chicago gigs were a case in point. The two performances were just six days apart but the critical reaction was like fire and ice.

Melody Maker's American correspondent reported, "In the auditorium 9,100 frenzied teenies started chanting 'T.Rex, T.Rex, T.Rex'. The guards, backed by a crew of flashlight-flicking ushers, awaited a riot.

"By the time the houselights went out, pandemonium had already begun to set in… When the lavender spotlight hit Marc, the cheers began. They didn't stop for an hour… By the time the more-than-an-hour set drew to a close with 'Bang A Gong', the house had gone absolutely bananas.

"It was, in one critic's words, a killer concert. Detroit had been primed for T.Rex… The concert couldn't just be a good one. It had to be a masterpiece. It was."

Contrast that with this cold-shouldered dismissal from Lynn Van Matre of *The Chicago Tribune*.

"When I left the auditorium last night at 11.30, the T.Rex concert wasn't over, but Marc Bolan's mic had just zonked out completely for what probably would be the first of many times and I decided to call it the end of a perfect evening. Perfect, that is, if you groove on mismanagement, 40-minute delays between sets, general screw-ups and noise, noise, noise.

"Bolan, the fey lead singer/composer of T.Rex…once wrote rather literate songs with poetic aspirations; now he's gone in for rock and roll with a few acoustic numbers thrown in. Admittedly, the sound system was terrible, but Bolan's not all that hot either. The sequins he had pasted on his cheekbones sparkled more than his music."

Comments like that hurt Bolan more than he would admit and being of a rather fretful disposition, he brooded on the bad reviews and looked for someone to blame.

On returning to Britain, Marc sacked Secunda claiming that he had only enlisted his expertise to negotiate the setting up of his own label and to help break 'Get It On' in the States. Now that both items had been achieved, Tony and he had parted amicably and he would consider managing his own affairs from now on.

As 'Telegram Sam' stormed to number one just two weeks after release, the fans remained ignorant of the pressures piling up on their idol and in the absence of hard

"Ringo was like a father to us." June Bolan (Photo: reprinted by special permission of the Estate of the late Keith Morris, Getty Images)

news they were relying on rumours. *Jackie* magazine was reporting that their offices were being inundated with more than 800 letters a week, every week, from distraught fans who had heard rumours that Marc had contracted a fatal illness and wouldn't be touring again.

"I like being loved," Marc mused. "Isn't it nice that someone can like you enough to put your picture on the bedroom wall?... The frightening thing is the sheer strength of it all, but I know they don't want to hurt me."

He admitted that it was impossible for him to leave home, which was now an upmarket flat in Little Venice at 31 Clarendon Gardens which June had furnished with antiques, expensive tapestries and oriental rugs. A nifty little sports car and a second-hand white Rolls-Royce had also been acquired and could be revved up and out of the underground garage like Thunderbird 2 before the fans realised the object of their daily vigil had eluded them. It was an unreal existence and was fun at first, but it quickly became tiresome and claustrophobic.

Marc: "I have a feeling all the time of being pinned against the wall by hundreds of invisible people. All the time. Consequently, I totally retreat. I don't go out anymore, ever.

"The thing about success, certainly in the rock and roll business, is that it gives an incredible amount but what it takes away is irreplaceable... Sometimes I get a funny feeling inside me that I shan't be here very long and I'm not talking in terms of things like success. It frightens me sometimes."

June: "It was great for him at first, having 200 hundred girls camped outside the flat every single day calling for him to come out and sign their autograph books and let them touch his hair. But it was no way to live. All summer we had to crawl about on all fours so we couldn't be seen. We hoped they would give up after a while and go away but they were persistent. They wouldn't leave until they'd seen him and it became a real pain. He couldn't just wave from the window. They wanted more. It was a hot summer and we had to spend it inside like prisoners. That's the downside of fame, the part nobody thinks about until it happens to them. And then you can never go back to the easy time when you could go out and not be chased down the street by a pack of screaming teenagers. We even had to take our rubbish in the boot of the car to a friend's house down the street because the fans had started to go through our dustbin and leave all the rubbish they didn't want scattered on the steps."

But there were compensations. If they couldn't go unmolested in England or Europe, they would just have to go where no one knew him. Barbados, for instance. With money no object, Marc and June flew First Class to the West Indies for their first real holiday abroad that summer, alone without minders, press or personal assistants. For two weeks they stayed in a luxury hotel and spent all day browning in the sun and clubbing at night. Two days after they returned to London they went back again in the company of Ringo Starr who had befriended Marc and felt protective towards him. "He was like a father to us," June has said, "he taught us loads of things, a wonderful person."

As the rock circus rolled on, Marc found himself surrounded by an increasing number of liggers and hangers-on: journalists, DJs, record company reps, assistants, flunkies, freeloaders and friends of friends whose role was never fully explained but who laughed loud and readily at his jokes, drank his champagne and shared the groupies who gathered back stage in the vain hope that some of the glamour might rub off on them.

It was a life many young men would dream of, but those who could see the dangers knew that it was time to split. The first to leave was publicist B.P. Fallon who excused himself by saying that he had achieved what he had set out to do for T.Rex and would now take his talents elsewhere to break in a new band. He had a point. Even Marc's old albums were charting without any assistance from the artist, or his well-oiled publicity machine. The first four Tyrannosaurus Rex albums were repackaged as doubles in April and November 72 and both sold three times as many as when first released, while a second compilation of early tracks misleadingly titled *Bolan Boogie* had been rushed out by Fly in May and immediately topped the chart (an earlier compilation, *The Best of T.Rex*, had been released in March 71 to capitalise on the success of 'Hot Love' although the only genuine 'hit' included was 'Debora'!) 'Debora' had also been reissued as a four-track EP, entering the top 10 in April 72. But although these unwelcome reissues swelled Bolan's bank balance, they did nothing to stem his increasing anxiety as EMI warned of the dangers of over-exposure. Nothing could kill a career faster than flooding the market with 'inferior product'.

By October the music press were comparing T.Rex to The Beatles and even Lennon and McCartney were acknowledging the group as their natural successors, as far as fan adulation went. Ringo was more effusive, calling the group "fantastic" and one of his favourites. He was even considering making a TV documentary about the phenomenon that had captured the imagination of both the music press and the national media who were scrambling for a new superlative to describe the scenes of mass hysteria that greeted the group at every venue. It had come to publicist B.P.Fallon in a vision, or so he claimed, as he sat on a train travelling between meetings. What word, he wondered could capture the excitement? Then he saw it, surrounded by flames before his inner eye. 'T.Rextasy!'

Chapter 15
Born to Boogie

I've become a kind of Elvis Presley figure. The kids have seen me in 'Born To Boogie' and come to think of me as a cut-out cardboard figure, some of them are surprised to find out that I really exist.
Marc to Michael Benton, Disc, December 1973

They came from all over Britain wearing T.Rex T-shirts, Bolan badges, scarves and rosettes to demonstrate their devotion to their pocket-sized idol at the venue where many of their older brothers had gathered just months before to venerate the mighty Led Zeppelin and just a short walk from Wembley Stadium, the site of England's historic victory over Germany in the 1966 World Cup Final. Now it was the Hackney hustler's turn to make history and a total of 20,000 fans were there for two shows on March 18, 1972, to witness it. Distance and money was no object for the faithful who made the pilgrimage to be in his presence, hundreds having had their hair curled to ape their idol, many attired in satin with glitter and sparkling stars under their eyes. They came by train, coach and car to vent their pent up passions with those who shared their obsession. A few denim and leather clad rockers rode up on motorbikes, wary of being seen as part of the sea of (mostly) teenage girls. Thousands crammed themselves into the overcrowded carriages of the tube trains converging on Wembley from every corner of the capital, before spilling out onto the platforms like an unruly school outing, though without their teachers to remind them to stay together and be quiet at the back.

Once past the touts, souvenir sellers and the officious uniformed commissioners who manned the turnstiles they found themselves inside the largest indoor venue most of them had ever seen, many soon wishing they had taken a chance to fight their way through to the crash barriers in front of the stage. The wait was almost unbearable, made all the more agonising by having to wait for the support act, Quiver, to finish their set. Then the lights dimmed and DJ Emperor Rosko strode on stage to whip them into a frenzy of expectation.

"Are you ready?" he asked. Screams of "Yeaaaaah!" "Are you ready over there?" More screams. "Are you ready over here?" How long would he drag it out? "Are you sure you're ready?" he taunted them. "Then let's hear it for the almighty – T.Rex!"

Lungs at bursting point, anticipation almost beyond endurance, all but the first dozen rows strained through the darkness to make out the four tiny figures who had trouped onto the stage and at one in particular. He was dressed in a sparkling silver-white jacket, a T-shirt bearing his own image, green satin trousers and dainty white girl's shoes. There was a strange stifled silence for a few moments as the fans waited for a sign that it had begun, a familiar voice to reassure them that it was real, but there was confusion as instruments were plugged in, amplifier settings were altered and anxious looks were exchanged. Then all of a sudden an eruption of sound like the roar of a feral beast and the time for thinking was over. Ten thousand teens abandoned themselves to the glorious clamour that reverberated off the cavernous walls and exulted in the new cult of T.Rextasy.

From the first number the band were steaming, Bill giving it some serious stick, Mickey flaying the congas and Steve stalking the spaces in between as Bolan hammered out thick wads of power chords interspersed with some finger blistering solos. If this was teenybop, the term needed redefining. This was rock, pure and simple. It had backbone, it had balls and it had everyone working up a sweat.

Visually speaking, it was no spectacle. A modest light show bathed the plain blue backdrop and picked out the only props – two large posters and a couple of life-sized cardboard cut-outs of the main man. But that afternoon and again at the evening performance, he proved himself a consummate showman – gliding across the stage with almost feline grace. This wasn't the empty posturing of a poseur, this was a rock star at the peak of his powers, in his element and in his prime.

And he was loving every minute. Bolan was clearly having as much fun as his fans, his impish smile breaking out across his face with every piercing scream. They screamed when he sang, they screamed when he let rip a throaty yelp like Little Richard's little white cousin and they screamed when he wiggled. And he wiggled a lot. They even screamed when he raised his glass to them during the three-song acoustic set and again when he gave tiny guttural gasps at the tail end of 'Spaceball Ricochet' when he'd run out of words. They didn't scream when he played a tasty solo or added a neat little fill, but then they wouldn't have heard the telling details through the din. But most of all they screamed and sighed when he acted the part he was born to play, sashaying across the stage, his guitar slung low, mimicking the moves of his childhood heroes who, if they'd been there, would have urged him on with cries of 'Go, Johnny, Go!' and raising two hands above his head as if to say 'Here I am, take me'. At the time it looked more like a cultural phenomenon rather than a musical event. It is only with hindsight that Bolan's iconic status has been recognised and the two concerts at Wembley seen as the apex of his all too brief tenure at the top.

There were no giant video screens back in 1972 so those who were more than ten rows back or in the tiered seating round the sides didn't see much, nor did they hear much for that matter, certainly not amidst the cacophony of shrieks and squeals. But they could say they'd been there, on 'The Day That Pop Came Back', as the press dubbed it. And that was what it had all been about.

Record Mirror journalist Rosalind Russell was in the audience and remembered it clearly.

"I was there with my little brother and I was under strict instructions from my mother not to let anything happen to him! We had seats near the front, but the fans were climbing over the seats to get to the stage, so a security man asked if we wanted to go into the pit with the photographers to be safe. We were then just three feet in front of the stage and I was scared because the barriers were all that were between us and the fans who kept trying to surge forward and there were only these old commissioners to hold them back. If they'd broken through the barriers I'd have been flattened and my brother could have been killed. But it was a great day – a wonderful day.

"However, I have to say the sound was appalling. I don't know whose fault it was. Sometimes he was just unlucky with places that weren't suitable for rock bands back then, or he played badly. Playing guitar was really secondary to his performance. I really don't think he put that much effort into playing guitar on stage – it was just an appendage. He was a great singer and songwriter and a great personality. He didn't stick in my mind as a great guitarist."

Wembley was much more than a personal victory for Bolan and those who had stuck by him through the lean times. For B.P. Fallon and roadie Micky Marmalade who watched proudly from the wings, for June and Chelita in the orchestra pit and Tony Visconti, overseeing the only official live recording the group would make from inside the Rolling Stones Mobile, Wembley was a validation of everything Bolan personified, the redemptive

power of pop. Now 20,000 fans confirmed what Bolan had known since he was a kid – he was a star, bigger than Eddie Cochran or Gene Vincent had been, as significant a figure in the pop pantheon as Elvis and Jagger. Bigger even than The Beatles, at least in Britain during that surreal year of success. And if proof were needed, five cameramen captured the coronation of the new Prince of Pop, one of whom was Ringo Starr.

It had been Ringo's idea to film the Wembley shows for a series of TV documentaries that he was planning on the cult of celebrity, but Bolan thought television would diminish the spectacle, so Ringo suggested they make it into a movie. Judging by the record sales and the demand for T.Rex concert tickets it would be a guaranteed hit. The only problem they could foresee was that the group rarely played sets longer than 50 minutes including encores, which was far too short for a main feature. But that was quickly resolved when Marc suggested they add 'surrealistic' scenes inspired by whatever took their fancy on the day, an approach which The Beatles had experimented with on their second feature, *Help!*, and their critically panned TV special *Magical Mystery Tour*. Improvisation was also the preferred MO of Marc and Mickey's favourite filmmaker Federico Fellini. But Ringo, bless him, was no Fellini, and even if he had possessed the unerring eye and imagination of the great Italian director, it was doubtful that he could have restrained his star's enthusiasm and channelled it into something constructive. Instead the concert footage became the core of a big budget home movie in which fragmentary improvised scenes with no logical purpose or entertainment value were intercut with footage of the Wembley concerts to pad the film out to the required 65 minutes. The only extra scenes worth more than a second look were two studio performances, 'Children of the Revolution' and 'Tutti Frutti', recorded with Ringo on drums and Elton John on piano which were filmed in the basement of the Apple Corps offices (a version of 'Long Tall Sally' didn't make the final cut) and the Mad Hatter's Tea Party sequence in which Marc played an acoustic medley accompanied by a string quartet who had to pretend to play as Marc was improvising and so their parts hadn't been scored.

I don't claim to be a guitarist, but I've got fucking hands and bleeding fingers." (Photo Chris Foster, Rex Features)

The film also brought one matter to a head that had been festering for many years. Marc always had trouble fine tuning his guitar, many self-taught pop musicians found it difficult in the days before digital tuners, but Marc made it an issue whenever Tony Visconti suggested that he might want to check the tuning before recording. Visconti knew that if he confronted Marc with the problem in the presence of others, there would be an almighty row as Bolan didn't want to lose face, so Visconti would wait for a quiet moment and fine tune Marc's guitar when no one else was around. On tour Micky Marmalade would perform that function. But when it came to mixing the soundtrack for the film, Visconti couldn't let the poor tuning pass and Marc went apoplectic with rage at the mere suggestion that he had been out of tune at Wembley and hadn't noticed it. His rhythm guitar was eventually re-recorded and a second added to fatten the sound and add a few fills, but the acoustic guitar couldn't be dubbed without re-recording the vocal as well, so it remains very clearly out of tune. Worse, restored footage of the second set included on the *Born to Boogie* DVD shows Marc struggling with the tuning and clearly uncertain how to rectify it.

Of course, the fans were delirious to have the opportunity to see Bolan on the big screen and sit through his repeated attempts to recite a verse of an old Presley song before convulsing into giggles, or watch as he was driven oh so slowly toward them up a long runway to recite a few lines of poetry while Ringo, dressed as a dormouse, sat and squeaked and a dwarf ate a chocolate wing mirror from the car. The critics, however, were not so forgiving. They savaged the self-indulgent scenes while grudgingly admitting that the concert footage would appeal to 'the kids'. Bolan who had been lauded for not putting a foot wrong since his meteoric rise to fame was now pilloried by the press who knew that controversy would do their circulation no harm at all. It was the first obvious example of the 'build-them-up-to-knock-them-down' policy that would determine the fortunes of future stars, but Bolan hadn't been prepared to be pilloried and he took it very badly. When the film was taken off the circuit after only the briefest run, Bolan was bullish in his defence of it.

"It was slated by everyone. But they all put it down for the wrong reasons, which is why it didn't worry me… it was made for T.Rex fans, for no one else. That's what upset the critics… I get off on it."

Steve Currie: "The film *Born To Boogie* was really a total ego trip… There was Marc and Ringo clashing their egos, trying to impress each other."

Industry trade paper *Music Week* slated the film, savaging its "meaningless indulgent sketches" although it singled out the sequence with Ringo and Elton jamming with Bolan in the basement of Apple as a "rock revelation".

Nick Kent of the *NME* took the opportunity to make a personal attack on Bolan. "The most embarrassing part of the film…is when Marc decides to play acoustic. New heights of fey precociousness are reached as Bolan strums the most blatantly out-of-tune guitar I've possibly ever heard, and whines obnoxiously for over five minutes." Though he, too, had to admit the jam with Ringo and Elton was rather splendid.

"Here the band really do rock and just when you think it's too good to be true they move into a fine, fine version of 'Children of the Revolution', which cuts the single to pieces. Ah, if only the film had ended there, but no… it's time for more Wembley Pool histrionics."

But surrealism and self-indulgence were par for the course for rock movies in the early seventies. Until the advent of the music video and MTV in the early Eighties, bands felt obliged to offer something more than a simple document of their stage act to draw fans into the cinema. At least *Born To Boogie* could boast concert footage that captured T.Rex at their very peak between their two classic albums, *Electric Warrior* and *The Slider* as well as presenting Bolan at his most charismatic before drink and drugs, cynicism and suspicion, dulled the spark that made him shine.

Ironically, at the very moment that Marc was where he had always dreamt of being and could yell, "Look, Ma, top of the world!", he realised he couldn't cope with fame on such a scale, although he would never admit as much to himself. It wasn't so much the loss of privacy, the debilitating lack of sleep that plagued him night after night, or the threat to life and limb posed by hysterical fans. It was the tightening screw of expectation to deliver one hit single after another, to better the chart topping run of the previous release, as well as producing an album a year, every year, that was sapping the strength and resolve of the man-child who wanted to saviour stardom, not repeatedly campaign for the crown. It was an exhausting contest and he had seriously underestimated the stamina and willpower required to stay the course.

Noddy Holder and Jim Lee, the main songwriters in Slade, had the down-to-earth Dave Hill and Don Powell to raise their spirits when they flagged, Elton had silent partner and lyricist Bernie Taupin, Suzi Quatro and Sweet had Chinn and Chapman to write their songs for them and Gary Glitter collaborated with Mike Leander. Bowie was the only major solo artist of the Glam Rock era who also wrote his own material, but even he had the sense to take a break at a critical point in his career by recording the *Pin Ups* collection of cover versions which gave him the breathing space to consider his options. He also had the support of guitarist Mick Ronson and trusted the advice given by manager Tony DeFries. Though Bowie was at one time in awe of Bolan and readily acknowledged the debt he owed to his friend in paving the way for his own ascent, it was Bowie who was fated to win the exhausting race because he had the intellect and self-awareness, the courage and imagination to reinvent himself periodically and so stay one step ahead of his rivals and defy expectation. Bolan, however, was alone, desperate to defend his besieged position, increasingly isolated from those he could have confided in and in self-denial. He could not and would not admit his shortcomings, even to himself. He was becoming estranged from June and was too paranoid to delegate responsibility. Managers were appointed to carry out Bolan's instructions, not give career advice to the star. His band, too, were mere employees and producer Tony Visconti had resigned himself to his new role as a glorified engineer for an artist who believed himself to be a better producer than the man he was paying to do the job.

Visconti: "He had the charisma, he had the guts, he had the leadership, he had almost everything except technique and actual academic background for some of the things he wanted to do."

Bolan also had the respect of his peers, but he couldn't confide in them either, not without letting his guard down. He had to play the star even for those who knew him better. Some found it endearing, others found it merely exasperating. Bowie paid him the ultimate tribute by immortalising Marc as 'the boy in the bright blue jeans' who 'jumped up on the stage' in 'Lady Stardust' (a song performed during the *Ziggy Stardust* tour of '72 when Marc's face would be projected on to a large screen behind the band), and again in 'All The Young Dudes' in the line 'who needs TV when we got T.Rex', which Bowie gave to Mott The Hoople to kick start their flagging career. Even Elton John and lyricist Bernie Taupin were inspired to pen 'Teenage Idol' which gently mocked the earnest intensity of Bolan's ambition and there would be superstar sessions with Alice Cooper, Donovan, ELO, Ringo and Ike and Tina Turner (see discography) throughout '72 and '73, but no one thought it their place to suggest that he might consider varying his style. They knew he wouldn't have listened.

Steve Currie: "He wouldn't listen… But that was the thing that made him successful in the first place."

Tony Visconti: "He was very reluctant to take any musical advice".

When Mickey Finn heard the acoustic demo of 'Metal Guru' for the first time he had an idea for a rhythm that would make it more interesting than the standard four-to-the-floor foot tapper that would propel it to number one, but Marc was already talking Steve and Bill through the changes and ordering Visconti to roll the tape before Mickey could get a word in. After that, he kept his thoughts to himself.

Chapter 16
The Slider

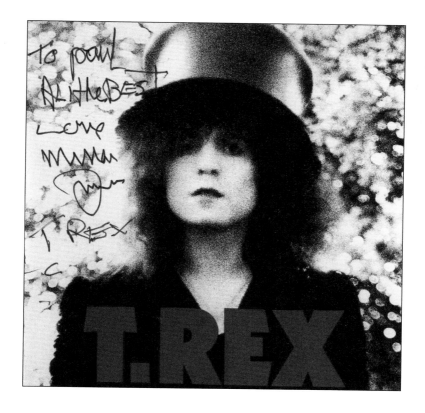

 I think I am a child. Everything blows my mind.
Marc Bolan

I t was the eyes that did it. When the camera zoomed in for a close up during the first mimed performance of 'Metal Guru' on *Top of the Pops* on May 11, it betrayed the toll that success had taken on Marc Bolan. The pupils were dilated and dull, the lids heavy and half closed as if ready for sleep and ringed with thick black mascara. The face had filled out, no longer the winsome boyish charmer with the wide smile and the mischievous twinkle in the eye, but a jet-lagged and jaded rock star going through the motions. It didn't look much like fun anymore.

The danger signs were there even before the Wembley concerts, but no one knew what to say or how to handle the situation. Bolan was under severe strain and drinking heavily. But how could they tell an old friend – one who paid their wages – that he was careering out of control when they knew that he wouldn't believe them and that he could never accept criticism, even if it was offered with the best of intentions? So they kept their concerns to themselves and they kept their jobs, but there was an unspoken understanding that things were not going to improve if they continued to ignore it.

On route to the Chateau D'Heuroville outside Paris to begin work on *The Slider*, Marc drained a bottle of cognac and grew loud and obnoxious. Tony and Steve stared out of the windows of the limousine at the scenery and prayed it would pass. Mickey made the mistake of humouring Marc and was drawn into a drunken sing-along to keep the peace. On arrival at the studio, Marc picked a fight with roadie Mick O'Halloran who was physically a formidable figure but, inside, a real softie. When Marc ordered him to clear the owner's belongings out of the master bedroom so that he could use it, O'Halloran hesitated. "Do it now!" Marc yelled. So O'Halloran went upstairs but soon returned, red faced with emotion. "You can't talk to me like I'm a fucking animal and I'm not going to treat other people like they're fucking animals. I won't do it".

Marc sobered up almost immediately. No one had ever spoken to him like this. He rose from his chair and tried to intimidate a friend that he now considered a mere servant. O'Halloran stood his ground. This time there was no breaking into laughter. Marc backed down. He took Mick aside. "OK," he said, "let's talk this over."

When Elton or Bowie hired the Chateau they would move in with their own cook

and make a party of it for a month, but Bolan had everyone working flat out. The best part of the album was in the can in just five days and the band packed up and on board the plane back to Britain before they'd time to savour the French cuisine or even admire the scenery. Visconti admits that it was at this point that he stopped being a fan. There seemed to be no creative input for him to make. There was now a standard set-up for recording T.Rex tracks, a predetermined process that they didn't waver from in which effects were applied without considering if there might be an alternative and the whole lot put through a compressor like processed meat in a sausage factory. Mixes were being finalised in 30 minutes instead of several hours and it didn't seem to bother anyone, least of all Marc who just grinned and said, 'Cheap, isn't it?'

Recording 'The Slider' at Rosenberg Studios, Denmark. Marc's lead vocals were routinely double tracked. (Photo Jorgen Angel). Previous page: 'The Slider' was recorded using a 2" state-of-the-art 16 track analogue machine mixed down to a ¼" master. Edits had to be performed with razor blades and tape. Marc confides in engineer Freddy Hansson. (Photo Jorgen Angel)

1972 was the peak year of productivity for the T.Rex hit factory, but already the formula was wearing thin and Visconti was beginning to resent having to work 17-hour shifts when there was the money available to take things more leisurely, to consider the options rather than always rely on the obvious approach and instrumentation. Bill Legend would often still be in the process of learning a song when Marc would pass a run through as a take. There were even instances when Visconti had not finished patching through the drum mikes when Marc demanded they press on with the next track. A notable example being 'Jitterbug Love', one of two tracks slated for the B-side of the next single, 'Children of the Revolution'. It was recorded with a 'dead' snare mike which weakens the effect of the drum fills. Such a cavalier attitude and lack of consideration for the other members of the band undermined their confidence as they rarely had the chance to give their best before being ordered to move on to the next song.

Bill complained that the band were now "speeding" and stockpiling tracks that might have benefitted from a little more work, or the addition of another section to avoid endless repetition of the chorus. Several promising songs that could have beefed up the album were shelved before the band had a chance to develop them simply because Marc didn't give himself time to write the additional parts that would have completed them. Other top drawer tracks such as 'Thunderwing', 'Cadilac' (Marc's misspelling), 'Jitterbug Love' and 'Sunken Rags' were consigned to B-sides because Bolan would compile an album from the completed tracks produced during the sessions that had been set aside for that project and so if stronger songs were taped at subsequent sessions, it would be too late to consider them for inclusion. It's arguable that *The Slider* might have been more favourably reviewed and held in even higher regard today if only he had taken

the time to consider his options and replaced the insipid 'Mystic Lady' and 'Main Man' with 'Thunderwing' and 'Cadillac', the latter being dropped in after 'Ballrooms of Mars' so the album would end with 'Chariot Choogle'. But armchair critics always compile the best albums.

It was ironic that Marc, who hadn't worried about money in the early days, had developed an almost pathological fear of losing it as soon as he began to accumulate vast sums. The punitive British tax system was partly to blame, demanding that the rich pay 99p in the pound and forcing many artists to become tax exiles. To avoid excessive tax demands, Bolan's royalties were siphoned off into offshore accounts and he was advised to record abroad and tour overseas so that he could minimise the time he spent in the UK. All this at a time when he needed the stability of a home life and the security of familiar surroundings.

June: "Librans are home makers and Marc being an uncommonly strong Libran – he had several Libran aspects in his birth chart – was at his most creative when he felt comfortable and secure, when he felt he was where he belonged. Being on the road and working abroad was not the ideal situation for him."

Nevertheless, as a character in the Elvis movie *Jailhouse Rock* remarked, no matter how big a star gets they can never afford to ignore the records. Bolan was now a movie star and all four Beatles rolled into one as far as fan adulation and record sales were concerned, but he couldn't afford to stop recording or touring.

On Friday 31st March 1972, Marc and Mickey flew from Munich, where they had accepted an award from *Bravo* magazine, to Copenhagen to continue work on *The Slider*.

Danish photographer Jorgen Angel had taken some stunning shots of Marc during a Tyrannosaurus tour of Scandinavia in 1970, but when Jorgen heard that T.Rex were booked to record in Copenhagen's Rosenberg Studios over the weekend he was determined to see if he could get even closer.

"I have always prided myself on not being a paparazzo, but this was one time when I had to behave like one and fortunately it paid off. I was only 20 when Bolan came to Copenhagen to record sessions for *The Slider*, but I had already established a good reputation with touring bands because they knew I wouldn't intrude on their privacy. I had an instinctive feeling when it was right to take pictures and when I should stay in the background, so they felt comfortable around me.

"I'd befriended Tony Reeves, the bass player in Colosseum who was in Denmark to produce several local bands, and while he was working at the Rosenberg Studios he happened to see a telegram lying on the office desk informing the engineer Freddy Hansson that T.Rex had booked a session for that weekend. Tony told me about this at a party a few days before and I thought I would try and see if I could get any candid shots before they kicked me out. So on the Sunday, an hour or so before Bolan was scheduled to arrive, I staked out a window on the second floor of the two-storey building where the studio was housed and waited. Eventually a limo drew up and Bolan got out wrapped in a black fur coat. B.P.Fallon must have heard the camera because I have a shot of him pointing up at me and saying something to Marc which I assume was, 'Look, there's an idiot up there with a camera'.

"After I'd taken a few more shots I got up my courage and went down to see if I could persuade them to let me stay a bit longer and to my surprise Marc wasn't annoyed.

He was really friendly and told me I was welcome to come inside, provided I didn't take pictures when they were actually recording in case the flash distracted them or I fell over something and made a noise!

"Marc looks pretty serious in some of the shots but that's because he was concentrating on setting up his stuff and getting the sound he wanted. He was working and he took his work seriously. But after he had set up, Marc was smiling and making funny faces for me behind the mixing desk. I got the impression that the rest of the band did what 'the boss' told them to do and that it was Marc and Tony Visconti who made all the creative decisions.

"After a couple of hours I thought I had better say 'goodbye', but Marc said I could stay if I wanted as they were sending out for hotdogs and I could eat with them. But I didn't want to overstay my welcome so I left.

"I met him twice again the following year when I was invited to accompany a journalist who was going to interview him for a Danish magazine in his suite at the Palace Hotel in Copenhagen. Marc was having caviar and champagne and kindly offered me some. I remember he had this portable hi-fii stack in his room and was playing Bob Dylan which I thought was an unusual choice for a pop star but Marc told me, 'He's my man!' That night at the gig he spotted me at the front of the stage and played up to me, posing for my camera. He was always very acutely aware of publicity and the power of image.

"Later that year, '73, we met again in London when I went to interview him at his office. I must admit I wasn't very well prepared, but the magazine wouldn't publish the photos without some quotes

so I had to think up a few questions in the taxi on the way to his office. He made a bit of fun of my poor English pronunciation, but he rose to the occasion when I started taking photographs. I had the impression that he preferred posing and playing the star to answering questions. Later I read that some people thought he could be selfish and would do anything to further his career, but I always found him to be a very nice man."

While the movie was being edited T.Rex embarked on yet another British tour, but this time the critics were considerably cooler.

Howard Fielding slated their Birmingham Odeon show on June 9th saying, "The T.Rex phenomenon is no longer about music. It's an act." According to Fielding, Marc was merely going through the motions. "But there's a lack of conviction to the smile. A hint of boredom in the hip shaking... There's no musical progress."

The simple fact was that Marc was flying on fumes and, instead of taking a break and a long hard look at where he was heading, he refuelled with more coke and cognac and pushed himself even harder.

If there is indeed a fine line between genius and madness, Marc teetered perilously close to it on *The Slider*, the album that found him at his most compelling and charismatic, alternating between the teasing, mischievousness *enfant terrible* and the preening, pouting rock god. It was the album that Syd Barrett might have made had he had a kick-ass band behind him and could keep it together long enough to get through a take. Assuming too, of course, that Barrett might have wanted to boogie, though no one did that better than Bolan. Through a supreme effort of will power and with the assistance of Visconti and the band, Marc held it together just long enough to create a classic album on which all the elements of his fantasy fused into a deliciously camp cartoon of seventies' rock excess.

The deliberately over-exposed cover shot, taken by Visconti (but which Marc credited to Ringo) on the set of *Born To Boogie*, conveys the prevailing mood. Marc is the Mad Hatter musing on the surreal situation that he now found himself in and bemused by his own superstar status.

After opening strongly with 'Metal Guru', the minimalist mantra which managed to be both inane and irresistible at one and the same time, quality control dipped for the indifferent 'Mystic Lady', but picked up for the soft-centred 'Rock On' which found Marc cruising in third before easing into the sensual, shuffle rhythm of the title track with its dark droning strings and melancholic chorus which he sang languorously as if emerging from an opium-induced dream. But if Lewis Carroll and Salvador Dali had supplied the lyrical inspiration for some of the songs, Bolan had reduced much of it to a meaningless nursery rhyme, "I have never nailed a nose before, that's how the garden grows," he mused, tongue firmly in cheek while strumming a chord sequence reminiscent of Donovan's 'Hurdy Gurdy Man' and Lennon's 'I Am The Walrus'. Someone had been taking too much coke and cognac and it had evidently burnt out their brain cells. Either that or they had simply given up trying. And yet perversely, it was this air of arrogant indifference which makes *The Slider* pop's equivalent of Warhol's celebrity silkscreen prints. Bolan had raised attitude to an art form.

For the autobiographical 'Spaceball Ricochet' he came on like a cute boyish guru with a winsome smile, entreating his critics to excuse his excesses ("With my Les Paul I know I'm small but I enjoy living anyway.") The title referred to the feeling that he was nothing more than a cosmic pinball being bounced from one life to the next and left wondering what the purpose of it all might be. But addressing profound questions in such a flippant way seemed little short of sacrilegious to those critics who could never take him seriously. But they were trying too hard and should have known better. Hadn't Bolan told them life's a gas? If they wanted a profound, philosophical treatise on the meaning of life they could decipher *Tales from Topographic Oceans* and good luck to them. Bolan was the Cosmic Dancer, not the Dalai Lama. His populist philosophy was gleaned from reading science fiction, watching TV news reports and from fleeting impressions of American city life seen through the windows of his limousine, not from the deep study of a spiritual tradition. The clue to his entire ethos could be found in the intro to 'Baby Strange' as he counted the band in with 'One-and-a-two-and-a-bobbly, bobbly boo-boo. Yeah!' It was Bolan's answer to Little Richard's "Awopbopaloobopalopbamboom!" and it would be pointless to look any deeper.

'Ballrooms of Mars', for example, was meant to emulate the grandeur of Bowie's 'Life On Mars', but settled for a vague impression of a futuristic disco and some characteristic name dropping. Bob Dylan, John Lennon and DJ Alan Freed ('Moondog') were the stars that orbited Marc's universe, with himself at its centre, needless to say. 'Baby Boomerang' was inspired by a meeting with punk poet Patti Smith, but no one would know that from the obscure reference to a 'New York witch' and a 'belladonna child' (an allusion to Patti's strict Catholic upbringing) and 'Rabbit Fighter' (the album's original working title) sketched the back street mugging of a drug dealer in terms that were deliberately obscure (describing a 'dude unscrewed' and 'badly burned').

Only the hard riffing 'Chariot Choogle' and 'Buick Mackane' betrayed his burning ambition to emulate the guitar gods and be accepted as their equal by those who had written him off as a preteen phenomenon. Of the latter he crowed, "It's like Zep Rex. It's yer heavy rock… Buick Mackane is a chick. If you wanna get inside a chick it's gotta be called Buick Mackane, man, to get off with me."

True, there were rather too many crass and lazy rhymes to justify his claims to be a 'street poet' as he coupled the image of a heart filled with pain to one of toes filled with rain (!) and his much professed 'semi-autobiographical' songs were only skin deep, offering no personal insights and no sense of irony, but the hardcore fans kept the faith, writing out the lyrics by hand and pressing them in their school exercise books for ritual dissection, deliberation and debate at break time.

They bought the music weeklies just to see which reviewers had been nice and which had been nasty to their Marc. None expected an analysis of the lyrics or a description of the music.

Melody Maker's Michael Oldfield conceded that there were "no dud tracks on *The Slider*", but concluded that it was an album created to please the converted. "All the familiar ingredients are here", he wrote, it's only fault was the absence of something new to spice up the "winning formula".

While *Penny Valentine* in Sounds called it Bolan's "hottest album yet" and "much more important than *Warrior*, which tended to be a bridge between the old and new Bolan", its 13 tracks were "directed totally toward T.Rex's audience, many of which could be whipped off as a single at any time."

To Marc's chagrin the first album on his own label failed to reach number one, despite pre-orders in excess of 100,000. It peaked at number 4 in the UK and 17 in the US.

CHILDREN OF THE REVOLUTION

Words and Music by MARC BOLAN

Recorded by

T. REX

WIZARD ARTISTS LTD.
sole selling agents
KPM MUSIC GROUP, 21 Denmark Street, London WC2H 8NE   20p

MUSIC LIFE 1973 10

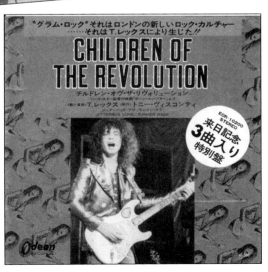

Evidently there was still a substantial fan base in the summer of '72, but the uncommitted felt no obligation to remain loyal, especially now that there was stiff competition from Bowie, Slade, Sweet, Gary Glitter, Mott The Hoople, Roxy Music and a whole horde of gate crashers to the Glam Rock party. Even more demoralising was the album's absence from the ten best-selling LPs of the year. No doubt the lukewarm reviews were partly to blame and the glut of reissues that had stolen some of its thunder, but there were other factors, not the least of which was the public perception that Bolan was getting far too big for his boots and was eager to distance himself from the teenyboppers who were already deserting him in droves. After 'Metal Guru', T.Rex no longer offered eminently danceable pop. The next single, 'Children of The Revolution', released in September, was simply too 'heavy' for the kids, the leaden riff (a lethargic reworking of the Kinks' 'All of the Day and All of the Night') left them floundering on the dance floor, unsure of what to do, and it was too crass for the critics who were outraged that a political slogan should have been hijacked by a politically illiterate pop star. Had Marc recorded it in the manner performed in the film with Elton's Leon Russell-styled gumbo groove, it might have fared better. But the most decisive factor in his decline, and the one that was to prove the most difficult for Bolan to accept, was the fact that the teens had simply lost interest. Many had defected to David Cassidy and The Osmonds whose saccharine sweet marshmallow music and soft-focus, peaches and cream, boy-next-door looks made them ideal teen dream material, in contrast to Bolan whose overt cock-rock posturing and increasingly heavy use of make-up was a distinct turn off for the under 16s.

On Friday 8th September, the day T.Rex were to play the first gig on their five week tour of North America, the next single was released in the UK. 'Children of the Revolution' garnered good reviews, but even before it stalled at number 2 it was clear that Bolan wouldn't have a clear run at the top slot from now on.

"(It) is much heavier than anything the band have done singles-wise before…but will it capture the imagination of the record buying public who are forever looking for new heroes?" asked Chris Welch in *Melody Maker*.

But the *NME* were not prepared to pronounce T.Rex passé, just yet.

"While scarcely revolutionary in concept, it's a different sound from Marc that should ensure that the phenomenal flow of hits is maintained."

That night in Montreal, Marc was all keyed up for another crack at North America.

"Bolan and his band literally barnstormed their way through the set… he pulled out every stop and then some, leaving few doubting that Bolan's time to conquer America has come." Ritchie York, *NME*.

But the next night in Toronto saw another uphill battle for the band.

"(T.Rex) brought a new sell-out crowd on Saturday night to Massey Hall," admitted Jack Batton of the *Globe and Mail*, but added "on any strictly musical terms Bolan isn't awfully impressive." Batton found the acoustic set a comedown with Bolan's voice exposed as a "thin, harsh, nervous thing".

A week later it was hard work again at the Academy of Music in New York. It must have seemed to Marc as if America was standing with its collective arms folded demanding that he impress them.

"It is to Marc Bolan's credit that he did take what started out to be a lethargic audience and bring them to their feet by the end of the set…" Lisa Robinson, *Disc*

"America hasn't exactly been propelled into action, transported into the electrified mysticism of *The Slider*. 'Telegram Sam' inspires some energy, but even during that, the brotherhood of the faithful has yet to truly boogie… the performance itself offered little evidence of the mystique that has galvanised European audiences. Bolan was lithe, energetic, charming in his openness, admirable in his determination to win the audience… Will Bolan finally win them over? We can only stay tuned." Sam Sutherland, *Record Mirror*.

Five long, tiring weeks later, the tone of the reviews hadn't changed.

"This was supposed to be the tour that would plant T.Rextasy into a previously resistant America," wrote *Melody Maker* correspondent Richard Cromelin of the penultimate date at the Civic Auditorium, Santa Monica, "but that hasn't quite been the way it's worked out." Cromelin admitted to loving the albums but found the live band "a terrific disappointment… Marc and his band do manage to build an intensity during some of his long, boring guitar solos, but then – snap! – the song ends, they dawdle and tune and wait for the energy to fade away before starting on the next one. Pacing is an elementary requirement of a good rock and roll show, but T.Rex indicate no consciousness of its necessity or existence… his movements are repetitive, empty and forced. He's trying much too hard and the result is a total lack of spontaneity."

Rock stars are expected to behave like shits, especially during the first rush of success when they suddenly find themselves the focus of almost religious adoration, their every wish granted without question. It is an unreal situation and few emerge unaffected. For someone with an artistic temperament and a tendency to narcissism, the effect of sudden elevation to God-like status can be destabilising, to say the least. Add a cocktail of cognac, champagne and cocaine to the mix and it's even money Mr Hyde is going to get the better of Dr Jekyll nine times out of ten.

According to his close associates, Bolan initially coped well with fame, but once he acquired a cocaine habit and began drinking to excess, he became overbearingly arrogant, aggressive and selfish.

The psychological side effects of cocaine, a short-term stimulant far stronger than amphetamines, are over-confidence, paranoia and anxiety and, though it is said not to be physically addictive when snorted, it can induce a craving to re-experience the sensation of being acutely alert and on top of one's game. But when cocaine is cut with other substances, such as sugar to make it go further, the risks of serious side effects are dramatically increased and if alcohol is added the two can produce a toxin that poisons both mind and body.

At first, Marc's entourage would make excuses for his tantrums which would be followed by profuse declarations of friendship and the offer of expensive gifts in lieu of an apology. But when the bouts of boorish behaviour became his reaction to every perceived slight or setback, their lives became intolerable. Being on the road with a rock star and sharing the excesses of success might sound like the world's best day job, but when the star in question turns on you every time things don't go his way, no amount of gold watches or guitars can ease the feeling of resentment. After the third or fourth time, it felt like their loyalty was being bought.

But it wasn't only their friend's once placid temperament that was adversely affected. His music, too, began to reflect his inner turmoil as he veered violently between rage and wounded pride, depending on the quality of the coke and the amount of cognac and champagne he used as a chaser. One night he wanted to be the rock god indulging in sprawling solos, the next night the sensitive poet, baring his soul and bleeding heart. And in between he strove to find himself. But the Marc Bolan who had once known exactly what he wanted and how he would achieve it had been lost somewhere in the struggle.

In truth, Marc Bolan had never existed. The idol of millions was a projection of an ideal created by shy, insecure, sexually conflicted Mark Feld. The camp pop poseur and the aggressively macho cock rock star were both a front, the embodiment of two complementary aspects of his personality writ larger than life. Mark was born, married, divorced and died as Mark Feld. He even signed contracts as Mark Feld and his son was registered as Rolan Seymour Feld, not Bolan. The only thing Marc Bolan signed in that name were autographs. Legally and officially Marc Bolan did not exist. He was an *alter ego* for a very private person who freely confessed in his songs to being lonely, incomplete and a "contradiction". The latter referred to his self-confessed bisexuality that helped him to play both Queen Bitch and Zinc Alloy with conviction.

Steve Currie: "I think his make-up was AC/DC: I mean, sexually he liked women but there was still the other side where he preferred the company of men."

Visconti: "I'm sure he was bisexual, but Bowie beat him to it by announcing in the press officially that he was bisexual. And I think Marc was a bit bitter about that."

Marc's bitterness was not the result of mere professional jealousy or the fact that Bowie had beaten him to a 'good story'. It would seem that Marc had been struggling to reconcile the two conflicting aspects of his sexuality since his teens and was only just coming to terms with it when Bowie stole his thunder.

"To make love (with a man) wouldn't be repulsive to me. It would just be a bit of a bore with bums, and it would hurt." Which doesn't sound like a comment made by a promiscuous bisexual.

June: "All this thing about him being gay in the papers came up later because it was fashionable to say you were. But he actually loathed making love to men."

Although Marc was comfortable with his male sexuality, he was intimidated, or perhaps even ashamed of his latent feminine aspect which expressed itself in his choice of clothes, make up, mannerisms and deportment. In the early days of Glam Rock he revelled in his image as the androgynous pixie, the Peter Pan of Pop and his look was stylish and subtle, but it would swiftly become gaudy and ostentatious, degenerating into drag queen camp when he lost his looks in the mid-seventies. It is revealing that he referred to this outrageously camp self as female and commented, "I didn't like her at all." The repression of that feminine aspect would have created a conflict which the intolerable pressures of fame, lack of privacy and artificial stimulants would have exacerbated into a crisis until the only escape would be in fantasy and more numbing narcotics. Adulation helped to stabilise this volatile cocktail of emotions, but when his audience turned away, he was forced to face the fact that his fantasy had become unsustainable.

His personal problems were aggravated by his inability to admit that he needed another person to provide stability, be it a lover to steady or share the roller coaster of emotions he was riding, or a producer and friend to contain and channel his conflicting creative urges.

But just when he needed the reassurance that both June and Tony Visconti had provided, Bolan was alienating both of them. June discovered that she couldn't cope with the pressure of running her husband's day-to-day business affairs and had hired Tony Howard from the NEMS agency to be Secunda's successor while she concentrated on renovating their newly-purchased country retreat, a dilapidated rectory in the Forest of Dean. Visconti was still on a retainer from Essex Music which required him to drop everything whenever Marc felt the urge to record, but this was becoming more infrequent as partying with Ringo, Elton and Harry Nilsson became more tempting than working. Besides, making hit singles was easier than picking foxes from a tree, as Marc phrased it on the final single of '72.

'Solid Gold Easy Action' had been pulled together in less than half an hour during a recording session at the Chateau in August after 'Children of the Revolution' and a number of backing tracks for the follow up album to *The Slider* were in the can. Marc had heard Bill and Steve fooling around with a speeded up shuffle rhythm which had distinct possibilities and, not being one to let an opportunity slide, he asked them to repeat it while he worked out a verse and chorus. Bolan took sole writer's credit, of course, and the satisfaction of watching it glide up to number 2 in December, the second T.Rex single to be held off the coveted top spot. Marc later admitted he might have taken it too fast but, unbeknown to him, across the Atlantic in New York, three kids from Queens – Jeffrey Hyman, John Cummings and Douglas Colvin (later to rename themselves Joey, Johnny and Dee Dee Ramone) – latched onto the 'Hey Hey Hey' chant and considered cranking it up even faster.

"Now I feel like I'm writing out of a sense of desperation," Marc admitted. "As though I have the feeling I'm not going to be around much longer."

They say that six months is a long time in politics, but political infighting is a leisurely pastime in comparison to the bear baiting that passes for the music business. Six months after the Wembley shows, T.Rextasy was already on the wane and a new bloodsport was in vogue – Bolan baiting. In the pubs and private clubs, the Fleet Street hacks drew on their fags, swilled their beer and joked that he'd brought it on himself with his boasting, comparing himself to the likes of Dylan and Lennon and bragging that he was making "£40 a second". They didn't care whether he had ripped off Howling Wolf, The Rolling Stones or Mother Teresa, for that matter. This had nothing to do with music. It was about selling newspapers. In their eyes Marc had committed the one unforgivable sin – immodesty – which made him fair game for ridicule. The British are generally very tolerant of sexual peccadillos and they positively treasure 'eccentricity', but they abhor those who practise double standards and they actively shun those who brag and boast. There were one or two who lowered their eyes when they laughed, because they'd genuinely liked him and he'd always given them good copy. But there were more than a few who thought he was a conceited little fag and had it coming. And now they had something to chew on.

Keith Altham: "Marc was the perfect PR subject, he knew what the media wanted to hear. If someone said, 'Tell us about your millionaire lifestyle, Marc', he'd say, 'Oh yes, you know, the gold Rolls-Royce and the gold boat and the gold house'. He didn't have any of those things, of course, but he gave them that sense of excitement that people in that area of national newspapers wanted. They wanted a glamorous figure. He never had as much money as people thought he had. It's always a bit like that. Usually money is invested in various areas or it comes in very much later because of publishing and record royalties, those sort of things. Sometimes you don't see money from a million-selling single for about four years.

"He was a glamorous figure because he played up to it. It was a pose in the same way that Bowie's things are always poses. He'd just as easily go in and charm somebody in an accountant or solicitor's office in a suit and tie as he would dress up in the most flamboyant furs and frills and things and charm the editor of…*Gay News!*

"You couldn't ever influence him. He'd totally made up his mind about what he was going to do before he did it. Whether it was fashionable or not didn't matter one iota.

"He'd do an interview with Judy Simons of *The Daily Express* who really liked him, and quite genuinely during the course of the interview she'd say, 'Oh, I like your hat' or something and he'd give it to her. It was probably a favourite hat of his, but he'd just give it to her.

"You'd get the situation where he'd be a 'Walter Mitty' man himself. He'd talk himself into a situation. Because in this game if you don't believe in yourself, then no one else is going to. So a silver disc immediately became a gold one, a gold disc became a platinum one and a platinum disc became a double platinum. He knew that people always wanted something larger than life, so he always exaggerated. And sometimes he actually began to believe that himself. The facts got a bit mixed up in his own mind. He started quoting his own sources which were himself quite often. But that was all part of the game – it's only a game anyway. He would tell the most gross stories if it was for a Sunday paper or a daily paper like *The Mirror* or *The Sun*, not caring for a moment if it was true, because he realised that was what they wanted. If you came to him from a teenage magazine, he would tell you just what they wanted, and if the music papers came to him, he would happily string them along as well.

"He was always a star. Bowie said that. 'Marc was always a star.' He was a very nice man actually. He had a very good memory for personal detail, but many people who have a strong artistic streak also have a strong fantasy streak and can lie convincingly. As long as he was speaking to music paper journalists he could get away with it. Fleet Street don't really care, they're only concerned with what sells newspapers. He could fantasise the whole time and I think there was a considerable gap between what was really going on in his mind and what he was trying to convince the world outside."

But before champagne and cocaine clouded his brain, Bolan demonstrated an acute sense of self-awareness. At a strawberries and cream buffet for the press at Newton's Restaurant in the King's Road in the summer of '73 he told journalists that he didn't read his reviews, but he always checked out how many column inches he'd been given and whether or not the paper had used a recent photo. "After all, a fan can cut out a photo and stick it on the bedroom wall – but no one wants to do that with newspaper stories, do they?"

In December *Born To Boogie* premiered to snide reviews and played to less than full houses. Having talked it up as something Fellini himself might have made, Marc was now faced with the brutal fact that his fans didn't care to see him clown around with his music biz mates. They simply wouldn't sit still for a plotless pop movie. They emerged from the cinema confused and perhaps even a little disappointed. The film did fair box office in the provinces but failed to secure a wider distribution deal and was quietly withdrawn. Marc was said to be "gutted".

There was more bad news that month. Tickets for the two 'T.Rexmas' shows in London had not sold as well as expected. The expanded T.Rex line-up, which now included three female backing singers and saxophonist Howie Casey, was a welcome development, but at the end of the Brixton show on December 23 as Bolan dropped to his knees to indulge yet again in his guitar and tambourine schtick, showered in fake snow, the temptation to allude to the copious amounts of fairy dust he was said to be sniffing up his nose back stage was almost too tempting for journalists to resist.

Reviewing the 22nd December show at the Sundown, Edmonton Charles Shaar Murray of the *NME* admitted, "despite the melee, it seems to these ears that T.Rex are playing more proficiently than they were earlier this year at Wembley. But…it's impossible to say that they're a really kick-ass hot action destructo band. It rattles along OK… Bolan played a gig to around 5,000 people, and he gave them a really fine time. Which I can dig, despite the rather low-grade music."

Instead of touring Britain to promote *The Slider* and the singles, Bolan had taken their success for granted and spent the autumn on another fruitless assault on North America. Already the UK press were comparing his gigs unfavourably with the extravagant stage shows presented by Bowie with his face paint and chameleon costume changes, the schlock horror spectacle offered by Alice Cooper, the crowd pleasing party time atmosphere generated by Slade and Sweet and the glitzy pantomime performances offered by old school showman Gary Glitter who knew how to whip the weenyboppers into a frenzy. In contrast, Bolan, they said, was taking himself far too seriously, testing the patience of his pre-teen audience with lengthy rambling guitar solos and tedious pauses between songs while he tuned his guitar. Even the band looked embarrassed as Bolan turned his back on his fans and made no attempt to engage them or put on a show unless it was to go through a routine of choreographed moves that were looking increasingly contrived with every performance. A second guitarist might have helped to thicken the sound and given him someone to trade licks with, but Bolan was loath to share the limelight and needed to be free to do a 'Chuck Berry' when he felt the urge (meaning altering the structure of a song as he played, something which didn't give bass, drums and congas too much of a problem, but which would have thrown another guitarist into a panic). If truth be told, a power trio was not the ideal format for a glam band. Bolan, of course, denied that T.Rex had ever been a glam band. They were a 70s' rock group who happened to attract a younger audience and, although that was true, turning his back on his audience and trying to force-feed them sub-Hendrix solos and heavy rock riffs was not the way to endear himself to teenage girls.

A ten-day tour of the Far East and Australia in November had promised a repeat of the scenes that had greeted the group at the start of the year, but America remained stubbornly indifferent.

June: "He became obsessive about cracking the States. Everything had happened in Britain just the way he had foreseen it, so he assumed that America would follow, but over there they marketed T.Rex as a teenybopper band and the critics didn't take him seriously. Japan had been great for him but they have a very different mentality. They loved the visual aspect and the heavy rock stuff. I think America was confused because he had been over there as part of Tyrannosaurus Rex which was clearly part of the Hippie underground movement and then he returned with a band but it wasn't hard rock and it wasn't exactly The Monkees either. He burned himself out trying to break America, trying to convince them to listen to him. But he just couldn't let it go. I think that ultimately it destroyed him."

In December, while on tour in Japan, Marc explained the idea behind 'Metal Guru' to journalist Nobuyuki Yoshinari and, in doing so, hinted at the increasing sense of isolation he felt as he sat day after day besieged in his plush new office. "Metal Guru is very much like one of your local deities… I mean it's a personal god… a superhero if you want, you know, it's someone who would help you, and I was just trying to get down some… a religious sentiment without it being religious, you know, sort of rock n' roll god… at the time when I wrote it I was being fucked up with telephones. I don't like telephones, and it was ringing all the time, so my idea of where god would be at would be all alone without a telephone… For me it was being on my own, you know."

The rock and roll circus is not the ideal environment for the creative individual, who is likely to be acutely sensitive, in need of constant reassurance, highly strung and under constant pressure to perform and conform in an effort to sustain their celebrity status and preserve their public persona. No rock star is going to step off the money-go-round once it's in motion and freely submit to analysis or treatment for substance abuse. And that was even truer in the early seventies when checking into rehab would have been a public admission of weakness and failure.

Bolan's endearing charm and need to be acknowledged as the Ace Face masked his insecurities in the early days, but after '72 when he became boorish and boastful, it was assumed that his latent megalomania had been aggravated by substance abuse and his inability to handle fame on a scale few well-adjusted personalities could have coped with.

But it was not that simple. There is no doubt that Marc Bolan exhibited symptoms of narcissistic personality disorder once he had acquired a serious cocaine habit and was drinking to excess.

The typical narcissist craves constant attention and admiration to compensate for their fragile self-esteem, inflating their accomplishments and overestimating their own abilities because they find it impossible to accept their limitations. In Bolan, this trait manifested in idle boasting, an air of superiority and the devaluing of the achievements of others, all of which were in evidence in his behaviour and interviews between '73 and '76.

"From the beginning I saw my place alongside people like Dylan and Pete Townshend… I've played with Pete and I know I'm as good as Pete. And he knows I'm as good as he is."

"On 'Cold Turkey' Lennon was trying to sound like me. I mean he told me."

"We still sell the most records in England out of anybody. We sold 39 million records, ten and a half in England in two years."

Unable to accept criticism, the narcissist will typically denounce those who rejected him as unworthy of making those observations and claim that he could do it better if only someone gave him the opportunity. Insensitivity, a lack of empathy and a lack of interest in anyone but themselves are all characteristics of NPD as well as miserliness which would take the form of overworking those in their employ and forming relationships primarily to further their own careers.

The narcissist will have developed a sense of entitlement and will create elaborate fantasies of unlimited success that give the impression of extreme self-confidence and even a sense that their success has been foreseen. The narcissist is arrogant, envious and quick to blame those who do not meet their expectations or their needs, a tendency which led Marc to dismiss a succession of managers and take on most of the responsibility himself with Tony Howard as a mere functionary and figurehead.

Howard liked to give the impression of being a hard negotiator but, in reality, he did little more than oversee the day-to-day running of the Marc Bolan business empire from their plush offices in New Bond Street, which must have been the only corporate headquarters to have a rocking horse for the star to ride while entertaining offers for merchandise and personal appearances.

In a misguided effort to shield Marc from demanding fans, press and general hassles, Howard appointed Alphi O'Leary as his chauffeur, gofer and bodyguard. The gentle Irish giant was the brother of Laurie O'Leary, Marc's accountant, and was assumed to be the group's 'bag man' responsible for ensuring the band got paid. If a promoter was reluctant to honour their contract, it was Alphi who was sent round to encourage them to reconsider. Alphi wouldn't have hurt a fly, but his imposing presence gave rise to the joke that the room would go dark when he walked past. Unfortunately, Alphi became overprotective and wouldn't allow anyone direct access to Marc other than Tony Howard which caused considerable inconvenience and irritation for road manager Mick O'Halloran who needed to consult Marc on an almost daily basis when a tour was being arranged.

Alphi became a surrogate father to Marc and was the only person allowed to be in the studio when he wrote his lyrics, which he routinely did after approving a backing track. Marc didn't believe in taking a rough mix back to his flat to listen to and see if it inspired him. Writing lyrics was a magical ritual which required him to sit alone in a dimly lit studio while everyone else took a break and to channel the first words that came through. It hadn't always been that way, of course. In the early days he had written the words to the songs while sitting cross-legged on the sofa at home with only June as a witness. But now cocaine, not Poon, fuelled a stream of consciousness that drummer Paul Fenton described as coming from "somewhere between Marc and the stars".

The worst-case scenario for a narcissist is the loss of their looks, whether in reality or only in their mind. Self-image is all. And when self-love turns to self-loathing it leads inevitably to self-destruction, a vicious circle which can only be broken by a supreme effort of will, or by the influence of someone who loves them unconditionally and has the strength of character to restore their self-esteem.

As Marc admitted the following year, "Certainly there was a period when I was fucked up and probably needed help. But there was nobody there – there never is when you need them."

Chapter 17
20th Century Boy

I lie a lot, you know. I feel that my credibility as a poet allows me to make things up.
Marc Bolan, Spring 1973

B olan was the personification of the cocksure seventies rock star, but it wasn't image alone or even his songs that earned him a place in the pantheon of rock gods. It was the energy and attitude that informed his music and the panache with which he presented it that elevated him above more technically proficient musicians who didn't have that indefinable quality that he possessed. And it was that spirit that he summoned in a Tokyo studio in December '72 for one last glorious two fingered salute to all those who had already written him off.

'20th Century Boy'[1] was the single many would remember him for, although its belligerent hard rock riff, honking sax and soaring female backing vocals were in contrast to the lean, seductive swagger of 'Hot Love' and the earlier hits. The chords were the very same he'd used on 'Get It On' and half a dozen album tracks in between, but he laid into them with the intensity of a man game for a scrap with those who had bruised his ego. His voice had hardened, acquiring an abrasive edge to match his stroppy attitude and the lyrics betrayed desperation to reassert his masculinity.

"Basically the content is erection rock," Marc explained on its release on March 2, 1973. "…it's purely an energy record and if you listen to the words it quotes from a lot of people including Muhammad Ali. I think that every young man in the 20th century is a superstud and the record is meant for him."

Penny Valentine was unconvinced, calling it "another variation on 'Telegram Sam'" and regretting that Bolan hadn't released something "unexpected" that might have "extended his musical capabilities".

Melody Maker detected similarities to 'I Wanna Be Your Man' (written for The Stones by Lennon and McCartney), but found it "full of nervous energy" and praised it for being "more danceable than 'Easy Action'".

The anonymous *NME* reviewer confessed that they thought Bolan might have "lost his touch" after a string of successful singles, but was pleasantly surprised to find it his best since 'Telegram Sam'.

It peaked at a very respectable number 3, but wasn't seen as a defining statement until a decade after his death when he was reclaimed by an older, more male-orientated

---

1 In 2000, manga artist Naoki Urasawa created the award winning graphic novel '20th Century Boys' inspired by Bolan's song and published in the US by VIZ Media.

Above: A rare shot of the double drum line-up taken during the 'Truck Off' tour. (Photo Nick Rogers, Rex Features). Below: By the 'Truck off' tour Marc was entering his 'fat Elvis' period and critics were claiming his performances were becoming predictable (Photo Nick Rogers, Rex Features)

audience who saw past the Glam Rock trappings that he had been lumbered with during his lifetime.

"I don't feel involved with it," he declared referring to Glam, "even if I started it… personally I find it very embarrassing." And as for being a teeny bop idol, he was less than flattered, "If someone seriously put me alongside Donny Osmond and David Cassidy I'd feel very insulted, for that takes away the fact that I'm a writer. However, on a photographic level I don't mind 'cause they're real sweet studs."

The first sign that Marc was willing to risk his cock rock credibility by appearing on kitsch family entertainment TV came with his appearance on *The Cilla Black Show* on January 27th. After miming to 'Mad Donna' from the forthcoming *Tanx* album, Marc joined Cilla for a live duet of 'Life's A Gas' (an event comparable to witnessing Jimmy Page jamming with Rolf Harris). Perhaps he thought he could broaden his audience as Elvis had done, but this wasn't the fifties. Rock had its niche and being seen to 'slum it' on a light entertainment variety show was positively detrimental to the image.

But Marc was unrepentant.

"No one expected us to do the show. I knew Cilla and her husband from quite a way back. I took some persuading to do it, but I think she's a good singer and I think it might break some sort of barrier… It was out of place, but that's why we did it."

One year on from Wembley found Marc in combative mood defending himself against those who accused him of recycling his own riffs. "Everyone else has revamped 'Get It On' and 'Telegram Sam' except T.Rex. Certainly on 'Metal Guru', 'Children of the Revolution', 'Solid Gold Easy Action' and '20th Century Boy', the key, the structure, the tempo, are totally different. I've only got one voice so if you think my voice sounds the same on every record, you could say the same about Mario Lanza. 'Children of the Revolution' is nothing like 'Solid Gold Easy Action'. One uses strings, the other black chicks. One is slow, the other superfast."

In the days leading up to the release of the last official T.Rex album, *Tanx*, on March 16, he appeared almost resigned to having it panned by the critics.

"Marc Bolan is changing, it's just that people aren't really listening."

Tanx was intended to broaden his appeal. The addition of mellotron and a more prominent role for piano and sax demonstrated a willingness to enrich the trademark T.Rex sound to produce an almost mellow West Coast densely textured soft rock sound palette, which was mistaken at the time as evidence that its star was taking it easy and taking its success for granted. But from the strident and defiant opener, 'Tenement Lady', to the soulful, gospel flavoured closer, 'Left Hand Luke', there was a distinct progression in comparison to the earthy early Sun sound of *Electric Warrior* and the bubblebum boogie of the Spectorish *Slider*. Bolan was writing as feverishly fast as ever and committing initial run-throughs and first takes whenever he felt they had the spontaneous feel and energy he was after, but he was persuaded by Visconti to take time with the overdubs to convince the critics that he was finished with the formula, as he repeatedly claimed in interviews.

The songs, with one or two exceptions ('Life Is Strange' and 'Highway Knees'), were as strong as on the previous albums and there were no obvious fillers, as before, although the raunchy 'Born To Boogie', 'Shock Rock' and 'Rapids' offered nothing new. He claimed 'Mad Donna' dated back to the days of John's Children and that he'd written the genuinely touching 'Broken Hearted Blues' at the age of 12 (!), but Mickey Marmalade

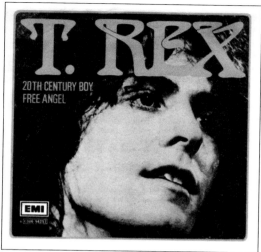

had the impression that Bolan had begun the sessions without any new material and wrote it all in the studio.

Bolan often bragged that he was just a 'street punk' and was laughed out of court by those who couldn't see beyond the feather boas and the face paint, but the album contains some deliriously surreal imagery which was overlooked on its initial release and which makes a compelling case for *Tanx* being the most unjustly neglected and underrated album of his career.

'Tenement Lady', for example, offers a thumbnail portrait of a homophobic street vendor that any modern rapper would give it up for, 'Count Lurch Hearse Head, Prince of the snick snacks, Got a pierced ear mind fear of the sailors with their perfume,' while the choice of words in 'Rapids' has a conversational quality suggestive of the ghetto. "Your mama said, 'Clean out your head boy, don't lay nothing on my child'. And again in 'Left Hand Luke' as he articulates the loneliness and wretchedness of the beggar, 'Call yourself friend and look me in the eye, I'll unstrap my knees and I'll apologise' and 'Ain't nobody's someone and it hurts deep inside'. Elsewhere there are fleeting glimpses of an uncommon facility with words as in the choice of the adjectives 'misshapen, forlorn and toothless' in 'Broken Hearted Blues', but also the ability to suggest a back story in a line or less. In 'The Street And Babe Shadow' the backstage dramas of a travelling circus or freak show are suggested with the equivalent of a single brush stroke ("Tiger Tim the tightrope walker tried to steal the drag queen's daughter'). But most of the time words were mere building blocks for the child-like poet to play with. 'Painted toes and purple earlobes, life's a gas but it's such a scene though.' ('The Street and Babe Shadow')

The veneer of sophistication on several of the more laidback tracks, (specifically 'The Street and Babe Shadow', 'Mister Mister' and 'Electric Slim And The Factory Hen'), suggested Bolan was indeed changing, or rather maturing. Unfortunately, it was also evident from the slurred and more aggressive vocals (including some distinctly off-key wails) that his alcohol consumption was affecting his performance. However, even when pie-eyed Bolan could still knock out killer songs – he just couldn't help himself.

Mickey Marmalade's abiding memory of the sessions was of Marc continually engaging in a drunken rant and storming out when his authority was questioned. But if it was an unpleasant experience for those involved, the bad vibes didn't translate to the record which was generally buoyant and optimistic.

The reviews, however, were lukewarm.

"(Bolan) understands rock 'n' roll and he's been nearly as good at it as he says he is – but lately he seems to have lost the crucial knack of writing good hooks… To his credit he's been trying to vary the pace… *Tanx* is a nice album… He's relaxed on it… Side one has some goodies… the second side just passes me by." Richard Williams, *Melody Maker*

"Overall the 13 tracks tend to vary enormously in merit, with a substantial amount of the standard T.Rex thump 'n' grind coming somewhere in between… For me, it's the calmer more relaxed tracks that are the most palatable… On the other hand, 'Shock Rock' is an abomination made utterly banal by two lines of lyrics…which are just repeated a few times.

Over on side two, though, interest begins to wane…as it gets back to the standard T.Rex we all know, if not exactly love." James Johnson, *NME*

Familiarity was beginning to breed contempt.

In a surreal moment Marc described it as "a gospel album", which was patently absurd, and claimed that he played slide guitar on every track (!), but although it only hinted at a tentative flirtation with American R&B, it was clearly a calculated attempt to distance himself from Glam Rock which by mid-73 resembled a tawdry provincial

pantomime. The track 'Shock Rock' was his answer to those who insisted on lumping T.Rex with the beer-bellied brickies in loon pants and platform boots who thought crotchets and quavers were a new brand of cheesy snack.

"So that's what the song is saying – if you can rock it doesn't really matter if you wear pink satin trousers and a feather boa. Glam Rock is sham rock... The greatest thing (Gary Glitter) ever did was to own up to saying it was mindless crap, which was amazing. That's very truthful. He plays body music but I think he underestimates himself. I don't think it's mindless. They've worked out their riff very well. I'd like to see them rock on... I didn't want to get sucked into second generation glam rock... the whole thing got too cheeky. I wore gold suits and that sort of shit for a while, but it was a flash. Billy Fury wore them four years before; it wasn't an innovation. I don't put down anyone who is involved in it, but once the vision takes over from the music they're in bad shape."

Not that he'd be abdicating his rock star status any time soon. It was too much fun and the perks were unreal.

"'Rapids' is the story of a guy being rejected by the daughter's parents, but then it turns out that although the mother doesn't want the daughter to go with the guy, she wouldn't mind going with him herself!

"It's a situation that I find very real...we get letters from the mums that say 'come to tea' or 'meanwhile, if you want to come while the kids are at school...'

"Of course what we do is sexual. But the sexual atmosphere is a fun thing; very warm, very sensual, very nice. Not something you should take too seriously, because if you do then anything you do on stage degenerates, becomes obscene and disgusting. It's possible to be sexy without being sleazy. It's ironic really, being called a male sex symbol – when I'm prettier than most chicks... Sure I often get accused of being a queer, a fag, but I'm not. (Sorry, boys)... I've checked out the other scene, I check everything out – but it just doesn't get me off... It's like that ludicrous idea that A Real Man Doesn't Cry. Why not? When I'm upset, I cry. All it means is that one is sensitive... I won't stand and be jeered at when I'm doing something that's a craft I've worked at hard for seven years or more. I've never felt so insecure or such pain as I do now because I'm so exposed musically."

If that remark was a serious admission of his state of mind, it went unheeded by the one person who needed to acknowledge that he was now in danger of suffering serious mental and emotional fatigue. But instead of taking a break, Bolan returned to the studio in Copenhagen the very same month that *Tanx* and '20th Century Boy' were released to record the last in the run of classic T.Rex singles, 'The Groover'.

As if to shout down his impertinent rivals, Marc urged his supporters to rally behind the band with a rousing chant of 'T-R-E-X!'

"Some call me Jeepster, some call me lame," he sang, needing no greater inspiration for a song than his own surreal success story, "but when I'm on the floor the kids yell for more, more, more". Such sentiments welded to yet another variation of the 'Get It On' melody and a suspiciously familiar tug-and-release rhythm, albeit taken at a faster tempo, were guaranteed to incite his critics, but it was just what the fans wanted – more of their beloved Bolan boogie.

"Very much the same mixture as before," lamented Charles Shaar Murray in the *NME*.

"Instantly recognizable as a T.Rex single," agreed Steve Peacock in *Sounds*, adding "any competent producer could have fed in the relevant information from their past singles and made this one just as well."

If Marc knew it was his last hurrah, he wasn't letting on.

"I doubt whether I'll be releasing any more records with the same sound," he announced as 'The Groover' ran out of steam after gliding to number 4 in June, to secure his last Top 10 hit. He'd taken the trademark T.Rex sound as far as it could go. There was no room for development.

Tony Visconti: "There were times he wanted to be a musician and there were times he just simply wanted to be a star... this was his conflict... Unfortunately, most of the time he wanted to be a star."

This would have been the moment to announce his retirement, temporarily at least, and grab a few more headlines in the process, turning his back on the music business for self-imposed exile like the legendary Garbo or Gloria Swanson. As the flash bulbs popped he could have heaved a deep sigh and waved away all requests for a final interview with a few choice quotes citing the unbearable pressures of fame and the toll it had taken on his artistic energies. It was regrettable but the world would have to do without Marc Bolan for a while.

Then he could have taken a few years to take stock and consider his next move, to sort out his convoluted business arrangements, perhaps build a home recording studio and work on the projects he had often talked about. He could have collaborated with new musicians and a producer whose fresh perspective might have re-vitalised him and helped him create a new sound. This would have been the time to write the novels and scripts he so often bragged about and complete that second volume of poetry he had planned.

Who could tell what lucrative offers and interesting projects might be forthcoming if he sat back and gave publishers, filmmakers and TV producers the opportunity to approach him without the distraction of scheduling recording dates and exhausting tours? Visconti often advocated a break, but Marc had the same stock reply. "Not now, Tony, I've got to give the kids one more album."

But perhaps it was easier to daydream than to muster the self-discipline necessary to see these projects through to completion? After all, why spend months of hard graft draughting a film script that might never reach the screen, or write a novel that if published might not sell and most likely will be panned, when in half an hour you can knock out a hit single? Why risk facing the possibility that you were deluding yourself, that you are getting high on illusions of grandeur, when you are already a star and don't need to prove it to anyone but yourself?

Drummer Paul Fenton, who sat in for Bill Legend on the *Zinc Alloy* album sessions in October '73, is adamant Bolan would never have considered retirement. "Even when the records stopped selling he wouldn't have taken the idea seriously. He was still in his mid-20s and was constantly on the move. If you're a poet or a song writer, you don't stop being that or having the urge to write and create just because your books or records aren't selling as well. The seeds were constantly germinating. He wasn't ruling anymore, he'd been relegated and was constantly being challenged, so not surprisingly he got aggressive, bullish. He must have been asking himself, 'Why is this happening to me?' In the music business you don't get a chance to make too many mistakes. Very few artists make it big and stay there for the long term. For most who make it big, the only way is down. But Marc was always a contender and had his eyes on the horizon, thinking about his next move. He wouldn't have given the competition the opportunity to overtake him. Even when he was down as low as he would go in popularity and was floundering, uncertain of which way to go during the *Bolan's Zip Gun* and *Futuristic Dragon* period, he didn't want to be beaten. He kept changing tactics looking for a way back, whether it was the metal-disco approach of *Zip Gun* or the light funky pop on *Futuristic Dragon*. He thought he could simulate the formula Visconti had created, but he needed someone to contain those ideas that were continually pouring out of his head, someone to keep him straight. He couldn't afford to give up or admit defeat. A builder's got to build. Besides, whenever we went to leisure out at the Speakeasy he wanted to be recognised. He needed to know he still mattered."

It was the need continually to reassert his status that prevented Marc from reaping the rewards of all those years of hard work, the reason why he could never sit back and enjoy a 'real' life with wife June, family and friends. Marc Feld of Hackney might have relished playing lord of the manor on an English country estate, flicking the long grass with his elephant-head handle walking stick and giving the gardener orders, but his flamboyant *alter ego* would never have been content to watch his music business friends leave his farewell party while he remained behind with his memories of being yesterday's hero. Marc Bolan was a workaholic who craved adoration, attention and applause. It was the very lifeforce that sustained him and gave him reason to live.

"If I didn't work I'd freak out," he said in '73, "I'd OD in two years and be found in the gutter somewhere." But as soon as he'd made that statement, he'd contradict himself and admit that constant touring was affecting his health. "The whole strain in your head warps your mind… I'm still not sure of my sanity half the time, seriously… The pressure is fantastic. I'm a million pound industry, but I'm only a kid really."

And there was the ever-present spectre of America taunting him like the great white whale that drew the obsessive Captain Ahab to his doom. Until he conquered the States Marc could not believe he was a *bona fide* star.

And so he drove himself on, dusting off the trite 'Truck On ('Tyke') which he had shelved as substandard in 1971 and stretching it out with 63 repetitious choruses for the final single of '73.

"It wasn't one of the Bolan greats," Marc conceded, "but it was still a good single."

The week it was released John Peel drew the short straw and found himself reviewing the singles for *Sounds*. He damned it as "curiously lifeless and colourless" and wondered whether "this particular space age cowboy is last year's space age cowboy". But most off putting for him was the fact that "for the last seventy seconds (there's) little but the title oft repeated to a listless guitar riff."

Melody Maker, too, found it "disappointing" with a "heavy emphasis on a rather worn out hook phrase" and felt that the acoustic B-side, 'Sitting Here', was infinitely more interesting.

It was only when 'Truck On' failed to crack the Top 10 that Marc finally acknowledged that he would have to call time on T.Rex.

Mickey Finn confided to the author that he lost faith in Bolan when Marc insisted on releasing 'Truck On (Tyke)' as his next single. "That's really when the songs started to sound too similar for my liking. Marc thought he had a formula for making hits – he said as much to me. He seemed quite happy about it. But as far as I was concerned he was still rehashing 'Ride a White Swan' three years after its release. When we played live all Marc would do were the hits. I don't blame him for playing more or less the same set year after year –he knew that's what the kids wanted. But it's frustrating when you knew he could do so much more."

George Tremlett: "Of course, it didn't help when none of his much talked about plans came to nothing – the film roles, the novels, science fiction scripts and so on. Journalists soon tired of his idle boasts and he only made it worse by making even more exaggerated claims to try and keep their interest. But perhaps the thing that distracted so fatally from his music was his insistence on wearing increasingly outrageous costumes. I interviewed him several times during '73 and on one occasion he appeared in a red jumpsuit with batwings and another time he greeted me in a pink Lurex evening suit, a black and silver waistcoat, a black top hat and thick makeup. The critics regarded him as a joke and yet he was a considerable figure, but he couldn't let the music speak for itself. He had a compulsion to tell everyone how great he was.

There are some artists who take years to develop and he was one of those. It was all coming together when he died. That's what's so sad about it."

Chapter 18
Whatever Happened to the Teenage Dream?

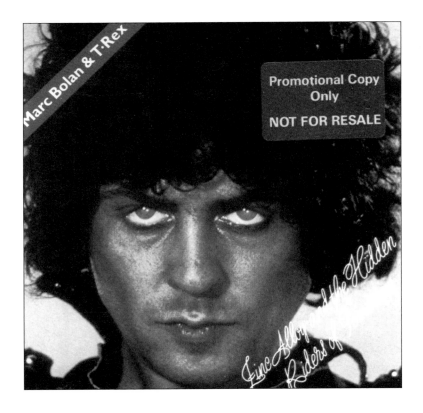

Musically that Zinc Alloy/Zip Gun period was really bad… looking back I was way off beam. I should've just retired for a couple of years… I'd get into the studio with all the songs and I didn't want to play them.
Marc to Paul Morley, NME March 1977

It was a scene Fellini would have loved. A bloated, coke snorting rock star, sprawled in an armchair in his luxury London apartment with a glass of cognac in one hand and an half empty bag of coke on the glass-topped table in front of him as he watches an old movie in which a faded film star gazes adoringly at her younger self on screen and contemplates the fickle nature of fame. *Sunset Boulevard* had been one of Marc's favourite films, the tragic story of an aging silent movie star who lives a life of isolation in the Hollywood Hills, sustained by the false belief that she is still adored by her fans and that one day she will make a glorious comeback. But now, in the late summer of 1973, it had assumed a bittersweet irony not lost on its inconsolable viewer.

June had just left him, exhausted by the intensity of his mood swings, shocked by his violent outbursts and fearing for her safety after he had thrown a magnum of champagne at her which lodged in a plaster partition an inch from her head. She framed it like a pop art exhibit but, after they'd laughed about it, he continued to beat himself up when things went wrong, head-butting a wall after a bad gig, breaking guitars and screaming at anyone within range. "I didn't throw TVs out of the window," he'd admitted, "but I used to smash mirrors all the time. I was ultra violent." June could see that he hated the way he looked, what he had done to himself, but she couldn't tolerate his tantrums and self-pitying rants any longer. She was simply worn out.

It wasn't his womanising either. After all, he had always come home to her to beg forgiveness and there had only been three or four affairs, which wasn't as humiliating as the serial sleeping around some rock widows had to put up with. It was the fact that he had to fall in love with the object of his obsession. Three full-blown romantic affairs were three too many.

The latest was 29-year-old American singer-songwriter and producer, Gloria Jones, queen of Tamla Motown. Gloria, the Ohio-born daughter of a Pentecostal preacher, was more than a flirtation, she was a fixture. Marc was not merely attracted to her, he was infatuated and fascinated by the fact that she had been baptised in gospel music, had sung on sessions for The Rolling Stones, The Supremes, Ike and Tina Turner and Phil Spector and had co-written hits for The Jackson Five, Gladys Knight, The Four Tops, Marvin Gaye and Diana Ross.

She had also co-written and recorded several minor hits for Motown under her own name, including the original version of Northern Soul staple 'Tainted Love' and was on the eve of promoting her own solo album in June '73 when she received a call from Tony Howard inviting her to a week-long session at the Musicland Studio in Munich to record with T.Rex.

During those sessions in the basement studio of the Arabella Hotel, it was clear that the relationship between Bolan and Visconti was breaking down, having been under strain since August 1972 when Marc instructed his solicitors to beat the producer down from the standard 2% royalty to 1%, instead of offering to raise it, as he should have done, to cement their partnership. In spite of this demeaning and mean-spirited insult, Tony remained at the helm of the T.Rex hit factory until it became clear that Marc was not going to evolve musically and that his substance abuse was affecting both his judgement and his temperament. At the end of the Munich sessions, which produced 'Truck On' and the basis of *Zinc Alloy*, Visconti agreed to finish the album, his last with T.Rex, after the band returned from their forthcoming American tour after which Marc would be free to find a new partner or produce the records himself.

Had they chosen to record elsewhere it is possible the sessions might have been more productive and Marc's mental health might not have deteriorated to the extent that it did, for unknown to Bolan and Visconti the studio had been built beneath a building which was said to be notorious for the number of suicides that had taken place there. Several people had jumped to their deaths from the roof and Marc himself was reduced to tears one night after claiming to have been aware of the restless spirits of those who died on that spot in the Second World War. Steve Currie was shaken to see Marc in such an emotional state and spent the entire night calming him down. But Bolan wasn't the only artist to be affected by the unusual atmosphere in Munich. Queen recorded what the group and many of their fans regard as their worst album, *Hot Space*, at Musicland and they blamed the building for the 'bad vibes' which made their sessions an extremely unpleasant experience and for the depressing ambience which they claim encouraged Freddie to indulge in the activities which contributed to his death.

But the bad vibes were not entirely to blame for Marc's disintegration. His world was beginning to fall apart and he seemed powerless to prevent it. His ego simply wouldn't allow him to back down and acknowledge that he needed experienced collaborators as much as they needed his intuitive talent. However, it wasn't only his professional life that was cracking under the strain.

June had flown out for the start of the six-week American tour on which T.Rex supported Three Dog Night, a band with a reputation for partying as hard as they played. After a few days she had to return to the UK and when she re-joined them in Seattle on August 15, it was clear from the awkward looks and embarrassed silences she received from the other members of the band and the road crew that something had occurred. That night she confronted her husband who confessed that he and Gloria had begun an affair. June gave him an ultimatum to break it off, but he demurred. Hurt and infuriated, she flew back to Britain, refusing a reconciliation when he returned to Bilton Towers on September 14, the high security apartment complex near Marble Arch into which they had moved after vacating the flat in Little Venice.

She didn't have the strength for a protracted fight and certainly not when drink and drugs were in the mix. She owed it to herself to walk away and find, if not happiness, then at least contentment elsewhere. Marc would always be the love of her life, an irreplaceable splinter of her soul, but now it was better to walk away while she still could, before she did something she knew she would regret – before she did something foolish.

Marc had hoped that he could have both, the wife and the mistress, and that somehow both women would accept the arrangement. Hadn't he read somewhere of the Pre-Raphaelites keeping a wife and a mistress, the one offering stability and the other inspiration? The mother and the muse? Couldn't they see that he loved them both? One no more no less than the other? Why had they made it so difficult for him? Why couldn't June have been more reasonable?

When she'd walked out on him in Seattle, he'd called Mick O'Halloran to his hotel room and broke down after telling the roadie that they had separated. But by September he told himself he no longer cared. Nobody could hurt him again. He numbed the pain with champagne and cocaine and in a curiously childish act of defiance, he began eating meat as if to erase her influence, but of course the only person who suffered the consequences was Bolan himself. He ate alone, he lived alone and he slept alone.

Gloria was still living in America in the process of extricating herself from her first marriage and trying to reconcile separation from her son who she would rarely see if she came to England to live with her new love. She wouldn't be free until November.

With no one willing to listen to his private troubles he confided to his tape recorder, signing off after one home demo with the words, "Marc Bolan, summer of '73 and I'm lonely." Later he would admit that he had only been unfaithful because he couldn't abide being alone. He loved Gloria, but he might have stayed faithful to June if he hadn't been desperate for company. "My problem was loneliness," he later admitted. "That's why my marriage broke up."

June had cut his hair short before leaving Bilton Towers for the last time and there were still a couple of corkscrew curls lying on the plush carpet at his feet that teenage girls would once have died for. But now there was no one to clean or cook for him. There were visitors of course, old friend Pete Sanders, newer mates like Steve Harley and Donovan, business partners such as Tony Howard and Visconti and a succession of session musicians Bolan was considering working with, all of whom were witness to the shocking transformation that had taken place. Session drummer Paul Fenton found Marc still had his impish sense of fun when he was sober, but was incapable of making his guest even the most basic meal without burning it. Every morning Fenton ate his "carbonised breakfast" with a fixed grin so as not to hurt Marc's feelings, but when he was coked Bolan was not to be reasoned with and not much fun to be around.

The new haircut was meant to make him look younger, but when he caught the reflection of himself on the screen he realised it wasn't right. It was a distortion. He'd become a bloated, puff-eyed, potbellied caricature. In '68 he'd joked that if he got a hit he'd rename himself Zinc Alloy and wear an aluminium suit – now he had become that phoney prefabricated pop star. He could have been bigger than Bowie. Now, he was shocked to see himself as Gary Glitter with tits.

On screen, silent queen Norma Desmond was fixated on the translucent iridescent image of her former self. "We had faces then," she purred rising from her chair, her face caught in the beam of the projector. "I'll show them. I'll be great again!"

Marc gripped the glass until it shattered in his hand.

Success rarely comes overnight and likewise decline. More often than not, it creeps up like old age, the process of decay accelerated by drugs and alcohol which, like an anaesthetic, numb the mind to the critical condition of the body, until one day the star who has traded on his youth and his looks as much as his talent, looks in the mirror and realises he's had the one summer everyone is entitled to and there won't be another.

In the early days of Tyrannosaurus Rex, Bolan had created a fantasy world over which he had complete control and his image was a true reflection of his congenial personality. Now he found himself alone in an illusory world over which he had no influence whatsoever and he was playing a part contrived to capture the headlines and keep him in the public eye.

Even if he could conjure that old white magic to write another irresistible hit, it wouldn't be enough to put him back on top where he believed he belonged and he knew it. He'd lost something that couldn't be retrieved. And it wasn't only the disintegration of his private life or the souring of his relationship with Visconti. Marc was grieving for something even dearer to him than the loss of another human being. Only those who have known fame can appreciate how devastating it can be to have it taken away. It's the one form of loss a performer is never prepared for and which few can accept, which is why many go on long after their time has passed. The

love of fans, of an audience, is entirely different from the affection shared with family and friends. A true artist gives something of themselves, of the very core of their being to what Norma Desmond called "those wonderful people out there in the dark", and when that psychic connection is severed, the sensitive artist will suffer a form of bereavement, no less intense than any other form of loss. They will go through the five stages of grieving – denial, depression, bargaining, anger and, finally, for the lucky ones, acceptance. But there is little chance of emerging from that tempering process if the mind is dulled by artificial substances and the star is surrounded by sycophants who isolate them from the truth.

June's friends blame those insidious influences for the break up of their relationship and the troubles that followed.

"June never really got over her break up with Marc," confides best friend Lani Herdmann. "I met her in '74, a year after she had broken up with him. She had been in Mexico to get as far away as possible and do some serious thinking about what she should do next. When she came back to England she had to go on the dole because he had ordered his minions to change the locks at their flat leaving her with nothing but the clothes she was wearing the day she left. She was cut off from him completely. It was a cruel and heartless way to end a relationship, but she never blamed him. She never spoke badly about him in all the years I knew her. I told her I thought he was a real shit, but she would never say a word against him. And she didn't blame Gloria. She blamed the people he had surrounded himself with and the drink and drugs which had turned his brain to mush. She would only say that he was weak and unworldly and allowed himself to be manipulated. June was always trying to protect him, but his management people blocked her out and poisoned his mind against her. They were trying to get as much out of him as they could and wanted to get her out of the way. They planted seeds of discontent so he wouldn't confide in her anymore. He wouldn't have cut her out like that if he'd known how unhappy she was. But she didn't have the strength to fight back. She kept defending him, saying it wasn't his fault and that allowed her to keep her memories untainted.

"She formed other relationships but they were never as special as the love she had for Marc. He was the love of her life and she never recovered from his rejection. It ruined her life. She became an alcoholic. She was a very loyal person and so felt betrayed when he didn't treat her the same way. It was very sad."

Roadie Mickey Marmalade concurs. "His split with June knocked him for six. He tried to arrange it so that he could have both June and Gloria but June wasn't going to have any of that. When she left him he went into a spiralling decline. Before then he had just been a social drinker, then he started emptying bottles of brandy and vodka before breakfast. But even so, he was never an alcoholic. He could leave it for a few months if he felt like it. What did for him was seeking comfort in food to compensate for his low self-esteem. June had encouraged him to be a veggie and live on pulses and stuff that kept him artificially thin. If you look at pictures of Marc's mother and brother, Harry they are both pretty heavy. I think Marc was always fighting a natural tendency to be stocky and when he switched to eating fatty chicken, fry ups and burgers, he just ballooned out of all proportion. He went from 8st 7lbs to over 11 stone in a few months in mid '74 and the more he worried about his appearance and the effect it was having on his career, the more he ate and drank to make himself feel better. He made the odd effort to work it off like checking in to a clinic with Gloria in '75 but it didn't work. Another time when he was living in LA I went out with him to buy an exercise bike, but he never used it. I also remember we even went jogging once, but Marc didn't have a natural interest in fitness or sport. He didn't stick with it. His only interests were music, movies and watching TV. If you sat next to him on a plane for any length of time you'd quickly find out that he didn't have a lot to talk about. Only those who were really close to him knew he was actually quite shy

and inhibited. He was a great one for bragging and bravado, but it was all a facade. "

As Bolan sank deeper into a morass of drugs and booze so his mood swings became more violent and Mickey had to harden himself to Marc's increasingly childish outbursts and fits of pique. "I was sacked virtually every day," he says, "but when Marc wanted someone sacked permanently he'd always get someone else in the office to do it for him while he was well out of the way. And once fired they were never mentioned again. The trouble with Marc was that he was cocooned; he didn't live a natural life. I used to get up very early in the morning when we were on tour and go sightseeing. And then come back and tell him about what I'd seen. I could tell he was excited about the world outside but he was afraid to go out into it."

Twenty-five years on, Mickey asserted that Bolan's reputation as a party animal during this period is exaggerated. Nevertheless, he concedes that Bolan's drinking and drug taking were inevitably debilitating.

"Cognac and cocaine made him lethargic and killed his inspiration as far as new songs were concerned, but they never dulled his enthusiasm for recording. On one occasion after a long tour he was almost dead on his feet from drink and jet lag, but insisted on going into the studio as soon as he landed. Steve Currie was drunk too and they soon ended up fighting in the control room – but it was like two girls slapping each other around. It was easy to separate them and send them home in cabs. The trouble with Marc's cocaine habit was that it led to him making endless retakes and losing the spontaneity that was often there in take one. It also distorted his perception of who he thought he was and what he was trying to do. When he made the disappointing *Bolan's*

Zip Gun and *Futuristic Dragon* albums he really saw himself as a better producer than Tony Visconti. By then he was blinkered and had lost it completely."

Sadly much of this personal tragedy had been played out in public as Bolan launched yet another fruitless assault on America beginning in Milwaukee on July 20 and criss-crossing the continent all through August and into the first week of September.

Judith Sims saw no need to hold back in her review of the Santa Monica show on August 11.

"Like his two previous attempts to knock America on its glitter ass, he still misses the punch and falls flat on his little pug nose. This time he's playing louder and strutting more confidently and his band have improved enormously... (which) means they now keep time and play most of the right notes."

Previously the American critics had complained that the shows were too short. Now they complained that they were too long and that all the songs sounded the same. In extending the "catchy" three- or four-minute tracks to ten, twenty or thirty minutes in concert, Sims grumbled "those same songs go way past boredom". Adding, "Mercifully, there was no encore."

Robert Hillburn, reviewing the same concert for *The Los Angeles Times*, was of the opinion that the group had been "all but written off" by American audiences after the "extremely disappointing" *Tanx*, but put on a "vigorous" performance for a "generally enthusiastic" but "ultimately unconvinced glitter and rouge audience." Bolan had become "a desperate performer", reduced to using "every imaginable rock cliché" and extending his small repertoire to insufferable lengths. The band were in better form than last time around, Hillburn conceded, but their efforts were undermined by Bolan's posturing and insincerity. "He may make it with a young audience that hasn't seen it all before, but that's a rather empty victory. It's too bad because Bolan really knows how to produce some good rock and roll."

Local journalist Peter Jay Philbin, writing for *Melody Maker*, commented, "For Marc Bolan a crowded American auditorium is a rare and welcome sight, yet it is not enough to help a flawed concert in a floundering career. T.Rex peaked before they reached America and the band has nose-dived here ever since.

"(Bolan) displays no grace and he knows neither style nor subtlety. Instead, he parades aimlessly across the stage, drowning in his own feedback... It's hard for an American concert-goer to understand how T.Rex climbed so high in the English rock scene."

The poor reviews and Marc's increasing frustration had a detrimental effect on the morale of the band.

Bill Legend recalls, "He was coming adrift during *Zinc Alloy*. He was trying too hard and listening to too many people. His new cronies were all into soul music, and he wouldn't let his old mates into that clique. He wouldn't give us credit for being able to get that together for him. He didn't realise what good people he had around him, both in the band and supporting him in general. He forgot to delegate. He tried to do everything himself. After '73, Marc tried to be something he wasn't, and messed with the fundamental elements which made his music special and had brought him success. At that point I knew I had to get out."

Bill left in November '73 at the end of a two-week tour of Japan and Australia, sacked by Tony Howard on the orders of a boss who blamed the drummer's impaired hearing for his own poor performance. His departure marked the end of T.Rex. Bolan would record and perform with a number of experienced session musicians in the last three years of his life, but their precision and professionalism were no match for the tight-but-loose feel generated by Bill Legend, Steve Currie and Mickey Finn.

Tony Visconti had left the previous month, citing Marc's aggressive and abusive behaviour for the breakdown in their relationship.

Paul Fenton believes the break with Visconti made it almost impossible for Marc to stage a comeback.

"Visconti made Marc Bolan a star. He was an exemplary producer, a genius. He had finesse, the brains and the musical know-how to take that very simplistic material and make it sound extraordinary and distinctive. He was continually trying to encourage Marc to try new things. But he also knew the value of being prepared. Tony would write out the dots so that the additional instruments would complement the guitar runs, colouring in the sound without giving the impression that it was over-produced. That's an art in itself. He devised a trick to thicken the sound without making it too heavy. He would ask the piano player and the strings to double the vocal melody instead of backing it because Marc had quite a thin voice and the piano and strings would blend into the vocal and strengthen the melody line. Visconti wanted to be different, to create a new sound and surprise people, but once Marc had a winning formula he wouldn't divert from it, so Visconti got frustrated and found a more willing partner in Bowie.

"If only Marc had stayed with Tony there is no limit to where they could have taken that music. It never would have dried up, but they fell out over some stupid little problem. Tony was in the middle of recording some other artist when Marc called and demanded Tony walk out of the session he was producing to answer the summons, and when Tony refused, Marc took over. Marc had been watching how Visconti produced their hits and when he got coked up he thought he could do it just as well, if not better. That was his fatal mistake."

It now became a matter of pride to prove himself both a better producer than anyone else and to validate his new musical direction. So for the greater part of late '73 and early '74 he devoted his energies to producing a solo album for backing singer Pat Hall, which remained unfinished when he abandoned it in March '74.

His tours, TV appearances and recordings now became subject to the law of diminishing returns, each sounding more strained and contrived than the last until he became a parody of his former self and his records a pastiche, a faint echo of former glories.

Bolan was a born fighter and in no mood to abdicate, but the crown had already been snatched from him in a bloodless coup and there was no chance of a comeback until a new wave could sweep the old guard aside.

The years '74-'76 were a dispiriting time for anyone who believed in pop's pleasure principle, the gratification of desire distilled into a three-minute single. The original Glam Rock party poppers were pooped out after a vainglorious effort to top each other in the excess stakes and the arrival of a decidedly tacky bunch of latecomers – Showaddywaddy, The Rubettes, Kenny, Pilot, The Bay City Rollers *et al* – only hastened the end. Pop had lost its impetus and its relevance. The charts were as lifeless as they had been when Bolan had burst through in 1970. One look at the singles charts for any week during those dire days tells a pitiful story – Pussycat, Our Kid, The Brotherhood of Man, ELO, Fleetwood Mac, The Wurzels… a long and lamentable list of bland AOR acts, inane novelty hits, sentimental schmaltz for the mums and dads and saccharine sweet pop confection for those with a sweet tooth and no discerning taste. The bland leading the bland. A few quirky pop art acts offered some evidence that pop still had a pulse – Sparks, Roxy Music, Cockney Rebel with Queen providing the cabaret – but otherwise 1974-6 was the pits, pop's lowest point. *Top of the Pops*, Britain's barometer of popular taste, had deteriorated into a tacky family variety show featuring acts that would have been jeered off a seaside end of the pier show. Even the hardest of hard rock acts appeared to have run their course with Deep Purple mutating into a blue-eyed soul band on *Stormbringer* and *Come Taste The Band*, Black Sabbath dabbling with synths and strings on *Sabotage* and an enervated Zeppelin losing their edge on *Houses of the Holy*. In a period when Abba's anaemic Europop reigned supreme there was no place for larger-than-life personalities. Elton had passed his most productive period, Rod Stewart was adrift in mid-Atlantic, Bowie was wandering a post-apocalyptic wasteland on *Diamond Dogs* and Pink Floyd were holed up in Abbey Road wishing Syd would return and offer them one decent idea so they wouldn't have to wallow in self-pity for another 40 minutes.

Pop had become soulless and soporific, lacking in spirit and substance. Bolan had backed himself into a dead end, but he wasn't the only one to have lost his way.

In such a climate the idea of fusing soul music with white man's rock didn't seem so outlandish.

Marc had loved R&B since his Mod days, when he would hang around the DJ's booth at The Lyceum and Le Discothèque, sneering at the third class tickets who could never hope to cut such a cool figure as the Hackney hustler. More recently, he'd assimilated contemporary black music at source while listening to the local soul stations during the long hours of tedious travelling coast to coast, but whether he would have attempted a synthesis of rock and soul without the urging of Gloria Jones, is very doubtful indeed. There was no question of his being unduly influenced by her, as no one could have persuaded him to pursue an idea he didn't totally believe in, but certainly without her voice and those of the other black singers she brought in to back him, the *Zinc Alloy* album would not have had the authentic 'Interstellar Supersoul' sound that he was after and he would have been forced to pursue other avenues.

Paul Fenton: "Gloria came from Motown, that was her comfort zone, so naturally she tried to influence Marc into fusing soul music with rock, which didn't really work, but Marc went along with it because he liked R&B and he loved her. He was always willing to try something if it sounded like it had possibilities. But in this case it was a compromise, not a new form of music. It didn't gel. Visconti was OK with it because it was sounding good when they started, but by the mixing stage the coloured singers that Marc called the Cosmic Choir were far too prominent. They almost drowned out the star! Visconti knew they were way too far out front and the whole balance of the record was wrong, but by then Marc was infatuated with Gloria and she was a very strong personality. They were both leaders and they would argue and fight pretty frequently. It could be very confrontational and I think Visconti realised that it wasn't just between him and Marc any longer. He didn't want to get mixed in so he quit."

Fenton became a close friend during the *Zinc Alloy* sessions at Scorpio Studios in London's West End in October '73, sitting in initially as a session musician and subsequently becoming a full-time member of T.Rex.

"I got involved with T.Rex through Tony Visconti who had produced a band I was in called Carmen. Bill Legend had already been replaced at this point by Davey Lutton, but Marc and Visconti wanted top flight session musicians on the record. They knew they had to have the best and if that meant getting people in to re-record parts that had been played by the band then they would do that. It was standard practice in the seventies. Getting the right feel was everything and if the regular drummer, or whoever, couldn't hack it, then too bad, you brought in someone who could nail it in one take. The session guy didn't expect to get a credit on the album. He accepted that was the way it worked.

"The first half dozen tracks I did were the most difficult because I had to play over Bill Legend's parts, keeping in perfect time but playing with a more funky feel. They must have been rehearsal tapes which Marc wanted to use as the basis of the album but were too rough to keep.

"Marc had left it to Tony to get the best people in because he trusted Visconti totally.

"Bolan was a genius – what else do you call someone who wrote all those hits and

that book of poetry when he was barely out of his teens? – but he wasn't a producer. He was an instinctive songwriter and a superlative rhythm guitarist – the best in the country in my opinion, and I've played with the best – but his solos were erratic. He was a busker, in the nicest sense of the term. He played what he felt ought to fit but sometimes his passing notes were unconventional, or off key, to put it bluntly. He never claimed to be a Segovia. That wasn't his style. It's like comparing Muddy Waters' technique with that of Eric Clapton. You can't say one is better than another. They're both highly effective, but each has their own approach. Marc looked at guitar playing from the point of view of an artist, not a musician. Visconti was there to put him right on that when Marc was in the mood to listen, but by the end of *Zinc Alloy*, Marc wasn't listening anymore. And you don't argue with someone on coke. They're not strolling, they're running. That's why they call it marching powder. It intensifies your powers of concentration and it brings your anxieties, discontentment and other stuff to the surface. Then you're on red alert."

The cruellest side effect of cocaine addiction is that it can deceive a musician into believing that they can become a virtuoso merely by playing the same part over and over again. In their mind each new solo is infinitely superior to the last, but in reality their subsequent performances are deteriorating in quality. This was the case with Marc, who would often insist that Visconti stayed up with him all night to perfect a 30-second solo which Visconti would erase after Marc had finally gone to bed and revert back to the first or second take which, unbeknown to Marc, had been bounced on to a safety track to save it for the final mix.

Fenton: "But when he was off coke and relaxing in private with his friends he didn't come across as egocentric. That was an act for the press. Just like that androgynous image which he'd cooked up with Chelita Secunda to get one over on Bowie. The only reason he wore those feminine clothes was that they didn't make sparkly things like that for men in those days. That was the only reason. There is no way he was half-man/half-woman. That was BS, believe me. I stayed with Marc for days at a time in Bilton Towers, that exclusive apartment complex he rented off the Edgware Road, and I can tell you, no way was that guy gay. He was as straight as an arrow, but he liked to wind up the press and when he camped it up he could say things that made great copy that he couldn't have said if he played it straight. He was a bit of an actor, very good at cameo parts. He played the camp star, the lovelorn and bruised poet, the macho male rock star. You name it, he played it. His outward appearance changed over the years as he went from committed vegetarian to comfort-eating carnivore and back to skinny health freak, but his mind remained the same. Drugs and drink affected his behaviour but not his personality, not long term at least. Underneath it all he was still a barrow boy from the East End. And I loved him to bits."

But Bolan was finding it hard to love himself.

His weight affected his live performances on the six-date 'Truck Off' tour of the UK, his first for 18 months, which began in Newcastle on January 21 1974 and featured a ten-piece line-up but few new songs. Whereas before he had flitted across the stage, preening and pouting with feline grace, he now ambled around like a middle-aged man striking a serious of stock poses while additional guitarist Jack Green, Pat, Gloria, two saxophonists (Howie Casey and Dick Parry) and two drummers (Paul Fenton and Davey Lutton) hammered out a thick slab of sound that drowned the remaining screamers. The endless bingeing on drugs, alcohol and rich food had left him bloated, sluggish and had dulled his mind. He was stumbling incoherently through a 'fat Elvis' period while still in his mid-20s.

George Tremlett: "A lot of drinking went on. His records stopped selling as well as they had done. And when your records don't sell you don't get television time and when you don't get television you don't get tours. He went through a down period, he drank a lot. I remember there was a gap of six or nine months between me seeing him and seeing him again. His face and body were puffed out, his clothes were bursting at the seams, he'd changed a great deal... he went to seed and looked it."

The critics could be cruel, but the truth of the matter is that even those who had borne the bragging and bullshit because they genuinely liked Marc and his music were growing tired of hearing the same songs at every gig. The ever-amiable Chris Welch caught the first show of the Truck Off tour at Newcastle City Hall and was sorry to report that he "attacked his guitar with perhaps more enthusiasm than expertise" and that the extended jams were "a trifle monotonous".

Zinc Alloy – A Creamed Cage In August was not well received on its release in February 1974. It was a bloated, stodgy pudding of an album: overwrought, over produced and largely indigestible. Its star was fatally self-absorbed and indulging in instrumental exhibitionism sounding not unlike Hendrix on 'Midnight Lightning', the drug fuelled jam sessions spliced together from cuttings swept up from the studio floor and overdubbed after his death. The 'Cosmic Choir' (Gloria, her brother Richard and Pat Hall) is predominant to the point where they threaten to submerge the lead vocals, particularly on 'Sound Pit' which contains some of the worst lines Marc penned in

his entire career (rhyming 'Metal Guru' with 'loo' and 'glue') and 'Liquid Gang' which sees Bolan wedged in between badass gospel wailing and overpowering brass.

The centrepiece of the album, '(Whatever Happened To) The Teenage Dream?' is as overblown and empty a number as Meatloaf's AOR pastiche, 'Bat Out Of Hell', but unlike Meatloaf, Marc was deadly serious. "The idea of the song is whatever happened to the enthusiasm one felt at the age of 12 and why is one's first screw a drag, however good the second one is. The whole song doesn't necessarily apply to me although the verses do. The song is about growing up."

Not that you'd know it from the obtuse imagery which threw in The Wizard of Oz, the Silver Surfer and a couple of characters of Marc's own creation who 'ruled' his girl with 'Teutonic teeth' (?) and turned her mouth green. This wasn't poetry, it was pop at its most pretentious and it charmed no one.

It was Cecil B. De Bolan on steroids, an already inflated ego pumped up to deliver a facile monologue that would make Jim Steinman's protégé sound restrained by comparison. What made it particularly painful for the older fans was the realisation that it was a reworking of the 'Cat Black' chord sequence which had been the basis of a beguiling musical fantasy only five years earlier but now only emphasised the depth of Bolan's decline.

When he was not camping it up and trying too hard to sound profound, as on the absurdly titled 'Painless Persuasion V The Meathawk Immaculate', Marc sounded positively playful. 'Interstellar Soul', 'The Avengers (Superbad)' and 'The Leopards Featuring Gardenia And The Mighty Slug' clearly provided the template for Prince to become a squiggle and style icon in the eighties. And if at least half a dozen tracks betrayed a careless indifference to his craft as a lyricist, including two songs that were little more than fragments edited together to create a track, it is also true to say that the album closed with two that found Marc at his tongue-in-cheek and teasing best, 'The Avengers (Superbad)' and 'The Leopards', proving that his poetic powers had not deserted him entirely. 'I know that we know that they know it's wrong to spend your life inside a song' and 'Mincing Quincy dropping bop drops down the drain' ('The Leopards').Love him or loathe him, it was difficult to deny he was one of a kind.

What he failed to appreciate, or had forgotten, however, was that albums are not simply star vehicles, but a collection of songs, and record buyers want songs that they can dance to, hum or relate to in some way, even if the experience described isn't one they have shared. Whether the artist is Sinatra, The Rolling Stones or The Sex Pistols the listener needs to be able to relate to a sentiment, an idea or an emotion. Only Captain Beefheart could get away with unfathomable lyrics and atonal sound collages because he was first and foremost a performance artist who was dabbling in rock and roll. Bolan was not a painter. He was a rocker who lost his way and with it, his audience.

But then again, as the album was originally to be credited to Zinc Alloy And The Hidden Riders of Tomorrow and not T.Rex, perhaps it should be viewed as a vanity project, just like the 'Blackjack'/'Squint Eye Mangle' single he had released under the moniker Big Carrot in August of the previous year (damned by John Peel as "egocentric drivel"). Those tracks were little more than an edited instrumental jam session with Marc wailing away furiously under the influence of Jack Daniels and his guitar god complex and as such shouldn't be taken too seriously. *Zinc Alloy* could be looked upon as more of the same.

For all its faults, and they are considerable, *Zinc Alloy* qualifies, if not as the last essential T.Rex album, then at least as a guilty pleasure and as such shouldn't adversely affect Marc's overall credit rating. Taken in isolation, tracks such as 'Venus Loon', 'Galaxy', 'Change', 'Nameless Wildness', 'The Avengers' and 'The Leopards' are tightly focussed and funky, and not entirely unsuccessful in blending rock and soul. But there was still a racial divide in popular culture at this time that affected the album's reception. Reviewers were confused. Blaxploitation movies were just beginning to find a wider white audience and R&B was still considered the prerogative of Stax. The early seventies was not the time for a white boy to sing soul unless he had a real feel for black music and his name was Van Morrison.

Boley was way ahead of the game on this one. He just needed more time.

The album's poor chart placing, nosing no higher than number 12, prompted Bolan to admit, for the first time, that he was losing ground and that his fans were falling by the wayside. "My fans are the most important thing in my life, but they have to dig me for what I'm doing."

Sadly, many of them had ceased to care or to follow his declining fortunes. And when his few friends in the music press openly expressed their doubts and disappointment, Marc retreated into a bunker mentality, repelling all attacks with stoic defiance.

Reviewing 'Teenage Dream' for *Sounds* a weary John Peel declared that it was both "pretty different" and at the same time "pretty much the same" with the lyrics being "not an entirely happy mixture" of Marc's own surrealism and a parody of mid-period Dylan.

Roy Carr in the *NME* called the single "an amazingly inarticulate mean teen lament" featuring a guitar solo which sounded like a ferret being suffocated, but was quite right in identifying the intro as having been 'borrowed' note for note from Paul Anka's classic fifties ballad 'Diana'.

Only Chris Welch had something positive to add, "at last, it really is the new T.Rex sound… a beautifully produced Wagnerian rock ballad."

The album reviews made for sorry reading, proof if needed, that not all publicity is good publicity.

"A thousand curses on his baco-foil jackets and may his mascara run all over his lip gloss in the heat of the spotlights," ranted Steve Peacock in *Sounds*. "My idea of purgatory would be to be marooned on a desert island with a gramophone and a copy of this album," while trade weekly *Record and Radio Mirror* mused, "Not bad at all… No one can say Marc Bolan is out of the game yet."

Andrew Tyler of the *NME* strained himself trying to be fair but found it hard going. "I was hoping the spangled dwarf was going to pull off something approaching musical competence… With the opening reverberation of 'Venus Loon' I was ready to believe Bolan had finally pulled himself and his music together… But the Loon toon, along with 'Teenage Dream' and a few guitar passages on 'Explosive Mouth' and 'Liquid Gang' are the album's only plausible moments."

Only Chris Welch had a positive word to say. "There's a lot more life, guts and twists of the unexpected here than on many a more serious work," and he singled out 'The Leopards' as having "the ring of true greatness". He ended by making a very perceptive remark, one which Marc would have done well to take to heart. "If the fantasy was replaced by substance and the words took on true meaning, then Marc could achieve his dream – to gain real respect as an artist."

But by mid '74 Marc had maxed out on his credit as a serious artist and been discounted as a teenage idol which left him floundering in a creative no man's land. His commercial value was in meltdown. He was no longer a priceless asset, but an expensive liability. EMI couldn't justify the expense of a luxury latticed gatefold sleeve for *Zinc Alloy*, but finally agreed to a limited edition of 1,000 copies in the special packaging as their tape lease agreement with Wizard Artists meant that they didn't have to pick up the studio bill. That spring Warners dropped T.Rex from their roster, having lost a small fortune promoting poorly attended US shows with disappointing record sales failing to make up the loss. It left Marc without an American label for the first time since 1969.

He put a brave face on it as always, and even managed to put a positive spin on his diminishing number of TV appearances.

"It's got to a point now where I'm such a legendary thing that people aren't really sure if I exist. People look at me in disbelief if I get out of a car or something. They almost whisper, 'There's Marc Bolan'. There's a definite air of mystique now which wouldn't have been there had I been doing *Top of the Pops* every year and putting out 95 records a year, like everyone else seems to be doing at the moment."

Germany had been a strong market for T.Rex from the days when the group would appear regularly on *Musikladen* and *Beat Club*, but one can only imagine what the German viewers made of his shameless mugging as he mimed to 'Teenage Dream' on *Disco* on April 13, 1974. It was an embarrassing performance, made more so by his decision to appear in a black bat-winged costume that was two sizes too small for his spreading waistline while hamming it up like a pantomime dame.

Whatever happened to the teenage dream, indeed? Marc didn't expect a response to his rhetorical question and it was just as well, as it would not have been to his liking.

Chapter 19
Exile

The final scene of David Puttnam's fictional rock and roll biopic *Stardust* (1974) sees rock star Jim Maclaine (David Essex) holed up in a private castle in Spain, separated from his wife and child, exiled from his native Britain, bored out of his brain and just one bad trip away from the morgue. Author and journalist Ray Connolly had based the tragic rags-to-riches fable on elements gleaned from incidents in the lives of The Beatles, Jim Morrison and Janis Joplin, but when the book was adapted for the screen, the filmmakers modeled the central character's look on Marc Bolan. Although the timeline is out – Maclaine sports corkscrew curls and satin jackets in '69 - the allusion is undeniable. Maclaine even plays a guitar solo in the Bolan manner copied move for move from a scene in *Born to Boogie*, but unbeknown to Puttnam and Connolly, that year art was imitating life in an eerily accurate fashion.

In the spring of '74 Bolan turned his back on Britain to go into self-imposed exile, first in Spain, then to LA, the South of France and back to LA. For the next 15 months or so, he jetted back and forth between half a dozen exotic destinations including Nice, Los Angeles, Chicago, Paris and Munich recording two decidedly underwhelming solo albums with top flight session musicians and consoling himself with copious amounts of alcohol and cocaine.

He was now playing dates to less than enthusiastic audiences in Europe and North America with a slimmed down four-piece band that included ex-Beach Boys keyboard player Dino Dines whose contribution to the records was minimal to say the least and positively detrimental, if truth be told.

Dino joined Steve Currie, Mickey Finn, Gloria and drummer Davey Lutton for the first time in August in Nice to rehearse for an autumn tour of the US, the last American tour of Marc's career. The punishing eight-week schedule saw T.Rex in a supporting role to Blue Oyster Cult and only occasionally headlining with popular domestic acts ZZ Top, Kiss and Black Oak Arkansas being better received than Bolan's band, no matter how much effort and energy they put into it.

Reviewing the opening night of the tour at the Tower Theater in Upper Darby, Pennsylvania for *Zoo World* magazine, Steve Weitzman remarked on the vast improvement he noticed in the band's performance ("a highly cohesive unit") and in Marc's guitar work in particular. Only 'Zip Gun Boogie' (which was announced as being the next single, but never released in US) was a disappointment with its "lame lyrics and unimaginative and repetitive guitar progressions", but after tambourining his strat to death, whipping it with the lead and throwing it against an speaker cabinet rigged to explode on impact, Bolan had left the crowd "wide-eyed".

But it was downhill, reviews-wise, from there on.

Don Stanley, reviewing the Pacific Coliseum concert of October 21st for *The Vancouver Sun*, wrote that T.Rex faced a "rough" and "hostile" audience who were "fatigued from a long, slow warm-up" and suffered poor acoustics that muffled Bolan's "adenoidal drone", compressing the songs into a "thick textured boogie rock sludge". Stanley ended his report by saying that as the crowd drained away before the end even the white neon star that lit up behind Marc "seemed to mock him".

The Calgary concert on October 23rd was also savaged in the Canadian press. The band were damned as "mediocre" and Bolan was accused of sounding "like a guy who used to know how to play guitar and forgot…" Gloria's backing vocals were the one saving grace, according to reviewer Eugene Chadbourne, her powerful, tuneful voice strengthening the "slick little melodies".

At Edmonton, Alberta, the next night, the band fared little better with reporter Joe Somberger of *The Edmonton Journal* remarking that, "The only thing that saved T.Rex's act from being totally boring was the offensive loudness." Somberger condemned Marc for being "rude" to a heckler then proceeded to trash T.Rex for playing "a degenerate form of rock music", a comment which the band must have found extremely offensive.

The lack of audience response and the negative critical reaction drained Marc's once irrepressible enthusiasm and the travelling left him listless and irritable. Concerts were cancelled at short notice and substituted with others in remote or unsuitable rowdy bar 'n' grill venues which were less than ideal for a band the Americans still considered a teenybop attraction. Marc was battering his head against a brick wall and getting nothing but a headache. Sometimes, it was said, he took his frustration out on whoever was within range, although Gloria maintains that he never hit her intentionally. She would insist she had sustained her black eye and bruises wrestling a bottle from him or trying to manhandle him back to bed. But if she thought she was protecting him by justifying or denying his drunken outbursts, she was only making matters worse for both of them.

In LA Marc was often heavily made up and, according to Gloria, often mistaken for another chick. (the Estate of Keith Morris, Getty Images)

That final US tour was planned to promote *Light of Love*, an album specially compiled for Neil Bogart's independent Casablanca label from recordings made at MRI studios in Los Angeles in May '74 and beefed up by three tracks from *Zinc Alloy*, an album which Bogart had turned down. Consequently, *Light of Love* was only available as an import in the UK. Marc's British fans would have to wait until February '75 to hear the MRI sessions which were then augmented with new tracks and released as *Bolan's Zip Gun*.

The stacks of tapes amassed from endless all-night sessions at MRI in LA and elsewhere give the false impression that this was a particularly productive period, but listening to the hours or unreleased recordings reveals an artist in crisis. There are meandering, shapeless jams, undeveloped ideas that are worked to death in the hope that inspiration might provide the missing ingredient (namely a decent chorus), and pseudo-sanctified soul tracks that sound as if Gloria is leading Marc to the Promised Land when he should have been going back to the crossroads before it was too late.

Steve Currie witnessed Marc drinking himself into "sheer alcoholic megalomania" during these sessions which would typically run from two o'clock in the afternoon until five o'clock the next morning. When Marc thought he had an idea the band would have to learn it before he called for a take. "Then he'd wipe out the guitars and just use the bass and drum tracks and build over it," Currie remembered, adding "That's not the way to write a song."

'Sky Church Music' is just one example of the futile avenues Bolan was prepared to explore, ostensibly to please his new muse, but also so he could say that he'd tried everything once. Unfortunately, it wasn't only once, but countless times over a succession of nights until he'd exhausted the musicians and the engineer, Gary Ulmer, whose limitless patience allowed Marc to indulge his fruitless fantasies. Sky Church Music was the name Hendrix had coined to describe any music of a spiritually uplifting nature, be it choral music, soul or heavy metal. Unfortunately, Bolan appeared to be under the impression that the Almighty had given him a mission to combine all three. It was *Stardust* all over again, but for real. In the film, Jim Maclaine becomes such a huge star that no one tries to dissuade him when he proposes recording a choral concept album in praise of womanhood (which he was inspired to start scribbling during his mother's funeral – just so we know he's off his trolley). Fortunately, in real life Bolan came to his senses, or ran out of coke at a critical point, and instead transposed the tune for a rock band to produce his second single of 1974, 'Zip Gun Boogie', which was not as godawful as some critics have complained, although Dino's twee keyboard noodling actually makes matters worse.

Colin Irwin in *Melody Maker* tried to be even handed.

"Fantastic start with really vicious guitars and what sounds faintly like a fairground organ… Then in comes Marc whining and groaning… There's an initial catchiness about it… but by the time we've heard about the Zip Gun Boogie for the three hundredth time, it's just another boring Bolan record (which) will do little to challenge his rapidly diminishing status in pop."

Steve Clarke in the *NME* dismissed the single as "ugly" and the lyrics as "banal even by Bolan's standards" with a heavy riff that boasts "all the panache of Uriah Heep."

If *Zinc Alloy* can be considered a guilty pleasure, then the verdict on *Bolan's Zip Gun* and its two singles, 'Light of Love' (July chart placing: 22) and 'Zip Gun Boogie' (November chart placing: 41), is an emphatic 'guilty as charged'. And there were no

BOLAN'S

New Album on EMI

ZIP·GUN

BLNA 7752

Available on Cassette and Cartridge

EMI Records Limited.
20 Manchester Square, London W1A 1ES

mitigating circumstances. This is the album that even hardcore Bolanites pass over when looking for something new to play. It could be argued that Marc was again ahead of the game in attempting a fusion of disco and techno, at a time when the latter term had not even been coined, but even so, the ham-fisted execution makes the entire album as painful an experience as tooth extraction without anaesthetic. It's simply too leaden and sterile to appeal. It's soul music without a soul.

Marc and Gloria at MRI Recorders in Hollywood. Their all night sessions failed to produce a viable blend of rock and soul despite Marc's lifelong love of R&B. (the Estate of Keith Morris, Getty Images)

Marc was mesmorised by the mirror ball and with no greasy thumb guitar licks to prove that there was a human being at the helm, the pneumatic beats and funky-lite clavinet parts just drone on and on, the repetitive, puerile choruses consisting of little more than the title sung over and over again. The song titles reveal the paucity of imagination he was attempting to palm us off with – 'I Really Love You Babe', 'Girl In The Thunderbolt Suit', 'Space Boss', 'Precious Star', 'Solid Baby' and the sorriest apology for a song ever released, 'Light of Love'. Bolan was scraping the bottom of the barrel and coming up empty. Only two tracks can be salvaged from the wreckage, 'Till Dawn', a fifties-style teen ballad pastiche and 'Token Of My Love', an equally melodramatic, lumbering 12-bar blues, both sounding as if they might be outtakes from 'The Rocky Horror Show'. It's a sad fact that while Bowie's coke intake would bring forth the Thin White Duke, Bolan's snorting exposed Dr Frank N. Furter.

The use of a still from Warner's greatest gangster flick *The Roaring Twenties* may have been intended to reinforce the image of Bolan as a 'street punk', but it suggests rather that he knows he's committed a musical mugging, a crime against good taste and needs all the muscle he can get to strong arm anyone to buy it. Around the time of its release he confessed to having just discovered Lou Reed and, if so, it sounds like he'd been listening to the wrong album, Lou's industrial noise project *Metal Machine Music*, instead of the three-chord street anthems from the *VU* days that might have stimulated his addled brain. Needless to say, the album failed to chart.

Sounds dubbed it a collection of "inferior exercises in self-indulgence" and speculated if someone else might have taken Marc's place, as it seemed inconceivable that this could

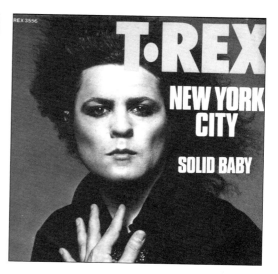

be the work of the same man who had given us *Electric Warrior* and *The Slider* only a few years before. The vultures were circling, sensing easy prey.

As Chris Welch observed, "The jackals of the industry swoop in for the kill, pleased to sink claws into a sitting target… this is Marc Bolan and he can't do anything right."

"A far cry from the pure voices and guitars of the old Rex days," grumbled Kate Phillips in the *NME*. "And yes, it might drive you mad, except that after six or seven minutes you don't really notice whether it's playing or not… this looks like the end of T.Rex as we knew them… Farewell, Mugger Pixie."

It was a sentiment echoed in *Melody Maker*, "England's best-selling poet bites the dust. So long Marc, it's been good knowing you."

If kids didn't buy into the 'just say no to drugs' campaign, they only had to play *Bolan's Zip Gun* to hear what damage substance abuse can do to the little grey cells. It looked like a sad and sorry end to a once glittering career, but it wasn't quite over yet.

In early December, Marc and Gloria moved out of their suite at the Beverly Wilshire Hotel in LA and were renting a luxury bungalow in Benedict Canyon in the Hollywood Hills close by celebrity neighbors Ingrid Bergman, Jacqueline Bisset and Roseanne Barr. Residents of the exclusive neighborhood were assured of their privacy by local law enforcement who patrolled day and night with powers to arrest any tourist who lingered too long or dared to ask for an autograph. It was an ideal retreat for a movie star, but isolation was the last thing Bolan needed at this point in his life. As with his fictional counterpart in *Stardust*, Marc was directionless and adrift, a stranger in a strange land, free to do whatever he wanted but with no idea at all of what that might be. He lacked motivation and he lacked inspiration, none of which were likely to come his way in a picture postcard setting where the sun shone bright and hot each and every day.

He would spend hours sitting by the swimming pool draining bottle after bottle of champagne, cognac or vodka and making plans for projects which would never see the light of day. Gloria imagined that her patience and pampering would heal his bruised ego and that she might become his new muse, but when the ideas didn't come he became frustrated, irritable and quarrelsome. Then he opened another bottle and sank into a chair with a scowl that said, should I drink it, or throw it through the window?

The only other inhabitant of the house was live-in road manager Mickey Marmalade whose duties included hiding half-finished bottles of vodka and getting Gloria out of harm's way when his boss became violently drunk.

They both made excuses for his drinking, she hoping in vain that he would renounce the demon alcohol and find salvation in the religion she still devoutly believed in, Mickey offering more practical help such as driving Bolan to the liquor store via the scenic route so that it would be long closed by the time they arrived.

At one point Gloria called on her Minister father for help, but all he could do was urge her errant lover to take Jesus to his swelling bosom and accept the gift of a cross. It was enough to sober Marc for a moment and bring a broad smile to his lips. Marc thanked the Reverend Jones and assured him that he was wasting his time on a nice Jewish boy who didn't need saving, just another hit single.

In the meantime Gloria prayed her companionship might be enough to compensate for the homesickness that only grew greater every day and dispel the dreams that haunted him.

There was one dream in particular that would cling to him like a damp clammy cloth until he went into the shower to wash it off. It always began backstage at Wembley with the noise of the expectant crowd muffled in the distance as the band waited in the dressing room, nervous but excited. Then a roar would greet them as they mounted the steps to the stage and adjusted the amps and instruments. But then Marc would find himself alone. The guitar would be out of tune and he wouldn't be able to tune it no matter how hard he tried. He'd call for a roadie but no one would come. Then he'd walk to the front of the stage and peer out into the darkness to ask the crowd to be patient, but there was only silence. Then the house lights would go up and there would be no one there.

There were other dreams too. Recurring dreams which never varied. The one which stayed with him the longest, found him travelling in the front passenger seat of a small car. That was unusual in itself as he always sat in the back of the limo or the Rolls. In the dream, Gloria was driving and it was dark - night time, or maybe early morning. There were no street lights, only the white line in the middle of the road to guide them. It was strangely comforting, like being wrapped in a warm blanket and at the same time he felt anxious and expectant. They were going somewhere very special, but he didn't know if he really wanted to go there, not yet anyway. Then it got very dark inside the car and there was no sound, but the car was still moving forward. Only Gloria was not driving. She'd gone. Then suddenly there was a brilliant white light illuminating the inside of the vehicle. It was more intense than any light he'd ever seen, blinding, yet he couldn't take his eyes from it. Everything was strangely calm. He didn't want the dream to end, but he knew it would. And then he would wake up. He would lie still for what seemed like a long time then he would get up and go to the window and look out at the wooded garden at the back of the house where the deer would come down to forage and drink from the pool. He would walk round the pool and breathe in the scent of the orange trees and he would try and recall the dream in detail. But the harder he tried, the more it receded until he returned to bed and sleep. But he never drank after having that dream. He didn't seem to need it.

1974 had been Marc's *annus horribilis*, a year in which he had been confronted with the unpalatable fact that he would never be successful in the States and that his popularity in Britain and Europe was on the decline. It was also the year that he had invested his artistic integrity in a failed experiment to fuse rock, soul and techno and emerged bankrupt and bruised. A year in which he had lead a double life, and been content with neither.

Things could only get better.

"I haven't slipped, not in my chart. I'm still number one." (Marc Bolan 1975)
January 1975 saw Marc and Gloria relocating to Monaco, a 14th floor apartment in the Avenue Princesse Grace with spectacular views overlooking the Mediterranean and the Alps. But the couple found little to amuse themselves there. Marc would sit on the balcony in a fedora and shades to shield his skin from the sun reflecting off the sea, flicking though magazines, with a glass of vodka in the other hand and the TV continually on in the background. When the sun went down they would stroll down to their favourite restaurant and afterwards Gloria might while away a couple of hours at the casino. Visitors were few and infrequent. Ringo would be invited, but even though he lived less than an hour away, he found he was not as free as he used to be. Reminiscing didn't appeal to him.

On January 29, Marc flew back to Los Angeles with Gloria to continue the marathon recording sessions at MRI. Before the flight he had phoned Tony Howard and told him to fire Mickey Finn. Mickey had been AWOL for some weeks having lost interest in playing second fiddle to his former friend who no longer seemed to notice whether his sidekick was there or not. Mickey had stopped attending rehearsals and was hoping he would be allowed simply to fade into the background, but Marc had to make the split official so he ordered Tony to make the call and ensure there were no loose ends, no unsightly scenes and no 'unreasonable' demands for unpaid royalties. Marc didn't even bother to say goodbye.

Mickey tried to pick up the pieces of his former life with girlfriend Sue Worth who had left him during his womanising and binge drinking in the early seventies. Together they opened an antiques business with what little was left from his royalties, but the business soon went bust. They married in '78, but Mickey was badly affected by Bolan's death and the couple split up shortly afterward.

"I was very upset by the split," Mickey told me in '97. "We had been very close and then suddenly it was over and we didn't even have the chance to talk about it. We had been together almost every day for seven years and the next day I was alone. Then just before he died he contacted me and talked about getting back together to do an acoustic show that had been organised by the fan club. I was up for it, but we didn't get the chance to make it right between us. I didn't expect to be so badly affected by his death as I was. It really shook me. I went to pieces."

Bolan, too, was in bad shape in '75. The drugs and alcohol which had numbed him to the damage he was doing to himself and others had taken its toll on his health. After suffering a spate of dizzy spells in the spring he had agreed to check in to an exclusive health resort near Cannes for a complete check-up.

There he learned the full extent of the damage he had inflicted on his body. He was suffering the effects of high blood pressure, his liver was in bad shape and he had the heart rate of a 70-year-old man.

"The doctor said I had been very lucky. It had been a warning. But if I kept living the way I was, I would die. I was told to rest for a month and during that month I had plenty of time to think... I'm going to live like a sane human being because I intend to be around for a long time yet."

It wasn't only the fear of death that brought Bolan to his senses. During their stay at the clinic, Gloria learnt that she was pregnant.

Marc was determined to be fit and together for the baby, but not just yet.In March he returned to the Chateau d' Herouville outside Paris with Gloria and the remaining members of T.Rex – Steve Currie, Dino Dines and Davey Lutton – in the hope that the studio would rekindle the old magic. But he couldn't resist one last orgy of coke and cognac. The sessions ground to a halt leaving two tracks incomplete and the engineer vowing that he would never work with Bolan again. The two songs which remained in the can until long after Marc's death, were reputedly for a rock opera based on the life of a 25th century Dickensian urchin, 'Billy Super Duper'. Although half a dozen tracks were written and recorded at various studios with others demoed at home, there is no record of a plot outline that would link them all together. It seems likely that Marc never got around to writing it.

Another project which he proudly announced but which never saw the light of day was *Obsession*, the film in which he was to play a psychopath opposite David Niven and continental starlet Cappucine. It has often been cited as yet another example of Marc's boasting, but the author uncovered a recording of Marc practising his lines with Micky Marmalade.

Micky can be heard explaining the scene then Marc comes in with his line: "Shut up! Or I really will shoot you this time!" Micky advises him to tone it down. Then Marc repeats the line in a sinister undertone sounding not unlike a young David Essex.

In February he had produced a copy of the script to silence a sceptical interviewer, but the project failed get the funding required and nothing more was heard of it.

"It's a very dramatic script, I play a psychotic who has sexual problems and sells dope. I kill three people and end up in a nuthouse so altogether it's quite a lovely role which is certainly gonna screw a lot of heads up. Here's the script." [throws it into the interviewer's lap] "I'm trying to learn it, but it's very difficult 'cos there's such a lot of dialogue... I have been waiting for a straight part for a long time - about four years - and this is too good to turn up, I mean the part's a gem - I'm the star and it all revolves around me, which is really nice. It won't be easy playing a killer, but I can do it... I'll have a try. I mean I've given it a lot of thought... it's a real emotional part... They chose me

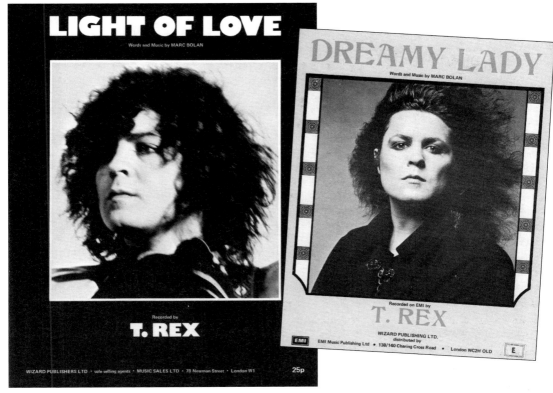

'cos they thought I was the only one who could do it… it's yer real legit film. It's not a musical, it's yer Robert Redford touch."

In that same interview he candidly admitted to having been so low at one point during his self-imposed exile that he seriously considered committing suicide.

"I've thought about it, y'know. Everyone has to if they're under a lot of pressures, but it would be so easy to kill yourself, it's a cop out. Like you can just jump out of that window over there and that's it, you're a gonner. But whatever way you go, you'll be reincarnated… I've been back about three times, that I know of. I mean I get these flashes and things. I was a minstrel and that would most probably explain why I'm interested in literature, poems and music… I can remember being a cavalier as well. You know I remember this place in France that I visited; it was a 16th century house which I'd never been to before and yet I remembered having been there before."

Having been effectively barred from the Honky Chateau, Marc decamped for Munich in March to continue work on the 'opera' and other songs at Musicland. But even recurring chest pains were not enough to persuade him to cut down on his drinking. The sessions were finally abandoned with little of use in the can, though Marc returned to 'supervise' a Donovan session which saw him telling the patient Scot what to play and how to play it.

There was only one solution, as Gloria saw it, and that was to return to Britain in the hope that familiar surroundings and the support of his family and friends would sober and stabilise him.

Marc was determined that the baby should be born in England and saw the sense of sharing the care of the child with his parents who were more than willing to babysit for their grandchild so that Marc and Gloria could pursue their careers. Gloria, for her part, was prepared to turn her back on California and see her own family only periodically if it meant Marc would take responsibility for his and perhaps finally exorcise the depression that had dogged him ever since the hits had dried up.

The move proved even more efficacious than either of them could have imagined. Within weeks of moving into a rented house at 25 Holmead Road, Fulham, in May, Bolan was back in the Top 20.

'New York City' was described by its composer as a 'boogie mind poem', a three line verse inspired by watching Gloria emerge from a limo with a Kermit the frog puppet given to her by a fan, which he repeated over a riff lifted from an earlier, minor hit, 'One Inch Rock'. Its very simplicity was the key to its appeal, the upbeat immediacy of classic T.Rex driven by a strong backbeat and lightness of touch that acknowledged it was fun and funky, not the techno treacle he'd asked fans to wade through on *Bolan's Zip Gun*.

"The grave is dug," wrote Colin Irwin for *Sounds*, "the coffin buried and earth poured on top, but still comes the cries from within, 'I'm not dead, I'm still the King of Pop'… But he's gonna need something really exceptional to lift him from that coffin now. And this trivia, though better than of late, is scarcely enough. Miss!"

Sorry to contradict, Colin. It was a hit, rising to number 15.

'New York City' was hard to dislike, unlike Marc's new high-price hooker look – thick pancake foundation, blue eyeshadow, rouged cheeks and a golden quiff highlight that made him look more feminine than his lover. On occasion he was seen wearing golden sling back high heeled sandals. Gloria is convinced that the only reason they didn't get abuse from racists in America who saw them together was that men mistook him for another chick.

The fans didn't care if he camped it up in a zip-up cat suit, miming amid soap bubbles and wearing more make up than Barbara Cartland, so long as their hero was back on form and on TV.

The fact that the show on which he appeared regularly that autumn, *Supersonic*, was little more than a teatime children's show didn't bother them either if it offered a glimpse of the once reclusive star. Marc's willingness to submit to whatever ludicrous setting producer Mike Mansfield and his team dreamed up was all credit to his showmanship, but not to his judgement. He was filmed emerging from a rocket, being raised on the infamous star-shaped dais like the Bride of Frankenstein with the blond highlights to match and riding on a white swan like a carnival queen in a faux Italian look that made him look like Dave Vanian's dad.

As B.P. Fallon later remarked, "If that was the only surviving footage of Marc, I'd be disappointed.' And 'Beep' was being extremely diplomatic. *Supersonic* was a circus, a burlesque for fading stars to squeeze their spreading waistlines into ridiculous outfits and parade before the cameras, a grotesque parody of their former selves. It was not, as DJ and comedian Kenny Everett, would say, "in the best possible taste", but it did give Marc and his mates a last chance to strut their stuff. And it was all that was on offer at the time.

Live shows were far more risky and, as Marc couldn't face the prospect of playing to a few hundred fans in big city venues which he had once filled to overflowing, he agreed to a low key four-date tour of out-in-the-sticks seaside towns where no one would know if he bombed. It may have been a humiliating comeback for the dethroned prince of pop to play Douglas on the Isle of Man, Great Yarmouth, Hastings and Folkestone, but there were many fans who had been too young to witness T.Rextasy first time round and for whom this was their first glimpse of a legend in the flesh.

HASTINGS PIER BALLROOM

MARC BOLAN

AND

T . R E X

Plus SUPPORTING ARTISTE

Friday 25th July 1975   8.00 - 11.45pm

LICENSED BAR & BUFFET

£1.25 In advance

£1.50 At door

N⁰ 1267

They didn't notice that it was not only low key but also decidedly low budget. Gone was the 'T.Rex' backdrop picked out in light bulbs and the hydraulic star. In their place hung a painted cardboard backdrop depicting Marc riding a dragon and a lot of dry ice to fill in the blank spaces.

Roadie Mick O'Halloran told this writer in '79 that the dragon was the only surviving prop from an elaborate stage show that Marc had planned and for which he had written several songs describing his character's "travels through the universe". It would have been a "futuristic musical drama" with dialogue and effects and a large animatronic dragon which sadly proved too costly to build. According to O'Halloran several of those songs were used on the *Futuristic Dragon* album released in January '76 and if fans juggled them around they could work out the story Marc had neglected to write, a concept that would combine elements of *2001: A Space Odyssey*, *The Children of Rarn* and *A Clockwork Orange*.

But after the aimless indolence of LA and Monaco, there were now so many distractions that Marc could be forgiven for forgetting what he had promised his public in the excitement of the moment.

Reborn and bopping, Bolan was back on *terra firma* and determined not to blow his comeback. A hit, a stable relationship and the prospect of fatherhood had pacified him and brought him back to reality. His new driver, Tony Hall, found him affable and not at all the arrogant star he had expected to meet. "He was a very ordinary bloke, very natural when I knew him, very well-mannered and polite although he didn't have to be. He could have looked down his nose at the 'hired help', but that wasn't in his nature.

"I liked Gloria too. They were always happy to chat. They were never distant or acting snooty. They would invite me in for a cup of tea or something stronger so I wouldn't have to sit in the car outside the house if they weren't ready, and whenever I went to pick Marc up from the studio he would ask me to join in on backing vocals, but I was too shy for that. I remember once they invited me into the house so I wouldn't have to wait in the car and there was Marc watching old videos of himself on *Top of the Pops* with Tyrone Scott his backing singer at the time. Marc was curious to see how he looked and to show Tyrone what it had been like back then. He must have been quite proud of it though because he turned to Gloria and said, 'This will be something to show the grandchildren.'

"That's when they told me that they were going to call the baby Rolan Bolan whether it was a boy or a girl!"

Tony was stunned when he was invited to the christening after the couple discovered that he shared their birth sign.

"They were both Librans and when they found out that I had the same star sign they were like little kids! They didn't have to be so friendly and open as I was only their chauffeur, but they put a lot of value on people's star signs and chose their friends accordingly. They seemed a very loving, close and warm couple. I never witnessed an argument between them.

"Marc never played the star to impress me, except once when he was trying out guitars in his living room and one didn't sound right, so he smashed it against the bare wooden floorboards and it shattered into pieces. I kept a bit as a souvenir, but unfortunately I didn't think to ask him to autograph it for me!"

There was another witness to this incident. George Underwood had been invited to the house that afternoon to talk over Marc's ideas for the cover art of the forthcoming album, *Futuristic Dragon*.

"I had seen Marc a couple of times, very briefly, since I had made the pen and ink drawings of him and Mickey Finn for the inner bag of *Electric Warrior*, which I'd done originally from photos, and then added some elaborate embellishments. Also, I'd done that painting with the frogs in his hair back in '72 which had originally been done for *Jackie* magazine which Marc loved because he said I'd caught his likeness.

"So I was a bit surprised to see how much he had changed. He'd put on a bit of weight and when I arrived at the house he was watching some old videos of himself on the TV. He seemed very subdued, maybe a bit sad, I thought, because he was watching his younger, slimmer self at the height of his fame and success and perhaps he thought he couldn't get it back – I don't really know, but one thing was quite apparent – there had been one hell of a party the night before and Marc was feeling a bit worse for wear! He hadn't seen me for quite a while but he was pleased to see me albeit somewhat hungover. I noticed what remained of a once nice guitar lying in pieces in the hall and living room. Marc told me that the guitar had been given to him by the famous jazz guitarist Barney Kessel. Marc and Barney Kessel seems a strange combination, but they must have met somewhere and Barney had given Marc this guitar as a present. And there it was in pieces. I knew he had a bad temper and when he drank he could be unpredictable. Gloria always tried to make light of it afterwards and find excuses, saying they'd "had a bit of a thing the night before", but he could get very stroppy after a few drinks.

"There were always two sides to Marc. He could be very funny and take the mick out of himself, but you had to be careful not to criticise him. Most of the time he was fine and even spoke of himself in the third person sometimes as if he was referring to someone else, but he could also be very touchy and he had a bit of a hair-trigger temper. It was always difficult talking to him about money, even when he knew he owed you for the work that you had done. He would also run hot and cold. One week you were his best mate and the next you were sidelined for someone else.

"He could be great fun. I had some great laughs with him. Just after that meeting at the house we went to the record shop that used to be at World's End along the King's Road and he kept stopping strangers in the street and asking them if they recognised him. It was bizarre. Then when we got to the shop he pulled out a copy of *My People Were Fair* and told the guy at the counter that here was the artist in his shop and he should be suitably impressed! It was funny at the time even though I was a bit embarrassed.

"Tony Visconti was always very considerate and polite. He got me involved doing paintings for other bands he was producing and was always very complimentary about my work. Marc on the other hand was somewhat more erratic, so I never knew exactly where I was with him. But with all his faults he was extremely likeable and I do miss him being around. We all loved Marc."

In October, Marc found himself in the hot seat as a chat show host having impressed the producer of Thames TV's *Today* programme by taking over from the show's regular presenter during a three-way interview with Telly Savalas.

Among Marc's guests during a five-week slot were Angie Bowie, Stan Lee, John Mayall, Roy Wood and Keith Moon. The Stan Lee interview gave Marc the chance to enthuse about his love for *Marvel* comics, a subject he went into at greater length when he himself was interviewed for a *Marvel* magazine feature.

"I've been into *Marvel* since 1967. The Silver Surfer in particular was one I liked. Dr Strange was another. I'm a bit bored with the primeval breed of hero, all that's kinda cute, but I like my heroes to be able to walk into a discotheque just as they are... I love Son of Satan. I like the idea that downstairs in his house was Hell. He could open a trap door and go down it to try to find his dad."

The inspiration for the forthcoming *Dandy in the Underworld* album, perhaps?

"My new album, *Futuristic Dragon* has a spoken introduction which sounds very much like the intro to a Dr Strange story... David Bowie and I have written a film script together. It's a science fiction thing, like a futuristic Knights of the Round Table."

Around the same time he told a music journalist, "(*Marvel Comics*) might be using some of my characters... My *Electric Warrior* character was meant to be a sort of Conan actually, except that he didn't follow the conventional boring barbarian pattern. The Silver Surfer was always my hero though. In fact, I used him in a song, didn't I? Was it 'Wind Quartets'? I've always liked Michael Moorcock as well, though he tends to be a little flimsy with his heroes. I've always liked his character... Elric... I toyed with actually giving up music and concentrating on writing 'Sword And Sorcery' tales at one time. I've got a book coming out in the New Year called *Wilderness Of The Mind* in fact, containing recollections, science fiction stories, horror stories - I was very into Arthur Machen and H. P. Lovecraft a while back..."

Whether Marc had any serious intention of following through with any of these projects is open to question, but his fans were just happy that the juices were flowing again. He had pulled out of a long slow dive at the very last moment, but could he stay on the level? Had he plucked another hit out of the hat, no matter how derivative, the fans would have flocked back, but he blew it with 'Dreamy Lady', a mawkish dollop of disco that David Soul would have turned down if offered it as the follow up to his similarly styled 'Silver Lady'.

"Ought to merit some marginal disco action," wrote Lester Bangs in the *NME* comparing the vocal to Bryan Ferry at 78 rpm.

There was a collective groan from the remaining fans who were now resigned to disappointment. At least they wouldn't have to wait long for the new album to hit the bargain bins.

Marc wasn't complaining though. He was home and he was newsworthy again, even if the tone of the interviews was gently mocking and more Quentin Crisp than Quentin

Hogg, the flamboyant politician known for his theatrical stunts. 'Dreamy Lady' scraped the Top 30 in September and that month Rolan Seymour Bolan was born at a private nursing home in St John's Wood.

"I delivered him myself," bragged the proud father, "very expertly too... I was a bit nervous about it but it just sort of popped out!... and suddenly there was this big soul voice – 'Oh yeah' [impersonates James Brown]."

While talking excitedly of his pride at the prospect of family life he made a revealing comment. "I don't feel like I'm a father, I feel like his brother, cos you know I'm not a dad type. I never think about dads. My mum was my person, the one I related to... This baby's made all the difference to my life... Whenever I feel myself getting silly and maybe thinking of slipping into my old ways I just imagine myself dying and Rolan never really having known me. That's a horrible thought. He's really held me together and he hasn't said a word."

With the cameras rolling again and the press clamoring for a quote, Marc played the drama queen for all it was worth.

"I was nearly over the edge. I'd had five nervous breakdowns and gone crazy about eight times. You couldn't do what I did and still remain sane."

But he had sworn to clean up his act for his son's sake.

"1976 is going to be a clean year for me. I'll be getting my kicks from playing to the kids again for the first time in three years. You could say I've rediscovered my original dream all over again."

He may have felt that way, but the music he was making was far removed from the dirty 'n' sweet Bolan boogie that his fans wished he would return to.

Chapter 20
Sensation Boulevard

In this crazy world where jive's the game, they got lonely me gold plated on their brain.
Sensation Boulevard

Futuristic Dragon had been compiled from tapes recorded in Chicago, Los Angeles and London between late '74 and Spring '75, but its release was postponed until January '76 in the hope that the two singles taken from it might create sufficient interest to justify its release. It just managed to scrape into the Top 50 and it stayed for one week only.

If Marc thought he could recapture former glories simply by commissioning artist George Underwood to design the cover, he was cruelly deluded. Underwood's new illustration recast the pastoral poet of *My People Were Fair* as a comic book sword and sorcery hero astride a fiery dragon, an image which might have been appropriate for the *Children of Rarn* project, but it only highlighted the yawning chasm that separated the earlier flights of fancy from the pallid, powder puff pop Marc was now serving up with a straight face.

Living in LA had taken the edge off his music where all he'd seen were palm trees, blue skies and golden beaches and this bleached out featureless landscape was reflected in his music – airbrushed squeaky clean plastic pop for people who spent all day working on their suntan. The lyrics were equally banal. "If your sting was like the bee, would you die only for me?" being one awful example and "Come on little girl, won't you hold my hand" a fair summing up of the rest.

It all meant sweet FA to the fans back home in a Britain beset by endemic unemployment, inner city decay and rising violent crime. West Coast AOR, as exemplified by Fleetwood Mac and The Eagles was dominating the airwaves and the British charts, but there was already a groundswell of resentment against such music and the artists who made it, all of whom meant nothing and said nothing to the Blank Generation. Nobody was cruising down the highway in an open topped convertible in Manchester or Birmingham.

Bolan, the shrewd East End toughie, should have sensed the gathering storm, but he was spending more time in front of the mirror than on his music, re-inventing himself as a disco diva and waving imperiously to a parade that had long passed him by.

"*Futuristic Dragon* is by no stretch of the imagination a great album," opined Geoff Barton of *Sounds* in a classic understatement, "and will no doubt be seen by many merely as additional vinyl fuel for Bolan's musical pyre."

Within a year Marc would be trying to distance himself from the album and its predecessor.

"Both the albums I put out after *Zinc Alloy* were not albums that I put together properly, they were very bitty, because I was going through a very indecisive time. The problem was that I was living in three countries at the same time for tax reasons and wasn't really on top of what I was doing and wasn't really happy with the overall direction… I've had my lean period. Last year was very bad for me. The records I made were very below par." It was a rare admission of failure but he immediately felt it necessary to blame his tools and cite other reasons for delivering a substandard product. "After *Tanx* the band was stale, but there was a product commitment… I had to release two albums a year and five singles." In actual fact, his tape lease deal with EMI did not stipulate a specific number of releases in any given period, but it looked better if he could play the victim. And he did it so well. "I didn't want to play on *Zinc Alloy*," he sighed, pouring on the agony. It was, he admitted, "very patchy".

He claimed he could still write songs in the 'old style' if he wanted to, but hadn't released any because he didn't think that they would sell.

"'The high woods filled with the bones of broken gods'… I wrote that the other day, it's a lovely line, isn't it? You see, my idea of rock and roll…is that 'Subterranean Homesick Blues' feel. Surrealistic rock and roll, that's what I like. That's what I've always wanted to do. I think I got close to it when I wrote the line 'cloak full of eagles'. It's a great idea, you open up a cloak and it's full of golden eagles…"

But instead of fulfilling that promise, in February '76 he knocked out 'London Boys', the runt in a litter of indifferent singles, backed by 'Solid Baby', a track from the dire *Bolan's Zip Gun*.

Left Top and Bottom: After returning to the UK Marc hedged his bets by agreeing to play a low key seaside tour' Folkstone Lees Cliff Hall July 76 (Photos courtesy Marc Arscott Archive). Above: Fan shot taken on the low-key 'Seaside tour' promoting 'Futuristic Dragon' (Courtesy Gary Smith Collection)

"Would have been a gas ten years ago," mused Alan Lewis in *Sounds*. "Today, it sounds like a lot of energy expended to little effect, although I can never bring myself to dislike anything from Bolan, one of British rock's few true originals."

The A-side was extracted from his next ambitious project, *The London Opera*, and offered a look back at his Stoke Newington roots, presumably in celebration of his homecoming.

"I had an obsession with being top Mod. I changed my clothes five times a day… ridiculous. It was a time when you daren't turn up at a club dancing last week's dance steps. I had competition then, more than I've had in pop. I felt more famous then too."

That was an odd and telling remark because it was clear by now, even to the supreme fantasist himself that times had changed.

The month long 18-date UK tour through February and into March to support the new album was a dispiriting experience for both Bolan and his fans. "It looked great but it didn't feel right," was *Sounds'* summing up, while Alan Jones of *Melody Maker* said it was "the saddest spectacle" he'd witnessed in years. "There were no more than a thousand people there to see him and he paraded himself before them like a faded old tart looking for one final trick before fading into final obscurity… It really was all so pathetic." Jones was to take back his words a year later when he admitted Bolan had recovered his old "zip and rush" and had to "congratulate the old campaigner for coming through." But in '76 it looked as if Bolan was bowing out.

"Born to boogie or born to waltz?" asked the *NME*. "Marc Bolan isn't quite as flash as he used to be, though the red rhinestone suit and the bleached streaked hair were as loud as his five piece band… The old Bolan magic circle warble's wearing a little thin

Marcos Bolantino – a new look for the 'Rollin Bolan' TV special 1976 (Photo Natasha Goy, Rex Features)

after all these years… The crown was lost years ago and I don't think he'll get it back."

The inclusion of a short acoustic set and a noticeable effort to acknowledge his audience gave the fans the impression that he was no longer as aloof and unapproachable as before. But then, he couldn't afford to be, he needed every one of those fiercely loyal fans if he was going to have a chance of resurrecting his career.

In June, against all the odds it appeared as if he might do precisely that.

There could be no denying that 'I Love To Boogie' was a shameless rip off of an obscure rockabilly single, 'Teenage Boogie' by Webb Pierce, and that Bolan had done little more than add some whimsical lyrics and that quavering voice, hell, he'd even copied the guitar solo! But it was a glorious slice of prime cut T.Rex with no surplus fat and it gave the fans hope that they might be treated to more of the same. But Bolan was dissuaded from recycling other rockabilly riffs by the threat of a law suit for plagarism brought by Pierce's publishers who later dropped the case when it was pointed out to them that 'Teenage Boogie' was itself a copy of several earlier R&B tracks. With the threat of an injunction lifted, Marc was free to promote the single which earned a very respectable chart placing of number 13, making it his last Top 20 hit. Ironically, it had been recorded as a demo at a tiny studio in Stamford Hill and its success suggested that

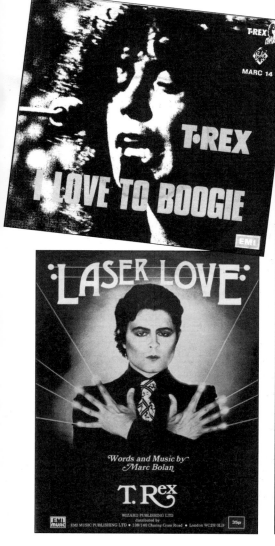

Marc might have been well advised to make an album of short, sharp gutsy 'demos' and resist the temptation to over-produce his next offering to please a disinterested AOR audience.

"So it's we love T.Rex time again… A hit." Caroline Coon, *Melody Maker*.

"The time is right, I reckon, for a Bolan revival… wonderfully basic." Geoff Barton, *Sounds*.

The success of the single and the attendant publicity persuaded ITV bosses to green light a T.Rex *Supersonic* special, a five-song set broadcast on August 28 under the title "Rollin' Bolan". It would see the first appearance of second guitarist Miller Anderson and the last of Steve Currie and Davey Lutton before Marc brought in session musicians to complete the final line-up.

Currie, a modest man who liked nothing more than going to his local pub for a quiet pint every night when not on tour, was drained after years of almost continual touring. Remarkably, Currie remained loyal to Marc despite having been palmed off with a minimal wage that saw only a £10 rise in six years and third class travel on long haul flights. He blamed all problems on management and even after Marc's death he wouldn't countenance criticism of his friend. "He was very good to me. I'll defend him to my death. He was a good bloke: always treated me fairly: never any bullshit." Currie emigrated to Portugal with his girlfriend in 1980 and died there in a car crash the following May. It is likely that Marc never knew how much he owed to Steve Currie for the success of T.Rex.

It was Jeff Dexter's idea that Marc should bring in session men, and none but the best if he was to have a chance of competing with the new wave. The snotty nosed upstarts from the inner city tower blocks and 'sink estates' may have lacked technique, but they had an excess of energy and attitude to give the old farts a good kicking. Lanky bassist Herbie Flowers was as uncool as they came, but he had a list of credits as long as the M1 (500 hits by the end of the decade including his own novelty hit 'Grandad' which had kept 'Ride A White Swan' off the top spot in 1970) and had been on the road with Bowie as part of the *Diamond Dogs* tour. Drummer Tony Newman, likewise, had an impeccable track record including sessions for Jeff Beck and Donovan – he'd also played on the soundtrack of Ken Russell's film version of *Tommy* – and could be relied upon to keep their new boss on his toes. He, too, had backed Beckenham's local boy made good in '74. Everyone in the business respected Bowie, but many secretly admitted to having a soft spot for Bolan.

Herbie Flowers: "Meeting Marc was like meeting a little fairy, an elf. He was everything in life like he was on stage. A beautiful guy, no question about that. Everything about him was so thoroughly warm. Working with Bowie was OK, but it was still a singer out front… Bolan actually played great guitar and moved great – it wasn't a question of being professional. It was a question of it being absolutely right."

Newman too was in awe of the man he called 'the last great pop star'.

The new line-up (Miller Anderson, Dino Dines, Herbie Flowers and Tony Newman) made their debut on the *Today* programme in October performing 'London Boys' and a second song from the aborted *London Opera*, the far stronger 'Funky London Childhood', which could and should have been issued as the next single.

(A further four songs survive only as home demos, proving that Marc was serious about some of these projects, but he was plagued by nagging doubts as to his ability to

Marc always made time to meet and sign autographs for his fans. (Photos: Steev Burgess, Nikki Sudden, Dave Rooney and others unknown. Courtesy Gary Smith Collection)

put together such an ambitious concept and so took the easy way out, breaking them up and issuing the stronger songs as tracks on a regular album.)

Instead, the tepid 'Laser Love' was released in September backed by 'Life's An Elevator', the first acoustic track Bolan had released since 'Sitting Here' in '73. To get the press talking about the single, Marc gave himself a makeover, emerging as Marcos Bolantino, the great matinee idol in a dark Italian suit with his hair streaked down with brilliantine, but there was more mileage in his new image than the music.

If the title, 'Laser Love', was intended to suggest a more passionate take on 'Hot Love', it was an empty promise. A disinterested public gave it the brush off, leaving it to expire just outside the Top 40.

"Didn't Marc Bolan already make this record?" Angie Errigo, *NME*.

"Don't knock him, he's an original." Susanne Garrett, *Sounds*.

Despite its groan worthy chorus ('Life's an elevator, it goes up and down') the flip side signalled a more promising departure, but unfortunately Marc failed to see the potential. Miller Anderson played a picked acoustic guitar figure against a diminished chord instead of the straight major and minor chords Marc had played on the demo and vocal group Alfalpha added chromatic harmonies (more prominent on the demo than on the finished mix). Had Marc been working with a name producer, it is almost certain he would have suggested this tentative foray into acoustic music as a possible new approach, a natural development of Marc's earlier offerings, offset perhaps by raw electric tracks in the style of 'I Love To Boogie' to create a mix of atmospheric acoustic cuts and edgy electric songs in the manner of *Electric Warrior*.

But Marc wasn't worried about reclaiming his artistic credibility. He wanted hits – at any price.

That autumn he toyed with the notion of making a Christmas novelty record, knowing that he could count on support from Mike Mansfield and *Supersonic*, but after recording the vapid 'Christmas Bop', he withdrew it, scheduling a schmaltzy duet with Gloria for a New Year release instead. Their cover of the old Phil Spector song, 'To Know Him Is To Love Him', failed to chart and now seems eerily prescient for Marc's first single of '77, as Spector had taken the title from the sentiment engraved on his father's headstone.

The best Steve Clarke of the *NME* could say for the single was that it was "fairly innocuous" and "entirely unoffensive (sic)", while *Melody Maker*'s Caroline Coon quipped, "This is less a duet than Marc sounding as if he's singing to himself about himself, naturally."

Marc had wasted no time in contacting old friends to let them know that he was back in town. The first to receive the royal summons was his oldest friend, Stephen Gold, who was invited to a Guy Fawkes party Marc and Gloria were holding at a restaurant in the King's Road, Chelsea.

"I was a bit reluctant to go in case he'd changed a lot so I phoned the venue to get a feel of it and Gloria must have asked who was inquiring about the party because she came on the line and said, 'Of course you're coming. Get your ass down here. Marc can't wait to see you.' When I arrived he left whoever he was talking to and rushed over to hug me. He wouldn't let me go for three hours. We talked about old times and just laughed the whole time. It's not true that he was self-centred, at least he wasn't with family and friends. He wanted to know what I was doing and when I visited his house later he took me into a room filled wall to wall with albums and he showed me that he had one of mine from '72. He had kept up with my career. He told me he was planning to start his own label and he wanted to sign me if I was free. Later he phoned me up and invited me to sing backing vocals and add handclaps to a session he was doing at Air Studios for the 'Christmas Bop' single, which he decided not to release for some reason. It was the only time we had an argument because he insisted on paying me and I refused to take any money for doing that. It was the last time I saw him alive. He was a real *mensch* (gentleman) and a loyal friend."

That autumn also saw Marc, Gloria and the baby move from the rented house in Fulham to a large Victorian property in East Sheen, a short drive from the council flat in Putney where Marc's parents were still living. The new house at 142 Upper Richmond Road was situated behind high walls in its own grounds at the end of a row of middle class terraced houses and adjacent to a busy main road. Research by this author suggests that Marc paid in the region of £55,000 for the property which was in need of extensive renovation (at a time when the average family home outside London would have been around £15,000) which suggests that Marc may not have been the multi-millionaire he claimed to be, although the couple owned a second home in Malibu at the time.

As plasterers, painters and carpenters worked on the house, Marc confined himself to the master bedroom where he began writing material for a new album.

Bolan's career may have been looking up at the end of '76 but his financial affairs are thought to have been in a mess and it is believed that he was in the process of untangling it and dispensing with the services of those he felt he could no longer entrust with his investments. The offshore companies set up in his name in 1972 to reduce his UK tax liabilities were being managed by a firm of accountants and investment consultants in whom Marc was said to have lost confidence[1]. It is believed that various ventures had not paid the dividends he had hoped for and though no suggestion of sharp practice was ever made, the labyrinthine structure of the companies that had been set up in his name made determining what had been spent, on what and by whom very difficult indeed.

No fewer than five companies had originally been set up between 1972-74 to channel royalties into offshore accounts – Wizard (Bahamas), Wizard (Jersey), Wizard (Delaware), Wizard Artists and Wizard Publishing, but a trawl through the records in Companies House by the author failed to uncover any revealing documents, presumably because all paperwork relating to Wizard (Bahamas) Ltd is held in Nassau.

---

1 *It is likely, that Marc's 'missing millions' will never be located or recovered, if they were channelled using a tax avoidance strategy known as laddering. In this practice, the account will not be held in the client's own name, but in a trust in a tax haven such as the Bahamas or in what Nicholas Shaxson★ calls a conduit haven, such as Delaware in the USA. The trustees who control the account will typically be living in another country and the beneficiaries might be a corporation registered in yet another tax haven. Directors will be professional nominees whose names appear on dozens, if not hundreds, of such companies and who are connected to the next person on the ladder via a lawyer who is prevented from divulging any details under client–attorney privilege. This barrier is invariably reinforced by what is known as a Turks and Caicos trust with a "flee clause", which automatically transfers the financial structure to another jurisdiction as soon as an enquiry is detected. (★Nicholas Shaxson, Treasure Islands, Bodley Head, 2011)*

An approach to Theodore Goddard, the firm of solicitors administering the copyright for Marc's publishing company, also proved a dead end. Senior partner James Harmon admitted that Marc's financial affairs were "extremely complex", but denied that any royalties had been misappropriated.

June had been a 40 per cent shareholder in Warrior Music Projects Ltd. in which Marc was the majority shareholder, holding the remaining 60 per cent. But after the couple separated, the assets of the company were transferred to Wizard Publishing and Wizard (Delaware), rendering her shares practically valueless. It may be that she was concerned that, if the vast sums that had been squirrelled away could not be recovered, then she might find herself liable for unpaid taxes. If so, her fears were well founded, for on the day of Marc's death the New Bond Street offices were said to have been visited by representatives from the Inland Revenue brandishing a demand for five million pounds in unpaid taxes.

It has been claimed that June sold some of Marc's master tapes after his death to finance a holiday to Turkey where she died of a heart attack on September 1, 1994. But there is no evidence for this. When the author knew her, she possessed only a shoe box of personal mementoes from her life with Marc including, ironically, the one-sided acetate of 'Gloria (The Road I'm On)' he had recorded in '64.

Her friend, Lani Herdmann, is insistent that there were no secret meetings between Marc and June, as has been stated in a previous biography.

"She only saw him once after the split, about three months before his death. I'd found her a job with an audiotape company that I was working for and one day he pulled up in his limousine outside our offices in Fulham Palace Road and she went out to talk to him. It couldn't have been for more than half an hour. When she came back in she was quite stunned and wouldn't talk about it. That was the last time she saw him."

They had arranged to meet after bumping into each other at a Music Therapy Awards luncheon. In the back of the limo he had poured out his heart to her, blaming their separation for his personal and professional problems. "If you hadn't left," he told her, "none of this would have happened."

"She found some stability from that job but she never had money," Lani maintains, "the money she was entitled to. She didn't get anything from him until after his death except a few thousand pounds from his will – the only will he made – and because it had been drawn up while they were still married it caused difficulties for Rolan and Gloria who were of course, not included. June only received a sizeable payment when the divorce settlement finally came through and even that was so badly administered by her own lawyers that she didn't really benefit from it until just before she died. Everyone thinks that she and Marc couldn't bring themselves to finalise the divorce. But that's romantic nonsense. June had obtained a decree nisi in October 5, 1976, and the decree absolute came through a year later, just after his death."

Lani also believes that there is no sinister reason to account for Marc's 'missing millions', just mere old-fashioned incompetence.

"His royalties went to an offshore company in the Bahamas which had an account set up to administer a trust fund for their children. But Marc and June didn't have any children so she couldn't access that money after he died and neither could Rolan because under Bahamian law children born out of wedlock are not recognised as legitimate beneficiaries. June had a daughter with another partner but, as they weren't married, she couldn't get any money for her own daughter either. Then when her divorce settlement came through her own lawyers advised her to invest it all in a trust fund for her daughter so that she could avoid having to pay the higher rate of tax on a sum that would be considered 'unearned income'. But later when she needed money, those same lawyers raised all sorts of difficulties and would only release enough funds to cover her daughter's expenses. It was shameful. They were making so much money from administering these trusts that it paid them to drag the whole thing out as long as they could. I went with her to the last meeting of that trust fund with a lawyer friend six months before she died and we fought tooth and nail until we got them to agree to give her a pension of £40,000 a year and release £20,000 as a lump sum so that she could pay for a new car – she was driving around in a clapped out old banger by then. It was terribly sad."

Chapter 21
Dandy in the Underworld

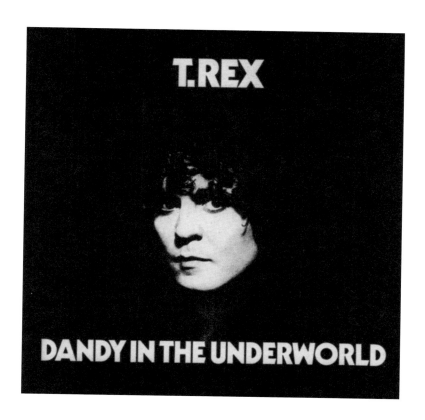

While the punks were gobbing all over Bolan's contemporaries, many of the new bands showed Marc respect and even reverence. It wasn't only because he was a self-taught, demonically driven East End working class tyke who'd made good on his air guitar ambitions. Or that he had mastered the art of the three-minute single using no more than three chords and was proud of it.

It was the fact that Marc didn't defer to anyone in this world or the next, with the possible exceptions of God and Elvis. "If God was to appear in the room I might cry but I wouldn't be humble," he'd once said. "He'd dig me like crazy." And that brazen attitude is what endeared him to the likes of Siouxsie and the Banshees, The Ramones and The Damned.

Punk sought to provoke, shock and outrage with a bizarre, aggressive asexual image – spiked dyed hair, safety pin-pierced flesh, ripped T-shirts, leather S&M gear and Nazi insignia, but for all its loud protestations that it was promoting an anarchic ideology, Punk was just another rock and roll swindle. Underneath the fetishistic facade it was essentially a visual movement and for that reason many of the New Wave identified with the man who had introduced the androgynous look which they were now taking to extremes.

Like the punks, Bolan didn't care what the critics thought of his image or his music as long as they gave him a buzz and the kids liked it. He'd even made a virtue of his limitations. He was an academic failure, but he had the balls to call himself a poet, and he was pretty good one too, for a while.

He also had an ego as large as King Kong. "I'm marvellous. I don't care what people say about me. I know I'm good", but he wasn't too proud to ham it up on kid's TV because, despite his declining popularity in the mid-seventies, he had cast-iron credibility and no one could take that away from him – he'd earned it. He had played the aloof, flamboyant star when the business needed glamour and he'd flirted with the rock aristocracy, but their snooty art school pretentions had gotten right up his nose. So when it was time to get real, he mixed in and made good on his boasts.

Initially he was wary of the New Wave, referring to punk as "electric skiffle" and even voiced his reservations in a weekly column in *Record Mirror* dictated on tape to his publicist Keith Altham who corrected his spelling and added some pithy social comment. But by February, as the new T.Rex prepared for a short French tour in support of the forthcoming album, *Dandy in the Underworld*, Marc was proclaiming himself 'the Godfather of Punk' with not even a mention of Iggy Pop or Lou Reed.

He lobbied for official recognition of his new status by posing for the cover of *Record Mirror* in a crown and sceptre with his tongue pink and protruding, as if blowing a raspberry at all those who dared to question his sovereignty. He was also intending to publish a 'no holds barred' exposé of the music business, documenting rock's Year Zero from the inside. But in the end, it boiled down to no more than a week's worth of entries in the style of Ian Hunter's best-selling *Diary of a Rock and Roll Star*, of which the following previously unpublished extracts are typical.

Day 1

O thou lazy rock star! Got up at eleven, felt good as today is the last day of rehearsal for the French tour; a kind of out of state dress run for the large British tour to follow in March. While I dress I play Bowie's new album (Heroes), he's such a scallywag – and also sly! Great band, only like one song though.

In car on way to rehearsal hall on Southbank I read Richard Williams' piece on New York's rock intelligentsia Television, great name so is Mink de Ville and Tom Verlaine, sounds like an interesting brain to bend notes with.

Day 2

Today Gloria and I do Supersonic. I enjoy working with Mr Maestro Mansfield, it's so unpredictable. Today Mike has me 25 ft. up in the air on a swing (heavily insured I believe) and with Jones – we sing our duet single 'To Know You Is To Love You' in a plastic bubble filled with what feels like washing up liquid. Waist high we croon, my toes and other things feel quite numb! A hard long day, but nevertheless fun. The tour awaits.

Day 3

Up at 6 a.m. I'd packed last night. I'd forgotten what touring was like. It's all coming back to me now. I fall out of bed, take a cold shower to the strains of 'New Rose' by The Damned. The car comes at 7.00 a.m., it's still dark. Through force of habit I don a pair of shades and cat-nap until we beach at Heathrow.

Gay-O-dear-Paris at 9.30 straight to the TV. Average telly day – screened live at 6.00… I do some Elvis wiggles and talk to the viewers in a Charles Boyer accent.

Day 4

The first gig. We're all excited – the place, a large club is what is known as a warm-up date, a gig to get sound cues, lights and heads all in the right space for the big ones. The show feels tight, we blow for an hour and it's magic. All ten days of intense rehearsal have paid off and I'm a hundred per cent pleased. It's been two years since I've worked full throttle and it feels great to be expressing myself in the way I was born to do.

Days 5 and 6
Driving though beautiful Bask (sic) countryside every view is like a French impressionists heaven, I wish I could paint as well as pick... I finish lyrics to several songs that seemed unfinished in the chaos of the city, but become clear complete sonnets on the motorways of France. Next stop Paris.

Paris Day
In the morning I went to the Louvre to look up a statue I'd enjoyed when I was in Paris at the cute age of 15. Hercules looked as great as I remember, also checked out Rodin's house, a museum with much of his work on view. Just the artistic inspiration to key the Bolan brain for boogie.

On his return from France, Marc hosted a launch party for the new album at the fashionable Roxy Club in Covent Garden on March 2 to which various members of The Sex Pistols, The Damned and Generation X were invited. The old guard too were in attendance that night – Paul McCartney, wife Linda, Donovan, Alvin Stardust and some less familiar faces from the Glam Rock era. For an hour or two they mingled, the tykes and the toffs, sipping champagne, nibbling on cucumber sandwiches and making polite conversation while the album rumbled from the speakers and waiters refilled their glasses. Had Karaoke been the rage back then, it's likely Marc would not have been able to resist treating his guests to an impromptu performance of each and every track. It must have taken every ounce of self-restraint for him to stand still in his mustard-yellow jacket and purple strides and be content to bask in the radiance of attention like a rare and exotic orchid.

He talked about the forthcoming UK tour and his decision to offer the support slot to The Damned, a shrewd move and a risky one, but he was more than confident he could show those upstarts a thing or two. Wait until they hear the raw electric version of 'Debora'! Old fart? Don't make me laugh! Dinosaur? Fuck off! He enthused about the arrival of punk and the effect it was having on a complacent establishment who had been sitting on their assets for far too long and growing fat between the ears as well as around the waist. He'd indulged too during his 'wilderness years', he admitted. "I was just bored. I got involved with drugs – particularly cocaine. And I started to drink a lot. I just didn't particularly want to be a rock star anymore." But now he was clean and trim. Almost back to his old svelte self. He'd rediscovered his passion for music and the new album proved he was on his way back.

"I have been sitting around waiting for the pop climate to change, for something like punk rock to come along. I consider myself to be an elder statesman of punk. Under this veneer of brilliantine and behind this perfect profile lurks a lad who knows what the punk movement is all about."

Dandy in the Underworld was well received and deservedly so. It was a pretty consistent collection of brittle-edged rock songs with a few soft centres and although, by no stretch of the imagination could it be said to be a return to the magnificence of *Electric Warrior*, it was a step in the right direction – backwards.

Marc: "The new album was cut very quickly with the new band. I wrote six tracks in the studio and the rest had been around some time."

The monochrome cover was in keeping with the minimalist approach, although Marc couldn't bring himself to ditch the cheesy seventies synths and replace them with a reedy Farfisa organ or a Vox Continental which would have given the album an authentic sixties tone to validate his 'Godfather of Punk' credentials. But for someone who had been written off as an artist adrift without a producer, he had made a pretty good job of it.

Admittedly, there was little evidence of musical development, other than the addition of a violin and flute on one track, and plenty to support the suspicion that he was prepared to recycle his own songs so long as the records continued to sell, but it was the confidence with which Bolan and his new band grasped the old material by the scruff of the neck and throttled some life into it that silenced all dissent. Even the title track resurrected the 'Cat Black' chord sequence for the umpteenth time, but it was performed as if they'd just discovered it.

Dandy began with a crescendo of descending chords to announce that Bolan was back in the guise of a 20th century bard with an abridged retelling of the Orpheus myth. "Distraction he wanted, to destruction he fell," he sang with all the pathos of an impassioned Italian tenor. "Now he forever stalks the ancient mansions of Hell.'

More comic book than yer actual classic Greek tragedy he would admit, but it was enough to dispel the execrable odour of 'Light of Love' and other unnameable horrors of yore.

Sadly, 'Funky London Childhood' had lost a lot in the re-write, appearing now under the title 'Visions of Domino' with the obligatory synth parps dulling its edge and pushing the riff deeper into the mix. 'Jason B. Sad' was not so much a 'distant friend of Johnny B. Goode', more the inbred offspring of 'Get It On' and a pale imitation of the original, while 'Groove A Little' and 'Hang Ups' borrowed other recognisable riffs and were little more than variations on a routine 12-bar with

a twist, but it was such a relief to have Bolan off the critical list, that it didn't matter too much if he sounded more like Shakin' Stevens on occasion than the real thing.

There was no way Marc would have risked his reputation by going all out for a rough 'n' ready garage rock sound, although it might have done his street cred the world of good to have used the likes of 'Mony Mony', 'Strychnine' and 'Crimson and Clover' as a template for his own songs, but he was too enamoured of pretty boy pop to get down and dirty. Instead, *Dandy* offered a polished and professional product with just a hint of string scraping and single note soloing as its star made a token gesture of solidarity to the New Order he hoped would embrace him.

Phil McNeil in the *NME* risked his street

cred to admit that he still had a soft spot for *The Slider* on which "T.Rex played like nobody else has ever played before or since" and that he regretted that on the last album, *Futuristic Dragon*, what had once been "appealingly simplistic" had become simply trite. However *Dandy* marked a return to form, although lyric-wise "the pseudo-innocence seems to have been replaced by pseudo-seriousness in places; the fey by the flippant."

Heartened by the positive reaction to the album, Bolan embarked on what was to be his final tour, one that was to be particularly memorable for all those involved. It kicked off at Newcastle City Hall on March 10 and included a triumphant night at the Rainbow Theatre in London which was recorded for a possible official live album (an incomplete recording of this show was released posthumously thus preserving a kinetic performance of Bolan on top form) before winding down at the Portsmouth Locarno where The Damned joined T.Rex to give 'Get It On' a good seeing to.

Writing in *Melody Maker*, Allen Jones made the point that, even if Marc couldn't fully persuade the critics of his regeneration, he had at least persuaded himself. The band's commitment infused even the oldies with energy and there was a hint of Patti Smith and The Stooges in Marc's new found voice and guitar licks, suggesting that Bolan had the astuteness to seek inspiration in the right places. Jones admitted to enjoying the show despite having anticipated disaster.

Robin Smith reviewing that first night praised the band for being "tight and anchor firm" and noted that Marc looked "relieved that the reaction was so good".

Steve Clarke of the *NME* conceded that Bolan was "back on form... looking thinner and fitter than he has for ages". Instead of the old arrogant aloofness he now treated his audience "with affection" and his rambling, self-indulgent solos were now "well constructed and relatively cliché free".

Marc was now exhibiting the benefits of a strict diet and exercise regime. He was so thin he looked almost anorexic and was high on adrenaline. The band had their work cut out keeping up with him as they pummelled the old songs into submission and gave the new ones a good drubbing while they were at it. The fans were ecstatic. Bolan was back and he was happy to meet and greet backstage. He even gave groups of fans a lift to the next gig in the coach and paid for some of them to stay in a Bed and Breakfast.

Herbie Flowers: "When we went on the road he was just a laugh, a very happy time for us all, wives, kids and everybody. It was just so easy, lovely and magical on stage. I've worked with hundreds of people in the business but he was really the one head and shoulders above the rest because it was like a proper group. All good music should just roll off your tongue and it really did. We didn't do a duff performance at any time.

"The Damned actually treated Marc with so much reverence it was beautiful. We'd all get on the coach and there would be a terrible racket, but if Marc said, 'Cut it out lads, I want to be quiet for ten minutes', they would all be as quiet as a mouse without there being any hard feelings.

"I remember one particular night we were driving back from Portsmouth about two o'clock in the morning and we stopped at a Little Chef. Tony Howard asked if anyone felt like egg and chips and we actually woke the manager and his wife up and said, 'Look, we'll give you 20 quid over the top if you give everyone egg, bacon, sausage, chips and beans, cup of tea and bread and butter'. And so there were 40 of us – the crew, fans, wives and kids and perhaps another 40 fans who had also piled in and we were there until five in the morning. It was the most gloriously happy thing. A couple of us would get up and do a little cabaret and everybody would muck in and make tea. That was the kind of feeling Marc had."

Captain Sensible was in awe of Bolan and was thrilled to see him back on top of his game. "I'd seen him in 1971," he told me, "during the days of so-called T.Rextasy, at the Fairfield Hall, Croydon, where I was working as a toilet cleaner. Another part of my job was showing punters to their seats and stopping them dancing in the aisles. But when T.Rex came on, all these young girls rushed to the front and I was carried along in the tide of writhing bodies. There I was, a bog cleaner, pinned against the barrier, gazing up at the biggest pop star of the day and I was hooked. The very next day, I stayed home learning the guitar."

The Damned's drummer, Rat Scabies, was also a fan. "At the time of T.Rex," he remembers, "people thought Yes and ELP were musical geniuses and Marc was just disposable trash culture. But that was good enough for us. Marc's whole philosophy was about communicating basic ideas through a simple tune. And when you're still learning to play guitar in your first band, those three-chord songs have a built-in usefulness. When he took us out on the *Dandy* tour, we were still more familiar with the image than the man himself, but it didn't take that long. He was very good at making you feel comfortable. He was very 'I'm the Godfather of Punk, get on the bus and let's show everybody!' We had a lot of respect for him, and the only trouble we had was the spitting on the first night.

"After we came off stage all their gear was covered with gob. They had a word with us, and when we explained there wasn't a lot we could do about it, they went out and bought a load of plastic sheets. I think that's the only problem I'm aware of. He was a nice guy full stop. The last time I saw him was at a Ramones gig, and then, well, he was gone. It was very sad."

It was not mentioned at the time, but Bolan paid the support band's expenses out of his own pocket, whereas it was common practice for the support act to subsidise the cost of the tour. "It must have come to two or three grand," says Captain Sensible. "But he really liked us. He knew we weren't out to destroy him – we were after those awful American country rock bands and dinosaur supergroups who were dominating the radio and the charts at the time.

"We admired him because as a rock star he was extremely left field, very English in his writing style, he was still knocking out two-and-a-half minute pop classics while all those old farts were churning out pretentious epics. He never played the star with us. He was very down to earth – a cosmic barrow boy. But he took the fan thing very seriously. He was very protective of them. Rat Scabies and I pulled a couple of girls

Mutual appreciation society. Marc with The Ramones. London 1977 (Photo Richard Young, Rex Features)

on the tour who were big Bolan fans by promising them that we would introduce them to Marc, and he told us off about that. He was quite upset about it. I think he genuinely craved the adulation and love from his fans. He didn't blame them for his commercial decline. He said it was because he had indulged in drink and drugs and had lost his direction. But if he was disappointed by all that, he didn't show it. He was a huge optimist and loved what he was doing. I remember he was very pleased with *Dandy*. And the press reaction was surprisingly quite favourable to the tour. The impression I got was at the end he didn't care too much about critical and commercial success anymore, as long as he could continue doing what he enjoyed – recording and playing live."

The final date of the tour at Portsmouth Locarno on March 20th was witnessed by Marc's brother Harry. It was only the second performance Harry had seen and it would also be the last time Bolan appeared live with T.Rex.

A gaunt faced Marc photographed by a fan on the final UK tour 1977. His punishing diet and exercise regime led some friends to fear for his health (Courtesy Gary Smith Collection)

"It gave me a real buzz to see him playing to all those adoring fans," Harry told me. "I was very proud of him. I wasn't surprised when he became a star, because that had always been his aim. He had convinced me that he would be famous when he was just a kid, but he then had to convince everybody he wanted to work with him. He had a strong will and belief in his own abilities, and that's what carried him through. But, underneath, he was very sensitive and shy. That was a characteristic of both of us. The over-confidence he is often criticised for was really a form of compensation. He had to give himself extra confidence, because he didn't really have much.

"What you saw on TV or on stage was the outside Marc – his front. The inside Marc was totally different. He was an extraordinary individual, a special talent. But at home, he was quite ordinary and very quiet – very normal, in fact. He put on a special persona when he went on stage because, like most performers, he was almost crapping himself before a gig.

"He wasn't addicted to the stage like Bowie or the Stones appeared to be. He would have been happy to become very private, and just make records and write poetry. In fact, he was talking seriously about retiring after his 30th birthday – which of course he never saw. He was going to concentrate on the business side and make more films. Family life with Gloria and Rolan had settled him, and he was happy and ready to take responsibility for them."

The tour was a commercial and critical success and the album made number 26 on the back of the publicity, but the accompanying single, 'Soul of My Suit', only managed a Top 50 placing, peaking at number 42, despite an appearance on *Top of the Pops*.

Caroline Coon suggested one possible reason for its failure. "Marc recorded this single before he listened to the New Wave sound, so, though his heart is in the right place, his music has not yet benefitted from association with his new found friends."

Undaunted, EMI issued the title track as a single in May, thinking that maybe they had chosen the wrong track, but that too bombed, failing to chart at all. Marc had given his fans reason to remain loyal, but he would have to come up with something special to convince the wider public.

In August he released his final single, 'Celebrate Summer', a cracking backing track complete with string scraping New Wave noise but let down by a flaky chorus and lyrics of the "Hey little girl would you like a dance" variety, although this time there was also "Hey little punk forget all that junk" which was both corny and condescending. Marc wouldn't have seen it that way. He wouldn't have given himself the time to consider the implications. The vocal would have been down and the track mixed while the ink was still wet in his yellow spiral-bound reporter's notebook.

"For one golden instant I thought Marc had finally pulled off the unalloyed pop triumph that he needs as a convincing viable follow up to 'Get It On'. This isn't it, but it's certainly the most likeable single he's made in a very long time…" Caroline Coon, *NME*.

It was typical of the uneasy compromise he had struck with himself as he tried to straddle the irreconcilable camps of pop and punk. It was almost as if he no longer believed in Marc Bolan, or couldn't take himself seriously, a suspicion given some credence by the fact that he had never taken the necessary steps to legalise the name change. Marc Bolan was as much a creation of Mark Feld's imagination as any of his fictional characters. And it appears that he never fully reconciled the two facets of his character, the shy boy with poetic aspirations and the showman.

"I still want to be known as a showman and *poseur*, but I also want people to take me seriously," he said back in April, seemingly unaware of the contradiction.

Only *he* knew what a beating his once implacable self-belief had taken in those years when the fans had deserted him *en masse*, the critics turned on him and the records failed to sell. As Cecil B. DeMille (appearing as himself) remarked in *Sunset Boulevard*, "A dozen press agents working overtime can do terrible things to the human spirit."

But there was every reason to believe that it would be only a matter of time before Bolan re-established himself as a contender and regained his credibility. In his August 6th column for *Record Mirror* he announced he was to host his own six-part teatime TV show for Granada beginning on August 24th. It was to be called *Marc* and would serve as a showcase for the best of the new bands, a few 'safe' faces and, of course, the Main Man himself, preening, pouting and pirouetting centre stage where he belonged.

"I'm back on the box… my own TV series is something I'm really excited about. It happened because Granada's big chief Johnny Hamp wanted someone to host a rock show which would bridge the gap between today and tomorrow and generate a genuine feeling for young people."

Marc was determined that he should be seen to embody Today while getting credit for introducing the artists of Tomorrow. The Jam, The Boomtown Rats and Generation X made their TV debuts on the show, which also featured a few names from Yesterday, namely Showaddywaddy, Mud, Hawkwind and Radio Stars featuring frontman Andy Ellison from John's Children.

"Watching him bopping about in front of the cameras was a revelation," Ellison confessed. "He was a completely different person to the shy boy I'd known in '67. He'd lost his inhibitions. He was polite with us, but he could appear very arrogant to those

Bowie and Bolan performing 'Standing Next To You' on the final 'Marc' TV show (ITV/Rex features)

he felt needed to see him as a star. He was very much in control and made sure he got his own way, and if he didn't, he'd throw a tantrum. I never knew if it was all just an act or not. I could never get close enough to find out what made him tick. He was still very reserved and withdrawn away from the spotlight. I believe he was still very insecure right at the end, but he'd found a way to deal with it."

"I never had any competition except from Marc Bolan… I fought like a madman to beat him." (David Bowie)

The final *Marc* show was filmed just days before Bolan's death and, in retrospect, events appear to have been arranged to allow him to bid a final farewell to his friends.

Andy Ellison had been invited to appear on the show after a chance meeting with Marc in the King's Road ten years after he left John's Children, while B.P. Fallon, Jeff Dexter and Steve Harley had taken turns to keep him company in the preceding weeks while Gloria was away recording a solo album in the States. He even been reunited with Helen Shapiro for ITV's Saturday morning children's show *Saturday Scene* on August 6th. Helen found him very positive and happy to talk about their old neighborhood, but she could not have failed to have been horrified by his cadaverous appearance which was giving his friends serious concern. Apparently he was refusing to eat and may have been popping pills to take the edge of his appetite.

Marc was determined to look leaner than ever so he would look good sharing the stage with special guest David Bowie who had agreed to fly in specially from his home in Switzerland for the final *Marc* show. No one had believed Bolan when he had told them that Bowie would appear. For once even Marc hadn't believed his own boast, but sure enough on September 7 a long black limousine pulled up outside the Granada studios in Quay Street, Manchester, and out stepped The Thin White Duke in his latest guise, immaculately attired in pale blue striped shirt and jeans, his eyes hidden behind the blackest shades. He was flanked by fashionable flunkies, publicists, management, image consultants and shadowed by a burly anonymous bodyguard. It was a combination of egos and officiousness that was guaranteed to cause friction in the hothouse atmosphere of a TV studio. There was trouble almost from the moment the entourage entered the lobby.

It appears that Bowie had insisted on a closed set during rehearsals and his minders interpreted that to mean that no one, but no one, was to be permitted in the studio other than the cameramen, sound crew and the producer. Never one to miss an opportunity for a good story, Marc's publicist, Keith Altham, had invited a coach load of journalists to witness the historic summit meeting and their appearance behind the scenes prompted Bowie's American publicist Barbara DeWitt to blow a fuse. The air was thick with accusations and abuse, not to mention a touch of unintended farce as a gaggle of journalists crept around the studio hiding behind the guests in an attempt to avoid the eyes of Bowie's bodyguard. 'Lurch' had been dispatched to clear the studio of strangers, but he turned on the wrong man. When he tried to eject the Head of the Technicians Union, a complaint was made to his handlers and he was ordered to back off. But it was already too late. Cameramen and lighting crew were calling for multiple retakes as the inexperienced guest artists missed their marks and disappeared out of shot. The floor manager was tearing out what little hair he had left when Marc, in a figure-hugging leopard skin outfit, began directing his own sequence. "When you've got your name up in lights, you've gotta take responsibilities," the star retorted. Then Generation X arrived three hours late without their equipment and threated to trash Marc's guitar if their spot was cancelled. Eddie and the Hot Rods had been threatening to walk out for hours because they had been hanging around the studio impatiently while Marc and Bowie rehearsed their co-written song 'Standing Next To You' which was to be the climax of the show. And in the midst of the chaos and recriminations stood producer Muriel Young who remained diplomatic and calm. Again, Fate seemed to be giving Marc the chance to say goodbye to those who had contributed to his career. Muriel had met Marc when he was a 15-year-old and she had been the presenter of *Five O'Clock Club*. She'd been charmed by his cheek, good looks and impish humour. The *Marc* shows had been her idea but they'd chosen the guests together and though she had initially been wary of having punk bands on a tea-time pop show, he had reassured her that punk was like any other pop music movement. It would eventually lose its abrasive edge and the better groups would become part of the establishment. So she agreed to his choices, trusting his judgment as he had invariably been proven right in the past.

But she drew the line at being abused herself. When the flak started flying from all quarters she retreated to the star's dressing room where Marc was watching the previous show being broadcast and together they waited for the heat to die down.

When they returned, Bowie was on the rostrum, mike in hand, waiting for the backing tape to roll.

Silence was called for and then David was counted in.

It was a complete coincidence, of course, but it was tempting to see something significant in the sentiment expressed in 'Heroes', a song honoring two star crossed lovers separated by the Berlin Wall. But today Bowie was the King and Bolan the Queen. They were heroes for just one day and for one of them that reign would be cruelly cut short.

When the tape ended and the director indicated that he was satisfied they had a take, Marc joined David on the rostrum and the cameramen took their positions. Then the director reminded everyone that time was tight so they had to crack on. The electrician's union had threatened to pull the plugs out at 7 p.m. on the dot in a dispute over pay and there would be no time for retakes if they overran. A make up lady stepped up to add a dash of foundation to take the shine off Bowie's face and then withdrew as Tony Newman counted the band in. But after a few bars Bolan yelled that he was getting electric shocks and called for a retake. It was almost 7 p.m. The floor manager called again for silence, but the band was already rehearsing for the next take. When the music ended Bowie leaned forward and asked nervously, "That wasn't the actual take, was it?' The answer was inaudible. Bowie's anger, however, was heard clear across the studio. "What do you mean, 'not really'?" The studio clock was approaching seven. Bowie must have sensed it was now or never. He counted them in again, almost catching Tony Newman on the hop. The riff restarted and Bowie came in late, "What can I do – do?" Marc leaned in toward his mike, misjudged the step and slipped off the rostrum. The music stopped.

Bowie looked down and laughed. "Someone get a wooden box for Marc."

★★★★★

At 6 a.m. on September 16, Sid and Phyllis Feld were woken by cries from Rolan's cot. Phyllis went to comfort him. "What's the matter, sweetie, bad dream?"

She picked him up and hugged him. "Daddy Marc is gone."

FREE 4-PAGE POP EXTRA ★ MARC BOLAN

Look-in

Junior TVTimes   Number 39   week ending 23 September 1972   Every Thursday 5p

BIGGER AND
BETTER WITH
PULL-OUT
DOUBLE-PAGE
COLOUR
PIN-UP OF
MARC!

BIG
COMPETITION!
REMOTE
CONTROL
RACING CARS
AND CINE
PROJECTORS
TO BE WON!

*Colour feature
Behind the scenes of*
BLACK BEAUTY

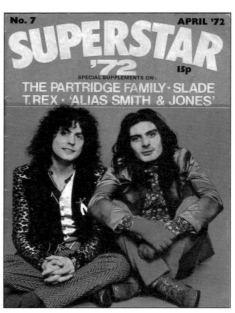

No. 7   APRIL '72

SUPERSTAR '72   15p

SPECIAL SUPPLEMENTS ON:
THE PARTRIDGE FAMILY · SLADE
T. REX · 'ALIAS SMITH & JONES'

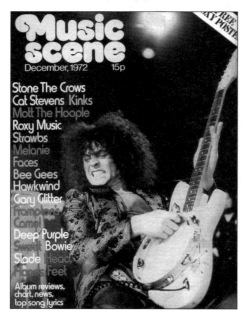

Music scene

December, 1972   15p

Stone The Crows
Cat Stevens Kinks
Mott The Hoople
Roxy Music
Strawbs
Melanie
Faces
Bee Gees
Hawkwind
Gary Glitter
Frampton's
Camel
Deep Purple
Sweet Bowie
Slade Head
Hands Feet

Album reviews,
chart, news,
top song lyrics

zigzag

NUMBER 21   THIRTEEN PENCE

Chapter 22
Broken-Hearted Blues

Sad to see them mourning you when you are there within the flowers and the trees.
'Child Star'

Captain Sensible was sitting in a deck chair in the garden of his parent's home in Croydon on the afternoon of September 16 when his mother returned from shopping with the news that a pop star had been killed in a car crash. "She was quite casual about it. She said it was somebody I knew, but couldn't remember his name. She said it was 'Roley somebody or other'. I leapt up and ran around to the paper shop, hoping it wasn't true, but there it was in big black headlines. I was devastated. I don't remember where I was when Kennedy was assassinated, but I'll never forget the day Marc Bolan was killed."

A month earlier, on the day Elvis collapsed and died at Graceland, aged 42, Marc had confided to his friend Steve Harley that he was glad he hadn't died that same day because he wouldn't have got more than a paragraph on page three. Four weeks later Marc was on the front pages once again. The ex-Stamford Hill mod had even managed to upstage the world famous opera diva Maria Callas who had died that very same day.

On the morning of Marc's funeral, Tuesday, September 20, Gloria lay in her hospital bed, her shattered jaw wired, a morphine drip to relieve the pain. She had been drifting in and out of consciousness for days. Now manager Tony Howard had to break the news they had been keeping from her. Howard later dismissed the notion that Marc had been fatalistic and foreseen his own death.

"Marc was a star. He was always a star and he wanted to live."

Howard had ordered the largest floral tribute on display that day, a four-foot high white swan constructed from chrysanthemums with 'Marc' spelt out in coloured flowers at the base. Other tributes were laid at the behest of Elton John, Keith Moon, Gary Glitter and Cliff Richard while David Bowie, Rod Stewart and Tony Visconti turned up in person to pay their respects. June Bolan kept her distance, unseen and unrecognisable in a large wide-brimmed hat and dark glasses. She had been forbidden from attending by Marc's parents because, in their grief, they blamed her for abandoning their son and precipitating his tragic and untimely death. But she couldn't leave without saying goodbye to the love of her life. She slipped quietly into the mortuary, stood for a moment then kissed him goodbye. His face was cold but unmarked. There was only a small scratch on his chin. He might have been asleep. "He was very beautiful, even in death."

Visconti remembers the funeral as the "saddest day of my life". It was also extremely traumatic. The producer and his wife, singer Mary Hopkin, were in shock never having imagined that someone so young and vital could have been taken so suddenly. The couple had been driven to the crematorium in a convoy of eight black limousines hired by EMI to take staff and other dignitaries including Marc's publisher David Platz, and when they arrived Visconti was horrified to see autograph hunters jostling through the mourners to pester the celebrities for their signature.

Among the crowds of grieving fans, friends, family members and celebrities at Golders Green Crematorium in North London stood a shaken Captain Sensible and other members of The Damned.

"I was choked," he told me. "I was a real Bolan fan and it was my first experience of death. I expected everyone to feel as gutted as I did, but Rod Stewart and Bowie and these stars who were supposedly Marc's mates rolled up in their big limos and turned it into a showbiz thing. The place was surrounded by heavies to keep the autograph hunters at bay. But what really shocked me was the bloodcurdling shriek that went up from Marc's mum when the coffin started moving. Christ, that was awful."

There was worse to come. It was alleged that a mortuary attendant had been attempting to sell the blood-soaked clothing in which Marc had died. But his plan to profit by it was thwarted when Harry, posing as a potential buyer, threatened the man with prosecution or worse if he didn't hand it all over there and then. Harry burned them that day.

And then there was the curious and rather distressing incident of the missing memorial plaque which the crematorium administrators had to replace several times before souvenir hunters tired of stealing it.

But more distressing of all for the family was the discovery that, while Gloria had lain helpless in hospital, their house at Upper Richmond Road West had been ransacked and almost everything the couple possessed had been taken. Marc's guitars, reels of unreleased recordings, boxes of handwritten unpublished poetry and diaries from the early days had vanished. The thieves had even emptied their wardrobes and stolen the clothes.

When Gloria was finally discharged from hospital after the Coroner's inquest on November 24, she and her brother Richard slipped out of the country without a single item to remind her of her life with Marc. She took Rolan to live with her in America some months later.

"I didn't come out of shock for over 14 years," Gloria admitted to Caroline Hedley of the *Sunday Mirror* in September 2007. "When I think about the accident now, I think about Rolan – because without him and my other son I don't know if I would have made it. Marc was my soul mate, but Rolan was nearly two when his father died – how could I not go on? Marc would not have wanted that."

Gloria, who has since remarried, now lives in Sierra Leone where she is supervising the building of a school of music for disadvantaged and orphan children in Marc's honour. She received nothing from Bolan's estate and neither did Rolan, so funding has had to come from friends and family. "Marc loved children – he would have been very proud to have this school in his name."

Whenever Gloria returns to the places she had shared with Marc, she often senses his presence. In the Beverly Wilshire Hotel in Los Angeles, she told Ms Hedley, "This was a very special place for us. Marc loved it here… We had some pretty rock 'n' roll times here. There'd be a knock on our door some nights and a couple of movie stars would turn up. It was always a suite. Marc always travelled first-class and only stayed in suites – did everything in style. He always put on his feather boa and his mascara even though it was a conservative hotel."

But there was another, less flamboyant aspect to him. When he tired of the all night parties he would take Gloria to parks, Disneyland and the zoo, in Florida and back in England after their move to London. "Marc loved tranquillity. Yes, there was the rock 'n' roll side, but then there was the humble Jewish boy."

He was a real family man, she says, who treated her first son as his own. He'd take the boy to Disneyland, sometimes several times in a single day, then go on somewhere else only to get bored with that and take the boy back to Disneyland.

When Rolan was just two months old, Marc didn't feel they had to be a conventional couple, limited to a life of nappy changing and so they went to Tramp, the London nightclub before the crowds arrived and, while the waitresses watched the baby, his parents took to the dance floor. Then he'd 'twirl' and tell her, "This is how it's done."

"There was always a lot of laughter in our life," Gloria remembered with a broad smile. Three weeks before the fatal crash he talked to her about getting married and moving to Malibu and having more children. "He was very much a man and a wonderful one at that."

Rolan admitted to me that he has no memory of his father, but nevertheless feels a connection that sometimes manifests in his dreams.

"The presence of my father has always been all round me. When I was a child it came through my mom and my grandparents, but recently I hear it whenever I hear his music or see a video or a photo of him.

"In those early years, just growing up without a father was hard. Being told about him was like a dreamworld for me. I had images of him rather than memories. Recently, I saw a home movie of him and me playing together, but by then the images and the stories had become indistinguishable from what I thought were real memories.

"My mom has been very reluctant to talk about him. The memory caused her so much pain. But for my sake she was willing to put her pain aside and made the sacrifice for me whenever I wanted to know what he had been like.

"It was a source of sadness and frustration for both of us not to have any of his possessions, which were stolen from the house on the day of his death. I would particularly have liked to have had one of his guitars, but that would only have been a physical possession. I have to be happy for what I do have and not sad for what I don't."

Rolan had ambitions to be a baseball player but a college injury put paid to that. Then, while auditioning for a college stage production, he discovered he had a talent for performing which led to his pursuing a musical career.

"My dad achieved a lot because he was determined to succeed," Rolan concludes. "And I must be equally single-minded. That's one thing I've learned from him. Unfortunately, he was not able to control what happened to his music once he was gone. My dad's music has been corrupted by the people who have been remixing and tampering with the unfinished tapes. I'm thinking about that appalling *Acoustic Warrior* album. It's not only a bloody cheek, it's also very badly done. I had thought of writing letters, but what good would it do. I'm just his son.

"But they can't tarnish my father's memory. His music is eternal and both it and his love for me have always been sacred to me. All of my family let me know how much my dad loved me. Now, although I have my own distinct personality, I know I will always be my father's son.

"One day we will make our connection."

Chapter 23
Legacy

In the weeks and months following the funeral, several high level meetings were held at EMI's headquarters in Manchester Square to finalise the company's winter and spring release schedule, but no plans were made to exploit the media interest generated by Bolan's untimely death. It was not, it seems, from fear of being seen to cash in on a tragedy. It was purely business. The marketing men were convinced that there was simply not sufficient interest in Bolan's music to justify the expense of a commemorative box set, or a trawl through the archives for unreleased material. It was their belief that T.Rex had been a teenybop phenomenon and that the group's audience had grown up and moved on. Besides, a box set of unreleased material was not a realistic option, even if there had been the will to compile something substantial, as the tape lease deal that Secunda had negotiated back in late '71 meant that all unreleased recordings were the property of Marc's production company Wizard Artists. The only tapes in EMI's possession were the master tapes of the albums and singles he had authorised for release and licensed to EMI. Any unreleased studio recordings from January '72 onwards were believed to have been 'liberated' from Marc's house on the morning of the accident along with dozens of reels of home demos.

It was known that Marc had begun work on a new album at Decibel Studios in Stamford Hill in April '77, but these sessions produced few finished mixes, certainly not enough material to fill a 40-minute album. Besides, both the tapes and their contents were the property of Wizard Artists and permission to release unreleased material would have to be obtained from the Estate which was being administered by the anonymous lawyers behind Wizard (Bahamas) Ltd. It was a bureaucratic labyrinth the EMI execs did not have the time, or the incentive, to explore. Consequently, EMI contented themselves by releasing *The Unobtainable T.Rex*, a mid-priced compilation of A and B-sides that had not been previously available on LP and then sat back and awaited bids from rival companies who had expressed interest in acquiring Bolan's back catalogue.

It was a different situation at the offices of Essex Music in Poland Street. Essex and its associated labels, Fly and Cube Records, possessed both the 2-inch multi-track tapes and the quarter-inch mix-down masters of everything Marc had recorded for them from '68-'71 and to which they owned the copyright, but they had no interest in digging through the archives to unearth unreleased recordings by an artist whose albums were then selling fewer copies than those by Joan Armatrading.

However, when Tony Visconti brought David Platz the original solo acoustic demo of *The Children of Rarn* and offered to sketch in light orchestration, the publisher agreed to release it as part of a double LP retrospective to be called *Marc – The Words and Music of Marc Bolan 1947-1977.* The album would complement a scrapbook of reminiscences and sheet music that Essex had planned to publish in the summer of '78. It was the least they could do to acknowledge the contribution Bolan's phenomenal sales had made to the success of the company.

In the absence of major label interest it was down to fanzines to keep the faith in those years before the advent of the internet and the proliferation of dedicated websites. The first British 'zine was *Cosmic Dancer* in 1978, published by this writer, but others were to follow as self-financed small press and Xeroxed 'scissors and paste' titles were superseded by professional desktop publishing programmes which gave every fan the opportunity to be their own publisher. And with so many unpublished poems, lyrics and short stories from Marc's notebooks in circulation, there was more than sufficient material to keep the completists happy, but not, it seemed sufficient interest to attract a major label into acquiring Bolan's back catalogue.

It was clear that if anything interesting was going to see the light of day it would have to be instigated by the more resourceful fans. The official fan club, which had organised a party for what would have been Bolan's 30th birthday at which he had agreed to play an acoustic set with Mickey Finn, had folded immediately following his death. In its place several rival factions vied for official status and an ugly squabble ensued. One of these groups successfully bid for the ownership of the master tapes that EMI appeared to have no interest in releasing themselves.

Their subsequent releases stirred some revival of interest in Bolan's music during the early eighties but divided fans between those who welcomed the opportunity to hear unreleased material in whatever form it was presented and those who were outraged that some of the tracks had been remixed and even overdubbed with new instruments by musicians who had no previous association with their idol.

But even more disturbing was the discovery that in some cases the original performances by Bill Legend and the other members of T.Rex had been erased to accommodate these new parts! If the masters been copied and the copies overdubbed, the damage would have been reversible but once the original parts had been recorded over, they were lost forever.

Superfan Danielz, frontman with tribute band T.Rextasy, made the horrifying discovery which he calls "an inexcusable act of destruction", when he and his business partners in Thunderwing Productions paid a small fortune for 150 of Marc's original master tapes in an effort to save them for posterity.

"In 1999, we formed a company to save the tapes which were in reprieve after having failed to find a buyer in an auction at Bonham's in London. It was likely that they would be sold off one reel at a time and they would have been scattered around the world to individual collectors who hadn't the facilities to look after them properly. With tapes of that age the oxide will come off if you play them without baking them first which means you lose all the high frequencies and eventually you won't be able to copy them or remaster from them at all because the playback heads will become clogged and there would be audible drop outs. You wouldn't get through a complete song without stopping several times to clean the heads.

"So my wife and I pooled our resources with three other Bolan-mad couples and raised enough money to buy a small house. We felt we had to act before the tapes deteriorated further or were sold off piecemeal to anyone who would pay. They'd been stored during the 1990s in a garage by the people who were running the 'fan club' and were in a terrible state. My wife and I were invited to their house to see the horde of material that EMI had handed over to them and when I looked through the gap in their garage door I could see the tapes stacked on shelves and some just piled on the floor. A few appeared to have bits gnawed out of the boxes by what I assume were mice. I couldn't believe what I was seeing. When these tapes were eventually sold to a third party a number of the original tape boxes had been thrown away because of the damp and damage done by vermin and, of course, that meant that the details of the recordings were lost. There were no dates or other information to help us catalogue these recordings, some of which would have been in Marc's own handwriting. Many of the unboxed tapes were just thrown into black plastic bin bags which were later sold by the 'fan club' to a record producer who hadn't realised that he was only purchasing the tapes, not the rights to release them. When he realised he couldn't do anything with them, he was willing to sell them to us. But now that we have them we can't release them either without the agreement of either Spirit Music in the USA (the current licensees) or Westminster Music in the UK. But at least we have cleaned, copied and catalogued every reel as best we can and have stored them in ideal conditions after taking advice from the London Museum's National Sound Archive, so the tapes and their contents are preserved."

There were no completed unreleased songs on the tapes, but there were a few solo demos, alternative takes, alternative guitar solos, jams and guide vocals with different working lyrics that Thunderwing were confident they could compile several albums with radically alternate versions of familiar songs.

In April 2000, they managed to secure the rights to release two compact disc compilations of outtakes and alternate versions, *Bump 'n' Grind* (TECI-24004) and *Shadowhead* (TECI-24055), which were initially released only in Japan. The tracks were mixed from the 2-inch multi-track tapes to match the original releases as closely as possible. Thunderwing added nothing, but took the opportunity to push instruments to the fore that had been hidden in the original mix. They also selected alternative guitar solos wherever possible and they allowed the tracks to play through to the end instead of fading to offer a fascinating alternative mix for hard core fans for whom previously unreleased versions are akin to discovering a lost scene from *Citizen Kane*.

Stripping the multi-tracks down to hear each individual performance, complete with false starts and studio chatter, also proved very revealing.

Danielz: "The first thing that struck me was how many false starts there were. That suggests that Marc wasn't as casual or in as much haste as Visconti and the band say he was. It's true, he didn't make more than two or three complete takes of a song, but he would abort the take time and again until he had exactly the right feel and tempo he wanted. That indicates a perfectionist and someone who was after the just right balance between spontaneity and 'feel'.

"We'd also find 'hidden' guitar solos as Marc played all through the song as he worked out the solo during the earlier verses and choruses, so that by the time he came to the solo it would be done in one or two takes. We could also hear how Marc worked with Visconti and the band. You could hear from his comments and tone of voice that he had great respect for Visconti and he never criticised Steve Currie, but he could be quite cruel to Bill. On one track he can be heard complaining, "Oh Bill, you play the same intro to every song, man" which just wasn't true. And on another, when Bill complains to Marc that he has a squeaky bass drum pedal, Marc dismisses it saying, 'Leave it Bill, we'll overdub that with dustbin lids!' Bill wasn't the best time-keeper it has to be said, and if you listen to 'The Groover' you can hear that it starts off at a steady clip and gets noticeably faster by the end, but Bill had a very individual style and played unconventional rhythm patterns that gave those early records a great bluesy rock feel that someone like Davey Lutton couldn't replicate on the later records.

"Doing an autopsy on the tapes revealed shortcuts that you would never guess they'd made. For example, the track 'Ballrooms of Mars' on *The Slider* ends after the solo. It just stops. So to lengthen it they spliced an earlier section in to finish it off. That's why the two solos in the middle and at the end are exactly the same! Also on 'Solid Gold Easy Action' underneath the shuffle rhythm on the snare there is the original straight drum track. So the shuffle rhythm was obviously an afterthought, which they just dubbed on top of the original recording instead of recording it again with a different rhythm. We also unearthed the legendary 'lost' saxophone version of 'Teenage Dream' which had only been heard once on *Top of the Pops* and which fans thought they would never hear again after the BBC wiped so much stuff from the seventies, (though a clip has now been found in private hands). It wasn't a live *TOTP* exclusive performance, but merely a special mix that Marc and Visconti made for the show. The 'missing' sax is actually on the original multi-track tape. And on '20th Century Boy' the heavy guitar chords that open the song are not multi-tracked as everyone assumed. That's a single guitar. Marc got so much power and such a thick overdriven sound from his set up and style of playing that he often didn't need to double track the rhythm guitars."

Being able to isolate Marc's guitars was invaluable to Danielz who had been striving to mimic Marc's trademark technique for more than a decade in order to recreate the highly distinctive T.Rex sound.

"Marc's guitar style was instantly recognisable from the first few notes. It was not just the instrument he chose or the set up. It was his touch, so even when he played a cheap guitar – and sometimes he picked up whatever was lying around the studio – it still sounded like him. Much has been made of the fact that he used a late '50s Les Paul or a certain effects pedal, but the effects were not that critical to the sound. A Screaming Tree, for example, is really little more than a treble booster and Marc didn't always play his Gibson. I've bought every item of equipment that Bolan used and had my guitar customised to replicate his Orange Les Paul but that alone wouldn't help me recreate his signature sound. It is down to 'feel'. You could transcribe one of his solos note for note and play it technically perfect and it wouldn't sound like Marc if you didn't have his touch and his musical 'sense'."

While one group were actively preserving Marc's musical legacy, another sought to conserve the crash site which had become a place of pilgrimage for fans the world over. At first the scarred tree on Gypsy Ride was festooned with sad little mementos and handwritten messages, but it soon began to look decidedly tacky and the surrounding area was in danger of being eroded by the steady procession of grieving fans and the morbidly curious. Being a notorious accident black spot, it was not an ideal place for sightseeing, so a number of concerned fans formed the T.Rex Action Group in 1999 and successfully campaigned to raise sufficient funds to purchase the site and erect a permanent memorial alongside a plaque that had been placed there by the Performing Rights Society on the 20th anniversary of Marc's death.

Another group purchased a permanent memorial plaque at Golders Green to replace the small markers that had been repeatedly stolen as macabre souvenirs. In September 2002 a second plaque bearing Marc's image and a small ceramic swan was unveiled at Golders Green Crematorium to commemorate the 25th anniversary of his death. The inscription reads "25 years on – his light of love still shines brightly".

A third group was less successful in lobbying English Heritage to bestow their coveted blue plaque at the site of Marc's first home at 25 Stoke Newington Common. In 2006 the committee rejected the proposal as they considered Marc to be of "insufficient stature or historical significance". However, the fans persistence eventually paid off as Hackney Council finally agreed to put up their own plaque to commemorate the childhood home of one of the borough's most famous sons.

Inevitably the passage of time burnished the music of the early seventies with a nostalgic glow, making it appealing to those who longed to relive their youth and to those who wished they had been there at the time. But Glam Rock by its very nature was almost impossible to take seriously. It was only when the Punk and post-punk generation spat out cover versions at triple the speed of the originals that latecomers realised that not all the performers in the rock and roll circus had been clowns.

The steady accumulation of cover versions (both live and studio recordings) by such influential artists as Siouxsie and the Banshees, Elvis Costello, The Undertones, Bauhaus and Blondie in the late seventies and early eighties conferred upon Bolan the credibility he had been denied in life. And in the nineties, when the Brit Pop generation reworked and recycled his riffs (as Oasis did with 'Get It On' for their own brazenly similar 'Cigarettes and Alcohol'), a younger generation inevitably began to forage for their roots, and in doing so unearthed the music of a man who had been effectively side-lined in rock history.

But it wasn't only the cover versions that prompted a new generation to back track. Since the early eighties Bolan's influence had been permeating the fabric of music by artists who were prepared to acknowledge the source of their inspiration: artists such as U2, Placebo, The Ramones, Guns N' Roses and The Smiths.

"The influence of T-Rex is very profound on certain songs of The Smiths, i.e. 'Panic' and 'Shoplifters'," guitarist and songwriter Johnny Marr admitted. "Morrissey was himself also mad about Bolan. When we wrote 'Panic' he was obsessed with 'Metal Guru' and wanted to sing in the same style. He didn't stop singing it in an attempt to modify the words of 'Panic' to fit the exact rhythm of 'Metal Guru'. He also exhorted me to use the same guitar break so that the two songs are the same!!!"

All of these endorsements served to establish Marc as a cult figure. But there would have to be a resurgence of interest in his music among the wider public to justify the wholesale reissue of his albums. But that, too, came in time, generated by the unlikeliest of sources. The use of a snippet of '20th Century Boy' in a Levi's advert in 1991 featuring Hollywood hunk Brad Pitt introduced Bolan to a generation who were not born when T.Rextasy was at its peak. On the back of that advert a mass-marketed compilation *The Essential Collection* (Universal Music) garnered significant sales to stimulate interest in the earlier albums, while the reissued single peaked at number 13. Other Bolan tracks began featuring in national advertising campaigns for a Robinsons soft drink and Mitsubishi cars, reaching an audience far in excess of those who had heard the original singles on UK pop radio in the seventies, and this exposure prompted the release of yet another compilation which also charted.

In 1992 specialist reissue label Edsel and its American partner Rhino acquired the rights to all the EMI releases from the Estate and began to repackage these together with albums of outtakes and home demos as part of the 'T.Rex Unchained' series, erasing all memory of the disfavoured "fan club" releases. And in 2004, prompted by public interest aroused by the use of Marc's music in a number of major movies, Universal subsequently acquired the Essex Music albums and reissued them with extra tracks, many of which were previously unreleased.

Filmmakers had been slow to feature T.Rex tracks largely because the group had failed to make an impression in America, but by the nineties Hollywood was ready to sentimentalise the seventies.

The earliest use of T.Rex on a soundtrack went unnoticed because it had been used incidentally, as background, in Martin Scorsese's 1976 art house road movie *Alice Doesn't Live Here Anymore*, but as soon as the unmistakable sound of T.Rex featured prominently on the soundtrack of major movies[1] such as *Jarhead, Moulin Rouge, Velvet Goldmine, School of Rock* and *Billy Elliot*, there was a resurgence of interest and a demand for the hits that rivalled the sales they amassed first time around. As a result Bolan has sold more albums in the three decades since his death than at the peak of his popularity, making an estimated total of 39 million records sold worldwide.

But where are the royalties? On each anniversary of his death, Marc's family were interviewed by the national press and maintained that they hadn't received a penny, only nominal sums of a few thousand pounds from his Will. At one point a TV documentary was commissioned to investigate but failed to reveal who had profited from 'Marc's Missing Millions'. Rumours were rife that shady characters in the underworld had siphoned off the proceeds, but nothing was ever proven and their whereabouts remain a mystery.

In 1985 Brian Dunham, a former music licensing consultant for Granada TV and the man responsible for facilitating the release of the 'Marc' shows on Video, was invited to join the Wizard group of companies as Music Publisher with a view to putting its house in order and to administer and enhance the value of the copyrights.

"It was a bit of a mess," he admits. "But I didn't find any evidence of anything sinister. There are all sorts of suspicions about Marc's so-called 'missing millions', but I found them unnecessary and unfounded. When Marc was advised to set up his various

---

1 *Bolan tracks have also been featured on the soundtrack of the following films: Breakfast on Pluto, Death Proof, Lords of Dogtown, Herbie: Fully Loaded, Breaking-Up, Hot Fuzz and Scott Pilgrim vs. the World. Velvet Goldmine features three Bolan songs, 'Diamond Meadows', 'Cosmic Dancer' and a cover of '20th Century Boy' performed by a fictional group featuring members of Placebo which was revived by Placebo and David Bowie at the 1999 Brit Awards ceremony. Moulin Rouge features a cover of 'Children of the Revolution' performed by Bono of U2 and Gavin Friday of the Virgin Prunes while Billy Elliot memorably features no less than five T.Rex tracks: 'Cosmic Dancer', 'Get It On', 'I Love To Boogie', 'Children Of The Revolution' and 'Ride A White Swan'.*

companies to serve as tax shelters he did so with his eyes open. It was standard practice at the time. When I was working with Chrysalis in the mid '70s I was aware of other Major Artists being offered the same advice and it worked very well for them.

"Marc was unfortunate though, in that he suffered from unscrupulous advisors. I have heard a particular story, which I can't verify, that on one occasion he wrote a cheque for 450,000 pounds and it never reached the account for which it was intended. But it was widely known that he was doing a lot of stuff at the time and he had slipped into a trough of despondency and so wasn't in the best state of mind to keep a track of things. He went off the rails when June left him and things got messy. June, I believe, was a co-Director in these offshore companies and so when they split up the infrastructure suffered and when Marc died before their divorce became absolute I believe she was left liable for the company's debts. When one party isn't talking to the other partner a lot of things are left unchallenged or unresolved and they can unravel pretty quickly. Success had gone to Marc's head and blurred his judgement. And there are so many areas of an artist's career that need to be constantly attended to if they are to get everything they have worked for – publishing, tour fees, record sales etc. So it was mismanagement more than anything else that was his undoing.

"I put it all down to his untimely death. If he had lived, he might have sorted out his financial affairs, but no one, as far as I could see, was keeping an eye on things. For instance, I've never seen any documentation on the T.Rex Wax Co., Marc's own label.

"When I had to clear the rights to release the 'T.Rex On TV' DVD in 2006 and the 'T.Rex Greatest Hits' CD the following year I discovered that the paperwork was all over the place. I had to retrieve it from various lawyers and negotiate with the bankers in the Bahamas who were not experienced in the music business.

"And then, I'm afraid to say, there are people who cannot be bothered when there is nothing in it for them. They simply aren't as motivated as myself and the Bolanistas I recruited to help me compile these releases. For three years I badgered Apple to locate the original prints of 'Born to Boogie' and was repeatedly told that they didn't know where they were. I was on the point of reluctantly accepting the same print I had used for the VHS release when the director of the documentary we were making about the film phoned Apple and happened by chance to be put through to the librarian who told him that the film was there in their vaults and we could have it – provided the Legal people gave him authorisation.

"When we went down to see what condition the cans of footage were in we found not 35 cans as we had been told but 272! Of course, the prints were in quite a bad state by then, but to their eternal credit Sanctuary Records agreed to a budget of 250,000 pounds to restore it to its former glory.

"That budget also enabled us to get Tony Visconti to remix the soundtrack, and include Rolan in a documentary about the whole process. All of this with a rightful share going to Ringo and Rolan."

In response to the question 'would you not have expected Ringo, being Marc's friend, to have taken more care of a film he had personally invested in,' Brian responded, "Perhaps, but Ringo and Marc had fallen out. I don't know the reason, but Marc was rather notorious for leaving friends behind and I suppose Ringo had no interest in the film after that. But it's to Ringo's credit that he would not even discuss the possibility of releasing a restored version of the film until Rolan could be guaranteed a share of the profits and that was only possible after a radical sea change at the Trust. After Visconti went to court in 2001 and secured a settlement from Wizard for unpaid royalties as the producer of the early albums, new lawyers were appointed and a more enlightened Trust Manager was brought in. They made Rolan a beneficiary and that is what reassured Ringo that Marc's son would get a cut. Only then was he willing to give us access to the unreleased footage and the original cans which were in dire need of restoration. Film deteriorates just like audio tape if it is not stored under the correct conditions. And these cans were rusting so we caught them just in time.

"The original release of 'BTB' on VHS had done very little in terms of sales, to be frank, but for the DVD we spent a small fortune restoring the print and sound and we had the added bonus of the second show in its entirety which had never been seen before. Plus Sanctuary Records commissioned a specially made documentary about the phenomenon that was T.Rextasy. So it was a great package and Visconti and Rolan took an active role in promoting it which helped take it to number one in the DVD sales charts in the UK in 2005. I was very proud of that and the number 3 placing we got for the 'T.Rex on TV' DVD that I prodded Demon to put together the following year. And with the creative help of uberfan Martin Barden we also put together a 'Greatest Hits' CD for Universal Music in 2007 which earned a Silver Disc. So I feel some justification in claiming that I was instrumental in Bolan's resurgence in the past ten years or so. "

But even that was not enough to satisfy Brian's burning ambition to create a permanent memorial to Marc in music.

"I thought Bolan suffered from the Glam Rock image he had created. It was so limited and he was much more than that. I had been into soul music during Marc's lifetime, but working on 'Born to Boogie' converted me into a real fan. I wanted to tell his story, but I didn't know how to do it. Then I went to see the film 'Billy Elliot' and realised that the five Bolan songs in the soundtrack had made a good movie into a great one. That inspired me to come up with the idea for a stage show, a musical using Marc's timeless songs but presenting them in a dramatic context to tell the story of his life. I had all the connections to the various publishers and felt I could get their support if I made what could be regarded a 'responsible treatment'. But I didn't want to simply stage his life story with actors playing the roles of Marc, Gloria and the band miming to the records. There had to be a creative and imaginative use of the music to depict events, and perhaps reflect Marc's state of mind and situation at various points in his career.

"Let me give you an example. I happened to attend the funeral of a fan who had taken his own life. His name was Sebastian Horsley and he had modelled himself after Marc. He dressed like Marc and had created a stage show in Soho called 'Dandy in the Underworld'. During the service they played only Marc's music and when the open coffin passed me while 'Cosmic Dancer' was playing I have to admit it choked me up. But it only served to convince me that the songs could comment on Marc's life instead of just being musical interludes. And that's how '20th Century Boy – The Musical' came into being. It took 3 and a half years of blood, sweat and tears to bring it to the stage, but on 8th September 2011 at the New Wolsey Theatre in Ipswich my dream came to fruition."[2]

The original fans have grown up, but not all of them have grown out of their obsession. Some found influence in the media[3] where they furthered their own agenda whenever the opportunity presented itself. And on every notable anniversary of his death Marc's music and irrepressible personality would be recalled to life to remind those who had kept a 'Marc in their heart' (to borrow the motto he had used on his Granada TV series) why they had loved the man and his music in the first place. One or two even moved into politics.

"What Marc Bolan did, I think, was he crossed over between what – in inverted commas – 'cool' people listened to and what people danced to. There was a time when the uncoolest thing a band could do was release a single and T. Rex made the single respectable again.

"I remember Marc Bolan sitting there cross-legged and saying 'more sound on microphone two' or something, and I remember being really thrilled. And you know the way the roadies used to go on and fix up the microphones? I'd look at them and think 'even that would be good'. You just wanted to be part of it. There's nothing like it, really." Tony Blair, British Prime Minister (1997-2004)

The new generation of Bolan fans are oblivious to the fact that critics once condemned him for grinding out a stream of formulaic hits and more significantly, they don't care. They are only sorry there isn't more of the same.

"He's actually bigger now than he was in the seventies. You've got kids of seven and eight wearing Marc's T-shirt because they used his music in Billy Elliot. *And all these stars are saying they were influenced by him. He'd be happy with that."* Gloria Jones

"Marc was rock and roll personified." Steve Harley

"He just wanted to be God." Holly Johnson

"I think Bolan was going to come back in a big way – a sort of David Bowie level. I'm convinced of it." George Tremlett

"He'll become like James Dean. To us he will always be as big a hero as Elvis Presley." Rosalind Russell

"On first meeting Marc, I was astounded by the amount of energy he radiated. He was a loyal friend and always totally committed to whatever he was doing. In a business where individualism is often cultivated, Marc stood out as an innovator and, above all, a lonely human being." Elton John

---

2 *Author's note: In February 1979 a Jersey court ruled against two trustees of the Bolan estate over what it called the "misuse" of $700,000 of Bolan's money which these trustees had allegedly invested in works of art. These were said to have declined in value, recouping only $277,000 at auction. Other sums have been and continue to be donated to charity under the provisions of Bolan's Will, one being the Performing Rights Society's Members' Fund which administers royalties to impoverished composers. It is estimated that the PRS receives approximately $97,800 a year from the Bolan estate to distribute among these members. The second beneficiary is the Ravenswood Foundation, a UK based charity which cares for people with learning disabilities. They receive an undisclosed sum on an annual basis.*

3 *In 2006, Marc was portrayed on the small screen by actor William Matheson in the BBC TV series* Life on Mars. *Time-travelling detective Sam Tyler spots Bolan in a bar in Manchester (!) circa 1973 and warns him not to take a lift in a mini while 'Get It On' can be heard in the background.*

"There was definitely a touch of genius there... to have gone so far with such a limited musical knowledge is amazing. I think you can only attribute that to genius." Tony Visconti

"He wasn't an angel, but he could still fly." B.P. Fallon

"He wasn't afraid of dying. He always believed he'd come back. There was never any doubt about that, never any question." June Bolan

*"He **was** the 'Cosmic Dancer'. It is my favourite song of his. Visconti wrote a beautiful string part for that and helped Marc make such wonderful music, music that will last forever."* Simeon (Sid) Feld (to the author, 1978)

Marc Bolan 1947-1997

Discography

Singles

Marc Bolan:
Nov 1965 The Wizard/Beyond The Risin' Sun (Decca F12288)
June 1966 The Third Degree/San Francisco Poet (Decca F12413)
Dec 1966 Hippy Gumbo/Misfit (Parlophone R5539)

John's Children:
May 1967 Desdemona/Remember Thomas A Beckett (Track 604 003)
July 1967 Midsummer's Night Scene/Sara Crazy Child (Track 604 005) Withdrawn
Aug 1967 Come And Play With Me In The Garden/Sara Crazy Child (Track 604 005)
Oct 1967 Go Go Girl/Jagged Time Lapse (Track 604 010)

Tyrannosaurus Rex:
April 1968 Debora/Child Star (Regal Zono RZ 3008)
Aug 1968 One Inch Rock/Salamanda Palaganda (Regal Zonophone RZ 3011)
Jan 1969 Pewtor Suitor/Warlord Of The Royal Crocodiles (Regal Zonophone RZ 3016)
July 1969 King Of The Rumbling Spires/Do You Remember (Regal Zonophone RZ 3022)
Jan 1970 By The Light Of A Magical Moon/Find A Little Wood (Regal Zonophone RZ 3025)
March 1970 Debora/One Inch Rock/Woodland Bop/Seal Of Seasons (Magnifly ECHO 102)

T. Rex:
Oct 1970 Ride A White Swan/Is It Love/Summertime Blues (Fly BUG 1)
Feb 1971 Hot Love/Woodland Rock/King Of The Mountain Cometh (Fly BUG 6)
July 1971 Get It On (Bang a Gong)/There Was A Time/Raw Ramp (Fly BUG 10)
Nov 1971 Jeepster/Life's A Gas (Fly BUG 16)
Jan 1972 Telegram Sam/Cadillac/Baby Strange (T.Rex Wax 101)
May 1972 Metal Guru/Thunderwing/Lady (EMI Marc 1)
Sept 1972 Children of the Revolution/Jitterbug Love/Sunken Rags (EMI Marc 2)
Dec 1972 Solid Gold Easy Action/Born To Boogie (EMI Marc 3)
Dec 1972 Xmas Fan Club Flexi (featuring Micky Marmalade and Alphi O'Leary)

March 1973 20th Century Boy/Free Angel (EMI Marc 4)
June 1973 The Groover/Midnight (EMI Marc 5)
Big Carrot:
Aug 1973 Blackjack/Squint Eye Mangle (EMI 2047)
T. Rex:
Nov 1973 Truck On (Tyke)/Sitting Here (EMI Marc 6)
Jan 1974 Teenage Dream/Satisfaction Pony (EMI Marc 7)
Marc Bolan:
June 1974 Jasper C. Debussy/Hippy Gumbo/The Perfumed Garden Of Gulliver Smith (Track 2094 013)
T. Rex:
July 1974 Light Of Love/Explosive Mouth (EMI Marc 8)
Nov 1974 Zip Gun Boogie/Space Boss (EMI Marc 9)
July 1975 New York City/Chrome Sitar (EMI Marc 10)
Sept 1975 Dreamy Lady/Do You Wanna Dance?/Dock Of The Bay (EMI Marc 11)
Nov 1975 Christmas Bop/Telegram Sam/Metal Guru (EMI Marc 12) Withdrawn
Feb 1976 London Boys/Solid Baby (EMI Marc 13)
April 1976 Hot Love/Get It On (Cube BUG 66)
June 1976 I Love To Boogie/Baby Boomerang (EMI Marc 14)
Sept 1976 Laser Love/Life's An Elevator (EMI Marc 15)
Marc Bolan and Gloria Jones:
Jan 1977 To Know Him Is To Love Him/City Port (EMI 2572)

T. Rex:
March 1977 The Soul Of My Suit/All Alone (EMI Marc 16)
May 1977 Dandy In The Underworld/Groove A Little/ Tame My Tiger (EMI Marc 17)
Aug. 1977 Celebrate Summer/Ride My Wheels (EMI Marc 18)

Albums

My People Were Fair And Had Sky In Their Hair But Now They're Content To Wear Stars On Their Brows
Regal Zonophone (SLRZ 1003)
Released July 7, 1968
Track listing: Hot Rod Mama/Scenescof/Child Star/ Strange Orchestra's/Chateau In Virginia Waters/Dwarfish Trumped Blues/Mustang Ford/Afghan Woman/Knight/ Graceful Fat Sheba/Wielder Of Words/Frowning Atahuallpa (My Inca Love)

Prophets, Seers And Sages , The Angels Of The Ages
Regal Zonophone (SLRZ 1005)
Released October 14, 1968
Track listing: Deboraarobed/Stacey Grove/Wind Quartets/ Conesuala/Trelawny Lawn/Aznagel The Mage/The Friends/Salamanda Palaganda/Our Wonderful Brown-Skin Man/O Harley/The Saltimbanques/Eastern Spell/ The Travelling Tragition/Juniper Suction/Scenescof Dynasty

Unicorn
Regal Zonophone (SLRZ 1007)
Released May 18, 1969
Track listing: Chariots of Silk/'Pon a Hill/The Seal of Seasons/The Throat of Winter/Cat Black (the Wizard's Hat)/Stones for Avalon/She Was Born to Be My Unicorn/ Like a White Star (Tangled and Far Tulip That's What you Are)/Warlord of the Royal Crocodiles/Evenings of Damask/The Sea Beasts/Iscariot/Nijinsky Hind/The Pilgrim's Tale/The Misty Coast of Albany/Romany Soup

A Beard Of Stars
Regal Zonophone (SLRZ 1013)
Released March 22, 1970
Track listing: Prelude/A Day Laye/The Woodland Bop/Fist Heart Mighty Dawn Dart/Pavilions of Sun/Organ Blues/ By the Light of the Magical Moon/Wind Cheetah/A Beard of Stars/Great Horse/Dragon's Ear/Lofty Skies/Dove/ Elemental Child

My People Were Fair/Prophets, Seers And Sages
Fly Records (Toofa 3/4)
Released April 2, 1972
Double album reissue

Unicorn/A Beard Of Stars
Fly Records (Toofa 5/6)
Released November 5, 1972
Double album reissue

T. Rex
Fly Records (Hi-Fly 2)
Released December 11, 1970
Track listing: The Children Of Rarn (Intro)/Jewel/ The Visit/Childe/The Time Of Love Is Now/Diamond Meadows/Root Of Star/Beltane Walk/Is It Love?/One Inch Rock/Summer Deep/Seagull Woman/Sun Eye/The Wizard/The Children Of Rarn (Reprise)

Electric Warrior
Fly Records (Hi-Fly 6)
Released September 17, 1971
Track listing: Mambo Sun/Cosmic Dancer/Jeepster/ Monolith/Lean Woman Blues/Get It On/Planet Queen/ Girl/The Motivator/Life's A Gas/Rip Off

Bolan Boogie
Fly Records (Hi-Fly 8)
Released May 5, 1972
Track listing: Get It On/Beltane Walk/King Of The Mountain Cometh/Jewel/She Was Born To Be My Unicorn/Dove/Woodland Rock/Ride A White Swan/Raw Ramp/Jeepster/Fist Heart Mighty Dawn Heart/By The Light Of A Magical Moon/Summertime Blues/Hot Love

The Slider
T.Rex Wax Co. (BLN 5001)
Released July 23, 1972
Track listing: Metal Guru/Mystic Lady/Rock On/The Slider/Baby Boomerang/Spaceball Ricochet/Buick McKane/Telegram Sam/Rabbit Fighter/Baby Strange/ Ballrooms of Mars/Chariot Choogle/Main Man

Ride A White Swan
Music For Pleasure (MFP 5274)
Budget priced compilation Released October 1972
Track listing: Ride A White Swan/Debora/Child Star/Cat Black (The Wizard's Hat)/Conesuala/Strange Orchestras/ One Inch Rock/Salamanda Palaganda/Lofty Skies/Stacey Grove/King Of The Rumbling Spires/Elemental Child

Tanx
T.Rex Wax Co. (BLN 50O2)
Released March 23, 1973
Track listing: Tenement Lady/Rapids/Mister Mister/ Broken-hearted Blues/Shock Rock/Electric Slim and the Factory Hen/Mad Donna/Born to Boogie/Life is Strange/ The Street and Babe Shadow/Highway Knees/Left Hand Luke

T. Rex Great Hits
T.Rex Wax Co. (BLN 5003)
Released September 27, 1973
Compilation
Track listing: Telegram Sam/Jitterbug Love/Lady/Metal
Guru/Thunderwing/Sunken Rags/Solid Gold Easy
Action/Twentieth Century Boy/Midnight/The Slider/
Born To Boogie/Children Of The Revolution/Shock
Rock/The Groover

Zinc Alloy And The Hidden Riders Of Tomorrow -
A Creamed Cage In August
T.Rex Wax Co. (BLNA 775)
Released February 1, 1974
Track listing: Venus Loon/Sound Pit/Explosive Mouth/
Galaxy/Change/Nameless Wildness/Teenage Dream/
Liquid Gang/Carsmile Smith Is The Old One/You Gotta
Jive To Stay Alive/Spanish Midnight/Interstellar Soul/
Painless Persuasion V The Meathawk Immaculate/The
Avengers (Superbad)/The Leopards Featuring Gardenia
And The Mighty Slug

MARC BOLAN
The Beginning Of Doves
Track Records (2410)
Released June 22, 1974
Track listing: Jasper C. Debussy/Lunacy's Back/Beyond
The Risin' Sun/Black And White Incident/Observations/
Eastern Spell/You Got The Power/Hippy Gumbo/Sara
Crazy Child/Rings Of Fortune/Hot Rod Mamma/The
Beginning Of Doves/Mustang Ford/Pictures Of Purple
People/One Inch Rock/Jasmine '49/Charlie/Misty Mist/
Cat Black/Sally Was An Angel

Get It On
Sounds Superb (SPR 90059)
Released December 1974
Budget priced compilation
Track listing: Get It On/Mambo Sun/Planet Queen/
Rip Off/Lean Woman Blues/Hot Love/Raw Ramp/
Summertime Blues/The Motivator/Cosmic Dancer/
Beltane Walk/Ride A White Swan

Bolan Zip Gun
T.Rex Wax Co. (BLNA 7752)
Released February 16, 1975
Track listing: Light of Love/Solid Baby/Precious Star/
Token of My Love/Space Boss/Think Zinc/Till Dawn/Girl
in the Thunderbolt Suit/I Really Love You, Baby/Golden
Belt/Zip Gun Boogie

Futuristic Dragon
T.Rex Wax Co. (BLN 5004)
Released January 31, 1976
Track listing: Introduction - Futuristic Dragon/Jupiter
Liar/Chrome Sitar/All Alone/New York City/My Little
Baby/Calling All Destroyers/Theme for a Dragon/

Sensation Boulevard/Ride My Wheels/Dreamy Lady/
Dawn Storm/Casual Agent

Dandy In The Underworld
T.Rex Wax Co. (BLN 5005)
Released February 11, 1977
Track listing: Dandy in the Underworld/Crimson Moon/
Universe/I'm a Fool for You/I Love to Boogie/Visions of
Domino/Jason B. Sad/Groove a Little/Soul of My Suit/
Hang-Ups/Pain and Love/Teen Riot Structure

Compact Discs

'The Maximum Sound Session'
(Zinc Alloy Records ZARCD 9006)
Multiple takes plus finished mixes of the Toby Tyler
demos 'The Road I'm On (Gloria)' and 'Blowin' In The
Wind'.

'The Beginning of Doves'
(Sanctuary Records CMRCD 491)
Track listing: Jasper C. Debussy/Hippy Gumbo/Misfit/
The Lilac Hand of Menthol Dan/Black and White
Incident/Jasmine '49/Cat Black/You Got The Power/
Eastern Spell/Charlie/I'm Weird/Pictures of Purple
People/Horrible Breath/Hippy Gumbo (Alternative
version)/Mustang Ford/Hot Rod Mama/Observations/
The Perfumed Garden of Gulliver Smith/Rings of
Fortune/Sarah Crazy Child/Lunacy's Back/Misty Mist
(Highways)/Beyond The Rising Sun/One Inch Rock/
Sleepy Maurice/Jasper C. Debussy (Alternative mix)/
Hot Rod Mama (Alternative version)/The Beginning of
Doves/Sally Was An Angel/Lunacy's Back (Alternative
version)/Beyond The Rising Sun (Alternative version)/
Observations (Alternative version)/Hippy Gumbo
(Alternative version)/Misfit (Alternative version)/Jasper C.
Debussy (Alternative version)/Observations (Alternative
version)/Hippy Gumbo (Alternative version)

'Love and Death'
(Cherry Red CDBRED 70)
(13 tracks from 'Beginning of Doves' overdubbed by
Simon Napier-Bell plus both sides of Bolan's first single
and recorded interview excerpts)
Track listing: You Scare Me To Death (Horrible Breath)/
You Got The Power/Eastern Spell/Charlie/I'm Weird/
Hippy Gumbo/Mustang Ford/Observations/Jasmine '49/
Cat Black/Black and White Incident/Perfumed Garden
of Gulliver Smith/The Wizard/Beyond The Risin' Sun/
Rings of Fortune/Interview Excerpts

'The Complete John's Children'
(New Millennium Communications)
Contains the five official singles, outtakes, a BBC session
and three Andy Ellison solo tracks.

'My People Were Fair' (Expanded Edition)
(Universal Music 982 250-9)
Tracks 1-12 original mono album. Tracks 14-25 Original
stereo mixes.
Bonus tracks: Debora/Child Star (outtake)/Chateau In
Virginia Waters (outtake)/Debora (outtake)

'Prophets, Seers and Sages' (Expanded Edition)
(Universal Music 982 251-0)
Tracks 1 -14 original album. Track 15 original single A
side. Tracks 16-28 outtakes.
Bonus tracks: One Inch Rock/Nickelodeon/Wind
Quartets/Conesuala/Trelawny Lawn/Aznageel The Mage/
Salamanda Palaganda/Our Wonderful Brownskin Man/O
Harley/Eastern Spell/The Travelling Tragition/Juniper
Suction/Scenescof Dynasty/One Inch Rock

Unicorn (Expanded Edition)
(Universal Music 982 251-1)
Tracks 1-16 original album. Tracks 17-19 original single A
and B sides. Tracks 20 – 31 outtakes.
Bonus Tracks: Pewter Suitor/King of the Rumbling
Spires/Do You Remember?/Pon A Hill/The Seal of
Seasons/The Throat of Winter/She Was Born To Be My
Unicorn/Warlord of the Royal Crocodiles/Evenings of
Damask/Iscariot/The Misty Coast of Albany/Romany
Soup/Pewter Suitor/King of the Rumbling Spires/Do You
Remember?

Beard of Stars (Expanded Edition)
(Universal Music 982 251-2)
Tracks 1-14 original album. Tracks 15–30 outtakes.
Bonus tracks: Ill Starred Man/Demon Queen/Once
Upon The Seas of Abyssinia/Blessed Wild Apple Girl/
Find A Little Wood/A Daye Laye/Fist Heart Mighty Dawn
Dart/Organ Blues/Wind Cheetah/A Beard of Stars/Great
Horse/Dragon's Ear/Dove/Elemental Child/By The Light
of the Magical Moon/Prelude

T.Rex (Expanded Edition)
(Universal Music 982 251-3)
Tracks 1-15 original album. Tracks 16-17 Original single
A and B side. Tracks 18-24 outtakes.
Bonus tracks: Ride A White Swan/Summertime Blues/
Poem/The Visit/Diamond Meadows/One Inch Rock/
Seagull Woman/The Wizard/The Children of Rarn

Electric Warrior (30th anniversary edition)
(A&M Records 493113-2)
Tracks 1-11 original album. Tracks 12-19 outtakes ('work
in progress').
Bonus tracks: Rip Off/Mambo Sun/Cosmic Dancer/
Monolith/Get It On/Planet Queen/The Motivator/Life's
A Gas

The Electric Warrior Sessions (outtakes)
(Burning Airlines/NMC Pilot 004)
Track listing: Get It On/Monolith/Cosmic Dancer/Life's
A Gas/Honey Don't/Woodland Rock/Monolith (2nd
version)/Summertime Blues/Jeepster/Baby Strange/Jewel/
Get It On (2nd version)

The Slider
(Edsel EDCD390)
Tracks 1-13 original album.
Bonus tracks: Cadillac/Thunderwing/Lady

**Rabbit Fighter (The Alternate Slider – demos and
previously unreleased versions)**
(Edsel EDCD 403)
Track listing: Metal Guru/Mystic Lady/Rock On/The
Slider/Thunderwing/Spaceball Ricochet/Buick Mackane/
Telegram Sam/Rabbit Fighter/Baby Strange/Ballrooms of
Mars/Cadillac/Main Man
Bonus tracks: Lady/Sunken Rags

Tanx
(Edsel EDCD391)
Tracks 1-13 original album.
Bonus tracks: Children of the Revolution/Jitterbug Love/
Sunken Rags/Solid Gold Easy Action/Xmas Message/20th
Century Boy/Free Angel

**Left Hand Luke (The Alternate *Tanx* – demos and
previously unreleased versions)**
(Edsel EDCD 410)
Track listing: Tenement Lady/Darling/Rapids
(Incomplete)/Mister Mister/Broken Hearted Blues/
Country Honey/Mad Donna/Born To Boogie/Life
Is Strange/The Street And Babe Shadow/Highway
Knees/Left Hand Luke/Children Of The Revolution
(Incomplete)/Solid Gold Easy Action/Free Angel/Mister
Mister/Broken Hearted Blues/The Street And Babe
Shadow/Tenement Lady/Tenement Lady/Broken Hearted
Blues/Mad Donna (Different Lyrics)/The Street And
Babe Shadow/Left Hand Luke

Zinc Alloy
(Edsel EDCD392)
Tracks 1-14 original album.
Bonus tracks: The Groover/Midnight/Truck On (Tyke)/
Sitting Here/Satisfaction Pony

**Change (The Alternate *Zinc Alloy* – demos and
previously unreleased versions)**
(Edsel EDCD 440)
Track listing: Venus Loon/Sound Pit (Parts 1&2)/
Explosive Mouth/Galaxy/Change (Signs)/Nameless
Wildness/Teenage Dream/Liquid Gang/Carsmile Smith
& The Old One/Spanish Midnight/Painless Persuasion
V. The Meathawk Immaculate/The Avengers (Superbad)/
The Leopards/The Groover/Midnight/Truck On (Tyke)/

Sitting There (Sitting Here)/Satisfaction Pony/Nameless Wildness/Carsmile Smith & The Old One (Solo)/ Carsmile Smith & The Old One (With Organ)/Painless Persuasion V. The Meathawk Immaculate/The Avengers (Superbad)/The Leopards

Bolan's Zip Gun
(Edsel EDCD 393)
Tracks 1- 11 original album
Light Of Love/Solid Baby/Precious Star/Token Of My Love/Space Boss/Think Zinc/Till Dawn/Girl In The Thunderbolt Suit/I Really Love You Baby/Golden Belt/ Zip Gun Boogie
Bonus tracks: Do You Wanna Dance?/Dock Of The Bay

Precious Star (The Alternate *Bolan's Zip Gun* – demos and previously unreleased versions)
(Edsel EDCD 443)
Track listing: Light Of Love/Solid Baby/Precious Star/ Token Of My Love/Space Boss/Think Zinc/Till Dawn/ Girl In The Thunderbolt Suit/I Really Love You Babe (Precision Debating)/Golden Belt/Zip Gun Boogie (Live)/ Do You Wanna Dance?/Dock Of The Bay/Solid Baby/ Till Dawn (Marc's Guide)/Till Dawn/Till Dawn/Girl In The Thunderbolt Suit (Blue Jean Bop)/Dishing Fish Wop (Golden Belt)

Futuristic Dragon
(Edsel EDCD 394)
Tracks 1-13 original album.
Bonus tracks: London Boys/Laser Love/Life's An Elevator

Dazzling Raiment – The Alternate Futuristic Dragon (demos and previously unreleased versions)
(Edsel EDCD 522)
Track listing: Futuristic Dragon Intro/Chrome Sitar/ All Alone/New York City/My Little Baby/Sensation Boulevard/Dreamy Lady/Dawn Storm/Casual Agent/ London Boys/Life's An Elevator/Futuristic Dragon Intro/ All Alone/Dreamy Lady/Casual Agent/Casual Agent/All Alone/Dreamy Lady/London Boys/Life's An Elevator

Dandy in the Underworld
(Edsel EDCD 395)
Tracks 1-12 original album.
Bonus tracks: To Know You Is To Love You/City Port/ Dandy In The Underworld (single version)/Tame My Tiger/Celebrate Summer

Prince Of Players (The Alternate *Dandy In The Underworld* - alternative versions, demos and mixes)
(Edsel EDCD 523)
Track listing: Dandy In The Underworld (live)/Crimson Moon/I'm A Fool For You Girl/I Love To Boogie/Funky London Childhood/Jason B.Sad/Groove A Little (live)/ The Soul of My Suit/Hang Ups (live)/Pain and Love/Teen Riot Structure

Bonus tracks: To Know You Is To Love You/City Port/ Tame My Tiger/Celebrate Summer/I Love To Boogie/ Soul of My Suit/pain and Love/Teen Riot Structure/ Celebrate Summer/Weird Strings

The Final Cuts
(Edsel DIAB8080)
Track listing: Hot George/Foxey Boy/Celebrate Summer/ Love Drunk/Write Me A Song/Mellow Love/Dandy In The Underworld/Crimson Moon/To Know You Is To Love You/Tame My Tiger/Shy Boy/20th Century Baby
Bonus tracks: Tame My Tiger/Mellow Love/To Know You Is To Love You

'Marc: Songs From The Granada TV Series'
(Edsel EDCD545)

Marc – The Words And Music Of Marc Bolan 1947-1977
(A&M Records 541008-2)
Track listing: Desdemona/Debora/Strange Orchestras/ Child Star/Afghan Woman/One Inch Rock/Stacey Grove/ eastern Spell/Salamanda Palaganda/Cat Black(The Wizard's Hat)/She Was Born To Be My Unicorn/Warlord of the Royal Crocodiles/Woodland Bop/By the Light of the Magical Moon/great Horse/Elemental Child/Cosmic Dancer/King of the Rumbling Spires/Beltane Walk/Ride A White Swan/Hot love/Get It On/Jeepster/Frowning Atahuallpa/The Children of Rarn Suite

Born To Boogie (The Soundtrack Album) 2 CD
CD1 The Motion Picture Soundtrack.
CD2 T.Rex In Concert 18th March 1972
(Sanctuary Records SMEDD 215)

Spaceball – The American Radio Sessions 2 CD
(Applebush Records CPSSPCD005)
CD1: Spaceball Ricochet/Jeepster/Cosmic Dancer/Main Man/Ballrooms of Mars/Mystic Lady/Girl/Baby Strange/ KLOS Jingle 1/Interview/Spaceball Ricochet/Interview/ Left Hand Luke/Interview/The Slider/Interview
CD2: T.Rex Album Advert 1/Interview/Cosmic Dancer/ Planet Queen/Elemental Child/Jewel/Hot Love/KLOS Jingle 2/Cosmic Dancer/Honey Don't/Planet Queen/Get It On Blues/WGLD Radio Jingle/Life's A Gas/Spaceball Ricochet/Sunken Rags/Everybody's Loose/Talking/T.Rex Album Advert 2

Great Hits 1972-1977 The A-Sides
(Edsel EDCD 401)
Track listing: Telegram Sam/Metal Guru/Children of the Revolution/Solid Gold easy Action/20th Century Boy/ The Groover/Truck On (Tyke)/Teenage Dream/Light of Love/Zip Gun Boogie/New York City/Dreamy Lady/ London Boys/I Love To Boogie/Laser Love/To Know You Is To Love You/The Soul of My Suit/Dandy In The Underworld/Celebrate Summer

Great Hits 1972-1977 The B-Sides
(Edsel EDCD 402)
Track listing: Cadillac/Baby Strange/Thunderwing/
lady/Jitterbug Love/Sunken Rags/Xmas Riff/Born To
Boogie/Free Angel/Midnight/Sitting Here/Satisfaction
Pony/Explosive Mouth/Space Boss/Chrome Sitar/Do
You Wanna Dance?/Dock of the Bay/Solid Baby/Baby
Boomerang/Life's An Elevator/City Port/All Alone/
Groove A Little/Tame My Tiger/Ride My Wheels
Both repackaged as a 2CD set **'The T.Rex Wax Co.
Singles: A's and B's'** (EDSEL MEDCD 714)

'Bump 'n' Grind' (alternative mixes, demos, outtakes
and working versions)
(Thunderwing Records TPLCD 4)
Track listing: The Groover/Jitterbug Love/Dishing Fish
Wop (Girl In The Thunderbolt Suit)Telegram Sam/Laser
Love/20th Century Boy/Silver Lady (Dreamy Lady)/
Metal Guru/Fast Blues (Easy Action)/Light of Love/
The Soul of My Suit/Thunderwing/Christmas Bop/The
Groover(demo)/Children of the Revolution

Twopenny Prince (rehearsals, demos and rare live
tracks) 2CD
(Easy Action EARS 021)
CD1 Track listing: Jeepster/Telegram Sam/Hot love/
Cadillac/Metal Guru/Truck On (Tyke)/Buick Mackane/
Jewel/Ride A White Swan/Elemental Child/Summertime
Blues/Life's A Gas/Oh Baby/Get It On/Salamanda
Palaganda/By The Light of a Magical Moon/Suneye
CD 2 Track listing: One Inch Rock/One Inch Rock/The
Children of Rarn/The Wizard/The Wizard/The Wizard/
The Children of Rarn/Woodland Rock

Box Sets

Bolan At The Beeb (BBC Radio Sessions) 3CD box set
(Polydor 5302923)
Disc 1 Track listing: Highways/Scenescof/Child Star/
Dwarfish Trumpet Blues/Pictures of Purple People/
Hot Rod Mama/Juniper Suction (poem and song)/The
Friends/Conesuala/The Seal of Seasons/Evenings of
Damask/Once Upon The Seas Of Abyssinia/Nijinsky
Hind/The Misty Coast of Albany/Chariots of Silk/
Iscariot/Poems/Jingle/Fist Heart Mighty Dawn Dart/
Pavillions of Sun/A Daye Laye/By the Light of a Magical
Moon/Wind Cheetah/Hot Rod Mama/Debora/Pavilions
of Sun/Dove/By the Light of a Magical Moon/Elemental
Child/The Wizard
Disc 2 Track listing: Ride A White Swan/Jewel/Elemental
Child/Suneye/Summertime Blues/Jewel/Hot Love/
Debora/Elemental Child/Ride A White Swan/Jewel/My
Baby's Like A Cloudfall/Funky Now Jam
Disc 3 Track listing: Woodland Rock/Beltane Walk/Hot
Love/Jeepster/Get It On/Electric Boogie/Sailors of the
Highway/Girl/Cadillac/Jeepster/Life's A Gas/Telegram
Sam/Bob Harris Jingle/Christmas Jingle

'The Electric Boogie – Nineteen-Seventy-One' 5CD
Box set
(Easy Action EARS 0014)
CD 1 Home Demos Track listing: Jeepster/Electric
Warrior/There Was a Time/Dark Lipped Woman/Guitar
Jam #1/Get It On/Guitar Jam #2/Planet Queen/Guitar
Jam#3/Guitar Jam#4/Jeepster/Life's a Gas/Gypsy Queen
(My Shaky Jane)/Girl/Guitar Jam#5/Get It On Blues/
Sailors of the Highway (demo)
CD 2 T. Rex Live Summer Tour '71 Track listing:
Cadillac/Ride A White Swan/Hot Love/Get It On/Jewel/
Beltane Walk/One Inch Rock/Spaceball Ricochet/Debora/
Jam/Elemental Child
CD 3 T.Rex Live Summer Tour Pt 2 Track listing: Beltane
Walk/Girl/Debora/Spaceball Ricochet/Girl/Cosmic
Dancer/Ride a White Swan/Get It On/Summertime
Blues/Summertime Blues (Soundcheck Rehearsal)/Jam
(Rehearsal)/Honey Don't (Rehearsal)/Summertime Blues
Version 2 (Rehearsal)
CD 4 Home Demos Track listing: Buick MacKane #1/
Buick MacKane (& The Babe Shadow)/Cadillac/Rock
On/Guitar Piece/The Slider/Baby Strange (acoustic)/
Telegram Sam/Thunderwing/Buick MacKane #2/
Spaceball Ricochet/Sunken Rags/Baby Strange/Rainy
Monday/I Knew a Girl/Guitar Piece/Baron of Wimpole
Street/Take Me Down to Birmingham
CD 5 The Electric Boogie Track listing: Electric Boogie
(unused mix)/The Electric Warrior Interview with
Michael Cuscuna Pt 1/Raw Ramp (unused mix)/Electric
Warrior Interview Pt 2/T.Rex Studio Jam/Jeepster/Life's
a Gas/Baby Strange/Children of Rarn Suite (original
solo demo)/Everybody's Loose (WGLG Chicago Radio
Session)
plus bonus DVD Contains live footage, interviews,
promo and TV clips

'A Whole Zinc of Finches' 5CD Box set
(Easy Action EARS 007)
CD1 The Final John Peel Perfumed Garden Program
14th August 1967
Track listing: John Peel Opening the Gates of the
Perfumed Garden/Rings of Fortune/Hippy Gumbo/The
Wizard/Highways/Desdemona/Winnie the Pooh (John
Peel)/Sarah Crazy Child/John Peel Closing the Gates of
the Perfumed Garden
CD 2 Demos & work in progress. Track listing: Child
Star/Highways/Sleepy Maurice/Chateau In Virginia
Waters/Deep Summer (instr)/Rock Me (Puckish Pan)/
One Inch Rock/Sea Beasts/Cat Black/Chariots of Silk/
Pilgrims Tale/Like A White Star Tangled and Far Tulip
That's What You Are/Prelude/King of the rumbling
Spires/June & Marc spoken word/Lofty Skies solo/
Dragon's Ear/The Wizard Vocal Extracts/Summer Deep/
Fist Heart Mighty Dawn Dart/Elemental Child/Organ
Blues/Pictures of Purple People Live/Demon Queen
CD 3 Live in London Lyceum Ballroom 11th April
1969 Track listing: Unicorn/Hot Rod Mama/Afghan

Woman/Debora/Mustang Ford/Stacey Grove/Salamanda Palaganda/Wind Quartets/One Inch Rock/Chariots of Silk/The Seal of Seasons/Conesuela/Nijinski Hind/Once Upon the Seas of Abyssinia/Do You Remember?/The Wizard/Conesuela

Live in London Pt 2 Queen Elizabeth Hall 13th Jan 1969. Track listing: The Seal of Seasons/One Inch Rock/Eastern Spell/Wind Quartets/Mustang Ford/Salamanda Palaganda/Strange Orchestras/Evenings of Damask/Chariots of Silk/Pewter Suitor/The Traveling Tragition

CD 4 Live In America. Café au go go New York 16th August 1969 Track listing: For the Lion and the Unicorn/Hot Rod Mama/Debora/Afghan Woman/Misty coast of Albany/Mustang Ford/The Seal of Seasons/Chariots of Silk/Strange Orchestras/The Wizard/Stacey Grove/One Inch Rock/Conesuela/Nijinsky Hind/Once Upon the Seas of Abyssinia/Salamanda Palaganda/Blue Thumb USA unreleased promo 45 Marc & John Peel 1969/The Wizard USA unreleased promo with Dwarfish Trumpet Blues Story

CD 5 A New Dawn Track listing: Interviews Chicago 23rd Aug 1969/Oh Baby/Universal Love - Dib Cochran & the Earwigs (Original A and B side)/Pavilions of Sun (live)/Jam session – Dib Cochran & the Earwigs/Oh Baby – Tyrannosaurus Rex version

Bonus DVD Unreleased footage

Debora & Mustang Ford (Kempton race course)/Stacey Grove/Salamanda Palaganda (both Paris, August 1968)/By the Light of the Magical Moon (Rotterdam, June 1970)/Children of Rarn/Suneye (both 'London Rock')/Kempton Race Course footage

Marc Bolan – A Wizard, A True Star 3CDs
(Demon/Edsel FBook 17)

Disc 1 Track listing: Interview Excerpt/Telegram Sam/Spaceball Ricochet/Cadillac/Metal Guru (Acoustic)/Baby Strange/Over The Flats/Thunderwing/Is It True/Interview Excerpt/Metal Guru/Rabbit Fighter/Pepsi Jingle/Sunken Rags/The Slider/Buick MacKane (Acoustic)/KLOS Radio Jingle/Would I Be The One/Rock On/Children Of The Revolution/Painted Pony/Solid Gold Easy Action/Xmas Flexi Message/20th Century Boy/The Street & Babe Shadow/I Wanna Go/Interview/You Got The Look/Electric Slim7The Groover/Sure Enough/Interview Excerpt/Highway Knees/Midnight/Untitled Poem/Left Hand Luke & The Beggar Boys

Disc 2 Track listing: Interview/Change/Every Day/Interview/Venus Loon/All My Love/The Leopards/Interstellar Soul/Carsmile Smith/Interview/Saturation Syncopation/Down Home Lady/Sky Church Music/Teenage Dream/Till Dawn/Jitterbug Love/Are You Ready, Steve?/Light Of Love/Sanctified/Think Zinc/Solid Baby/Bust My Ball/Token Of My Love (Live)/Children Of Rarn/Interview

Disc 3 Track listing: Brain Police/Futuristic Dragon Intro/New York City/Reelin' & a Wheelin'/Dreamy Lady/Christmas Bop/Talking To A Critic/Rip It Up/Teenager In

Love/Capital Radio Jingle/Jupiter Liar/Pale Horse Riding/Chrome Sitar/Piccadilly Radio Jingle/Jeepster Rap/Funky London Childhood/Dawn Storm/Casual Agent/20th Century Boy/I Love To Boogie/Interview/London Boys/Life's An Elevator/Dandy In The Underworld/Crimson Moon/Hang Ups (Live)/Hot George/21st Century Stance/Pain And Love/Interview/Celebrate Summer/Keep A Little Marc In Your Heart

20th Century Superstar 4CDs
(Universal) 2002

Disc 1 Track listing: The Road I'm On (Gloria) (as Toby Tyler)/Blowin' In The Wind (as Toby Tyler)/The Wizard/Beyond The Risin' Sun/The Third Degree/San Francisco Poet/Eastern Spell/Hippy Gumbo/Misfit/Jasper C. Debussy/Desdemona/Midsummer Night's Scene/Sara Crazy Child/The Lilac Hand of Menthol Dan/Sleepy Maurice/Highways (Misty Mist)/Child Star/Chateau In Virginia Waters/Puckish Pan/Lunacy's Back/Debora/Hot Rod Mama/Scenescof/One Inch Rock/Salamanda Palaganda/Conesuala/Juniper Suction/Nickelodeon/Pewter Suitor/The Seal Of Seasons/Catblack (The Wizard's Hat)/Chariots Of Silk/Iscariot

Disc 2 Track listing: King Of The Rumbling Spires/Do You Remember (Steve on vocals)/Do You Remember/Once Upon The Seas of Abyssinia/Ill Starred Man/Demon Queen/By The Light Of The Magical Moon/Lofty Skies/Elemental Child/Dove/The Prettiest Star by David Bowie (Marc on Lead Guitar)/Oh Baby (as Dib. Cochran & The Earwigs)/Ride A White Swan (Intro)/Ride A White Swan/Ride A White Swan (Outro)/Untitled Poem/Jewel/Diamond Meadows/Beltane Walk/Suneye/Childe/The Children of Rarn/Hot Love/King Of The Mountain Cometh/Mambo Sun/Cosmic Dancer/Get It On/There Was A Time/Raw Ramp/Rip Off

Disc 3 track listing: Jeepster/Life's A Gas/Sailors Of The Highway/Telegram Sam/Cadillac/Baby Strange/Metal Guru/Thunderwing/Spaceball Ricochet/Children Of The Revolution/Jitterbug Love/Xmas Flexi Message/Solid Gold Easy Action/Born To Boogie/20th Century Boy/Highway Knees/Electric Slim & The Factory Hen/Left Hand Luke/The Groover/Blackjack (as Big Carrot)/Truck On (Tyke)/City Port/Teenage Dream

Disc 4 Track listing: Venus Loon/Painless Persuasion v. The Meathawk Immaculate/Change/Till Dawn/Light Of Love/Zip Gun Boogie/Think Zinc/Solid Baby/New York City/Chrome Sitar/Dreamy Lady/Christmas Bop/Jupiter Liar/Dawn Storm/London Boys/I Love To Boogie/Laser Love/Life's An Elevator/To Know Him Is To Love Him/Teen Riot Structure/The Soul Of My Suit/Dandy In The Underworld (Album Version)/Celebrate Summer

Total T. Rex 5 CDs + DVD
(Easy Action EAR 001)
CD 1 US Radio Sessions 1972 (LA and Boston)
Track listing: Spaceball Ricochet/Jeepster/Cosmic Dancer/
Mainman/Ballrooms Of Mars/Mystic Lady/Girl/Baby
Strange/Spaceball Ricochet/Left Hand Luke/Slider/
Interview & Jingles
CD 2 Radio Sessions 1971 New York
Track listing: Cosmic Dancer/Planet Queen/Elemental
Child/Jewel/Hot Love/Cosmic Dancer/Honey Don't/
Planet Queen/Get It On Blues/Radio Advert
CD 3 Live (UK tour Aug '71 and Jan '72)
Track listing: Cadillac/Jeepster/Thunderwing/Baby
Strange/Spaceball Ricochet/Girl/Cosmic Dancer/Hot
Love/Get It On/Beltane Walk/One Inch Rock/Girl
CD 4 Live (UK May '71 and June '72)
Track listing: Jeepster/Cadillac/Baby Strange/Debora/
Spaceball Ricochet/Telegram Sam/Beltane Walk/One
Inch Rock/Spaceball Ricochet/Debora/Instrumental Jam/
Elemental Child
CD 5 Home Demos
Track listing: Electric Warrior/There Was A Time/Planet
Queen/Guitar Jam/Girl/Guitar Jam #2/Girl#2/Guitar
Jam#3/Get It On/Jeepster/Dark Lipped Woman/Life's
A Gas/Honey Don't (Rehearsal)/Summertime Blues
(Rehearsal)/Interview/Alligator Man/Sailors Of The
Highway/Children Of The Rarn Suite
DVD Film Footage
Recorded at the Taverne De L'Olympia, Paris '71
Jewel/Ride A White Swan/Elemental Child/Summertime
Blues (Recorded at Chateau D'Herouville, France '72)
Jeepster/Hot Love/Cadillac/Telegram Sam (Recorded at
the Cockpit Theatre, Marylebone '71)/Spaceball Ricochet
Unchained 8 CDs
(Edsel EDCD)
174 studio outtakes and home demos (many only
fragments) available as a box set or individually and
replicating many of the rare and unreleased tracks from
earlier box sets. Also two selective compilations culling
the better tracks 'Messing With The Mystic – Unissued
Songs 1972-1977 Edsel EDCD 404) and 'Best of
Unchained' (Edsel NESTCD 907)

Guest sessions
March 1970 - Marc plays guitar on David Bowie's original
single version of 'Prettiest Star' (Mercury MF1135).
August 1970 - Oh Baby/Universal Love (Bell 1121)
Marc wrote and played on this novelty single on which
Tony Visconti sings lead. Released under the name Dib
Cochran And The Earwigs.
November 1971 - Marc appears on Marsha Hunt's album
Woman Child (Track 2410101) singing one line on 'My
World Is Empty Without You'. He does not appear on the
three cover versions of his songs featured on the LP.
November 72 - Marc rumoured to have played on Alice
Cooper's 'Hello Hurray' and 'Slick Black Limousine' as
well as on cover versions that were never released. Other

guests included Donovan and Keith Moon.
April 1973 - Marc plays guitar on an ELO session which
produces 'Ma-Ma-Ma-Belle', 'Everyone's Born To Die'
and 'Dreaming of 4000' which are included on the CD
On The Third Day (Epic/Legacy 82796942712).
November 1973 - Marc plays guitar on Ringo Starr's Top
10 hit 'Have You Seen My Baby' included on the *Ringo*
album (Apple PCTC 252) and Marc inspired Ringo's
1972 hit 'Back Off Boogaloo', but is not thought to have
appeared on the track.
1973-4 - Marc produces and plays guitar on the aborted
Sister Pat Hall album *Marc Bolan Presents Sister Pat Hall*
(Edsel EDCD 449).
June 1974 - Marc contributes guitar to the flip side of the
Ike and Tina Turner single 'Sexy Ida Pt1'/'Sexy Ida Pt2'.
Dec 1976 - Marc produced and played guitar on Gloria
Jones' solo album *Vixen* (EMI EMC 3159) which utilised
some of the backing tracks recorded three years earlier for
the aborted Pat Hall album.
Spring 1977 - Marc played guitar on Gloria's single 'Go
Now' (EMI 2570), Alfalfa's 'If I just Can Get Through
Tonight' (EMI EMC 3213) and 'Amerika The Brave' on
Steve Harley's 'Hobo With A Grin' (EMI EMC 3254).

Cover Versions
1979 - Siouxsie and the Banshees released '20th
Century Boy' as the B-side to their single 'The Staircase
(Mystery)'.
1980 - Bauhaus released their cover of 'Telegram Sam'.
1980 - American band The Bongos charted with 'Mambo
Sun'. Singer Richard Barone went on to work with Tony
Visconti and recorded 'The Visit', 'Girl' and 'Ballrooms of
Mars' before producing sessions for Rolan Bolan.
1981 - Indie act Department S released a cover of 'Solid
Gold Easy Action' on the flip side of their single 'Is Vic
There?'.
1982 - Andy Ellison, Knox (of the Vibrators) and the
author released a cover of 'Hot George' under the name
Beau Brummel. The author also covered 'Iscariot',
'Meadows Of The Sea' and 'The Perfumed Garden Of
Gulliver Smith' on subsequent releases.
1984 - The Replacements released '20th Century Boy'
as the B-side to their single 'I Will Dare'. 19?? Adam
Ant featured a live version of '20th Century Boy' on the
bonus live disc of *Antmusic: The Very Best of Adam Ant*.
1985 - Power Station, with singer Robert Palmer and
members of Duran Duran charted with a cover of 'Get It
On' and performed the song with Michael Des Barres (in
place of Palmer) at the U.S. Live Aid.
1986 - The Violent Femmes recorded 'Children of the
Revolution' for their album *The Blind Leading the Naked*.
1990 - Baby Ford covered 'Children of the Revolution' on
their album *Oooh, The World of Baby Ford*.
1993 - Guns N' Roses included a cover of 'Buick
MacKane' on *The Spaghetti Incident?*
2006 - Def Leppard released '20th Century Boy' on their
covers album *Yeah.*

2008 - Australian singer Steve Kilbey, of The Church covered 'One Inch Rock' on a live DVD *Steve Kilbey Live.* 'Beltane – A Musical Fantasy' suite of Bolan songs in a pseudo Renaissance style Michel Laverdiere, arr. Robert Lafond, vocal Catherine Lambert, Lore Liege Ensemble (XXI, Canada).

Bolan References
Mentioned in The Who song 'You Better, You Bet' ("...to the sound of old T-Rex").
Mentioned in the Ramones song 'Do You Remember Rock and Roll Radio?' ("Do you remember Jerry Lee, John Lennon, T Rex and Old Moulty?")
Mentioned in Mott The Hoople's hit 'All The Young Dudes' ("Man, I need TV when I got T.Rex") which had originally been written for Marc by David Bowie.
Bolan inspired the Elton John/Bernie Taupin song 'Teenage Idol' on the *Don't Shoot Me, I'm Only The Piano Player* album.
Bolan also provided inspiration for David Bowie's 'Lady Stardust' on the *Ziggy Stardust* album.
The song 'Vampire Money' by My Chemical Romance features the line "glimmer like Bolan in the morning sun".

Index